PROFESSIONAL

iOS Database Application Programming

Second Edition

Patrick Alessi

wrox™

A Wiley Brand

Professional iOS Database Application Programming, Second Edition

Published by
John Wiley & Sons, Inc.
10475 Crosspoint Boulevard
Indianapolis, IN 46256
www.wiley.com

Copyright © 2013 by John Wiley & Sons, Inc., Indianapolis, Indiana

Published simultaneously in Canada

ISBN: 978-1-118-39184-6
ISBN: 978-1-118-39185-3 (ebk)
ISBN: 978-1-118-41757-7 (ebk)
ISBN: 978-1-118-72836-9 (ebk)

Manufactured in the United States of America

10 9 8 7 6 5 4 3 2 1

For general information on our other products and services please contact our Customer Care Department within the United States at (877) 762-2974, outside the United States at (317) 572-3993 or fax (317) 572-4002.

Wiley publishes in a variety of print and electronic formats and by print-on-demand. Some material included with standard print versions of this book may not be included in e-books or in print-on-demand. If this book refers to media such as a CD or DVD that is not included in the version you purchased, you may download this material at http://booksupport.wiley.com. For more information about Wiley products, visit www.wiley.com.

Library of Congress Control Number: 2013933611

For Cheryl—Without you, this would have never been possible.

CREDITS

ABOUT THE AUTHOR

PATRICK ALESSI has been fascinated with writing computer programs since he first saw his name flash across a terminal in 1980. Since then, he has written software using every language and hardware platform that he could get his hands on, including a brief and painful foray into Fortran on a VAX system during his engineering education. Patrick holds a BS degree in Civil Engineering from Rutgers University and an MS in Computer Science from Stevens Institute of Technology.

Professionally, Patrick has focused on data-centric applications for clients ranging from small business databases to large-scale systems for the United States Air Force. Currently, he is focused on the promise of mobility and developing connected applications for mobile devices such as the iPhone and iPad.

When he can back away from the computer, Patrick enjoys gaming (especially *Starcraft*), photography, traveling, and doing just about anything with his family. You can follow him on Twitter at pwalessi and read his blog at `iphonedevsphere.blogspot.com`.

ABOUT THE TECHNICAL EDITOR

MICHAEL GILBERT is a long-time systems programmer for various engineering firms. He got his start developing games for the Atari ST, and he was a frequent contributing editor for *STart* magazine. Over the years, he has continued to develop gaming software on PC and Mac for clients worldwide. He's also an expert Flash ActionScript programmer and has produced a popular Internet gaming environment called HigherGames. He now enjoys developing games for the iPhone and iPad, and currently has several games in the AppStore, with more on the way. In his spare time, he enjoys trying to defeat his wife Janeen in a friendly game of Scrabble.

ACKNOWLEDGMENTS

I WOULD LIKE TO TAKE THIS OPPORTUNITY TO THANK everyone who made this book possible. Mary James, my acquisitions editor, shepherded this second edition through the acquisitions process. My project editor, Brian MacDonald, was there to answer every question that I had about writing and the publishing process. Mike Gilbert, my technical editor, gave up valuable app development time to review my work. I would also like to thank all the other editorial and production staff that put many hours into this project to help get it to print.

I cannot thank my wife, Cheryl, and my stepdaughter, Morgan, enough for putting up with my fits, general crankiness, and lack of time for fun family activities as I worked my way through writing this book. Your patience with me is astounding. I want to thank my Mom for introducing me to computers at a very young age and teaching me the basics. Finally, I want to thank my Dad for pushing me to work hard and for showing me how to be a father.

CONTENTS

INTRODUCTION

WITH THE INTRODUCTION OF THE IPHONE, Apple revolutionized the mobile computing market. The iPhone transformed the mobile phone from a device that you could use to make calls, check e-mail, and look up movie times into a computer that could run almost any type of application. Since the iPhone's release in 2007, developers have written over 700,000 applications that run on iOS devices. These apps encompass many categories, including games, utilities, social networking, reference, navigation, and business, among many others.

The trend in the field of computing is moving toward mobility and mobile platforms, like the iPhone and iPad, and away from a desktop-based environment. Particularly in business and corporate environments, decision makers want convenient, 24-hour access to their data. The iPhone and iPad are ideal platforms for mobile computing because of their form factor and extensive set of libraries and APIs.

Although there are many terrific books about iOS software development on the market, I couldn't find one geared specifically toward the enterprise developer that needs to mobilize corporate data or business applications. My original goal for this book was to present these developers with the information that they would need to be able to get enterprise data from a back office server, display and manipulate that data on a mobile device, and then get the appropriate information back into their corporate information system.

As I worked through writing the book, it became clear that the tools and techniques that I cover in the book are applicable to many classes of applications in addition to the business use case I had in mind when I started. Developers of any type of application that needs to store data on iOS will certainly be interested in the extensive coverage of the Core Data API. Any developer attempting to send data to an external web service such as Facebook or Twitter can benefit from the section of the book dealing with XML and web services. Many applications need to display data using tables, which I also cover in detail. Finally, all iOS applications have a user interface, and I cover building user interfaces using storyboards. Even though my original goal was to write a book for enterprise developers, I believe I have written one that is useful when developing applications of just about any type.

WHAT'S NEW IN THIS EDITION

Since the first edition of this book, much has changed in the iOS development community. Apple continues to deliver new versions of iOS with new features that help developers build even better applications for Apple devices.

Apple has greatly simplified memory management in iOS applications with the introduction of Automatic Reference Counting, or ARC. The developer is no longer required to manually retain and release memory, ARC takes care of this for you. Therefore, I have updated the examples in this book to implement ARC and to be ARC-compatible.

Apple also streamlined the development of iOS UIs with the delivery of Storyboards. Storyboards replace the functionality that was formerly delivered in Interface Builder. Now, you can do all of your UI work right inside of Xcode in a Storyboard. I have modified the code and examples from the previous edition to use Storyboards where appropriate.

Finally, all of the screenshots and many of the other figures have been redrawn to reflect these and other changes to developing in the iOS ecosystem since the first edition.

WHO THIS BOOK IS FOR

As I mentioned, I started out writing this book for enterprise developers tasked with mobilizing corporate data and producing applications that could present and manipulate this data on a mobile device. During the process of writing the book, I became convinced that the tools, APIs, and development techniques I was covering were valuable for many categories of application development outside of the business realm. Anyone writing an application that deals with data in just about any way should find this book useful.

This should not be your first book on iOS application development. You will not find a "Hello World" iOS application here. There are many good books on learning to build basic iOS applications. I have aimed this book at developers who already understand how to build an iOS application, how to design and build a user interface using Interface Builder, and those who have a firm foundation in Objective-C. That is not to say that beginners will find nothing of use here, only that I write from a position that the reader already understands the basic architecture of iOS applications and knows his way around the Xcode tools.

WHAT THIS BOOK COVERS

This book covers the technologies that you need to understand to build data-centric applications for iOS. You will find a chapter on SQLite, the database engine that is included as a part of iOS. Here, you will learn how to import data into the database from different file formats and how to query that data on the device. I cover the UITableView control extensively, including different strategies for customizing the display of your data. Additionally, I cover using storyboards to build your application UI. You will also see extensive coverage of the Core Data API. You will find yourself using this terrific data persistence framework often, as you need to create and store data on the device. Finally, I cover handling and creating XML on iOS and integrating your applications with web services.

HOW THIS BOOK IS STRUCTURED

I've structured this book in three parts that loosely correspond to the flow of data in an enterprise application. The first part of the book covers getting data out of a large-scale database such as Oracle, MySQL, or SQLServer; getting it on the device; and displaying it. The second part of this book covers creating data on the device and the Core Data API. The final part covers getting data out of the device and communicating with web services. Although I have tried to present the material in a logical order from chapter to chapter, there is no need to read this book in order. If you are building a table view–based application and need to know how to customize the look and feel of your table, jump right into Chapter 3. If you are building an app specifically for the iPad, look at Chapter 4. If you need to implement Core Data, jump right into Part II. If you need to integrate with a web service, check out Chapters 10 and 11.

WHAT YOU NEED TO USE THIS BOOK

Because I geared this book toward intermediate to advanced iOS developers, you should already have all the tools you need to use this book. You need an Apple computer with Mac OS X to build applications for iOS. Additionally, you need to install the Xcode development environment that Apple graciously offers for free on the Mac App Store.

The only other requirement is that if you intend to install your applications on a physical device, as opposed to simply running your code in the iOS simulator, you need to join the iOS developer program. At the time of this writing, joining the program costs $99 annually and entitles you to build and run programs on your device and to submit your finished applications to Apple's iOS App Store for sale. If you are not currently part of the developer program, don't worry. There is little in the book that requires you to run on an actual device. Nearly everything works correctly in the simulator. Where there is a need to run on the device, I have noted that in the text.

CONVENTIONS

To help you get the most from the text and keep track of what's happening, we've used a number of conventions throughout the book.

> **WARNING** *Warnings hold important, not-to-be-forgotten information that is directly relevant to the surrounding text.*

> **NOTE** *Notes indicates notes, tips, hints, tricks, or asides to the current discussion.*

As for styles in the text:

➤ We highlight new terms and important words when we introduce them.

➤ We show keyboard strokes like this: Ctrl+A.

> ➤ We show file names, URLs, and code within the text like so: `persistence.properties`.

> ➤ We present code in two different ways:

```
We use a monofont type with no highlighting for most code examples.
```

We use bold to emphasize code that is particularly important in the present context or to show changes from a previous code snippet.

SOURCE CODE

As you work through the examples in this book, you may choose either to type in all the code manually, or to use the source code files that accompany the book. All the source code used in this book is available for download at `www.wrox.com`. Specifically for this book, the code download is on the Download Code tab at:

`www.wrox.com/remtitle.cgi?isbn=1118391845`

You can also search for the book at `www.wrox.com` by ISBN (the ISBN for this book is 978-1-1183-9184-6) to find the code. And a complete list of code downloads for all current Wrox books is available at `www.wrox.com/dynamic/books/download.aspx`.

Throughout each chapter, you'll find references to the names of code files as needed in listing titles and text.

Most of the code on `www.wrox.com` is compressed in a .ZIP, .RAR archive or similar archive format appropriate to the platform. Once you download the code, just decompress it with an appropriate compression tool.

ERRATA

We make every effort to ensure that there are no errors in the text or in the code. However, no one is perfect, and mistakes do occur. If you find an error in one of our books, like a spelling mistake or faulty piece of code, we would be very grateful for your feedback. By sending in errata, you may save another reader hours of frustration, and at the same time, you will be helping us provide even higher quality information.

To find the errata page for this book, go to

`www.wrox.com/remtitle.cgi?isbn=1118391845`

And click the Errata link. On this page you can view all errata that has been submitted for this book and posted by Wrox editors.

If you don't spot "your" error on the Book Errata page, go to `www.wrox.com/contact/techsupport.shtml` and complete the form there to send us the error you have found. We'll check the information and, if appropriate, post a message to the book's errata page and fix the problem in subsequent editions of the book.

P2P.WROX.COM

For author and peer discussion, join the P2P forums at http://p2p.wrox.com. The forums are a Web-based system for you to post messages relating to Wrox books and related technologies and interact with other readers and technology users. The forums offer a subscription feature to e-mail you topics of interest of your choosing when new posts are made to the forums. Wrox authors, editors, other industry experts, and your fellow readers are present on these forums.

At http://p2p.wrox.com, you will find a number of different forums that will help you, not only as you read this book, but also as you develop your own applications. To join the forums, just follow these steps:

1. Go to http://p2p.wrox.com and click the Register link.
2. Read the terms of use and click Agree.
3. Complete the required information to join, as well as any optional information you wish to provide, and click Submit.
4. You will receive an e-mail with information describing how to verify your account and complete the joining process.

> **NOTE** *You can read messages in the forums without joining P2P, but in order to post your own messages, you must join.*

Once you join, you can post new messages and respond to messages other users post. You can read messages at any time on the Web. If you would like to have new messages from a particular forum e-mailed to you, click the Subscribe to this Forum icon by the forum name in the forum listing.

For more information about how to use the Wrox P2P, be sure to read the P2P FAQs for answers to questions about how the forum software works, as well as many common questions specific to P2P and Wrox books. To read the FAQs, click the FAQ link on any P2P page.

PART I
Manipulating and Displaying Data on the iPhone and iPad

Introducing Data-Driven Applications

WHAT'S IN THIS CHAPTER?

➤ Creating a view-based application using Xcode

➤ Building a simple data model

➤ Neatly displaying your data in a table using the UITableView control

WROX.COM CODE DOWNLOADS FOR THIS CHAPTER

The wrox.com code downloads for this chapter are found at www.wrox.com/remtitle .cgi?isbn=1118391845 on the Download Code tab. The code is in the Chapter 1 download and individually named according to the names throughout the chapter.

Data is the backbone of most applications. It is not limited only to business applications. Games, graphics editors, and spreadsheets all use and manipulate data in one form or another. One of the most exciting things about iOS applications is that they enable you and your customers to take your data anywhere. The mobility of iOS devices gives the developer an amazing platform for developing applications that work with that data. You can use the power of existing data to build applications that use that data in new ways. In this book, you will learn how to display data, create and manipulate data, and send and retrieve data over the Internet.

In this chapter, you learn how to build a simple data-driven application. While this application will not be production-ready, it is intended to help you to get started using the tools that you will use as you build data-driven applications. By the end of this chapter, you will be able to create a view-based application using Xcode that displays your data using the UITableView control. You will also gain an understanding of the Model-View-Controller (MVC) architecture that underlies most iOS applications.

BUILDING A SIMPLE DATA-DRIVEN APPLICATION

Many applications that you will build for iOS will need to handle data in one form or another. It is common to display this data in a table. In this section, you learn how to build an application that displays your data in a table in an iOS application.

Creating the Project

To build applications for iOS, you need to use the Xcode development environment provided by Apple. Xcode is a powerful integrated development environment that has all of the features of a modern IDE. It integrates many powerful features including code editing, debugging, version control, and software profiling. If you do not have Xcode installed, you can install it via the Mac App Store or by downloading it from the Apple developer website at `https://developer.apple .com/xcode/index.php`.

To begin, start up Xcode and select File ➪ New ➪ Project. A dialog box appears that displays templates for the various types of applications that you can create for iOS and Mac OS X, as shown in Figure 1-1.

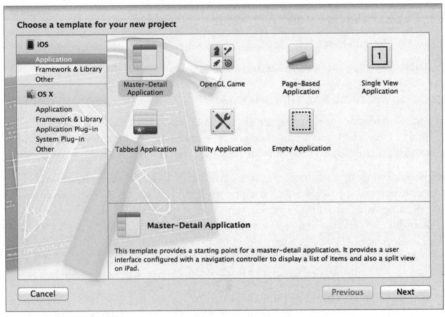

FIGURE 1-1: New Project dialog

Each option presented provides you with the basic setup needed to start developing your application. The default iOS templates are divided into three groups: Application, Framework & Library, and Other.

The Application group consists of the following templates:

➤ **Master-Detail Application:** This template provides a starting point for a master-detail application. It provides a user interface configured with a navigation controller to display a list of items and a split view on iPad. The Contacts application is an example of a Master-Detail Application. The contact list is the master table and detail is the individual contact information that you see when you tap a contact.

➤ **OpenGL Game:** This template provides a starting point for an OpenGL ES-based game. It provides a view into which you render your OpenGL ES scene and a timer to allow you to animate the view. OpenGL is a graphics language that you can use to build games and other graphics-intensive applications. You will not be using OpenGL in this book.

➤ **Page-Based Application:** This template provides a starting point for a page-based application that uses a page view controller. You can use this template to build applications that incorporate page layout and page turning animations like iBooks.

➤ **Single View Application:** This template provides a starting point for an application that uses a single view. It provides a view controller to manage the view and a storyboard or nib file that contains the view. The calculator application is an example of a single view application.

➤ **Tabbed Application:** This template provides a starting point for an application that uses a tab bar. It provides a user interface configured with a tab bar controller, and view controllers for the tab bar items. The Clock application is a tabbed application. The tabs at the bottom let you switch between the world clock, alarm, stopwatch, and timer.

➤ **Utility Application:** This template provides a starting point for a utility application that has a main view and an alternate view. For iPhone, it sets up an Info button to flip the main view to the alternate view. For iPad, it sets up an Info bar button that shows the alternate view in a popover. Weather is a utility application. It provides a simple interface and an information button that flips the interface to allow for advanced customization.

➤ **Empty Application:** This template provides a starting point for any application. It provides just an application delegate and a window. You can use this template if you want to build your application entirely from scratch without very much template code.

The Framework & Library template set consists of a single template: Cocoa Touch Static Library. You can use this template to build static libraries of code that link against the Foundation framework. You will not use this template in this book. However, this template is useful for building libraries of code that you can share amongst multiple projects.

The Other template set consists of only a single template: Empty. The Empty template is just an empty project waiting for you to fill it up with code. You will not use this template in this book, but it is useful if you want to start a new project and none of the existing templates is appropriate.

For this sample application, you are going to use the straightforward Single View Application template.

Select the Single View Application template from the dialog box and click the Next button. Set the Product Name of your project to **SampleTableProject**, leave the Company Identifier at its default setting, and choose iPhone from the Devices drop-down. Check the checkbox labeled Use Automatic

Reference Counting, and make sure that the other two checkboxes are unchecked. Click the Next button. Select a location to save your project, and click the Create button. Xcode creates your project and presents the project window. You are now ready to get started!

Xcode now displays the project window, as shown in Figure 1-2. In the project window, you will see the navigator in the left-hand pane. The navigator simplifies navigation through various aspects of your project. The selector bar at the top of the navigator area allows you to select the specific area that you want to navigate. There are seven different navigators that you can use.

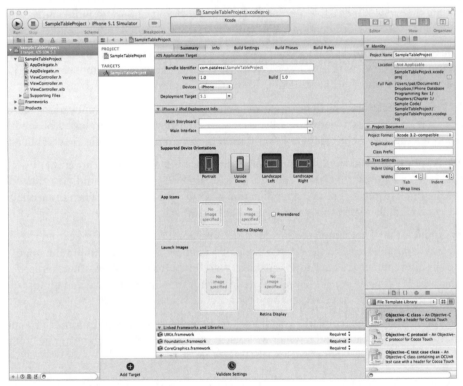

FIGURE 1-2: Xcode project window

The first icon in the navigator selector bar represents the Project Navigator. You use the Project Navigator to view the files that are part of your project. You can organize your files in folders and use the Project Navigator to drill down through these folders to get to the file that you want to edit.

Whatever item you select in the Project Navigator appears in the Editor area. Selecting a source code file (.m extension) will result in that file opening in the Editor area. If you select a user interface file (.xib extension), Interface Builder will open in the Editor area, allowing you to work on the user interface file. Double-clicking on a code file opens the code in a new tab, which can make your code easier to work with. If you prefer that double-clicking a code file opens the code in a new window, you can change this behavior in the General tab of Xcode ➪ Preferences dialog.

You can change various configuration settings for your project by selecting the project node at the top of the Project Navigator to open the project settings in the Editor area.

In addition to the Project Navigator, you can also find the Symbol, Search, Issue, Debug, Breakpoint, and Log Navigators in the left pane. You can use these various navigators to get different views of your project. Feel free to click on any of the folders, files, or navigator tab icons to explore how Xcode organizes your project. You can add additional folders at any time to help keep your code and other project assets such as images, sound, and text files under control.

Adding a UITableView

The most common control used to display data on iOS is the UITableView. As the name suggests, the UITableView is a view that you can use to display data in a table. You can see the UITableView in action in iOS's Contacts application. The application displays your list of contacts in a UITableView control. You learn much more about the UITableView control in Chapter 3.

Typically, when developing the interface for your iOS applications, you will use the Interface Builder. This tool is invaluable for interactively laying out, designing, and developing your user interface. However, the focus of this chapter is not on designing a beautiful interface; it is on displaying data on iOS. So instead of using Interface Builder to design the screen that will hold a table view, you will just create and display it programmatically.

To create the table view, you will be modifying the main View Controller for the sample project.

Model-View-Controller Architecture

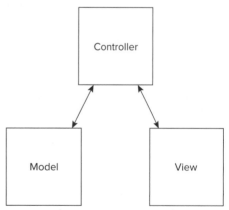

Before I move on with the sample, it's important that you understand the basic architecture used to build most iOS applications: Model-View-Controller. There are three parts to the architecture, shown in Figure 1-3. As you can probably guess, they are the model, the view, and the controller.

The *model* is the class or set of classes that represent your data. You should design your model classes to contain your data, the functions that operate on that data, and nothing more. Model classes should not need to know how to display the data that they contain. In fact, think of a model class as a class that doesn't know about anything else except its own data. When the

FIGURE 1-3: Model-View-Controller architecture

state of the data in the model changes, the model can notify anyone interested, informing the listener of the state change. Alternatively, controller classes can observe the model and react to changes.

In general, model objects should encapsulate all your data. Encapsulation is an important object-oriented design principle. The idea of encapsulation is to prevent other objects from changing your object's data. To effectively encapsulate your data, you should implement interface methods or properties that expose the data of a model class. Classes should not make their data available through public variables.

A complete discussion of object-oriented programming is beyond the scope of this book, but there are many good resources for learning all about OOP. I have included some sources in the "Further Exploration" section at the end of this chapter. Encapsulating your data in model objects will lead to good, clean, object-oriented designs that you can easily extend and maintain.

The *view* portion of the MVC architecture is your user interface. The graphics, widgets, tables, and text boxes present the data encapsulated in your model to the user. The user interacts with your model through the view. View classes should contain only the code that is required to present the model data to the user. In many iOS applications, you won't need to write any code for your view. Quite often, you will design and build it entirely within Interface Builder.

The *controller* is the glue that binds your model to your view. The controller contains all the logic for telling the view what to display. It is also responsible for telling your model how to change based on input from the user. Almost all the code in your iOS applications will be contained in controller classes.

To quickly summarize, the *model* is your application data, the view is the user interface, and the controller is the business logic code that binds the view to the model.

In the sample application, you will be creating a class that acts as the model for the data. Xcode creates a default controller for the application as part of the Single View Application code template, and you are going to add a `table view` as the view so that you can see the data contained in the model. You will then code the controller to bind the view and model.

Adding the Table View Programmatically

Now that you have a basic understanding of the MVC architecture, you can move ahead and add the `table view` to the application. Open the SampleTableProject folder in the Project Navigator pane by clicking the disclosure triangle to the left of the folder. Select the `ViewController.m` file to display its code in the code window.

Because you are not using Interface Builder to build the interface for this application, you will override the `loadView` method of the `UIViewController` to build the view. You are going to write code in the `loadView` method so that when the View Controller tries to load the view, it will create an instance of the `UITableView` class and set its `view` property to the newly created view. Add the following code to the `ViewController` class implementation:

```
- (void)loadView {
    CGRect cgRct = CGRectMake(0, 20, 320, 460);
    UITableView * myTable = [[UITableView alloc] initWithFrame:cgRct];
    self.view = myTable;
}
```

The first line creates a `CGRect`, which is a Core Graphics structure used to specify the size and location for the `table view`. You set it to have its origin at (0, 20), and defined it to be 320 points wide by 460 points high. The `table view` will cover the entire screen, but start 20 points from the top, below the status bar.

The next line creates an instance of a `UITableView` and initializes it with the dimensions that you specified in the previous line.

Just creating the `table view` instance is not enough to get it to display in the view. You have to inform the View Controller about it by setting the View Controller's `view` property to the `table view` that you just created.

You can go ahead and click the Run icon in the toolbar at the top left of the Xcode window to run the project. You will see that your application compiles successfully and starts in the iOS simulator. You should also see a bunch of gray lines in the simulator, as shown in Figure 1-4. That is your `table view`! Those gray lines divide your rows of data. Unfortunately, there is no data for your `table view` to display yet, so the table is blank. You can, however, click in the simulator and drag the `table view`. You should see the lines move as you drag up and down and then snap back into position as you let go of the mouse button.

FIGURE 1-4: Running an application with table view

Retrieving Data

A table is useless without some data to display. To keep this first example simple, you are going to create a very simple data model. The data model will be a class that contains a list of names that you would like to display in the table. The model class will consist of an array to hold the list of data, a method that will return the name for any given index, and a method that will return the total number of items in the model.

To create a new class in your project, begin by clicking the SampleTableProject folder in the Project Navigator in Xcode. Then select File ⇨ New ⇨ File. You will see the New File dialog that shows all of the types of files that you can create in an Xcode project.

Select Cocoa Touch in the left pane of the dialog box, select Objective-C Class as the type of file that you want to create, and click Next. On the next screen, name your class `DataModel` by typing **DataModel** into the Class text box. Then select `NSObject` in the drop-down box next to Subclass Of. The template allows you to create Objective-C classes that are subclasses of `NSObject`, `UIView`, `UIViewController`, `UITableViewController`, or `UITableViewCell`. In this case, you want to create a subclass of `NSObject`, so just leave `NSObject` selected. Click Next to move to the net screen.

In the final dialog screen, you can tell Xcode where to put your new file. The options in this dialog allow you to specify the location for your file, the group to contain your new class, and the build target to compile your file. Leave the options at their defaults and click Create to have Xcode generate your new class files.

Implementing Your Data Model Class

For your class to serve data to the `table view`, you'll need a method to return the requested data. So, you'll create an interface method called `getNameAtIndex` that will return the name from the model that corresponds with the index that is passed in.

Bring up your `DataModel.h` header file by selecting it in the Project Navigator in Xcode. Below the interface definition, add the following line of code to declare the `getNameAtIndex` interface method:

```
-(NSString*) getNameAtIndex:(int) index;
```

You will also need an interface method that tells users of the class how many rows you will be returning. So, add another method to the interface called `getRowCount`. Below the declaration for `getNameAtIndex`, add the declaration for `getRowCount`:

```
-(int) getRowCount;
```

Your header file should look like this:

```
#import <Foundation/Foundation.h>

@interface DataModel : NSObject
-(NSString*) getNameAtIndex:(int) index;
-(int) getRowCount;

@end
```

Now switch over to the data model implementation file `DataModel.m` and implement the new methods. You can quickly switch between a header and an implementation file in Xcode by using the shortcut key combination Ctrl+Cmd+Up Arrow. You can also use the Assistant Editor to view your source and header files side by side. The Assistant Editor is the second icon in the Editor menu bar on the top right side of the Xcode window. It looks like a tuxedo.

> **NOTE** *You will be well served to learn the keyboard shortcuts in Xcode. The small amount of time that you invest in learning them will more than pay off in time saved.*

Below the `#import` statement in your implementation file, add a local variable to hold the data list. Typically, the data in your application will come from a database or some other datasource. To keep this example simple, you'll use an `NSArray` as the datasource. Add the following line to the `DataModel.m` file below the `#import` statement:

```
NSArray* myData;
```

Now, inside the `@implementation` block, you add the implementation of the `getNameAtIndex` method. Add the following code stub between the `@implementation` and `@end` tags in `DataModel.m`:

```
-(NSString*) getNameAtIndex:(int) index
{

}
```

Before you get to the lookup implementation, you need to initialize the data store, the `myData` array. For this example, you do that in the initializer of the class. Above the function stub `getNameAtIndex`, add the following code to initialize the class:

```
-(id)init
{
    if (self = [super init])
    {
        // Initialization code
        myData = [[NSArray alloc] initWithObjects:@"Albert", @"Bill", @"Chuck",
                    @"Dave", @"Ethan", @"Franny", @"George", @"Holly", @"Inez",
                    nil];
    }
    return self;
}
```

The first line calls the superclass's `init` function. You should always call `init` on the superclass in any subclass that you implement. You need to do this to ensure that attributes of the superclass are constructed before you begin doing anything in your subclass.

The next line allocates memory for the array and populates it with a list of names.

The final line returns an instance of the class.

Now that you have the data initialized, you can implement the function to get your data. This is quite simple in this example. You just return the string at the specified location in the array like so:

```
-(NSString*) getNameAtIndex:(int) index
{
    return (NSString*)[myData objectAtIndex:index];
}
```

This line of code simply looks up the object at the specified index in the array and casts it to an `NSString*`. You know that this is safe because you have populated the data by hand and are sure that the object at the given index is an `NSString`.

> **NOTE** *To keep this example simple, I have omitted bounds checking that you would add in a production application.*

To implement `getRowCount`, you simply return the count of the local array like this:

```
-(int) getRowCount
{
    return [myData count];
}
```

At this point, if you build your project by selecting Product ⇨ Build from the menu or pressing Cmd+B, your code should compile and link cleanly with no errors or warnings. If you have an error or warning, go back and look at the code provided and make sure that you have typed everything correctly.

I am a big proponent of compiling early and often. Typically, after every method that I write or any particularly tricky bit of code, I attempt to build. This is a good habit to get into, because it is much easier to narrow down compile errors if the amount of new code that you have added since your last successful compile is small. This practice also limits the number of errors or warnings that you receive. If you wait until you have written 2,000 lines before attempting to compile, you are likely to find the number of errors (or at least warnings) that you receive overwhelming. It is also sometimes difficult to track down the source of these errors because compiler and linker errors tend to be a little cryptic.

Your completed data model class should look like this:

```
#import "DataModel.h"
NSArray* myData;

@implementation DataModel

-(id)init
{
    if (self = [super init])
    {
        // Initialization code
        myData = [[NSArray alloc] initWithObjects:@"Albert", @"Bill", @"Chuck",
                    @"Dave", @"Ethan", @"Franny", @"George", @"Holly", @"Inez",
                    nil];
    }
    return self;
}

-(NSString*) getNameAtIndex:(int) index
{
    return (NSString*)[myData objectAtIndex:index];
}

-(int) getRowCount
{
    return [myData count];
}


@end
```

Displaying the Data

Now that you have the view and model in place, you have to hook them up using the controller. For a table view to display data, it needs to know what the data is and how to display it. To do this, a UITableView object must have a delegate and a datasource. The datasource coordinates the data from your model with the table view. The delegate controls the appearance and behavior of the table view. To guarantee that you have properly implemented the delegate, it must implement the UITableViewDelegate protocol. Likewise, the datasource must implement the UITableViewDataSource protocol.

Protocols

If you are familiar with Java or C++, protocols should also be familiar. Java interfaces and C++ pure virtual classes are the same as protocols. A *protocol* is just a formal contract between a caller and an implementer. The protocol definition states what methods a class that implements the protocol must implement. The protocol can also include optional methods.

Saying that a table view's delegate must implement the UITableViewDelegate protocol means you agree to a contract. That contract states that you will implement the required methods specified in the UITableViewDelegate protocol. Similarly, a class that will be set as the datasource for a table view must implement the required methods specified in the UITableViewDataSource protocol. This may sound confusing, but it will become clearer as you continue to work through the example.

To keep this example as simple as possible and to avoid introducing more classes, you make the ViewController the delegate and datasource for the table view. To do this, you have to implement the UITableViewDelegate and UITableViewDataSource protocols in the ViewController. You need to declare that the ViewController class implements these protocols in the header file. Change the @interface line in the ViewController.h header file to add the protocols that you plan to implement in angle brackets after the interface name and inheritance hierarchy like so:

```
@interface ViewController : UIViewController
    <UITableViewDataSource, UITableViewDelegate>
```

If you try to build your project now, you will get some warnings. Go to the Issue Navigator in the navigator pane by clicking the Issue Navigator icon at the top of the navigator pane or by using the shortcut Cmd+4. Your screen should look something like Figure 1-5.

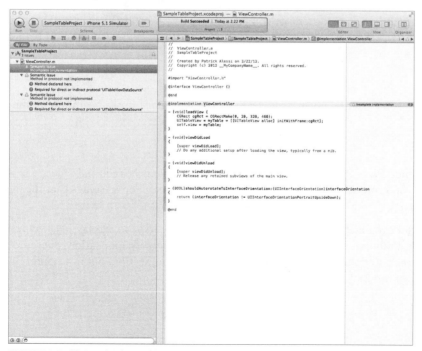

FIGURE 1-5: Using the Issue Navigator

You should see warnings associated with the compilation of ViewController.m; specifically, you should see the warnings "Semantic Issue incomplete implementation" and "Semantic Issue Method in protocol not implemented."

These warnings are clear. You have not implemented the protocols that you claimed you would implement. In fact, if you expand the issues in the Issue Navigator, you can use the navigator to see the required methods that you failed to implement. Expand the first "Semantic Issue Method in protocol not implemented" issue, and you will see two items. Click on the item labeled "Method declared here," and you will see the protocol definition in the editor pane with the method that you did not implement highlighted. In this case, it is the tableView:numberOfRowsInSection: method. If you click on the item labeled "Required for direct or indirect protocol 'UITableViewDataSource,'" the editor window changes back to your source code where you declared that you were going to implement the UITableViewDataSource protocol.

If you have any doubt about which methods are required to implement a protocol, a quick build will tell you and show you the exact method or methods that you have failed to implement.

Implementing the UITableViewDataSource Protocol

You can get rid of those warnings and move one step closer to a working application by implementing the UITableViewDataSource protocol.

Because you will be using the DataModel class in the ViewController class, you have to import the DataModel.h header file. In the ViewController.h header file, add the following #import statement just below the #import <UIKit/UIKit.h> statement:

```
#import "DataModel.h"
```

Now that you've imported the DataModel class, you have to create an instance variable of the DataModel type. In the ViewController.m implementation, add the following declaration below the @implementation keyword:

```
DataModel* model;
```

To actually create the instance of the model class, add the following code to the beginning of the loadView method:

```
model = [[DataModel alloc] init];
```

Now that you have an initialized model ready to go, you can implement the required UITableViewDataSource protocol methods. You can see from the compiler warnings that the methods you need to implement are cellForRowAtIndexPath and numberOfRowsInSection.

The numberOfRowsInSection method tells the table view how many rows to display in the current section. You can divide a table view into multiple sections. In the Contacts application, a letter of the alphabet precedes each section. In this example, you have only one section, but in Chapter 3, you see how to implement multiple sections.

To implement `numberOfRowsInSection`, get the number of rows that the datasource contains by calling the model's `getRowCount` method:

```
- (NSInteger)tableView:(UITableView *)tableView
    numberOfRowsInSection:(NSInteger)section{
    return [model getRowCount];
}
```

If you look at the Issue Navigator now, you will see that the warning about not implementing `numberOfRowsInSection` is gone.

The `cellForRowAtIndexPath` method returns the actual `UITableViewCell` object that will display your data in the table view. The table view calls this method any time it needs to display a cell. The `NSIndexPath` parameter identifies the desired cell. So, what you need to do is write a method that returns the correct `UITableViewCell` based on the row that the table view asks for. You do that like so:

```
- (UITableViewCell *)tableView:(UITableView *)tableView
        cellForRowAtIndexPath:(NSIndexPath *)indexPath
{
    static NSString *CellIdentifier = @"Cell";

    UITableViewCell *cell = [tableView
                            dequeueReusableCellWithIdentifier:CellIdentifier];
    if (cell == nil) {
        cell = [[UITableViewCell alloc]
                initWithStyle:UITableViewCellStyleDefault
                reuseIdentifier:CellIdentifier] ;
    }

    NSUInteger row = [indexPath row];
    cell.textLabel.text = [model getNameAtIndex:row];
    return cell;
}
```

The first few lines of code return a valid `UITableViewCell` object. I will not go into the details of exactly what is happening here because I cover it in detail in Chapter 3, which is dedicated to the `UITableView`. For now, suffice it to say that for performance purposes you want to reuse table view cells whenever possible, and this code does just that.

The last few lines of code find the row that the caller is interested in, look up the data for that row from the model, set the text of the cell to the name in the model, and return the `UITableViewCell`.

That's all there is to it. You should now be able to successfully build the project with no errors or warnings.

Delegates

In designing the iOS SDK and the Cocoa libraries in general, Apple engineers frequently implemented common design patterns. You've already seen how to use the MVC pattern in an application design. Another pattern that you will see all across the Cocoa and Cocoa touch frameworks is delegation.

In the *delegate* pattern, an object appears to do some bit of work; however, it can delegate that work to another class. For example, if your boss asks you to do some work and you hand it off to someone else to do, your boss doesn't care that you or someone else did the work, as long as the work is completed.

While working with the iOS SDK, you will encounter many instances of delegation, and the table view is one such instance. A delegate for the table view implements the `UITableViewDelegate` protocol. This protocol provides methods that manage the selection of rows, control adding and deleting cells, and control configuration of section headings along with various other operations that control the display of your data.

Finishing Up

The only thing left to do with the sample is to set the `UITableView`'s `delegate` and `DataSource` properties. Because you have implemented the `delegate` and `DataSource` protocols, in the `ViewController`, you set both of these properties to `self`.

In the `loadView` method of the `ViewController.m` file, add the following code to configure the datasource and the delegate for the table view:

```
[myTable setDelegate:self];
[myTable setDataSource:self];
```

The final code for the `ViewController.m` should look something like Listing 1-1.

LISTING 1-1: ViewController.m

```
#import "ViewController.h"

@interface ViewController ()

@end

@implementation ViewController
DataModel* model;

- (NSInteger)tableView:(UITableView *)tableView
 numberOfRowsInSection:(NSInteger)section{
    return [model getRowCount];
}

- (UITableViewCell *)tableView:(UITableView *)tableView
        cellForRowAtIndexPath:(NSIndexPath *)indexPath
{
    static NSString *CellIdentifier = @"Cell";

    UITableViewCell *cell = [tableView
                    dequeueReusableCellWithIdentifier:CellIdentifier];
    if (cell == nil) {
        cell = [[UITableViewCell alloc]
                initWithStyle:UITableViewCellStyleDefault
```

```
                        reuseIdentifier:CellIdentifier] ;
    }

    NSUInteger row = [indexPath row];
    cell.textLabel.text = [model getNameAtIndex:row];
    return cell;
}

- (void)loadView {
    model = [[DataModel alloc] init];

    CGRect cgRct = CGRectMake(0, 20, 320, 460);
    UITableView * myTable = [[UITableView alloc] initWithFrame:cgRct];
    self.view = myTable;

    [myTable setDelegate:self];
    [myTable setDataSource:self];

}

- (void)viewDidLoad
{
    [super viewDidLoad];
    // Do any additional setup after loading the view, typically from a nib.
}

- (void)viewDidUnload
{
    [super viewDidUnload];
    // Release any retained subviews of the main view.
}

- (BOOL)shouldAutorotateToInterfaceOrientation:
                    (UIInterfaceOrientation)interfaceOrientation
{
    return (interfaceOrientation != UIInterfaceOrientationPortraitUpsideDown);
}.

@end
```

You should now be able to build and run your application in the simulator. You should see the table populated with the names that are contained in your DataModel class, as in Figure 1-6.

Congratulations! You have successfully built your first data-driven application! If you feel adventurous, feel free to go back and modify the DataModel to use a different datasource, like a text file.

FIGURE 1-6: Running table view with data

FURTHER EXPLORATION

In this chapter, you learned how to build an iOS application that uses the `UITableView` control to display data. You also learned a little bit about design patterns — specifically the Model-View-Controller pattern that is prevalent in iOS application development. In the next chapter, you learn how to use the SQLite database as your datasource. Then, in Chapter 3, you master the `UITableView` control. By the end of Chapter 3, you should be able to build a data-centric iOS application on your own.

Design Patterns

If you are interested in writing maintainable, high-quality software, I highly recommend *Design Patterns: Elements of Reusable Object-Oriented Software* by Erich Gamma, Richard Helm, Ralph Johnson, and John Vlissides (Addison-Wesley, 1994). This is the bible of OO design patterns. The book illustrates each pattern with a UML model, very readable explanations of the patterns and their implementation, and code samples in both C++ and Smalltalk. If you don't already have this masterpiece of computer science, get it now — you won't regret it.

I would also recommend *Object-Oriented Design and Patterns* by Cay S. Horstmann (Wiley, 2005). Although the code in the book is in Java, you will find that the explanations of the patterns introduced are outstanding and will help you further understand the patterns and their importance in implementing high-quality software.

Even if you are not interested in either of these titles, do yourself a favor and search Google for "design patterns." There is a reason why there is a lot of literature on design patterns. It doesn't make any sense to try to reinvent the wheel. Others have already discovered the solutions to many of the problems that you will find in your software designs. These solutions have become design patterns. The point of these design patterns is to present well-tested designs to developers in a form that everyone can understand. The patterns are time proven and offer a common vocabulary that is useful when communicating your design to other developers.

Reading a Text File

If you are interested in making your simple table-viewing application more interesting, it is easy to read data from a text file. The following code snippet shows you how:

```
NSError *error;

NSString *textFileContents = [NSString
    stringWithContentsOfFile:[[NSBundle mainBundle]
    pathForResource:@"myTextFile"
    ofType:@"txt"]
    encoding:NSUTF8StringEncoding
    error:&error];

// If there are no results, something went wrong
if (fileContents == nil) {
    // an error occurred
    NSLog(@"Error reading text file. %@", [error localizedFailureReason]);
```

```
    }

    NSArray *lines = [textFileContents componentsSeparatedByString:@"\n"];
    NSLog(@"Number of lines in the file:%d", [lines count]  );
```

This code reads the contents of the file `myTextFile.txt`, which should be included in your code bundle. Simply create a text file with this name and add it to your Xcode project.

The first line declares an error object that will be returned to you should anything go wrong while trying to read your text file. The next line loads the entire contents of your file into a string.

The next line is an error handler. If you get `nil` back from the call to `stringWithContentesOfFile`, something went wrong. The error is output to the console using the `NSLog` function.

The next line breaks up the large string into an array separated by \n, which is the return character. You create an element in the lines array for each line in your file.

The final line outputs the number of lines read in from the file.

MOVING FORWARD

In this chapter, you learned how to build a simple data-driven application using an `NSArray` as your datasource. You also explored the project options available when creating a project in Xcode. Then you learned about the Model-View-Controller architecture and how the table view fits in with that design. Finally, you looked at the important concepts of protocols and delegates.

In the next chapter, you will learn how to get data from a more robust datasource, the SQLite database. This is the embedded database that is included as part of the iOS SDK. Learning to use this database will enable you to build rich, data-driven applications for iOS.

The iOS Database: SQLite

As an application developer, you have several options when it comes to storing the data used by your iOS application. You could use plist files, XML, or plaintext. Although any of these solutions is acceptable in certain situations, not all provide the best efficiency for your application. None of these formats allows you to query for specific data quickly, nor does any provide an efficient way to sort your data. If you have designed your application to work with a large data set and you would like to be able to query and sort it, you should consider using SQLite.

In the previous chapter, you learned how to display a small dataset that was stored in a simple array. As you move on to build more complicated applications, chances are that your data set will grow. Hard-coded arrays will probably not meet the demanding requirements of a more complicated application. You will find as you progress with your iOS development that you need a data storage solution more robust than a simple array.

In this chapter, you will learn about the database engine that backs many iOS applications: SQLite. By the end of this chapter, you will be able to build an application that uses SQLite as its backing data store.

To use SQLite, you will first learn to create a database using the command-line application provided with Mac OS X. This tool will enable you to create the schema of your database, populate it with data, and perform queries.

Next, you will learn how to deploy your database with an iOS application, connect to it in code, and display the results or your SQL queries.

By the end of the chapter, you will know how to build a fully functional database application that you can use to view data that has a master-detail relationship: in this case, a product catalog.

WHAT IS SQLITE?

SQLite is an open source library, written in C, that implements a self-contained SQL relational database engine. You can use SQLite to store large amounts of relational data. The developers of SQLite have optimized it for use on embedded devices like the iPhone and iPad.

Although the Core Data application programming interface (API) is also designed to store data on iOS, its primary purpose is to persist objects created by your application. SQLite excels when pre-loading your application with a large amount of data, whereas Core Data excels at managing data created on the device.

The SQLite Library

Because SQLite is a fully self-contained SQL database engine, all the data required to implement the database is stored in a single, cross-platform disk file. Because SQLite is self-contained, it requires few external libraries and little support from the operating system. This is the prime reason that it is ideal for a mobile platform like iOS.

Apple has adopted SQLite for use on iOS for other reasons as well, including its small footprint. Weighing in at less than 300K, the library is small enough to use effectively on mobile devices with limited memory. What's more, SQLite requires no configuration files, has no setup procedure, and needs no administration. You can just drop your database file on the device, include the SQLite library in your iOS project, and you are ready to roll.

Because SQLite implements most of the SQL92 standard, working with an SQLite database is intuitive if you already know SQL. You should keep in mind that there are some features of SQL92 that SQLite does not currently support. These include RIGHT and FULL OUTER JOIN, complete support for ALTER TABLE, FOR EACH STATEMENT triggers, writeable VIEWS, and GRANT and REVOKE permissions. For more detail on unsupported functionality, look at the SQLite website http://www .sqlite.org/omitted.html.

Because the interface to SQLite is written in C, and Objective-C is a superset of C, you can easily incorporate SQLite into your Objective-C–based iOS projects.

SQLite and Core Data

When you start a data-centric application for iOS, there is a significant architectural decision that you need to make. Should you use SQLite or Core Data for your data management needs?

Let's take a quick look at what Core Data is and is not. First, Core Data is not a relational database like SQLite. *Core Data* is an object persistence framework. Its primary purpose is to provide the developer with a framework to retain objects that the application creates. Core Data allows you to model your data as objects using a convenient graphical interface built into Xcode. You can then manipulate those objects in code with an extensive set of APIs. Designing and defining your data objects using the graphical interface can simplify the creation of the Model portion of the Model-View-Controller (MVC) architecture.

Core Data can use SQLite, among other storage types, as a backing store for its data. This causes some confusion for developers. It is a common misconception that because Core Data can use SQLite to store data, Core Data is a relational database. This is not correct. As mentioned, Core Data is not an implementation of a relational database. Although Core Data uses SQLite in the background to store your data, it does not store the data in a way that is directly accessible to the developer. In fact, you should never attempt to manually modify the backing database structure or its data. Only the Core Data framework should manipulate the structure of the database and the data itself. Feel free to open the SQLite database and look at it if you are curious, but making any modifications to the data or database structure will likely invalidate it and cause problems when trying to access it using Core Data.

Although Core Data is the preferred framework for dealing with data that you create on a device, SQLite remains a useful tool for iOS developers. If you need the functionality that a relational database provides, you should strongly consider using SQLite directly. However, if you only need to persist objects created during the use of your application, you should consider using Core Data. You explore the Core Data framework in detail in Part II of this book.

Core Data is the recommended framework for creating data on the device, but you may want to forego Core Data and use the SQLite API directly.

You might choose to use a SQLite database if you need to preload a large amount of data on the device. Take, for example, a GPS navigation application. Navigation applications need a great deal of data, including points of interest and the maps themselves. A good option for the architectural design is to create an SQLite database that contains all the point-of-interest (POI) and map data. You can then deploy that database with your application and use SQLite APIs to access the database.

It is easy to create an SQLite database using desktop tools. You can then use the same tools, scripts, or a desktop application to load your data into the database. After that, you can simply deploy the database to the device with your application.

In this chapter, you are going to build the database for a catalog application that a mobile sales force could use. The catalog will need to be preloaded with data, not populated on the device itself, so you will use SQLite as the back-end data store.

BUILDING A SIMPLE DATABASE

In this section, you will build the back-end database for your sales catalog application. Before you start designing the database and the application, you need to understand what the application will do. In the real world, you will (or should) get a detailed specification defining what the application should do and how it should look. Of course, the implementation, or how it should work, is up to the designer and developer. Here are some simple requirements for the catalog application.

The purpose of the application is to display your company's catalog of widgets. Each widget will have a manufacturer, a product name, some details about the product, the price of the product, the quantity on hand, the country of origin, and a picture of the product.

The application should start up by showing a list of products. Tapping on a product should bring up a detail page with detailed information about the product.

It is often helpful to mock up the user interface and design the database on paper as a first step in the design of an application. Often, the interface itself can help drive decisions about how to organize the data in the database. I like to use OmniGraffle by the Omni Group (`http://www.omnigroup.com/applications/OmniGraffle`) to do my design work. It is an easy-to-use yet powerful vector graphics application for the Mac that allows me to quickly do my design work. Additionally, the output of the application is good enough to use in presentations to managers and other stakeholders who may not be technically inclined. It is far easier to explain an application design with pictures than words!

I suspect that the database gurus out there are pulling their hair out right now because it is common wisdom that the user interface and the data should be completely decoupled and that you should normalize the data independently. However, when developing applications that you will run on an embedded device like the iPhone or iPad, performance is an important concern. Data that you have fully normalized, with no duplicated data, can have a negative impact on performance. Sometimes the cost to execute a complicated query is higher than the cost of maintaining the same data in two tables. I am not suggesting that you should not normalize your data at all; just keep in mind how you will display the data while working through the database design process.

Designing the Database

If you do not know, normalization is the process of breaking down your data in a way that makes it easy to query. Normalization helps to avoid common problems in database storage, such as duplication of data. For example, when creating your database, a designer may want to store all the data in a single table, as in Figure 2-1.

If you're unfamiliar with Entity-Relationship Diagrams (ERDs), the box represents an entity or table in the database. The ovals that are connected to the entity are the attributes of that entity or the fields of the table. So, this diagram shows one table with each attribute as a field in the table.

The problem with this database design is that you have not normalized it. There will be duplication of data if more than one product in the catalog is manufactured by the same manufacturer or if more than one product is manufactured in a specific country. In that case, the data may look something like Figure 2-2.

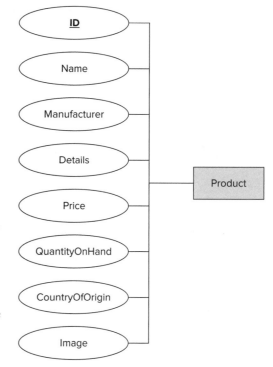

FIGURE 2-1: Storing the data in a single table

ID	Name	Manufacturer	Details	Price	QuantityOnHand	CountryOfOrigin	Image
						Product	
1	Widget A	Spirit Industries	...	...	...	USA	...
2	Widget B	Industrial Designs	...	...	...	Taiwan	...
3	Widget X	Spirit Industries	...	...	...	China	...
4	Widget Y	Industrial Designs	...	...	...	China	...
5	Widget Z	Design Intl.	...	...	...	Singapore	...
6	Widget R	Spirit Industries	...	...	...	USA	...

FIGURE 2-2: Data in a single table

You can see that the same manufacturer has more than one product in the database. In addition, there is more than one product made in a specific country. This design is a maintenance problem. What happens if the data entry person populating the database types in **Spirit Industries** for item 1 and **Spit Industries** for item 3? It will appear in the application that two different companies make these products, when in reality Spirit Industries manufactures both products. This is a data integrity problem that you can avoid by normalizing the data. You can remove the manufacturer and country of origin from the product table and create new tables for these fields. Then, in the product table, you can just reference the value in the related tables.

Additionally, this new design could allow you to add more detail about the manufacturer, such as address, contact name, and so on. For the sake of simplicity, you will not be doing that in this example, but proper normalization makes this type of flexibility possible.

The new design should look something like Figure 2-3.

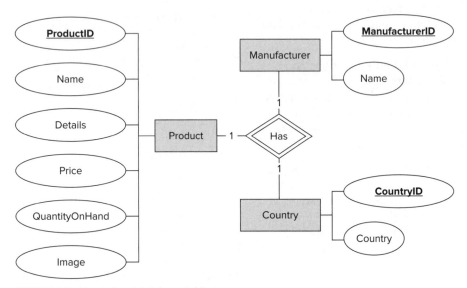

FIGURE 2-3: Normalized database tables

Figure 2-4 shows what the new normalized database will look like.

Product							
ID	Name	ManufacturerID	Details	Price	QuantityOnHand	CountryID	Image
1	Widget A	1	...	...	...	1	...
2	Widget B	2	...	...	...	2	...
3	Widget X	1	...	...	...	3	...
4	Widget Y	2	...	...	...	3	...
5	Widget Z	3	...	...	...	4	...
6	Widget R	1	...	...	...	1	...

Manufacturer	
ManufacturerID	Name
1	Spirit Industries
2	Industrial Designs
3	Design Intl.

Country	
CountryID	Country
1	USA
2	Taiwan
3	China
4	Singapore

FIGURE 2-4: Data in normalized tables

You can see that, instead of specifying the manufacturer and origin explicitly in the main Products table, you just reference the ID in the related tables. The fact that you can relate data in one table to data in another gives a relational database both its name and its power.

Although normalization is important, you can take it too far and overnormalize your data. For instance, you could create a separate table for price. In that case, all products that cost $1 would reference a row in a Price table that contains the value $1. While doing this would eliminate the duplication of data for all products that cost $1, it would be painful to write the code to maintain the relationship between the Product and Price tables. This is overnormalized, and you should avoid it.

As important as normalization is, you should know that laying out the data in a way that optimizes its display is important as well. Optimizing the user experience on the iPhone or iPad is often a difficult and tedious process. Users expect a fast and smooth user experience. If the data is overnormalized, it may be an optimal data storage strategy, but if accessing the data for display at runtime is too costly, the performance of the application will suffer. Remember that you are writing applications for a mobile platform with limited CPU capability. You will pay a penalty for using overly complex SQL to access your data. You are better off in some instances repeating data instead of using relationships.

Creating the Database

You can use a couple of different methods to create, modify, and populate your SQLite database. Let's first look at the command-line interface.

Using a command-line interface may not seem optimal in these days of graphical interfaces, but the command line does have its advantages. One feature that stands out is that you can create and populate a database using the command-line interface and scripts. For example, you could write a PERL script that gets data out of an enterprise database such as Oracle or MySQL and then creates an SQLite database with a subset of the data. Although scripting is beyond the scope of this book, I will show you how to create and populate a database using the command-line tool.

You can also use the command-line interface to import data from a file into a table, read in and execute a file that contains SQL, and output data from a database in a variety of formats, including these:

➤ Comma-separated values

➤ Left-aligned columns

➤ HTML `<table>` code

➤ SQL insert statements for TABLE

➤ One value per line

➤ Values delimited by `.separator` string

➤ Tab-separated values

➤ TCL list elements

To start the command-line tool, you need to bring up a terminal window. Next, change to the directory where you want to store your database file. For this example, you create the database in the root of your home directory and then copy it into the Xcode project that you will create later.

Start the command-line tool and create your new database by typing **sqlite3 catalog.db** at the command prompt. This command starts the command-line tool and attaches the database catalog.db. The ATTACH DATABASE command either attaches an existing database to the SQLite tool or creates a new database if the specified file doesn't already exist. You can attach multiple databases to a single instance of the command-line tool and reference data in each database using dot notation in the form *database-name.table-name*. You can use this powerful feature to migrate data from one database to another.

Aside from being able to execute SQL at the command line, the command-line interface tool has various metacommands that you can use to control the tool itself. You can display these by typing **.help** from the command line. You can see what databases you have attached to the current instance of the tool by typing **.databases** at the command line. You can quit the command-line tool by typing **.exit** or **.quit**.

To create your main Product table, type the **CREATE TABLE** statement at the SQLite command prompt as follows:

```
CREATE TABLE "main"."Product"
  ("ID" INTEGER PRIMARY KEY  AUTOINCREMENT  NOT NULL ,
    "Name" TEXT, "ManufacturerID" INTEGER, "Details" TEXT,
    "Price" DOUBLE, "QuantityOnHand" INTEGER,
    "CountryOfOriginID" INTEGER, "Image" TEXT );
```

A full discussion of the SQL language is beyond the scope of this book. You should pick up a copy of *SQL For Dummies* by Allen Taylor (Wiley, 2010) if you are interested in learning more about the SQL language.

The previous SQL statement creates a table called Product in the main database. It adds the fields that you designed in your ERD. Finally, it specifies that the ID field is the PRIMARY KEY and that it is an AUTOINCREMENT field. This means that you do not have to supply ID values; the database engine will generate them for you.

Now that you have created the Product table, let's move on to creating the Manufacturer and Country tables. Type the following SQL commands at the command prompt:

```
CREATE  TABLE "main"."Manufacturer"
  ("ManufacturerID" INTEGER PRIMARY KEY  AUTOINCREMENT  NOT NULL ,
  "Name" TEXT NOT NULL );

CREATE  TABLE "main"."Country"
  ("CountryID" INTEGER PRIMARY KEY  AUTOINCREMENT  NOT NULL ,
  "Country" TEXT NOT NULL );
```

At the time of this writing, the SQLite engine provided with the Mac OS X Lion operating system is version 3.7.7. This version supports foreign key constraints; however, for simplicity, I am not building the tables with foreign key constraints enabled.

Foreign key constraints allow the database to validate that the values used as a foreign key in a child table map to values stored in the parent table. In our model, the ManufacturerID field in the Product table is a foreign key that references values in the Manufacturer table. In the Manufacturer table, the ManufacturerID field is its primary key. If you wanted the database to enforce the rule that a manufacturer must exist in the Manufacturer table to use a ManufacturerID in the Product table, you would define the ManufacturerID in the Product table as a foreign key that references the ManufacturerID in the Manufacturer table.

You have just successfully created your database. You should have a database file that contains three tables: Product, Manufacturer, and CountryOfOrigin. Now you can put some data into the tables.

Populating the Database

Having a database is great, but the data is what really counts. You can populate your database one item at a time from the command line using INSERT SQL statements.

Creating Records with the INSERT Command

Figure 2-5 shows the syntax for the INSERT statement.

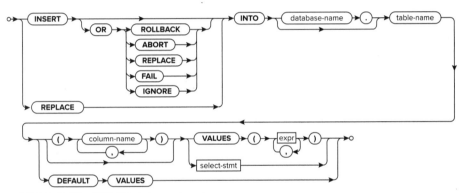

FIGURE 2-5: The INSERT statement syntax

In case you aren't familiar with SQL syntax diagrams, I'll quickly go over how to read them.

The open circles at the beginning and the end are terminators. They show where the SQL statement starts and ends. The arrow that comes out of the terminator indicates the main branch of the statement.

Keywords are in all caps. Keywords on the main branch are required. So, for the INSERT statement, INSERT, INTO, and VALUES are required for an INSERT statement to be valid SQL. Anything that is not on the main branch is optional. Choices for optional keywords are left aligned. For example, the OR after INSERT is optional. If you do use OR, you must pick one and only one of the options ROLLBACK, ABORT, REPLACE, FAIL, or IGNORE.

Text that is not in all caps is data that the user provides. Therefore, the INSERT SQL in Figure 2-5 indicates that the user needs to specify the database name and table name into which the data will be inserted. Additionally, the user must specify the columns into which the data will be inserted and, finally, the values to be inserted.

You can insert a row into the Product table using the following INSERT statement:

```
INSERT INTO "main"."Product"
  ("Name","ManufacturerID","Details","Price","QuantityOnHand",
  "CountryOfOriginID","Image")
  VALUES ('Widget A','1','Details of Widget A','1.29','5','1', 'Canvas_1');
```

Although it is possible, inserting data one row at a time using SQL is inefficient. I mentioned earlier that the command-line tool can import text files into the database. This can come in handy when dumping data from another database, Microsoft Excel, or simply a text file. Instead of typing in each INSERT statement, you can create a text file for each of the database tables and then use the import functionality to get the data into the database.

Create a text file in your home directory called products.txt and include the following data. Note that you use tabs between each field as a delimiter. You can also download the file from this book's companion website.

```
1    Widget A    1    Details of Widget A    1.29    5    1    Canvas_1
2    Widget B    1    Details of Widget B    4.29    15   2    Canvas_2
3    Widget X    1    Details of Widget X    0.29    25   3    Canvas_3
4    Widget Y    1    Details of Widget Y    1.79    5    3    Canvas_4
5    Widget Z    1    Details of Widget Z    6.26    15   4    Canvas_5
6    Widget R    1    Details of Widget R    2.29    45   1    Canvas_6
7    Widget S    1    Details of Widget S    3.29    55   1    Canvas_7
8    Widget T    1    Details of Widget T    4.29    15   2    Canvas_8
9    Widget L    1    Details of Widget L    5.29    50   3    Canvas_9
10   Widget N    1    Details of Widget N    6.29    50   3    Canvas_10
11   Widget E    1    Details of Widget E    17.29   25   4    Canvas_11
12   Part Alpha  2    Details of Part Alpha  1.49    25   1    Canvas_12
13   Part Beta   2    Details of Part Beta   1.89    35   1    Canvas_13
14   Part Gamma  2    Details of Part Gamma  3.46    45   2    Canvas_14
15   Device N    3    Details of Device N    9.29    15   3    Canvas_15
16   Device O    3    Details of Device O    21.29   15   3    Canvas_16
17   Device P    3    Details of Device P    51.29   15   4    Canvas_17
18   Tool A      4    Details of Tool A      14.99   5    1    Canvas_18
19   Tool B      4    Details of Tool B      44.79   5    1    Canvas_19
20   Tool C      4    Details of Tool C      6.59    5    1    Canvas_20
21   Tool D      4    Details of Tool D      8.29    5    1    Canvas_21
```

Each column, separated by a tab in the text file, represents a field in the database. The fields must be in the order that you created them using the CREATE TABLE command. Therefore, the order of the fields is ID, Name, ManufacturerID, Details, Price, QuantityOnHand, CountryOfOriginID, and Image.

To import your data file into the database, open the SQLite command prompt if you do not still have it open. Type the command .separator "\t" to specify that you are using the tab character \t as the field separator in the data file. Then type .import "products.txt" Product to import the file products.txt into the Product table. You should have successfully imported your data into the database.

Reading Your Rows with the SELECT Command

To verify that your data was successfully imported, you can display it using the SQL SELECT statement. The syntax for the SELECT statement appears in Figure 2-6.

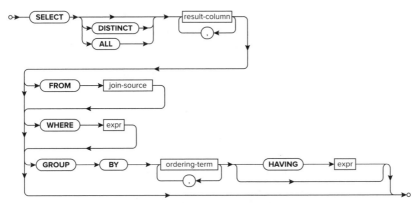

FIGURE 2-6: The SELECT statement syntax

Type `select * from Product;` to see all the rows in your product table. The output should look like this:

```
1    Widget A    1    Details of Widget A    1.29    5    1    Canvas_1
2    Widget B    1    Details of Widget B    4.29    15   2    Canvas_2
3    Widget X    1    Details of Widget X    0.29    25   3    Canvas_3
4    Widget Y    1    Details of Widget Y    1.79    5    3    Canvas_4
5    Widget Z    1    Details of Widget Z    6.26    15   4    Canvas_5
6    Widget R    1    Details of Widget R    2.29    45   1    Canvas_6
7    Widget S    1    Details of Widget S    3.29    55   1    Canvas_7
8    Widget T    1    Details of Widget T    4.29    15   2    Canvas_8
9    Widget L    1    Details of Widget L    5.29    50   3    Canvas_9
10   Widget N    1    Details of Widget N    6.29    50   3    Canvas_10
11   Widget E    1    Details of Widget E    17.29   25   4    Canvas_11
12   Part Alpha  2    Details of Part Alpha  1.49    25   1    Canvas_12
13   Part Beta   2    Details of Part Beta   1.89    35   1    Canvas_13
14   Part Gamma  2    Details of Part Gamma  3.46    45   2    Canvas_14
15   Device N    3    Details of Device N    9.29    15   3    Canvas_15
16   Device O    3    Details of Device O    21.29   15   3    Canvas_16
17   Device P    3    Details of Device P    51.29   15   4    Canvas_17
18   Tool A      4    Details of Tool A      14.99   5    1    Canvas_18
19   Tool B      4    Details of Tool B      44.79   5    1    Canvas_19
20   Tool C      4    Details of Tool C      6.59    5    1    Canvas_20
21   Tool D      4    Details of Tool D      8.29    5    1    Canvas_21
```

This is identical to the input data file, so you are ready to proceed.

Create another text file in your home directory called `manufacturers.txt` and include the following data:

```
1    Spirit Industries
2    Industrial Designs
3    Design Intl.
4    Tool Masters
```

Import the manufacturer data into the Manufacturer table by typing `.import "manufacturers.txt" Manufacturer`. You can again use the SQL SELECT statement to verify that your data has been imported correctly by typing `select * from manufacturer;`.

Finally, create another text file in your home directory called `countries.txt` and include the following data:

```
1   USA
2   Taiwan
3   China
4   Singapore
```

Import the country data into the database by typing `.import "countries.txt" Country` to import the file `countries.txt` into the Country table. You can again use the SQL SELECT statement to verify that your data has been imported correctly by typing `select * from country;`.

Now that you have your data in the database, feel free to experiment with all the standard SQL that you already know! For example, if you want to see all the products ordered by price, you can type `select name,price from product order by price;`. The result of that query is as follows:

```
Widget X      0.29
Widget A      1.29
Part Alpha    1.49
Widget Y      1.79
Part Beta     1.89
Widget R      2.29
Widget S      3.29
Part Gamma    3.46
Widget B      4.29
Widget T      4.29
Widget L      5.29
Widget Z      6.26
Widget N      6.29
Tool C        6.59
Tool D        8.29
Device N      9.29
Tool A        14.99
Widget E      17.29
Device O      21.29
Tool B        44.79
Device P      51.29
```

You can join your tables using standard SQL syntax. For example, you can show each product and the name of the country of origin using this SQL statement `SELECT name,country FROM Product,country where product.countryoforiginid=country.countryid;`. The results are as follows:

```
Widget A      USA
Widget B      Taiwan
Widget X      China
Widget Y      China
Widget Z      Singapore
Widget R      USA
Widget S      USA
```

```
Widget T    Taiwan
Widget L    China
Widget N    China
Widget E    Singapore
Part Alpha  USA
Part Beta   USA
Part Gamma  Taiwan
Device N    China
Device O    China
Device P    Singapore
Tool A      USA
Tool B      USA
Tool C      USA
Tool D      USA
```

You can also filter your data using a WHERE clause. To find all products manufactured in China, you can use the following query:

```
SELECT name, country FROM Product, country where
product.countryoforiginid=country.countryid and country.country="China";.
```

The result of this query is a list of all the products made in China:

```
Widget X    China
Widget Y    China
Widget L    China
Widget N    China
Device N    China
Device O    China
```

Tools to Visualize the SQLite Database

As powerful as the command-line interface to SQLite is, sometimes it is easier to use a graphical user interface (GUI) to examine the database. Many applications provide this functionality. You can find a list of them on the SQLite website at http://www.sqlite.org/cvstrac/wiki?p=ManagementTools.

Feel free to try out any or all of the applications listed on the SQLite site. These applications range in price from free to hundreds of dollars and offer a variety of capabilities, including import/export from various tools and commercial databases, graphical ER modeling, SQL editors with syntax highlighting, and many other advanced features. If you are going to use SQLite for enterprise applications, it may well be worth it to purchase one of these applications.

For developing simple iOS applications that do not require intense database development, I prefer to use the SQLite Manager plug-in for the Firefox web browser. This free plug-in, available at the Google code website (http://code.google.com/p/sqlite-manager/), provides the following features:

➤ Dialog interface for creation and deletion of tables, indexes, views, and triggers

➤ Ability to modify tables by adding and dropping columns

➤ Ability to create or open any existing SQLite databases

➤ Ability to execute arbitrary SQL or simply view all the data in your tables

➤ Visual interface for database settings, eliminating the need to write `pragma` statements to view and change the SQLite library settings

➤ Ability to export tables/views, such as CSV, SQL, or XML files

➤ Ability to import tables from CSV, SQL, or XML files

➤ A tree view that shows all tables, indexes, views, and triggers

➤ Interface to browse data from any table/view

➤ Ability to edit and delete records while browsing data

The plug-in is easy to install and use. You can use the plug-in to create new tables by clicking the Create Table icon. You are then presented with a dialog that contains all the data that you need to create a new table, as shown in Figure 2-7. I have populated the dialog with the fields from the ERD.

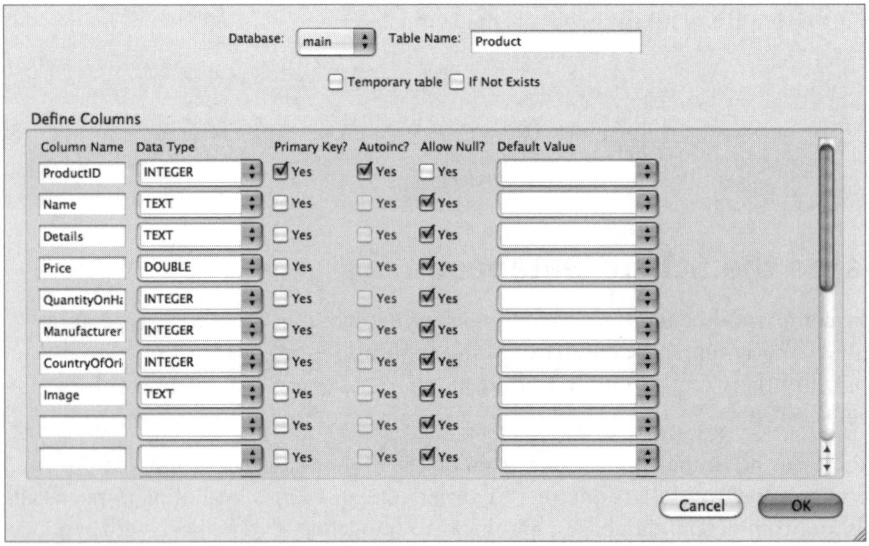

FIGURE 2-7: Creating a table with SQLite Manager

Click the disclosure triangle next to Tables in the left pane of the interface to see a list of all the tables in the database. Selecting a table, like Product in Figure 2-8, reveals the details of the table. You can see the SQL that you originally used to create the table, the number of fields in the table, the number of records, and detailed information on all the columns in the table. You can also add, alter, and drop columns from this view.

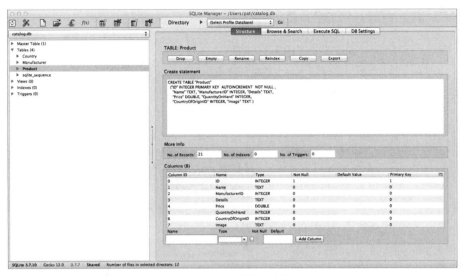

FIGURE 2-8: Viewing table definition data with SQLite Manager

You can select the Browse & Search tab at the top of the right pane to view and edit the data in the selected table, as shown in Figure 2-9.

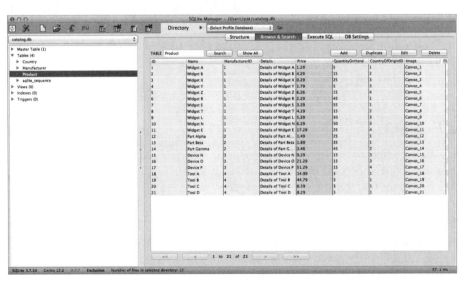

FIGURE 2-9: Browsing table data with SQLite Manager

Selecting the Execute SQL tab enables you to execute arbitrary SQL statements against the database. Finally, the DB Settings tab enables you to view and edit various database settings that are normally only available via `pragma` statements at the command prompt.

CONNECTING TO YOUR DATABASE

Now that you have a catalog database, you can write the iOS application that you will use to view the catalog. To do this, you'll need to create an application with a table view to display the catalog. Clicking a cell in the table view should navigate to a detail page that shows detailed information about the selected catalog entry. To build this interface, you need to be able to connect to your database and run SQL statements against it. You'll also use a Navigation Controller to implement a master-detail interface.

As I previously mentioned, it is often a good idea to mock up your application interface before you get started. It helps to get buy-in from customers that the interface you have designed meets their needs. It is far easier to move around interface items or redesign the look and feel of a mockup than it is to rework your actual application code. You want to find any problems with the design as early as possible to avoid costly and time-consuming changes to the software. A picture can go a long way in explaining to customers what the application will look like. Figure 2-10 shows a mocked-up interface in OmniGraffle.

The interface might not look pretty, but it will get the job done. You will spruce it up a bit in the next chapter. However, for now, it will demonstrate how to get data out of your SQLite database.

FIGURE 2-10: Application interface mockup

Starting the Project

For this project, you are going to implement a master-detail interface. As seen in the mockup in Figure 2-10, the main screen shows the entire product catalog, and tapping an item should display a screen with the details for that item. The UINavigationController is perfect for building this kind of interface. To get started, open Xcode and create a new project using the Master-Detail Application template.

When you create your project, set the Device Family to iPhone and check the Use Automatic Reference Counting checkbox in the Choose options for your new project dialog. You can leave all the other checkboxes unchecked, as in Figure 2-11.

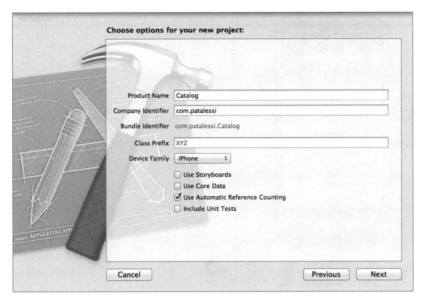

FIGURE 2-11: Project options dialog

This template creates a project that contains two Interface Builder xib files. The MasterViewController.xib file contains the table view that will hold your master data. The DetailViewController.xib file is a placeholder that you will fill with your detail data.

The AppDelegate contains a NavigationController that manages the navigation of the application. The AppDelegate sets the root view controller of the NavigationController to the MasterViewController. You can see this in the application:didFinishLaunchingWithOptions: method in the AppDelegate.

The UINavigationController

You use the Navigation Controller to display and manage a hierarchy of View Controllers. Any time that you need to display hierarchical data, consider using the UINavigationController. The Navigation Controller manages the state of the display using a "navigation stack." You push View Controllers that you want to display onto the navigation stack when you are ready to display them. Pressing the Back button causes the current View Controller to be popped off the navigation stack. At the bottom of the stack is the Root View Controller — in this example, the MasterViewController.

You will implement navigation in the catalog application using the UINavigationController. The diagram in Figure 2-12 shows the application mockup along with the navigation stack.

The left side shows the product catalog displayed in the UITableView, which is included in the MasterViewController. Selecting a row in the table view causes the DetailViewController to be pushed onto the navigation stack. You see this in the image on the right. The status of the navigation stack appears at the bottom of the figure.

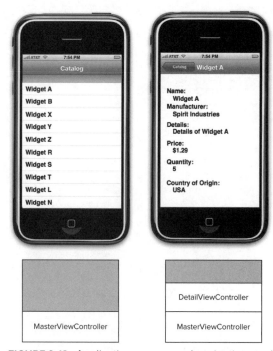

FIGURE 2-12: Application screens and navigation stack state

Tapping the Catalog button in the navigation bar at the top of the detail screen causes the `DetailViewController` to be popped from the navigation stack, thus displaying the `MasterViewController` again. The most important thing to remember is that the `UINavigationController` always displays the View Controller that is at the top of the navigation stack.

You can see what makes the Navigation Controller ideal for displaying hierarchical data. As a user navigates down a hierarchy, the application pushes View Controllers onto the stack. When the user presses the Back button, the View Controllers are popped back off the stack, navigating back up the hierarchy.

The UITableViewController

If you look at the code header for the `MasterViewController`, you will notice that the `MasterViewController` is not a subclass of `UIViewController` as in the previous chapter. Instead, it is a subclass of `UITableViewController`.

When implementing a View Controller that will control a table view, you can subclass the `UITableViewController` class instead of `UIViewController`. `UITableViewController` is a great shortcut to use. When you use a `UITableViewController`, you do not have to declare that you will be implementing the `UITableViewDataSource` and `UITableViewDelegate` protocols.

The `UITableViewController` also already has a table view associated with it. You can get a reference to the table view by using the `tableView` property. Because you are subclassing

`UITableViewController`, you don't need to worry about creating the table view as you did in the previous chapter. You simply need to implement the model and the controller. You are, however, still responsible for implementing the methods `numberOfSectionsInTableView`, `numberOfRowsInSection`, and `cellForRowAtIndexPath` as in the previous chapter.

The `#pragma mark - Table View` section highlights the table view methods that you must implement. You will notice that the template groups them at the bottom of the implementation file for the `MasterViewController` (`MasterViewController.m`).

Because the `UITableView` is being loaded from the XIB file for the `MasterViewController` (`MasterViewController.xib`), the `dataSource` and `delegate` properties are read from the XIB. These properties are both set to File's Owner in the XIB, which is `self` in code. This is fine because the `MasterViewController` will be the delegate and `dataSource` for your `UITableView`.

The Model Class

By simply creating a project based on the Master-Detail Application template, you get a lot of free functionality. In fact, if you build and run the application, you should get something that looks like Figure 2-13.

You have added no code, yet you already have a navigation bar (the blue-gray area at the top) and a table view (the lines). You also can add new rows with the plus button and edit the set of rows using the Edit button. Now you need to fill the table view with data.

In keeping with the preferred application architecture on iOS, you'll design this application by following the Model-View-Controller design pattern. You already have your views (in the XIB files) and controllers (Master View Controller and Detail View Controller); you just need a model. You need to design a model class that represents your data. The model class should also have a method that returns the number of rows in the database and provides access to the data for a specific row.

For this application, you will base your model on the `Product` class. The `Product` class will mirror the fields in the Products table in the database. Your model will be a collection of `Product` objects.

FIGURE 2-13: Running the Master-Detail Application template

To implement this model, create a new Objective-C class called `Product`. In the header, you will add a property for each database field. The following is the code for the header:

```
#import <Foundation/Foundation.h>

@interface Product : NSObject {
    int ID;
    NSString* name;
    NSString* manufacturer;
    NSString* details;
    float price;
```

```
    int quantity;
    NSString* countryOfOrigin;
    NSString* image;
}

@property (nonatomic) int ID;
@property (strong, nonatomic) NSString *name;
@property (strong, nonatomic) NSString *manufacturer;
@property (strong, nonatomic) NSString *details;
@property (nonatomic) float price;
@property (nonatomic) int quantity;
@property (strong, nonatomic) NSString *countryOfOrigin;
@property (strong, nonatomic) NSString *image;

@end
```

You can see that you simply declare a member variable for each database field and then create a property to access each field.

The implementation for this class is even easier:

```
#import "Product.h"

@implementation Product
@synthesize ID;
@synthesize name;
@synthesize manufacturer;
@synthesize details;
@synthesize price;
@synthesize quantity;
@synthesize countryOfOrigin;
@synthesize image;

@end
```

Here, you just synthesize all the properties declared in the header. At this point, it is a good idea to build and verify that there are no errors in your application.

The DBAccess Class

Now that you have your model class completed, you need to write the code to get the data out of the database and into your model. In general, it is a good idea to abstract away access to the database. This means writing a general class to perform common database functions. This gives you flexibility if you want to move to a different database engine later. To do this, you will create a database access class that talks to the database. This class will have methods to initialize the database, close the database, and most important, build and return an array of Product objects.

Before you get started on coding the database access class, you need to add your SQLite database to the Xcode project. Add the SQLite database to the project's Supporting Files folder by right-clicking on the Supporting Files folder and selecting Add Files to "Catalog." Navigate to your home directory or wherever you stored the catalog database, select it, and press Add in the dialog. Make sure that you have selected Copy items into destination group's folder (if needed), as in Figure 2-14.

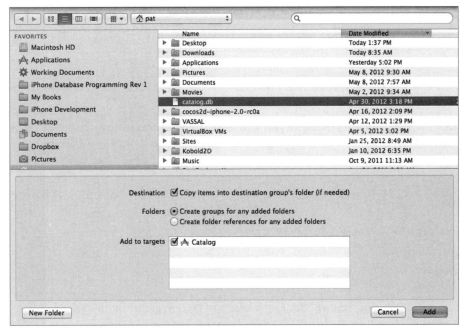

FIGURE 2-14: Adding an existing file to a project

To create the database access class, create a new Objective-C class called DBAccess. In the header, DBAccess.h, you need to add an import statement for sqlite3.h because you intend to use functions from the sqlite3 library in the data access class.

You also need to add three method signatures for the methods that you plan to implement: getAllProducts, closeDatabase, and initializeDatabase. closeDatabase and initializeDatabase are self-explanatory. The getAllProducts method returns an array of all the Product objects in the catalog. Because you will be referencing the Product object in this class, you need to add an import statement for Product.h.

The DBAccess.h header file should look like this:

```
#import <Foundation/Foundation.h>

// This includes the header for the SQLite library.
#import <sqlite3.h>
#import "Product.h"

@interface DBAccess : NSObject {


}

- (NSMutableArray*) getAllProducts;
- (void) closeDatabase;
- (void)initializeDatabase;

@end
```

In the implementation of the DBAccess class, add a class-level variable to hold a reference to the database:

```
// Reference to the SQLite database.
sqlite3* database;
```

You will populate this variable in the initializeDatabase function. Then every other function in your class will have access to the database.

Now you'll create the init function that callers use to initialize instances of this class. In init, you will make an internal call to initialize the database. The init function should look like this:

```
-(id) init
{
    //  Call super init to invoke superclass initiation code
    if ((self = [super init]))
    {
        //  Set the reference to the database
        [self initializeDatabase];
    }
    return self;
}
```

Your initializeDatabase function will do just that. It will go out, get the path to the database, and attempt to open it. Here is the code for initializeDatabase:

```
// Open the database connection
- (void)initializeDatabase {

    // Get the database from the application bundle.
    NSString *path = [[NSBundle mainBundle]
                        pathForResource:@"catalog"
                        ofType:@"db"];

    // Open the database.
    if (sqlite3_open([path UTF8String], &database) == SQLITE_OK)
    {
        NSLog(@"Opening Database");
    }
    else
    {
        // Call close to properly clean up
        sqlite3_close(database);
        NSAssert1(0, @"Failed to open database: '%s'.",
                sqlite3_errmsg(database));
    }
}
```

You can see that you need the path to the database file. Because you put the catalog.db file in the Supporting Files folder, the database will be deployed to the device in the main bundle of the application. There is a handy class, NSBundle, for getting information about an application bundle. The mainBundle method returns a reference to the main application bundle, and the pathForResource:ofType: method returns the path to the specified file in the bundle. Because you specified the resource as catalog and the type as db, the method returns the path to catalog.db.

Next, you use the C function `sqlite3_open` to open a connection to the database. You pass in the path to the database and the address to a variable of type `sqlite3*`. The second parameter is populated with the handle to the database. The `sqlite3_open` function returns an `int`. It returns the constant `SQLITE_OK` if everything goes well. If not, it returns an error code. The most common errors that you will encounter are `SQLITE_ERROR`, indicating that the database cannot be found, and `SQLITE_CANTOPEN`, indicating that there is some other reason that the database file cannot be opened. You can find the full list of error codes in the `sqlite3.h include` file.

You make sure that you got back `SQLITE_OK` and then log that you are opening the database. If you get an error, you close the database and then log the error message.

Next, you'll add a method to cleanly close the connection to the database. This is as simple as calling `sqlite3_close` and passing in a handle to the database like this:

```
-(void) closeDatabase
{
    // Close the database.
    if (sqlite3_close(database) != SQLITE_OK) {
        NSAssert1(0, @"Error: failed to close database: '%s'.",
                sqlite3_errmsg(database));
    }
}
```

The `sqlite3_close` function returns a value just like `sqlite3_open`. If the call to `sqlite3_close` fails, you use the `sqlite3_errmsg` function to get a textual error message and print it to the console.

At this point, you should try to build the application. The build fails because the SQLite functions are not found. Although you included the proper header files, the compiler doesn't know where to find the binaries for the library. You need to add the `libsqlite` framework to your Xcode project. Click on the Catalog project icon at the top of the Project Navigator. Select the Catalog Target on the left side of the Editor pane. At the top of the Editor pane, select the Build Phases tab. Expand the Link Binary with Libraries entry in the Editor pane and press the plus sign below the list of frameworks that are already included with your project. Select `libsqlite3.0.dylib` from the list of frameworks. Now you should be able to build your project successfully. You will still receive a warning that tells you that the `getAllProducts` method is not implemented, but you can fix that by implementing the function.

Now comes the heart of the database access class: the `getAllProducts` method. You will implement the `getAllProducts` method to return an array of `Product` objects that represent the records in the product catalog database. The method allocates an `NSMutableArray` to hold the list of products, construct your SQL statement, execute the statement, and loop through the results, constructing a `Product` object for each row returned from the query.

You'll start the method by declaring and initializing the array that will hold the products. You'll use an `NSMutableArray` because you want to be able to add `Product` objects to the array one by one as you retrieve rows from the database. The regular `NSArray` class is immutable, so you cannot add items to it on-the-fly.

ᵣₑᵣₑ is the beginning of your method:

```
- (NSMutableArray*) getAllProducts
{
    //  The array of products that we will create
    NSMutableArray *products = [[NSMutableArray alloc] init];
```

The next step in implementing `getAllProducts` is to declare a char* variable and populate it with your SQL statement:

```
//  The SQL statement that we plan on executing against the database
const char *sql = "SELECT product.ID,product.Name, \
Manufacturer.name,product.details,product.price,\
product.quantityonhand, country.country, \
product.image FROM Product,Manufacturer, \
Country where manufacturer.manufacturerid=product.manufacturerid \
and product.countryoforiginid=country.countryid";
```

The following is the SQL statement in a slightly more readable form:

```
SELECT product.ID,
    product.Name,
    Manufacturer.name,
    product.details,
    product.price,
    product.quantityonhand,
    country.country,
    product.image
FROM Product,Manufacturer, Country
WHERE manufacturer.manufacturerid=product.manufacturerid
    AND product.countryoforiginid=country.countryid
```

This book assumes that you already know SQL, so I will not go into all the details of writing SQL statements. However, I will quickly note that this SQL statement gets data out of the three tables noted in the FROM clause: Product, Manufacturer, and Country.

You can see which fields are selected from each table in the SELECT portion of the query. The form for specifying fields to select is *table.field*. Therefore, you are selecting the ID field from the Product table, then the Name field from the Product table.

Finally, you set up the joins in the WHERE clause. You only want data from the manufacturer table where the manufacturerID is the same as the manufacturerID in the product table. Likewise, you only want data from the country table where the countryID is the same as the countryoforiginID in the product table. This allows you to display the actual manufacturer name and country name in the query and in the application, instead of just displaying a meaningless ID number.

I recommend writing and testing your queries in an application such as SQLite Manager or at the command line. It is much easier to develop your query when you can run it and instantly see the results, especially as you get into queries that are more complex. Figure 2-15 shows the query running in SQLite Manager. You get the desired results when you execute this query.

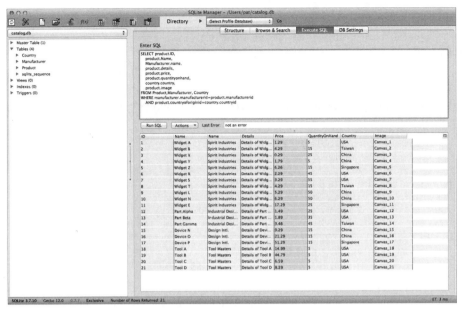

FIGURE 2-15: Testing a query using SQLite Manager

To run this SQL in your code, you need to create an SQLite `statement` object. This object will execute your SQL against the database. You can then prepare the SQL statement:

```
//  The SQLite statement object that will hold the result set
sqlite3_stmt *statement;

// Prepare the statement to compile the SQL query into byte-code
int sqlResult = sqlite3_prepare_v2(database, sql, -1, &statement, NULL);
```

The parameters for the `sqlite3_prepare_v2` function are a connection to the database, your SQL statement, the maximum length of your SQL or a –1 to read up to the first null terminator, the statement handle that will be used to iterate over the results, and a pointer to the first byte after the SQL statement, or `NULL` which you use here.

Like the other commands that you have run against SQLite in this chapter, `sqlite3_prepare_v2` returns an `int`, which will be either `SQLITE_OK` or an error code.

You should note that preparing the SQL statement does not actually execute the statement. The statement is not executed until you call the `sqlite3_step` function to begin retrieving rows.

If the result is `SQLITE_OK`, you step through the results one row at a time using the `sqlite3_step` function:

```
if ( sqlResult== SQLITE_OK) {
    // Step through the results - once for each row.
    while (sqlite3_step(statement) == SQLITE_ROW) {
```

For each row, allocate a `Product` object:

```
// Allocate a Product object to add to products array
Product  *product = [[Product alloc] init];
```

Now you have to retrieve the data from the row. A group of functions called the "result set" interface is used to get the field that you are interested in. The function that you use is based on the data type contained in the column that you are trying to retrieve. The following is a list of the available functions:

```
const void *sqlite3_column_blob(sqlite3_stmt*, int iCol);
int sqlite3_column_bytes(sqlite3_stmt*, int iCol);
int sqlite3_column_bytes16(sqlite3_stmt*, int iCol);
double sqlite3_column_double(sqlite3_stmt*, int iCol);
int sqlite3_column_int(sqlite3_stmt*, int iCol);
sqlite3_int64 sqlite3_column_int64(sqlite3_stmt*, int iCol);
const unsigned char *sqlite3_column_text(sqlite3_stmt*, int iCol);
const void *sqlite3_column_text16(sqlite3_stmt*, int iCol);
int sqlite3_column_type(sqlite3_stmt*, int iCol);
sqlite3_value *sqlite3_column_value(sqlite3_stmt*, int iCol);
```

The first parameter to each function is the prepared statement. The second parameter is the index in the SQL statement of the field that you are retrieving. The index is 0-based, so to get the first field in your SQL statement, the product ID, which is an `int`, you would use this:

```
sqlite3_column_int(statement, 0);
```

To retrieve text or strings from the database, you use the `sqlite3_column_text` function. I like to create `char*` variables to hold the strings retrieved from the database. Then I use the ternary operator (`?:`) to either use the string if it is not null, or use an empty string if it is null. Here is the code to get all the data from the database and populate your product object:

```
// The second parameter is the column index (0 based) in
// the result set.
char *name = (char *)sqlite3_column_text(statement, 1);
char *manufacturer = (char *)sqlite3_column_text(statement, 2);
char *details = (char *)sqlite3_column_text(statement, 3);
char *countryOfOrigin = (char *)sqlite3_column_text(statement, 6);
char *image = (char *)sqlite3_column_text(statement, 7);

// Set all the attributes of the product
product.ID = sqlite3_column_int(statement, 0);
product.name = (name) ? [NSString stringWithUTF8String:name] : @"";
product.manufacturer = (manufacturer) ? [NSString
    stringWithUTF8String:manufacturer] : @"";
product.details = (details) ? [NSString stringWithUTF8String:details] : @"";
product.price = sqlite3_column_double(statement, 4);
product.quantity = sqlite3_column_int(statement, 5);
product.countryOfOrigin = (countryOfOrigin) ? [NSString
    stringWithUTF8String:countryOfOrigin] : @"";
product.image = (image) ? [NSString stringWithUTF8String:image] : @"";
```

Finally, you add the product to the `products` array and move on to the next row:

```
// Add the product to the products array
[products addObject:product];
}
```

After you are finished looping through the result set, you call `sqlite3_finalize` to release the resources associated with the prepared statement. Then you log any errors and return your products array:

```
// Finalize the statement to release its resources
        sqlite3_finalize(statement);
    }
    else {
        NSLog(@"Problem with the database:");
        NSLog(@"%d",sqlResult);
    }

    return products;

}
```

The whole database access class should look like Listing 2-1.

LISTING 2-1: DBAccess.m

```
#import "DBAccess.h"

@implementation DBAccess

// Reference to the SQLite database.
sqlite3* database;

-(id) init
{
    //  Call super init to invoke superclass initiation code
    if ((self = [super init]))
    {
        //  Set the reference to the database
        [self initializeDatabase];
    }
    return self;
}

// Open the database connection
- (void)initializeDatabase {

    // Get the database from the application bundle.
    NSString *path = [[NSBundle mainBundle]
                      pathForResource:@"catalog"
                      ofType:@"db"];

    // Open the database.
    if (sqlite3_open([path UTF8String], &database) == SQLITE_OK)
    {
        NSLog(@"Opening Database");
    }
    else
    {
```

continues

LISTING 2-1 *(continued)*

```objc
        // Call close to properly clean up
        sqlite3_close(database);
        NSAssert1(0, @"Failed to open database: '%s'.",
                sqlite3_errmsg(database));
    }
}


-(void) closeDatabase
{
    // Close the database.
    if (sqlite3_close(database) != SQLITE_OK) {
        NSAssert1(0, @"Error: failed to close database: '%s'.",
                sqlite3_errmsg(database));
    }
}

- (NSMutableArray*) getAllProducts
{
    //  The array of products that we will create
    NSMutableArray *products = [[NSMutableArray alloc] init];

    //  The SQL statement that we plan on executing against the database
    const char *sql = "SELECT product.ID,product.Name, \
    Manufacturer.name,product.details,product.price,\
    product.quantityonhand, country.country, \
    product.image FROM Product,Manufacturer, \
    Country where manufacturer.manufacturerid=product.manufacturerid \
    and product.countryoforiginid=country.countryid";

    //  The SQLite statement object that will hold our result set
    sqlite3_stmt *statement;

    // Prepare the statement to compile the SQL query into byte-code
    int sqlResult = sqlite3_prepare_v2(database, sql, -1, &statement, NULL);

    if ( sqlResult== SQLITE_OK) {
        // Step through the results - once for each row.
        while (sqlite3_step(statement) == SQLITE_ROW) {
            //  allocate a Product object to add to products array
            Product  *product = [[Product alloc] init];
            // The second parameter is the column index (0 based) in
            // the result set.
            char *name = (char *)sqlite3_column_text(statement, 1);
            char *manufacturer = (char *)sqlite3_column_text(statement, 2);
            char *details = (char *)sqlite3_column_text(statement, 3);
            char *countryOfOrigin = (char *)sqlite3_column_text(statement, 6);
            char *image = (char *)sqlite3_column_text(statement, 7);

            //  Set all the attributes of the product
            product.ID = sqlite3_column_int(statement, 0);
            product.name = (name) ? [NSString stringWithUTF8String:name] : @"";
```

```
            product.manufacturer = (manufacturer) ? [NSString
                                    stringWithUTF8String:manufacturer] : @"";
            product.details = (details) ? [NSString stringWithUTF8String:details] : @"";
            product.price = sqlite3_column_double(statement, 4);
            product.quantity = sqlite3_column_int(statement, 5);
            product.countryOfOrigin = (countryOfOrigin) ? [NSString
                                    stringWithUTF8String:countryOfOrigin] : @"";
            product.image = (image) ? [NSString stringWithUTF8String:image] : @"";

            // Add the product to the products array
            [products addObject:product];

        }
        // Finalize the statement to release its resources
        sqlite3_finalize(statement);
    }
    else {
        NSLog(@"Problem with the database:");
        NSLog(@"%d",sqlResult);
    }

    return products;

}
@end
```

Parameterized Queries

Although I am not using them in this sample, it is possible and quite common to use parameterized queries.

For example, if you wanted to create a query that returned only products made in the USA, you could use the following SQL:

```
SELECT Product.name, country.country
FROM country,product
WHERE countryoforiginid=countryid and country='USA'
```

This query is perfectly fine if you always want a list of the products made in the USA. If you wanted to decide at runtime which countries' products to display, you would need to use a parameterized query.

The first step in parameterizing this query is to replace the data that you want to parameterize with question marks (?). So your SQL will become this:

```
SELECT Product.name, country.country
FROM country,product
WHERE countryoforiginid=countryid and country=?
```

After you prepare your statement with sqlite3_prepare_v2 but before you start stepping through your results with sqlite3_step, you need to bind your parameters. Remember that preparing the statement does not actually execute it. The statement is not executed until you begin iterating over the result set using sqlite3_step.

You use a series of functions to bind parameters in a manner similar to the way that you retrieve data fields. Here are the bind functions:

```
int sqlite3_bind_blob(sqlite3_stmt*, int, const void*, int n, void(*)(void*));
int sqlite3_bind_double(sqlite3_stmt*, int, double);
int sqlite3_bind_int(sqlite3_stmt*, int, int);
int sqlite3_bind_int64(sqlite3_stmt*, int, sqlite3_int64);
int sqlite3_bind_null(sqlite3_stmt*, int);
int sqlite3_bind_text(sqlite3_stmt*, int, const char*, int n, void(*)(void*));
int sqlite3_bind_text16(sqlite3_stmt*, int, const void*, int, void(*)(void*));
int sqlite3_bind_value(sqlite3_stmt*, int, const sqlite3_value*);
int sqlite3_bind_zeroblob(sqlite3_stmt*, int, int n);
```

You need to use the bind function that corresponds with the data type that you are binding. The first parameter in each function is the prepared statement. The second is the index (1-based) of the parameter in your SQL statement. The rest of the parameters vary based on the type that you are trying to bind. Complete documentation of the bind functions is available on the SQLite website.

To bind text at runtime, you use the `sqlite3_bind_text` function like this:

```
sqlite3_bind_text (statement,1,value,-1, SQLITE_TRANSIENT);
```

In this bind statement, `value` is the text that you would determine at runtime. In the example, that text would be "USA," but you could set it to anything that you want dynamically at runtime. That is the advantage of using parameterized queries. Of course, you could just dynamically generate your SQL each time, but parameterized queries offer the performance advantage of preparing and compiling the statement once, and then caching and reusing the statement.

Writing to the Database

If you modify the sample application or create your own SQLite application that attempts to write to the database, you will have a problem. The version of the database that you are using in the sample code is located in the application bundle, but the application bundle is read-only, so attempting to write to this database will result in an error.

To be able to write to the database, you need to make an editable copy. On the device, place this editable copy in the documents directory. Each application on the device is "sandboxed" and only has access to its own documents directory.

The following code snippet shows how to check whether a writable database already exists, and if not, create an editable copy.

```
// Create a writable copy of the default database from the bundle
// in the application Documents directory.
- (void) createEditableDatabase {
    // Check to see if editable database already exists
    BOOL success;
    NSFileManager *fileManager = [NSFileManager defaultManager];
    NSError *error;
    NSArray *paths = NSSearchPathForDirectoriesInDomains
        (NSDocumentDirectory, NSUserDomainMask, YES);
    NSString *documentsDir = [paths objectAtIndex:0];
    NSString *writableDB = [documentsDir
```

```
        stringByAppendingPathComponent:@"catalog.db"];
    success = [fileManager fileExistsAtPath:writableDB];

    // The editable database already exists
    if (success) return;


    // The editable database does not exist
    // Copy the default DB to the application Documents directory.
    NSString *defaultPath = [[[NSBundle mainBundle] resourcePath]
        stringByAppendingPathComponent:@"catalog.db"];
    success = [fileManager copyItemAtPath:defaultPath
        toPath:writableDB error:&error];
    if (!success) {
        NSAssert1(0, @"Failed to create writable database file:'%@'.",
            [error localizedDescription]);
    }
  }
}
```

You would then need to change your database access code to call this function and then refer to the editable copy of the database instead of the bundled copy.

Displaying the Catalog

Now that you have the DBAccess class done, you can get on with displaying the catalog. In the MasterViewController, you will implement code to retrieve the products array from the DBAccess class and display it in the table view.

In the header, MasterViewController.h, add import statements for the Product and DBAccess classes:

```
#import "Product.h"
#import "DBAccess.h"
```

Add a property to hold your products array:

```
@property (strong, nonatomic) NSMutableArray* products;
```

In iOS 6, you can optionally synthesize properties by adding an @synthesize directive to the implementation file. Synthesizing a property causes the compiler to generate the setter and getter methods for the property. In iOS 6, the compiler synthesizes properties for you automatically. However, you can alternatively define the getter, setter, or both methods yourself. The compiler fills in the blanks by defining either of these methods if you don't.

Continuing in the MasterViewController.m implementation class, you can add code to the view-DidLoad method to get your products array from the DBAccess class:

```
- (void)viewDidLoad
{
    [super viewDidLoad];
    // Do any additional setup after loading the view, typically from a nib.

    //  Get the DBAccess object;
    DBAccess *dbAccess = [[DBAccess alloc] init];
```

```
   //  Get the products array from the database
   self.products = [dbAccess getAllProducts];

   //  Close the database because we are finished with it
   [dbAccess closeDatabase];

}
```

Additionally, to keep this example simple, I've removed the default code to provide the Edit and Add buttons at the top of the screen.

You should also modify the `tableView:canEditRowAtIndexPath:` method to disallow editing row data:

```
-(BOOL)tableView:(UITableView *)tableView canEditRowAtIndexPath:(NSIndexPath *)indexPath
{
   // Return NO if you do not want the specified item to be editable.
   return NO;
}
```

Next, you have to implement your table view methods. The first thing you have to do is tell the table view how many rows there are by implementing the `numberOfRowsInSection` method as you did in the previous chapter. You will get the count of items to display in the table view from your products array:

```
- (NSInteger)tableView:(UITableView *)tableView
   numberOfRowsInSection:(NSInteger)section {
   return [self.products count];
}
```

Finally, you have to implement `cellForRowAtIndexPath` to provide the table view with the table view cell that corresponds with the row that the table view is asking for. The code is similar to the example from the previous chapter. The difference is that now you get the text for the cell from the `Product` object. You look up the `Product` object using the row that the table view is asking for as the index into the array. The following is the `cellForRowAtIndexPath` method:

```
// Customize the appearance of table view cells.
- (UITableViewCell *)tableView:(UITableView *)tableView
         cellForRowAtIndexPath:(NSIndexPath *)indexPath {

   static NSString *CellIdentifier = @"Cell";

   UITableViewCell *cell = [tableView
                            dequeueReusableCellWithIdentifier:CellIdentifier];
   if (cell == nil) {
      cell = [[UITableViewCell alloc]
            initWithStyle:UITableViewCellStyleDefault
            reuseIdentifier:CellIdentifier];
   }

   // Configure the cell.
   // Get the Product object
```

```
            Product* product = [self.products objectAtIndex:[indexPath row]];

            cell.textLabel.text = product.name;
            return cell;
    }
```

To set the Catalog text at the top in the Navigation Controller, navigate to the
`initWithNibName:bundle:` method in the `MasterViewController.m` implementation file. Change
the line that reads:

```
        self.title = NSLocalizedString(@"Master", @"Master");
```

to:

```
        self.title = NSLocalizedString(@"Catalog", @"Catalog");
```

You should now be able to build and run the application. When you
run it, you should see the product catalog as in Figure 2-16. When you
touch items in the catalog, nothing happens, but the application should
display the details of the product that is touched. To accomplish this, you
need to implement the table view function `didSelectRowAtIndexPath`.
However, before you do that, you need to build the view that you will
display when a user taps a product in the table.

Viewing Product Details

When a user taps a product in the table, the application should navigate to a product detail screen. Because this screen will be used with
the `NavigationController`, it needs to be implemented using a
`UIViewController`. A nice feature of the master-detail application template is that the template automatically creates the detail view controller
for you. Appropriately, the controller is called `DetailViewController`.

FIGURE 2-16: Running
the Catalog application

In the `DetailViewController.h` header, add Interface Builder outlets for the data that you want to
display. You need to add an outlet property for each label control like this:

```
        @property (strong, nonatomic) IBOutlet UILabel* nameLabel;
        @property (strong, nonatomic) IBOutlet UILabel* manufacturerLabel;
        @property (strong, nonatomic) IBOutlet UILabel* detailsLabel;
        @property (strong, nonatomic) IBOutlet UILabel* priceLabel;
        @property (strong, nonatomic) IBOutlet UILabel* quantityLabel;
        @property (strong, nonatomic) IBOutlet UILabel* countryLabel;
```

Because you will not be using it, you can delete the default Interface Builder outlet property that the
project template created:

```
        @property (strong, nonatomic) IBOutlet UILabel *detailDescriptionLabel;
```

You will use the outlets in the code to link to the user interface (UI) widgets. The basics of building
UIs in Xcode is beyond the scope of this book. There are several good books on building UIs for
iOS, including *iOS 6 Programming Pushing the Limits* by Rob Napier and Mugunth Kumar
(Wiley, 2012).

You will transfer the data about the product that the user selected to the detail view by passing a `Product` object from the `MasterViewController` to the `DetailViewController`. Because you will be referencing the `Product` object in your code, you need to add an import statement for the `Product` class to the `DetailViewController` header. The complete header should look like this:

```
#import <UIKit/UIKit.h>
#import "Product.h"     // model

@interface DetailViewController : UIViewController

@property (strong, nonatomic) IBOutlet UILabel* nameLabel;
@property (strong, nonatomic) IBOutlet UILabel* manufacturerLabel;
@property (strong, nonatomic) IBOutlet UILabel* detailsLabel;
@property (strong, nonatomic) IBOutlet UILabel* priceLabel;
@property (strong, nonatomic) IBOutlet UILabel* quantityLabel;
@property (strong, nonatomic) IBOutlet UILabel* countryLabel;

@property (strong, nonatomic) id detailItem;

@end
```

Now select the `DetailViewController.xib` file. In this file, you will add a series of `UILabels` to the interface as you designed in the mockup. Your interface should look something like Figure 2-17.

Next, you need to hook up your labels to the outlets that you created in the `DetailViewController.h` header file. Make sure that you save the header file before you try to hook up the outlets, or the outlets that you created in the header will not be available.

To hook up the outlets, make sure that you have the `DetailViewController.xib` file open. On the left side of the interface builder window, you should see two groups of objects: Placeholders and Objects. In the Placeholders group, select File's Owner. Make sure that you have the Utilities view open, and click the last icon at the top of the Utilities view to show the Connections Inspector. In this pane, you can see all the class's outlets and their connections. Click and drag from the open circle on the right side of the outlet name to the control to which that outlet should be connected in the user interface. When you are finished, the interface should look like Figure 2-18.

FIGURE 2-17: Product detail view

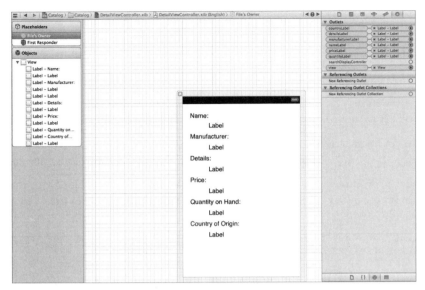

FIGURE 2-18: Building the detail view

In `DetailViewController.m`, implement the `configureView` method to set the text in the labels:

```
- (void)configureView
{
    // Update the user interface for the detail item.

    if (self.detailItem) {
        Product* theProduct = (Product*) self.detailItem;

        //  Set the text of the labels to the values passed in the Product object
        [self.nameLabel setText:theProduct.name];
        [self.manufacturerLabel setText:theProduct.manufacturer];
        [self.detailsLabel setText:theProduct.details];
        [self.priceLabel setText:[NSString stringWithFormat:@"%.2f",theProduct.price]];
        [self.quantityLabel setText:[NSString stringWithFormat:@"%d",
                                theProduct.quantity]];
        [self.countryLabel setText:theProduct.countryOfOrigin];

    }
}
```

The Master-detail application template creates the `configureView` method to give you a place to configure the view. You add your code to set the text in the labels inside of the `if (self.detailItem)` block to ensure that you have an object that you want to display. In this application, the `detailItem` will be a `Product` object, so you cast `self.detailItem` to a `(Product*)`. In general, because `detailItem` is of type `id`, you can use `detailItem` in your own applications to display data from any type of object.

The code in the template calls the `configureView` method in the setter for the `detailItem` property, as you can see in this code:

```
- (void)setDetailItem:(id)newDetailItem
{
    if (_detailItem != newDetailItem) {
```

```
        _detailItem = newDetailItem;

        // Update the view.
        [self configureView];
    }
}
```

Therefore, when you set the `detailItem` property from the master view controller, the detail view controller will use the object in that property to configure the view.

To be able to navigate to your new screen, you need to modify the `tableView:didSelectRowAtIndexP ath:` method in the `MasterViewController` to display the detail screen when a user selects a product.

In the `MasterViewController` implementation, modify the code in the `tableView:didSelectRowA tIndexPath:` method to set the `detailViewController.detailItem` to the object in the `products` array that the user selected:

```
- (void)tableView:(UITableView *)tableView
    didSelectRowAtIndexPath:(NSIndexPath *)indexPath
{
    if (!self.detailViewController) {
        self.detailViewController = [[DetailViewController alloc]
            initWithNibName:@"DetailViewController" bundle:nil];
    }

    self.detailViewController.detailItem = [self.products objectAtIndex:[indexPath row]];
    [self.navigationController pushViewController:
        self.detailViewController animated:YES];
}
```

That's all there is to it. Now you should be able to build and run your application. Try tapping on an item in the catalog. The application should take you to the detail page for that item. Tapping the Catalog button in the navigation bar should take you back to the catalog. Tapping another row in the table view should take you to the data for that item.

You now have a fully functioning catalog application! I know that it doesn't look very nice, but you'll work on that in the next chapter when you dive into customizing the `UITableView`.

MOVING FORWARD

Now that you have a functioning application, feel free to play with it as much as you like! Spruce up the interface, or add additional fields to the database tables and `Product` class.

There are a lot of good books on the SQL language, so if you were confused by any of the SQL used in this chapter, it may be a good idea to pick up a copy of *SQL For Dummies* by Allen Taylor.

Another resource that you should be aware of is the SQLite website at http://www.sqlite.org/. There you will find extensive documentation of the database and the C language APIs that are used to access the database.

Although you've learned how to get your data out of SQLite and into an iOS application, the catalog doesn't look that great. In the next chapter, you will learn how to display your data with more flair by customizing the table view.

3

Displaying Your Data: The UITableView

WHAT'S IN THIS CHAPTER?

➤ Customizing the table view by creating your own table view cells

➤ Searching and filtering your result sets

➤ Adding important UI elements, such as indexes and section headers, to your tables

➤ Avoiding and troubleshooting performance issues with your table views

WROX.COM CODE DOWNLOADS FOR THIS CHAPTER

The wrox.com code downloads for this chapter are found at www.wrox.com/remtitle .cgi?isbn=1118391845 on the Download Code tab. The code is in the Chapter 3 download and individually named according to the names throughout the chapter.

The focus of the book thus far has been on how to get your data onto the device and how to access that data on the device. This chapter focuses on how you can enhance the display of your data by customizing the table view cell. It also examines how to make your data easier to use by adding an index, section headings, and search functionality to the UITableView. In the next several sections, you take a closer look at how to use the table view to display your data in ways that make it more useful to your target audience.

CUSTOMIZING THE TABLE VIEW

You begin by looking at the default table view styles that are available in the iOS SDK. Then you learn the technique of adding subviews to the content view of a table view cell. If neither of these solutions meets your needs for customizing the display of your data, you will examine how to design your own table view cell from scratch using the interface builder in Xcode. If you had trouble using the interface builder in the previous chapter, now is a good time to review Apple's documentation, which you can find at http://developer.apple.com/.

Table View Cell Styles

Several precanned styles are available to use for a table view cell:

➤ **UITableViewCellStyleDefault:** This style displays a cell with a black, left-aligned text label with an optional image view.

➤ **UITableViewCellStyleValue1:** This style displays a cell with a black, left-aligned text label on the left side of the cell and an additional blue text, right-aligned label on the right side.

➤ **UITableViewCellStyleValue2:** This style displays a cell with a blue text, right-aligned label on the left side of the cell and an additional black, left-aligned text label on the right side of the cell.

➤ **UITableViewCellStyleSubtitle:** This style displays a cell with a black, left-aligned text label across the top, with a smaller, gray text label below.

In each style, you define the larger of the text labels with the textLabel property and define the smaller text label by the detailTextLabel property.

You can change the Catalog application from Chapter 2 to see what each of these styles looks like. You will change the application to use the name of the part manufacturer as the subtitle.

In the MasterViewController.m implementation file, add a line to the tableView:cellForRowAtIndexPath: method that sets the cell's detailTextLabel text property to the product's manufacturer:

```
- (UITableViewCell *)tableView:(UITableView *)tableView
        cellForRowAtIndexPath:(NSIndexPath *)indexPath {

    static NSString *CellIdentifier = @"Cell";

    UITableViewCell *cell = [tableView
                        dequeueReusableCellWithIdentifier:CellIdentifier];
    if (cell == nil) {
        cell = [[UITableViewCell alloc]
                initWithStyle:UITableViewCellStyleDefault
                reuseIdentifier:CellIdentifier] ;
    }

    // Configure the cell.
    // Get the Product object
```

```
Product* product = [self.products objectAtIndex:[indexPath row]];

cell.textLabel.text = product.name;
cell.detailTextLabel.text = product.manufacturer;

return cell;
}
```

When you run the application, you will see something like Figure 3-1 (a). Nothing has changed. You may be wondering what happened to the subtitle. When you initialized the cell, the style was set to `UITableViewCellStyleDefault`. In this style, the table only displays the cell's `textLabel`, along with an optional image, which you will add in a moment.

On the line where you initialize the cell, change the code to use `UITableViewCellStyleValue1`:

```
cell = [[UITableViewCell alloc]
            initWithStyle:UITableViewCellStyleValue1
            reuseIdentifier:CellIdentifier] ;
```

The table now displays the part name and the manufacturer, as shown in Figure 3-1 (b).

Changing the default to `UITableViewCellStyleValue2` results in a table that looks like Figure 3-1 (c).

Changing the default to `UITableViewCellStyleSubtitle` results in a table that looks like Figure 3-1 (d).

(a) UITableViewCellStyleDefault (b) UITableViewCellStyleValue1

(c) UITableViewCellStyleValue2 (d) UITableViewCellStyleSubtitle

FIGURE 3-1: Table view cell styles

Now you are ready to add images to the catalog items. You can obtain the images used in the example from the book's website. Create a new group in the Project Navigator to hold your images by selecting File ➪ New ➪ Group from the menu bar. Make sure that the new group is selected, and add the images to the new group by selecting File ➪ Add Files to "Catalog" from the menu bar. Next, add code to the `tableView:cellForRowAtIndexPath:` method that will look for the image in the application bundle using the image name from the database:

```
NSString *filePath = [[NSBundle mainBundle] pathForResource:product.image
                                           ofType:@"png"];
UIImage *image = [UIImage imageWithContentsOfFile:filePath];
cell.imageView.image = image;
```

Finally, you can add an accessory to each cell. The accessory is the little arrow on the right side of a cell that tells the user that selecting the cell will take him to another screen. To add the accessory, you need to include a line of code for the `tableView:cellForRowAtIndexPath:` method to configure the cell's `accessoryType`:

```
cell.accessoryType = UITableViewCellAccessoryDisclosureIndicator;
```

You can use a few different accessory types:

➤ UITableViewCellAccessoryDisclosureIndicator is the gray arrow that you have added. This control doesn't respond to touches. You use this style to indicate that selecting this cell will bring the user to a detail screen or the next screen in a navigation hierarchy.

➤ UITableViewCellAccessoryDetailDisclosureButton presents a blue button with an arrow in it. This control can respond to touches. You use this style to indicate that selecting the cell will lead to configurable properties.

➤ UITableViewCellAccessoryCheckmark displays a checkmark on the right side of the cell. This control doesn't respond to touches.

Figure 3-2 shows how a catalog looks after adding the images and a disclosure indicator accessory.

The final code for the cellForRowAtIndexPath: method should look like this:

FIGURE 3-2: Catalog application with images

```objc
- (UITableViewCell *)tableView:(UITableView *)tableView
        cellForRowAtIndexPath:(NSIndexPath *)indexPath {

    static NSString *CellIdentifier = @"Cell";

    UITableViewCell *cell = [tableView
                      dequeueReusableCellWithIdentifier:CellIdentifier];
    if (cell == nil) {
        cell = [[UITableViewCell alloc]
                initWithStyle:UITableViewCellStyleSubtitle
                reuseIdentifier:CellIdentifier] ;
    }

    // Configure the cell.
    // Get the Product object
    Product* product = [self.products objectAtIndex:[indexPath row]];

    cell.textLabel.text = product.name;
    cell.detailTextLabel.text = product.manufacturer;

    NSString *filePath = [[NSBundle mainBundle] pathForResource:product.image
                                                ofType:@"png"];
    UIImage *image = [UIImage imageWithContentsOfFile:filePath];
    cell.imageView.image = image;

    cell.accessoryType = UITableViewCellAccessoryDisclosureIndicator;

    return cell;
}
```

There are other properties you can use to provide additional customization for the table view cell. You can use the `backgroundView` property to assign another view as the background of a cell, set the `selectionStyle` to control how a cell looks when a user selects it, and set the indentation of text with the `indentationLevel` property.

You can further customize a cell by modifying properties that the `UIView` class exposes because `UITableViewCell` is a subclass of `UIView`. For instance, you can set the background color of a cell by using the `backgroundColor` property of the `UIView`.

Adding Subviews to the contentView

If none of the existing table view cell styles works for your application, you can customize the table view cell by adding subviews to the `contentView` of the table view cell. This approach is effective when the OS can perform the cell layout using autoresizing, and the default behavior of the cell is appropriate for your application. If you need full control of how the cell is drawn or wish to change the behavior of the cell from the default, you need to create a custom subclass of `UITableViewCell`. You will learn how to create this subclass in the next section.

Because `UITableViewCell` inherits from `UIView`, a cell has a content view, accessible through the `contentView` property. You can add your own subviews to this `contentView` and lay them out using the superview's coordinate system either programmatically or interactively using the interface builder component of Xcode. When you implement customization this way, you should avoid making your subviews transparent. Transparency causes compositing to occur, which is quite time-consuming and processor intensive. Compositing takes time and results in degraded table view scrolling speed. You look at this in more detail at the end of this chapter in the section on performance.

Suppose that your customer is not happy with the table in the current application. He wants to see all the existing information plus an indication of where the product was made and how much it costs. You could use a flag icon to represent the country of origin on the right-hand side and add a label to display the price, as shown in the mockup in Figure 3-3. It's not a beautiful design, but it's what the customer wants.

It's impossible to achieve this layout using any of the default cell styles. To build this customized cell, you will hand-code the layout of the cell.

Because you will be modifying the cell you display in the table, you will be working in the `MasterViewController.m` file and modifying the `tableView: cellForRowAtIndexPath:` method.

First, you need variables for the two images and three labels that you plan to display. At the beginning of the method, add the declarations for these items:

FIGURE 3-3: Catalog mockup with flags

```
UILabel *nameLabel, *manufacturerLabel, *priceLabel;
UIImageView *productImage, *flagImage;
```

Next, declare an `NSString` for the `CellIdentifier` and try to dequeue a cell using that identifier:

```
static NSString *CellIdentifier = @"Cell";

UITableViewCell *cell = [tableView
                        dequeueReusableCellWithIdentifier:CellIdentifier];
```

You have seen this code in previous examples, but until now, I haven't explained *how* it works. Creating table view cells is a relatively time-consuming process. In addition, memory is scarce on an embedded device such as the iPhone or iPad. It is inefficient to create all the cells and have them hanging around using memory while off-screen and not viewable. Conversely, because it takes time to create cells, creating them dynamically each time you needed them would be a performance hit.

To solve these problems, the engineers at Apple came up with a good solution. They gave the table view a queue of table view cells from which you can get a reference to an existing cell object. When you need a cell, you can try to pull one from the queue. If you get one, you can reuse it; if you don't, you have to create a new cell that you will eventually add to the queue. The framework handles the control logic by determining which cells are queued and available, and which the table view is currently using.

All you need to do as a developer is try to dequeue a cell and check the return. If the return is `nil`, you have to create the cell. If it is not, you have a valid cell that you can use. The type of cell that is dequeued depends on the cell identifier that you pass in when trying to dequeue. Remember that you set this identifier when you initialized a new cell with the `reuseIdentifier`.

The preceding code attempts to dequeue a cell using the `reuseIdentifier`, named `Cell`. The following `if (cell==nil)` block either creates a new cell with the `Cell reuseIdentifier`, or goes on to work with the cell that was dequeued.

If the cell needs to be created, the following code is executed:

```
if (cell == nil) {
    // Create a new cell object since the dequeue failed
    cell = [[UITableViewCell alloc]
            initWithStyle:UITableViewCellStyleSubtitle
            reuseIdentifier:CellIdentifier];

    // Set the accessoryType to the grey disclosure arrow
    cell.accessoryType = UITableViewCellAccessoryDisclosureIndicator;

    // Configure the name label
    nameLabel = [[UILabel alloc]
                initWithFrame:CGRectMake(45.0, 0.0, 120.0, 25.0)];

    nameLabel.tag = NAMELABEL_TAG;

    // Add the label to the cell's content view
    [cell.contentView addSubview:nameLabel];

    // Configure the manufacturer label
    manufacturerLabel = [[UILabel alloc]
                        initWithFrame:CGRectMake(45.0, 25.0, 120.0, 15.0)];
    manufacturerLabel.tag = MANUFACTURERLABEL_TAG;
    manufacturerLabel.font = [UIFont systemFontOfSize:12.0];
```

```
        manufacturerLabel.textColor = [UIColor darkGrayColor];

        // Add the label to the cell's content view
        [cell.contentView addSubview:manufacturerLabel];

        // Configure the price label
        priceLabel = [[UILabel alloc]
                      initWithFrame:CGRectMake(200.0, 10.0, 60.0, 25.0)];

        priceLabel.tag = PRICELABEL_TAG;

        // Add the label to the cell's content view
        [cell.contentView addSubview:priceLabel];

        // Configure the product Image
        productImage = [[UIImageView alloc]
                      initWithFrame:CGRectMake(0.0, 0.0, 40.0, 40.0)];

        productImage.tag = PRODUCTIMAGE_TAG;

        // Add the Image to the cell's content view
        [cell.contentView addSubview:productImage];

        // Configure the flag Image
        flagImage = [[UIImageView alloc]
                     initWithFrame:CGRectMake(260.0, 10.0, 20.0, 20.0)];
        flagImage.tag = FLAGIMAGE_TAG;

        // Add the Image to the cell's content view
        [cell.contentView addSubview:flagImage];
    }
```

The first line allocates a new cell and initializes it with the Cell reuseIdentifier. You have to do this because cell==nil indicates that no existing cells are available for reuse.

Each block thereafter is similar. You first create the object that you will add to the cell, either a UILabel or a UIImage. Then you configure it with the attributes that you want, such as fonts and text colors. You assign a tag to the object that you can use to get the instance of the label or image if you are reusing an existing cell. Finally, you add the control to the contentView of the cell.

The tag values for each control must be integers and are commonly defined using #define statements. Put the following #define statements before the tableView:cellForRowAtIndexPath: method definition:

```
#define NAMELABEL_TAG 1
#define MANUFACTURERLABEL_TAG 2
#define PRICELABEL_TAG 3
#define PRODUCTIMAGE_TAG 4
#define FLAGIMAGE_TAG 5
```

The position of each UI element is set in the initWithFrame method call. The method takes a CGRect struct that you create using the CGRectMake function. This function returns a CGRect struct with the x, y, width, and height values set.

Next, code the `else` clause that is called if you successfully dequeue a reusable cell:

```
else {
    nameLabel = (UILabel *)[cell.contentView
                        viewWithTag:NAMELABEL_TAG];
    manufacturerLabel = (UILabel *)[cell.contentView
                                viewWithTag:MANUFACTURERLABEL_TAG];
    priceLabel = (UILabel *)[cell.contentView
                        viewWithTag:PRICELABEL_TAG];
    productImage = (UIImageView *)[cell.contentView
                                viewWithTag:PRODUCTIMAGE_TAG];
    flagImage = (UIImageView *)[cell.contentView
                            viewWithTag:FLAGIMAGE_TAG];
}
```

You can now see how you use tags. The `viewWithTag` function of the `contentView` returns a pointer to the UI object that you defined with the specified tag. Therefore, when you create a new cell, you define the UI objects with those tags. When you dequeue a reusable cell, you use the tags to get pointers back to those UI objects. You need these pointers to be able to set the text and images used in the UI objects in the final section of the method:

```
// Configure the cell.
// Get the Product object
Product* product = [self.products objectAtIndex:[indexPath row]];

nameLabel.text = product.name;
manufacturerLabel.text = product.manufacturer;
priceLabel.text = [[NSNumber numberWithFloat: product.price] stringValue];

NSString *filePath = [[NSBundle mainBundle] pathForResource:product.image
                                            ofType:@"png"];
UIImage *image = [UIImage imageWithContentsOfFile:filePath];
productImage.image = image;

filePath = [[NSBundle mainBundle] pathForResource:product.countryOfOrigin
                                        ofType:@"png"];
image = [UIImage imageWithContentsOfFile:filePath];
flagImage.image = image;

return cell;
```

In this final section, you get an instance of the `Product` object for the row that you need to display. Then you use the `product` object to set the text in the labels and the images in the `UIImage` objects. To finish the method, you return the `cell` object.

If you add the flag images to the project, you should be able to build and run your application. The catalog should look like the mockup shown in Figure 3-3. You can see the running application in Figure 3-4.

Now that you know how to add subviews to the `contentView` for a table view cell, you have opened up a completely new world of customization of the table view cell. You can add any class that inherits from `UIView` to a cell. Now would be a good time to explore all the widgets that are available to you and to think about how you could use them in table views to develop great new interfaces.

FIGURE 3-4: Running the catalog with flag images

Subclassing UITableViewCell

If you need full control of how the cell is drawn or wish to change the behavior of the cell from the default, you will want to create a custom subclass of UITableViewCell. You can also eke out some additional performance, particularly when dealing with problems with table scrolling, by subclassing the UITableViewCell.

There are a couple of ways to implement the subclass. One is to implement it just as you did in the previous section by adding subviews to the contentView. This is a good solution when there are only three or four subviews. If you need to use more than four subviews, scrolling performance could be poor.

If you need to use more than four subviews to implement your cell, or if the scrolling performance of your table view is poor, it is best to manually draw the contents of the cell. You do this in a subview of the contentView by creating a custom view class and implementing its drawRect: method.

There are a couple of issues with implementing drawRect. First, performance will suffer if you need to reorder controls because of the cell going into editing mode. You should not perform custom drawing during animation, which happens when transitioning into editing mode or reordering cells. Second, if you need the controls embedded in the cell to respond to user actions, you cannot use this method. You cannot use this method if, for example, you have some buttons embedded in the cell and need to take different action based on which button was pressed.

In the example, you will be drawing text and images in the view, so implementing drawRect is a viable option. The cell will look like it contains image and label controls; however, in fact it will contain only a single view with all the UI controls drawn in. Therefore, the individual controls are not able to respond to touches.

Because the table view cell will have more than four controls, is not editable, and doesn't have subcontrols that need to respond to touches, you will implement the cell using drawRect. You will find that most, if not all, of the tables that you create to display data will fall into this category, making this a valuable technique to learn.

Getting Started

To work along with this example, download a copy of the original catalog project from the book's website. You will use that as the starting point to build the custom subclass version of the application.

In the project, you will first add a new Objective-C class. In the New File dialog, select Objective-C Class. Then, in the Options dialog, select subclass of UITableViewCell from the drop-down in the center of the dialog box. Call the new class CatalogTableViewCell. This will be your custom subclass of the table view cell.

In the header for CatalogTableViewCell, add an #import statement to import the Product.h header:

```
#import "Product.h"
```

The subclass will implement a method that sets the Product that you will use to display the cell.

Add a `setProduct` method that users will call to set the `Product` to what they want to be displayed in the cell:

```
- (void) setProduct: (Product *) theProduct;
```

Create a new Objective-C class that is a subclass of `UIView`, called `CatalogProductView`. This will be the custom view that your cell subclass uses to draw the text and images that you will display. This view will be the only subview added to the cell.

In the `CatalogProductView` header, add an `import` statement and instance variable for the `Product` object. Also, add a function `setProduct`. The cell uses this function to pass the product to the view. The view will then use the product to get the data used to draw in the view. The `CatalogProductView` header should look like this:

```
#import <UIKit/UIKit.h>
#import "Product.h"

@interface CatalogProductView : UIView {
    Product* theProduct;
}

- (void) setProduct: (Product *) inputProduct;

@end
```

Switch back to the `CatalogTableViewCell` header and add a reference and property for your custom view. The `CatalogTableViewCell` header should look like this:

```
#import <UIKit/UIKit.h>
#import "Product.h"
#import "CatalogProductView.h"

@interface CatalogTableViewCell : UITableViewCell {

}

@property (nonatomic, strong) CatalogProductView* catalogProductView;

- (void) setProduct: (Product *) theProduct;

@end
```

In the `CatalogTableViewCell` implementation file, you'll add code to `initWithStyle:reuseIdentifier:` to initialize the custom view to the size of the container and add the subview to the cell's content view:

```
- (id) initWithStyle: (UITableViewCellStyle) style
    reuseIdentifier: (NSString *) reuseIdentifier
{
    self = [super initWithStyle:style reuseIdentifier:reuseIdentifier];
    if (self) {
        // Initialization code
        // Create a frame that matches the size of the custom cell

        CGRect viewFrame = CGRectMake(0.0, 0.0,
```

```
                                          self.contentView.bounds.size.width,
                                          self.contentView.bounds.size.height);

        // Allocate and initialize the custom view with the dimensions
        // of the custom cell
        self.catalogProductView = [[CatalogProductView alloc]
                            initWithFrame:viewFrame];

        // Add the custom view to the cell
        [self.contentView addSubview:self.catalogProductView];

    }
    return self;
}
```

You will now implement the setProduct: method. All it will do is call the view's setProduct method:

```
- (void)setProduct:(Product *)theProduct
{
    [self.catalogProductView setProduct:theProduct];
}
```

Now let's get back to implementing the CatalogProductView. First, you need to implement the initWithFrame: method to initialize the view:

```
- (id)initWithFrame:(CGRect)frame
{
    self = [super initWithFrame:frame];
    if (self) {
        // Initialization code
        self.opaque = YES;
        self.backgroundColor = [UIColor whiteColor];
    }
    return self;
}
```

Here, you set the view to be opaque because there is a severe performance hit for using transparent views. If possible, always use opaque views when working with table cells. The next line sets the background color of the view to white.

Next, you implement the method setProduct that is called from the custom cell:

```
- (void)setProduct:(Product *)inputProduct
{
    // If a different product is passed in...
    if (theProduct != inputProduct)
    {
        theProduct = inputProduct;
    }

    // Mark the view to be redrawn
    [self setNeedsDisplay];
}
```

od does a couple of things. First, it sets the product that you want to display, and then he view to be redrawn. You should never directly call the drawRect method to redraw a view. The proper way to trigger a redraw is to tell the framework that a view needs to be redrawn. The framework will then call drawRect for you when it is time to redraw.

Implementing drawRect:

Now you get to the real meat of this example: drawing the view. This is done in the drawRect function and is relatively straightforward:

```
// Only override drawRect: if you perform custom drawing.
// An empty implementation adversely affects performance during animation.
- (void)drawRect:(CGRect)rect {
    // Drawing code

    // Draw the product text
    [theProduct.name drawAtPoint:CGPointMake(45.0,0.0)
                        forWidth:120
                        withFont:[UIFont systemFontOfSize:18.0]
                     minFontSize:12.0
                   actualFontSize:NULL
                    lineBreakMode:UILineBreakModeTailTruncation
               baselineAdjustment:UIBaselineAdjustmentAlignBaselines];

    // Set to draw in dark gray
    [[UIColor darkGrayColor] set];

    // Draw the manufacturer label
    [theProduct.manufacturer drawAtPoint:CGPointMake(45.0,25.0)
                                forWidth:120
                                withFont:[UIFont systemFontOfSize:12.0]
                             minFontSize:12.0
                           actualFontSize:NULL
                            lineBreakMode:UILineBreakModeTailTruncation
                       baselineAdjustment:UIBaselineAdjustmentAlignBaselines];

    // Set to draw in black
    [[UIColor blackColor] set];

    // Draw the price label
    [[[NSNumber numberWithFloat: theProduct.price] stringValue]
     drawAtPoint:CGPointMake(200.0,10.0)
     forWidth:60
     withFont:[UIFont systemFontOfSize:16.0]
     minFontSize:10.0
     actualFontSize:NULL
     lineBreakMode:UILineBreakModeTailTruncation
     baselineAdjustment:UIBaselineAdjustmentAlignBaselines];

    // Draw the images
    NSString *filePath = [[NSBundle mainBundle]
```

```
                    pathForResource:theProduct.image ofType:@"png"];
UIImage *image = [UIImage imageWithContentsOfFile:filePath];
[image drawInRect:CGRectMake(0.0, 0.0, 40.0, 40.0)];

filePath = [[NSBundle mainBundle]
            pathForResource:theProduct.countryOfOrigin ofType:@"png"];
image = [UIImage imageWithContentsOfFile:filePath];
```

Basically, you render each string using the `drawAtPoint:forWidth:withFont:minFontSize:actua`
`lFontSize:lineBreakMode:baselineAdjustment:` method. Boy, that's a mouthful! This function
accepts a series of parameters and renders the string to the current drawing context using those
parameters.

Therefore, for the product name, you draw it at the point (45,0) with a width of 120 points using
the system font with a size of 18. You force a minimum font size of 12 because the renderer
shrinks the text to fit within the width specified. You don't specify an actual font size because you
specified that in the `withFont` parameter. The `lineBreakMode` sets how the lines are broken for
multiline text. Here, you just truncate the tail, meaning that the renderer just shows ". . ." if you
reduce the text size to 12 and still cannot fit in the 120 points that you've allotted. Finally, the
`baselineAdjustment` specifies how to vertically align the text.

Now that you've drawn the product name, you set the drawing color to dark gray to draw the
manufacturer name. The next `drawAtPoint:` call does just that.

Next, you set the color back to black and draw the price string. Notice that you need to get a string
representation of the floating-point price field. You do that by using the `stringValue` method of the
`NSNumber` class.

Then you obtain the product image and the flag image just as you did in the previous example.
Finally, you render the images using the `drawInRect:` method of the `UIImage` class.

Finishing Up

Now that you have the new cell subclass and custom view implemented, it's time to put them to use.
In the `MasterViewController` header, add a #include for the custom cell:

```
#import "CatalogTableViewCell.h"
```

In the `MasterViewController` implementation, change the `tableView:cellForRowAtIndexPath:`
method to use the new cell control:

```
- (UITableViewCell *)tableView:(UITableView *)tableView
        cellForRowAtIndexPath:(NSIndexPath *)indexPath {

    static NSString *CellIdentifier = @"Cell";

    CatalogTableViewCell *cell = (CatalogTableViewCell *)
    [tableView dequeueReusableCellWithIdentifier:CellIdentifier];
    if (cell == nil) {
        cell = [[CatalogTableViewCell alloc]
                initWithStyle:UITableViewCellStyleDefault
                reuseIdentifier:CellIdentifier];
```

```
    }

    // Configure the cell.
    cell.accessoryType = UITableViewCellAccessoryDisclosureIndicator;

    // Get the Product object
    Product* product = [self.products objectAtIndex:[indexPath row]];

    // Set the product to be used to draw the cell
    [cell setProduct:product];

    return cell;
}
```

In this method, you replace the UITableViewCell with the new CatalogTableViewCell. When you try to dequeue the reusable cell, you must cast the return to a CatalogTableViewCell* because dequeueReusableCellWithIdentifier: returns a UITableViewCell*. If you are unsuccessful with the dequeue, you create a new CatalogTableViewCell just as you did with the UITableViewCell. Then, just as in the previous example, you set the accessory type and get the Product object that you want to display. Finally, you set the product that you want to display in the custom cell object and return the cell object.

Now all you have to do is add the flag images to the resources folder of your project, build, and run. You should get something that looks just like the previous example and Figure 3-4.

IMPLEMENTING SECTIONS AND AN INDEX

Now that you can create fantastic and highly performant table cells, you need a better way to organize them. In this section, you learn to partition your data into sections, display them with section headers, and allow the user to navigate them using an index.

If you have ever used the Contacts application on the iPhone, you should be familiar with section headers and the index. In Contacts, each letter of the alphabet appears as a section header, the gray bar with the letter. The Contacts application groups every contact whose name starts with that letter under the section header. You can use the index on the right side of the screen to quickly navigate to a section by tapping on the letter in the index that corresponds to the section.

You will be adding section headers and an index to the catalog application. When you are finished, your catalog application should look like Figure 3-5.

You need to organize the data that you use to populate your indexed table such that you can easily build the sections. That is, the data should be an array of arrays in which each

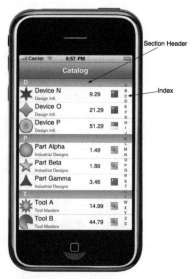

FIGURE 3-5: Catalog application with sections and index

inner array represents a section of the table. You can see the scheme that you will use in the catalog application in Figure 3-6.

You then order these section arrays in the outer array based on criteria that you provide. Typically, this ordering is alphabetical, but you can customize it in any way that you wish.

You can take care of sorting and organizing the table data yourself, but there is a helper class in the iOS SDK framework that Apple has designed to help you with this task: UILocalizedIndexedCollation.

The UILocalizedIndexedCollation class is a helper class that assists with organizing, sorting, and localizing your table view data. The table view data source can then use the collation object to obtain the section and index titles.

You will implement the indexed table using the UILocalizedIndexedCollation class. If you use this class, the data model object that you want to display in the table needs to have a method or property that the UILocalizedIndexedCollation can call when creating its arrays. It is also helpful for your data model class to have a property that maintains the index of the object in the section array. Because the product model class already has a name property, you can use that to define the sections. You need to add a property to hold the section number. Add the section property to the Product.h header like this:

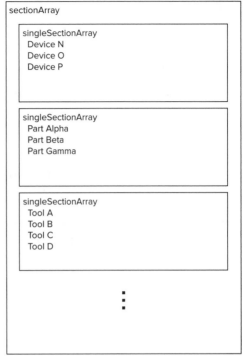

FIGURE 3-6: Data scheme for sectioned tables

```
@interface Product : NSObject {
}
@property (nonatomic) int ID;
@property (retain, nonatomic) NSString *name;
@property (retain, nonatomic) NSString *manufacturer;
@property (retain, nonatomic) NSString *details;
@property (nonatomic) float price;
@property (nonatomic) int quantity;
@property (retain, nonatomic) NSString *countryOfOrigin;
@property (retain, nonatomic) NSString *image;
@property NSInteger section;
```

The next thing that you need to do is load all the data from your data source into your model objects. In the case of the catalog application, you are already doing that in the getAllProducts method of the DBAccess class. If you recall, that method queries the SQLite database, creates a Product object for each row in the table, and adds each Product object to an array.

You will use this array along with the UILocalizedIndexedCollation object to create the sections. To create the necessary data arrays, you have to make some changes to the viewDidLoad method of the MasterViewController.m implementation.

Here is the new implementation of viewDidLoad:

```
- (void)viewDidLoad {
    [super viewDidLoad];

    self.products = [NSMutableArray arrayWithCapacity:1];

    NSMutableArray *productsTemp;

    // Get the DBAccess object;
    DBAccess *dbAccess = [[DBAccess alloc] init];

    // Get the products array from the database
    productsTemp = [dbAccess getAllProducts];

    // Close the database because you are finished with it
    [dbAccess closeDatabase];

    UILocalizedIndexedCollation *indexedCollation =
    [UILocalizedIndexedCollation currentCollation];

    // Iterate over the products, populating their section number
    for (Product *theProduct in productsTemp) {
        NSInteger section = [indexedCollation sectionForObject:theProduct
                                      collationStringSelector:@selector(name)];
        theProduct.section = section;
    }

    // Get the count of the number of sections
    NSInteger sectionCount = [[indexedCollation sectionTitles] count];

    // Create an array to hold the subarrays
    NSMutableArray *sectionsArray = [NSMutableArray
                                     arrayWithCapacity:sectionCount];

    // Iterate over each section, creating each subarray
    for (int i=0; i<=sectionCount; i++) {
        NSMutableArray *singleSectionArray = [NSMutableArray
                                              arrayWithCapacity:1];
        [sectionsArray addObject:singleSectionArray];
    }

    // Iterate over the products, putting each product into the correct subarray
    for (Product *theProduct in productsTemp) {
        [(NSMutableArray *)[sectionsArray objectAtIndex:theProduct.section]
         addObject:theProduct];
    }

    // Iterate over each section array to sort the items in the section
    for (NSMutableArray *singleSectionArray in sectionsArray) {
        // Use the UILocalizedIndexedCollation sortedArrayFromArray: method to
        // sort each array
        NSArray *sortedSection = [indexedCollation
```

```
                                   sortedArrayFromArray:singleSectionArray

                                   collationStringSelector:@selector(name)];
          [self.products addObject:sortedSection];
    }


    }
```

The first part of the method is largely the same as the previous example, except that now you have added code to initialize the new products property. You then proceed to get the array of Products from the database access class, just as before.

Next, you move on to getting a reference to the UILocalizedIndexedCollation object:

```
UILocalizedIndexedCollation *indexedCollation = [UILocalizedIndexedCollation
currentCollation];
```

After that, you iterate over all the products to populate the section index property:

```
for (Product *theProduct in productsTemp) {
      NSInteger section = [indexedCollation sectionForObject:theProduct
                                   collationStringSelector:@selector(name)];
      theProduct.section = section;
   }
```

You determine the section index using the UILocalizedIndexedCollation's sectionForObject :collationStringSelector: method. This method uses the property or method that you pass in as the collationStringSelector parameter to determine in which section the sectionForObject parameter belongs. Therefore, in this case, the method uses the name property to determine the correct section for theProduct. You can use any method or property to organize your sections, as long as it returns a string.

The next section of code gets a count of all the sections that you will need, creates the main array to hold all the section subarrays, and creates each subarray:

```
// Get the count of the number of sections
NSInteger sectionCount = [[indexedCollation sectionTitles] count];

// Create an array to hold the subarrays
NSMutableArray *sectionsArray = [NSMutableArray
                              arrayWithCapacity:sectionCount];

// Iterate over each section, creating each subarray
for (int i=0; i<=sectionCount; i++) {
    NSMutableArray *singleSectionArray = [NSMutableArray arrayWithCapacity:1];
    [sectionsArray addObject:singleSectionArray];
}
```

Next, loop through each product again, placing it into the correct subarray. Remember that the index to the correct subarray was determined before and stored in the new section property of the Product object:

```
// Iterate over the products, putting each product into the correct subarray
for (Product *theProduct in productsTemp) {
   [(NSMutableArray *)[sectionsArray objectAtIndex:theProduct.section]
       addObject:theProduct];
}
```

Finally, the last section of the code goes back over each subarray, sorts the data within the array using the `UILocalizedIndexedCollation`'s `sortedArrayFromArray:collationStringSelector:` method, and then adds the array to the `products` array:

```
// Iterate over each section array to sort the items in the section
for (NSMutableArray *singleSectionArray in sectionsArray) {
    // Use the UILocalizedIndexedCollation sortedArrayFromArray:
    // method to sort each array
    NSArray *sortedSection = [indexedCollation
                             sortedArrayFromArray:singleSectionArray
                             collationStringSelector:@selector(name)];
    [self.products addObject:sortedSection];
}
```

Now you have the `products` array set up as you need it. You have it organized as an array of arrays, each of which contains a sorted list of `Product` objects, as shown in Figure 3-6.

The next thing that you need to do is configure the table view to show the newly created sections. There are two table view delegate methods that you need to implement:

`numberOfSectionsInTableView:` and `numberOfRowsInSection:`.

The `numberOfSectionsInTableView:` method should return the number of sections that you will show in the table view. You implement this by returning the count of objects in the `products` array:

```
- (NSInteger)numberOfSectionsInTableView:(UITableView *)tableView {
    return [self.products count];
}
```

The table view uses the `tableView:numberOfRowsInSection:` method to return the number of rows in the requested section. To implement this, you just return the count of rows for the particular section that the table has requested:

```
- (NSInteger)tableView:(UITableView *)tableView
    numberOfRowsInSection:(NSInteger)section {
    return [[self.products objectAtIndex:section] count];
}
```

You also need to modify the `tableView:cellForRowAtIndexPath:` method to get the product from the `products` array by section and row. If you recall, when you had only the single array, you just indexed into it directly to get the `Product` object that you wanted to display. Now, you need to get the `Product` object that corresponds with the section and row that the table view is asking you to display:

```
Product* product = [[self.products objectAtIndex:[indexPath section]]
                    objectAtIndex:[indexPath row]];
```

You get the section from the `indexPath` and use that to index into the outer array. Then you use the row as the index to the subarray to get the `Product` object.

Another modification that you need to make in `cellForRowAtIndexPath:` is to change the cell's `accessoryType` to `UITableViewCellAccessoryNone`. You need to remove the accessory view because the index will obscure the accessory and it will look bad:

```
cell.accessoryType = UITableViewCellAccessoryNone;
```

The complete implementation of the `tableView:cellForRowAtIndexPath:` method should look like this:

```
- (UITableViewCell *)tableView:(UITableView *)tableView
        cellForRowAtIndexPath:(NSIndexPath *)indexPath {

    static NSString *CellIdentifier = @"Cell";

    CatalogTableViewCell *cell = (CatalogTableViewCell *)
    [tableView dequeueReusableCellWithIdentifier:CellIdentifier];
    if (cell == nil) {
        cell = [[CatalogTableViewCell alloc]
                initWithStyle:UITableViewCellStyleDefault
                reuseIdentifier:CellIdentifier];
    }

    // Configure the cell.
    cell.accessoryType = UITableViewCellAccessoryNone;

    // Get the Product object
    Product* product = [[self.products objectAtIndex:[indexPath section]]
                        objectAtIndex:[indexPath row]];

    // Set the product to be used to draw the cell
    [cell setProduct:product];

    return cell;
}
```

Now that you will be using headers in the table, you need to implement the method `tableView:titleForHeaderInSection:`. This method returns a string that will be used as the header text for the section. You obtain the title from the `UILocalizedIndexedCollation` by using the `sectionTitles` property:

```
- (NSString *)tableView:(UITableView *)tableView
    titleForHeaderInSection:(NSInteger)section {
    // Make sure that the section will contain some data
    if ([[self.products objectAtIndex:section] count] > 0) {

        // If it does, get the section title from the
        // UILocalizedIndexedCollation object
        return [[[UILocalizedIndexedCollation currentCollation] sectionTitles]
                objectAtIndex:section];
    }
    return nil;
}
```

Likewise, because you are implementing an index, you need to provide the text to use in the index. Again, the `UILocalizedIndexedCollation` helps. The property `sectionIndexTitles` returns an array of the index titles:

```
- (NSArray *)sectionIndexTitlesForTableView:(UITableView *)tableView {
    // Set up the index titles from the UILocalizedIndexedCollation
    return [[UILocalizedIndexedCollation currentCollation] sectionIndexTitles];
}
```

Once you've set up the index, you have to link the index to the section titles by implementing the `tableView:sectionForSectionIndexTitle:atIndex:` method. Again, using the `UILocalizedIndexedCollation` greatly simplifies this implementation:

```
- (NSInteger)tableView:(UITableView *)tableView
    sectionForSectionIndexTitle:(NSString *)title atIndex:(NSInteger)index {
    // Link the sections to the labels in the index
    return [[UILocalizedIndexedCollation currentCollation]
            sectionForSectionIndexTitleAtIndex:index];
}
```

If you build and run the application, it should run, and the table should be displayed with sections and an index. However, if you select a row, the application will not take you to the detail page. Because you modified the way the data is stored, you need to go back and modify the `tableView:didSelectRowAtIndexPath:` method to use the new scheme. This is as simple as changing the line of code that sets the `detailItem` in the `detailViewController` like this:

```
self.detailViewController.detailItem =[[self.products
                                    objectAtIndex:[indexPath section]]
                                    objectAtIndex:[indexPath row]];
```

The complete implementation of `tableView:didSelectRowAtIndexPath:` should now look like this:

```
- (void)tableView:(UITableView *)tableView
    didSelectRowAtIndexPath:(NSIndexPath *)indexPath
{
    if (!self.detailViewController) {
        self.detailViewController = [[DetailViewController alloc]
                                    initWithNibName:@"DetailViewController"
                                    bundle:nil];
    }

    self.detailViewController.detailItem =[[self.products
                                        objectAtIndex:[indexPath section]]
                                        objectAtIndex:[indexPath row]];
    [self.navigationController pushViewController:self.detailViewController
                                    animated:YES];
}
```

If you build and run again, all should be well. You should be able to navigate the application just as before, except that now you have a well-organized and indexed table for easy navigation.

IMPLEMENTING SEARCH

The sample application now has all the items in the corporate catalog neatly organized into sections based on the product name, with an index for quick access to each section. The final piece of functionality that you will add is a search capability. Users should be able to search for particular products within the catalog, without having to scroll through the entire thing.

You will implement functionality that is similar to the search capabilities of the built-in Contacts application. You will add a `UISearchBar` control at the top of the table and then filter the products list based on user input. The final interface will look like Figure 3-7.

When the user starts a search, you will remove the side index list and only show rows that meet the search criteria, as shown in Figure 3-8.

FIGURE 3-7: Catalog with search interface

FIGURE 3-8: Search in progress

Implementing search requires two controls: the `UISearchBar` and the `UISearchDisplayController`, which Apple introduced in the iOS SDK 3.0. The `UISearchBar` is the UI widget that you will put at the top of the table to accept search text input. You use the `UISearchDisplayController` to filter the data provided by another view controller based on the search text in the `UISearchBar`.

You initialize the `UISearchDisplayController` with a search bar and the view controller containing the content that the user wants to search. When a search begins, the search display controller overlays the search interface above the original view controller's view to display a subset of the original data. The results display is a table view that the search display controller creates.

The first step is to create the `UISearchBar` and add it to the table. In the `MasterViewController` header, add a property for the search bar:

```
@interface MasterViewController : UITableViewController

@property (strong, nonatomic) DetailViewController *detailViewController;
@property (strong, nonatomic) NSMutableArray* products;
@property (strong, nonatomic) UISearchBar* searchBar;
@end
```

You can now add the code to create the search bar to the header of the table view at the end of the viewDidLoad method:

```
// Create search bar
self.searchBar = [[UISearchBar alloc] initWithFrame:
                        CGRectMake(0.0f, 0.0f, 320.0f, 44.0f)];
self.tableView.tableHeaderView = self.searchBar;
```

Next, you will create and configure the UISearchDisplayController. You use this controller to filter and display the data in the MasterViewController's table view. In the header for MasterViewController, add a property for the search display controller:

```
@interface MasterViewController : UITableViewController

@property (strong, nonatomic) DetailViewController *detailViewController;
@property (strong, nonatomic) NSMutableArray* products;
@property (strong, nonatomic) UISearchBar* searchBar;
@property (strong, nonatomic) UISearchDisplayController* searchController;
```

Add the code to viewDidLoad to create and configure the display controller:

```
// Create and configure the search controller
self.searchController = [[UISearchDisplayController alloc]
                        initWithSearchBar:self.searchBar
                        contentsController:self];

self.searchController.searchResultsDataSource = self;
self.searchController.searchResultsDelegate = self;
```

Because you are going to be creating a new, filtered table, you need to create an array to hold the filtered product list. Add another property to the MasterViewController header for this list:

```
@interface MasterViewController : UITableViewController

@property (strong, nonatomic) DetailViewController *detailViewController;
@property (strong, nonatomic) NSMutableArray* products;
@property (retain, nonatomic) NSArray *filteredProducts;
@property (strong, nonatomic) UISearchBar* searchBar;
@property (strong, nonatomic) UISearchDisplayController* searchController;

@end
```

You have now completed adding the additional controls and properties that you need to implement the search feature. The next step is to modify the UITableView methods that you use to populate the UITableView.

In each function, you need to determine if you are working with the normal table or the filtered table. Then you need to proceed accordingly. You can determine which UITableView you are dealing with by comparing the UITableView passed into the function to the view controller's tableView property, which holds the normal UITableView.

The first method that you will modify is numberOfSectionsInTableView:

```
- (NSInteger)numberOfSectionsInTableView:(UITableView *)tableView {
    // Is the request for numberOfRowsInSection for the regular table?
    if (tableView == self.tableView)
```

```
    {
        // Just return the count of the products like before
        return [self.products count];

    }

    return 1;
}
```

The first thing that you do is compare the `tableView` that was passed into the method with the `MasterViewController`'s `tableView`. If they are the same, you are dealing with the normal table view, and you will determine the number of sections just as you did in the previous example. If you are dealing with the filtered table, you return 1 because you do not want to use sections in the filtered table.

Next, you modify the `tableView:numberOfRowsInSection:` method to check which table you are working with and then return the appropriate row count. You use the `NSPredicate` class to filter the data. You will learn more about predicates in Part II of this book, which focuses on Core Data. For now, the only thing that you need to understand about predicates is that they are a mechanism for providing criteria used to filter data. Predicates work like the WHERE clause in an SQL statement. Before you can use the predicate, you need to flatten the array of arrays that contains the data. You flatten the array and then use the `NSPredicate` to filter the array:

```
- (NSInteger)tableView:(UITableView *)tableView
  numberOfRowsInSection:(NSInteger)section {

    // Is the request for numberOfRowsInSection for the regular table?
    if (tableView == self.tableView)
    {
        // Just return the count of the products like before
        return [[self.products objectAtIndex:section] count];

    }

    // You need the count for the filtered table
    // First, you have to flatten the array of arrays self.products
    NSMutableArray *flattenedArray = [[NSMutableArray alloc]
                                      initWithCapacity:1];
    for (NSMutableArray *theArray in self.products)
    {
        for (int i=0; i<[theArray count];i++)
        {
            [flattenedArray addObject:[theArray objectAtIndex:i]];
        }
    }

    // Set up an NSPredicate to filter the rows
    NSPredicate *predicate = [NSPredicate predicateWithFormat:
                             @"name beginswith[c] %@", self.searchBar.text];
    self.filteredProducts = [flattenedArray
                             filteredArrayUsingPredicate:predicate];

    return self.filteredProducts.count;
}
```

This code uses the same methodology as the previous method for determining which table view you are dealing with. If you are working with the normal table view, you return the product count as in the previous example. If not, you need to determine the count of filtered products.

To accomplish this, you first flatten the `products` array of arrays into a single array. Remember that to implement sections, you should store your data as an array of arrays. Well, you need to flatten that structure to a one-dimensional array to filter it with the `NSPredicate`. To flatten the `products` array, you simply loop over each array and put the contents of the subarray into a new array called `flattenedArray`.

Next, you set up the `NSPredicate` object to filter out only rows that begin with the text that is input into the search bar. Then you apply the predicate to the `flattenedArray` and put the result into the `filteredProducts` array. You will use the `filteredProducts` array from here on out when dealing with the filtered table view. Finally, you return the count of items in the `filteredProducts` array.

Now that you have the correct row counts, you need to modify the `tableView:cellForRowAtIndexPath:` method to display the correct rows:

```
- (UITableViewCell *)tableView:(UITableView *)tableView
        cellForRowAtIndexPath:(NSIndexPath *)indexPath {

    static NSString *CellIdentifier = @"Cell";

    CatalogTableViewCell *cell = (CatalogTableViewCell *)

    [tableView dequeueReusableCellWithIdentifier:CellIdentifier];
    if (cell == nil) {
        cell = [[CatalogTableViewCell alloc]
                initWithStyle:UITableViewCellStyleDefault
                reuseIdentifier:CellIdentifier];
    }

    // Configure the cell.
    cell.accessoryType = UITableViewCellAccessoryNone;

    // Is the request for cellForRowAtIndexPath for the regular table?
    if (tableView == self.tableView)
    {

        // Get the Product object
        Product* product = [[self.products
                            objectAtIndex:[indexPath section]]
                            objectAtIndex:[indexPath row]];

        // Set the product to be used to draw the cell
        [cell setProduct:product];

        return cell;
    }

    // Get the Product object
```

```
        Product* product = [self.filteredProducts objectAtIndex:[indexPath row]];

        // Set the product to be used to draw the cell
        [cell setProduct:product];

        return cell;
    }
```

In this method, you do the same type of thing that you have done in the previous two methods. You create the cell just as you did in the previous example. The difference here is that if you are dealing with the normal table, you get the Product object from the self.products array, but if you are dealing with the filtered table, you get the Product object from the self.filteredProducts array.

Now you will modify the didSelectRowAtIndexPath: method to use either the normal or the filtered table:

```
- (void)tableView:(UITableView *)tableView
didSelectRowAtIndexPath:(NSIndexPath *)indexPath {

    Product* product;

    if (tableView == self.tableView)
    {
        // Get the product that corresponds with the touched cell
        product =  [[self.products objectAtIndex:[indexPath section]]
                        objectAtIndex:[indexPath row]];
    }

    else {
        product =  [self.filteredProducts objectAtIndex:[indexPath row]];

    }


    if (!self.detailViewController) {
        self.detailViewController = [[DetailViewController alloc]
                                    initWithNibName:@"DetailViewController"
                                    bundle:nil];
    }

    self.detailViewController.detailItem = product;

    [self.navigationController pushViewController:self.detailViewController
                                    animated:YES];


}
```

Again, in this method, you do the same thing that you did in the previous method. If you are dealing with the normal table, you get the Product object from the self.products array, but if you are dealing with the filtered table, you get the Product object from the self.filteredProducts array.

Finally, modify the `sectionIndexTitlesForTableView:` method to return the regular index for the normal table but `nil` for the filtered table because you don't want to show the index while displaying the filtered table:

```
- (NSArray *)sectionIndexTitlesForTableView:(UITableView *)tableView {
    if (tableView == self.tableView)
    {
        // Set up the index titles from the UILocalizedIndexedCollation
        return [[UILocalizedIndexedCollation currentCollation]
                sectionIndexTitles];
    }

    return nil;
}
```

You should now be able to build and run the code and have full searching capabilities. In a nutshell, you implement search by adding a search bar and a `SearchDisplayController` to your view controller and then modify your table view methods to handle dealing with either the normal or filtered data.

OPTIMIZING TABLE VIEW PERFORMANCE

In this chapter, you have explored how to use the table view in detail. You have learned how to customize the table view to look exactly as you want by using styles, adding subviews to the `contentView`, and creating your own cells by subclassing the `UITableViewCell` class. You have also learned how to organize your table and make it easy to use by adding sections, an index, and search capability. The final aspect of the table view that you will look at is how to optimize performance.

The iPhone and iPad are amazing devices, and users expect an amazing experience from their apps. Apple has set the standard with the preinstalled applications. You should strive to get your applications to function as fluidly and elegantly as the default applications.

The primary problem that you will encounter when building an application with a table view is poor scrolling performance. Several factors can cause this, as you will see in the following sections.

Reusing Existing Cells

Creating objects at runtime can be an expensive operation in terms of how much processor time you use to create the object. Additionally, objects that contain a hierarchy of views, such as the table view cell, can consume a significant amount of memory.

On embedded devices like the iPhone and iPad, the processors are generally not as fast as those on desktop and laptop computers, so you must try to do whatever you can to optimize your code for execution on these slower machines. In addition, on devices such as the iPhone and iPad, memory is at a premium. If you use too much memory, the OS on the device notifies you to release some memory. If you fail to release enough memory, the OS terminates your application. Random termination of your application does not lead to happy customers.

One step that you can take to optimize the code of your table views is to reuse existing cells when appropriate. The first step in debugging scrolling problems with the table view is to look at object allocations. If you are allocating objects as you scroll, there is a problem.

The designers at Apple have provided a private queue that you can use to store table view cells for reuse. In the `cellForRowAtIndexPath:` method, you can access this queue to get an existing cell from the queue instead of creating a new one. In fact, you have done this in the code examples in this chapter.

If you want to see the difference that this optimization makes in your sample code, change the following line in `cellForRowAtIndexPath:`

```
UITableViewCell *cell = [tableView
                    dequeueReusableCellWithIdentifier:CellIdentifier];
```

to this:

```
UITableViewCell *cell = nil;
```

Now the code does not try to use a cell from the queue; it creates a new cell each time the table view asks for a cell. The performance difference may not be too noticeable with a table that has only a few rows, but imagine creating all these cells if your data consisted of thousands of rows. Additionally, the final project is using subclassing and custom-drawn cells. Try going back and making this change to the code where you added subviews to the `contentView`. You should notice a significant slowdown in scrolling speed.

A common point of confusion with cell reuse is the cell identifier. The string that you provide in `dequeueReusableCellWithIdentifier:` is the identifier. This identifier does not define the cell's contents, only its style. When you plan to reuse the style of a cell, assign a string to the reuse identifier, and then pass that string into `dequeueReusableCellWithIdentifier:`. This allows you to create cells with different styles, store them with different identifiers, and queue them up for quick access.

When you call `dequeueReusableCellWithIdentifier:` the method returns either a cell that you can use, or `nil`. If the return is `nil`, you need to create a new cell to use in your table.

A final note about the `cellForRowAtIndexPath:` method. Do not do anything in `cellForRowAtIndexPath:` that takes a long time. I recently saw an example of a developer downloading an image from the web each time `cellForRowAtIndexPath:` was called. That is a bad idea! You need to make sure that `cellForRowAtIndexPath:` returns quickly, because the table view calls it each time that it needs to show a cell in your table. When it will take a long time to create the content for a cell, consider prefetching the content and caching it.

Opaque Subviews

When you are using the technique of programmatically adding subviews to a cell's content view, you should ensure that all the subviews that you add are opaque. Transparent subviews detract from scrolling performance because the compositing of transparent layers is an expensive operation. The `UITableViewCell` inherits the opaque property from `UIView`. This property defaults to `YES`. Do not change it unless you must have a transparent view.

Additionally, you should ensure that the subviews that you add to the UITableViewCell have the same background color as the cell. Not doing this also detracts from the performance of the table view.

It is possible to view layers that are being composited by using the Instruments application, which Apple provides free as part of Xcode. The tool is useful in debugging applications and can accomplish a lot of helpful things, including tracking memory leaks and logging all memory allocations. You can use the Core Animation tool in Instruments to show layers that are being composited. The Core Animation tool only works when it is running your application on a device.

To see where compositing is occurring in your application, first make sure that you have a device connected to your development machine and ensure that you have configured your build scheme to test on a device. Then start the Instruments tool by selecting Product ➪ Profile from the Xcode menu. When the tool starts, it asks you to choose a template for the trace document. In the left pane, choose iOS/All.

In the right pane of the dialog, select Core Animation. This opens the Instruments interface with a Core Animation instrument. If the bottom pane is not visible, click the second icon in the View icon group in the toolbar to expand the detail view. In the debug options on the left side of the bottom pane, select Color Blended Layers, as shown in Figure 3-9.

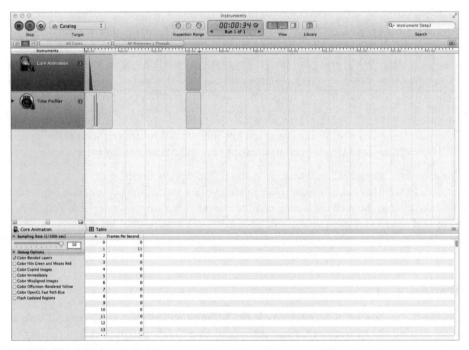

FIGURE 3-9: Instruments tool

Now when you run your application on the device, layers that are not composited appear green, and composited layers appear red.

To see the difference, you can make a change to the `MasterViewController` in the first version of the catalog application that you built in this chapter. If you do not have the first, nonsubclassed version, you can download it from the book's website.

In the `tableView:cellForRowAtIndexPath:` method, add a line to set `productImage.alpha = 0.9` under the line `productImage.tag = PRODUCTIMAGE_TAG`. The snippet of code should look like this:

```
// Configure the product Image
productImage = [[UIImageView alloc]
                initWithFrame:CGRectMake(0.0, 0.0, 40.0, 40.0)];

productImage.tag = PRODUCTIMAGE_TAG;

productImage.alpha = 0.9;

// Add the Image to the cell's content view
[cell.contentView addSubview:productImage];
```

Now run the application. You should see all the product images overlaid with red. The red overlay indicates which images are being composited. Remember that compositing images is processor intensive; avoid compositing if at all possible.

There is one final issue that you should be aware of regarding PNG images. If you are using PNG files, as in the sample, you should create them without an Alpha layer. Including the Alpha layer causes compositing regardless of how the opaque property is set on the `UIImageView`.

You examine how to use Instruments in more detail in Appendix A.

Custom Drawn Cells with drawRect

You examined this technique in the "Subclassing UITableViewCell" section of this chapter. The fastest way to render a cell is by manually drawing it in the `drawRect` method. It may take more work on the part of the developer, but there is a large payoff. If you are building a cell that will contain more than three subviews, consider subclassing and drawing the contents manually. This can dramatically increase scrolling performance.

The technique basically boils down to collapsing multiview table cells to one view that knows how to draw itself.

A subclass of `UITableViewCell` may reset attributes of the cell by overriding `prepareForReuse`. This method is called just before the table view returns a cell to the data source in `dequeueReusableCellWithIdentifier:`. If you do override this method to reset the cell's attributes, you should only reset attributes that are unrelated to content, such as alpha, editing, and selection state.

UI Conventions for Accessory Views

You should abide by the following conventions when adding accessory views to cells in your table:

➤ The `UITableViewCellAccessoryDisclosureIndicator` is a disclosure indicator. The control does not respond to touches and indicates that touching the row will bring the user to a detail screen based on the selected row.

➤ The `UITableViewCellAccessoryDetailDisclosureButton` does respond to touches and indicates that configuration options for the selected row will be presented.

➤ The `UITableViewCellAccessoryCheckmark` displays a checkmark indicating that the row is selected. The checkmark does not respond to touches.

For more information, read the iOS Human Interface Guidelines located at `http://developer .apple.com`.

MOVING FORWARD

In this chapter, you learned how to use the `UITableView` to display data in your application. Then you learned how to customize the display of your data by building custom `UITableViewCells`. Next, you learned how to allow users to manipulate the display of their data by searching and filtering the results. Finally, you learned how to avoid and troubleshoot performance problems with the `UITableView`.

In the next chapter, you will learn how to display and navigate your data using some of the unique UI elements that are available on the iPad. Then, in Part II, you will learn how to create and query data using the Core Data framework.

User Interface Elements

➤ Building a master-detail view using the split view controller and storyboards

➤ Displaying informational messages using the popover controller

➤ Recognizing and reacting to various user gestures using gesture recognizers

➤ Sharing files with desktop machines using file-sharing support

WROX.COM CODE DOWNLOADS FOR THIS CHAPTER

The wrox.com code downloads for this chapter are found at www.wrox.com/remtitle .cgi?isbn=1118391845 on the Download Code tab. The code is in the Chapter 4 download and individually named according to the names throughout the chapter.

In Chapter 3, you learned how to display your application data using the UITableView control. Then you took that knowledge a step further by building custom cells, adding search and filter capabilities, and implementing indexes and section headers.

In this chapter, you will learn about some interesting user interface elements and other features of iOS so you can build better data-driven applications.

You will explore the UISplitViewController and UIPopoverController, which you can use when building iPad applications. You will learn how to build your user interface using storyboards. You will also learn how to use the UIGestureRecognizer class and its subclasses to interpret user gestures. Finally, you will learn how to share files between an iOS device and desktop computers using file-sharing support.

BUILDING YOUR INTERFACE WITH STORYBOARDS

Data-driven applications often use many interconnected screens to allow users to view and manipulate the data. Xcode contains a user interface design feature called Storyboards, introduced in iOS 5, that you can use to help design the interface and flow of your applications. In contrast to the single screen editing in Interface Builder that you have used in previous chapters, a storyboard can contain all the screens of your application in a single file. You can use storyboards to lay out all the screens of your applications and link them with transitions.

Storyboards have two basic parts: scenes and segues. *Scenes* are your application's screens, which typically correspond to view controllers. *Segues* are simply the connections between the scenes. Storyboarding allows you to lay out the entire user interface of your application before you write a single line of code.

The best way to see the value of using storyboards is through an example. In this simple example, you will build a master-detail application, not unlike the catalog example that you are already familiar with, using storyboards. In this example, however, you will not be adding database code — or very much code at all, for that matter. You will simply create a new project based on the Master-Detail template, add two additional screens to the template project, and provide user navigation to those screens using the storyboarding interface. When you are finished, your storyboard will look like Figure 4-1. You will continue to use storyboards to build the examples throughout the remaining chapters of this book.

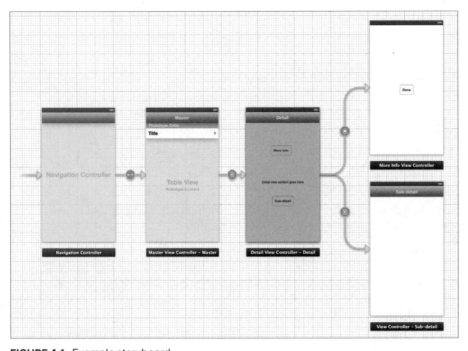

FIGURE 4-1: Example storyboard

In Figure 4-1, you can see the Master view controller and Detail view controller that you should be familiar with from previous examples. The beauty of storyboards is that they provide a visual representation of your application interface. The arrow between the Master view controller and Detail view controller makes it clear that the Master view controller transitions to the Detail view controller.

You will add the two screens to the right of the Detail view controller to provide additional details for the user. The More Info view controller will be a modal screen that the user can see by tapping the More Info button on the detail screen. You will use a flip style transition to make the Detail view controller flip over like a piece of paper with the More Info view controller on the back side. Users will navigate to the Sub-detail view controller by tapping on the Sub-detail button on the Detail view controller. You will add a Navigation Item to the Sub-detail view controller and use a Push transition so that you can push the Sub-detail screen onto the navigation stack. This will allow the Sub-detail screen to be integrated with the navigation controller and the overall navigation of the application.

Starting the Storyboard Example Application

Begin your example application by opening Xcode and creating a new project. Choose Master-Detail Application as the template for your new project. In the options for your new project, call the project **FirstStoryboard**. Set the device for the project to iPhone, check the Use Storyboards checkbox, and click Next. Select a location for your project, and click Create to create the project.

After you create your project, select the `MainStoryboard.storyboard` file in the Project Navigator. You should see a storyboard in the editing window that looks like Figure 4-2.

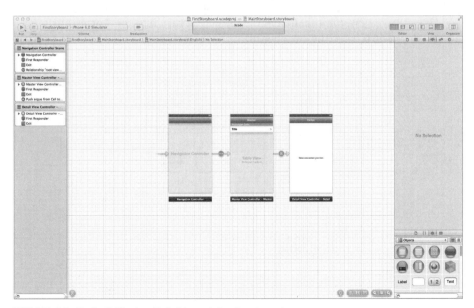

FIGURE 4-2: Default Master-Detail template storyboard

By default, projects developed for iOS 6 use Auto Layout, introduced in iOS 6, to arrange your interface elements on the storyboard. If you need to build an application that works with earlier versions of iOS, you can turn Auto Layout off by clearing the checkbox that says, "Use Autolayout" in the Interface Builder Document section in the File Inspector. For this example, you should disable Auto Layout.

The left side of the storyboard window lists all the scenes in the storyboard, while the middle pane displays the scenes and segues in your application. In the template, you see the navigation controller, which references the Master view controller. You can also see the segue relationship between the Master view controller and the Detail view controller. If you click on this segue and look at the Attributes Inspector in the Utilities pane, you see that this segue uses a Push style. This means that the Master view controller will transition to the Detail view controller by pushing the Master view controller off the screen, as you have seen previously in the catalog application.

To see what the template application does, run the application. You see the Master screen, which includes an Edit and a Plus (+) button in the navigation bar. Tap the + button to add date-timestamps to the table view. Then tap on one of the timestamps that you created to navigate to a detail view, which simply displays the timestamp.

Adding the Sub-detail Screen to the Storyboard

Now that you have the template application up and running, you will add two new screens. First, you will add the Sub-detail screen, and then you will add the More Info screen.

To add the Sub-detail screen, you will add a new view controller to the storyboard. If the Object Library pane in the Utilities view in Xcode is not visible already, select View ➪ Utilities ➪ Show Object Library. The first icon in the Object Library pane should be the view controller, as you can see in Figure 4-3. Drag a new view controller from the Object Library into the storyboard. This should create a new view controller in the storyboard.

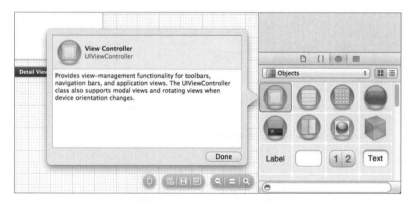

FIGURE 4-3: View controller object

Next, scroll down through the list of objects in the Object Library until you find the navigation item object. Drag the navigation item into the new view controller that you created in the previous step.

You need a way for the user to navigate to your new view controller, so drag a Round Rect button from the Object Library and drop it into the Detail view controller. Users will use this button to get to the Sub-detail screen. Change the text of the button to read **Sub-detail**. Now connect the button that you just created with the Sub-detail view controller by right-dragging from the button to the view controller. When you let go of the mouse button, you will see a pop-up asking you to choose an Action Segue. Choose Push from this pop-up. After you choose Push, you should see a navigation item appear in the Sub-detail view controller that says Title. You can change the title to **Sub-Detail** by selecting the navigation item and changing the Title property in the Attributes Inspector.

If you build and run the application now, you can see your new screen in action. Tap the plus sign at the top of the Master view controller to add a new row to the table. Then tap on the row to display the Detail view controller. Finally, tap the Sub-detail button that you added to navigate to the Sub-detail view controller. You should see the Sub-detail screen with an option in the navigation bar to navigate back to the detail screen. As you can see, it is easy to add new screens to your application using storyboards.

Adding a Modal Screen to the Storyboard

Now that you have the Sub-detail view in place, you are ready to add the More Detail view controller to your storyboard. In this case, the view controller will not be part of the navigation hierarchy; it will simply be a modal screen that you can employ to get more information about something in your application.

For this view controller, you will create a new code class that you will associate with the view controller. Create a new Objective-C class in your project called `MoreInfoViewController`, and make it a subclass of `UIViewController`.

Next, add a new view controller to your storyboard by dragging a view controller from the Object Library pane and dropping it onto your storyboard. Using the Identity Inspector, set the Class of the new view controller to be the `MoreInfoViewController` that you just created. Then drag a Label control from the Object Library, drop it into the More Info view controller, and change it to read **More Info**.

You need to add a way for users to be able to navigate to the More Info view controller, so add a new button to the Detail view controller and change the text of the button to say **More Info**. Right-drag from the new More Info button to the More Info view controller and select Modal from the pop-up. This creates a segue from the button to the view controller that opens the More Info view controller in modal mode. To enable the flip segue animation, click the segue and change the Transition to Flip Horizontal in the Attributes Inspector.

The last thing that you need to do is provide a way for users to dismiss the modal view controller and get back to the Detail view. Add a Round Rect button to the More Info view controller and change the text of the button to **OK**. You need to connect the OK button to a bit of code that will dismiss the modal view controller. You can easily make this connection using the Assistant editor.

Open the Assistant editor to display the storyboard and the code header `MoreInfoViewController.h` side by side. Right-drag the OK button from the storyboard into the code header file and let go of the mouse button right below the `@interface` declaration. In the pop-up that appears, select Action from the connection drop-down, set the name to `okTapped`, and click Connect. You will see that Xcode has added a new `IBAction` method called `okTapped:` to the header and a stub implementation to the code (`.m`) file.

Switch over to the code implementation file `MoreInfoViewController.m` and implement the `okTapped:` method with one line of code to dismiss the modal view controller:

```
- (IBAction)okTapped:(id)sender {
    [self dismissViewControllerAnimated:YES completion:NULL];
}
```

Now you are ready to build and run your application. Tap the plus sign at the top of the Master view controller to add a new row to the table. Then tap on the row to display the Detail view controller. Finally, tap the More Info button to display the More Info view controller. You should see a flip transition to the More Info screen. Tap the OK button to navigate back to the detail screen. Once again, you've easily added another type of functionality using storyboards and a minimal amount of code.

DISPLAYING MASTER/DETAIL DATA WITH THE SPLIT VIEW CONTROLLER

Quite often, when you're building a data-centric application, you will want to show data in a master/detail format. For instance, in an address book application, the master view typically consists of a simple list of contact names. Selecting a contact from the list then presents the details for that contact, such as address, phone number, and company.

When you develop an application for the iPhone, you generally build master/detail displays using the Navigation Controller. You would typically use a `UITableView` to show the master records. Tapping on a master record advances the user to a second screen that displays the details for the record that the user selected. Because the iPhone screen has limited space, two separate screens are necessary to display the master and detail data. The catalog application that you built in Chapter 3 uses this model, as shown in Figure 4-4.

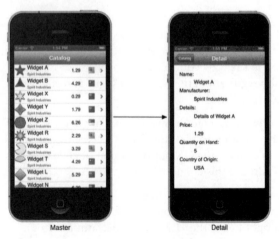

FIGURE 4-4: Master-Detail view on iOS

Introducing the UISplitViewController

With the extended amount of screen space available to you on the iPad, you have a better option than building master/detail displays using the Navigation Controller. Instead of displaying the master data and detail data separately on two different screens, you can combine the two so that all this information is visible at the same time by using the UISplitViewController. You can use this user interface element to display two distinct view controllers side by side in landscape mode, as you can see in Figure 4-5. This enables you to take advantage of the iPad's large screen.

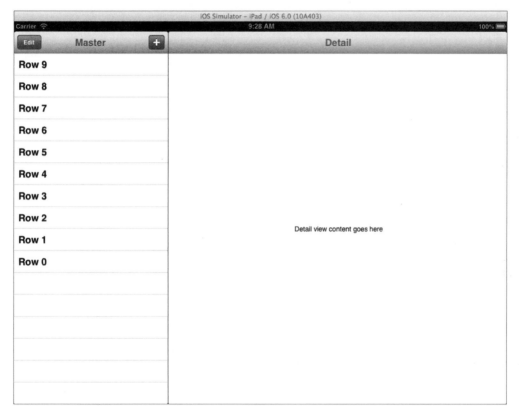

FIGURE 4-5: UISplitViewController in landscape mode

In portrait mode, the controller allows the user to view the detail data onscreen while popping up the master data on demand by tapping a button in the interface. Figure 4-6 shows the same view controller as Figure 4-5, but in this case, I have rotated the iPad into portrait mode. The UISplitViewController automatically changes the display of its child view controllers based on the orientation of the device.

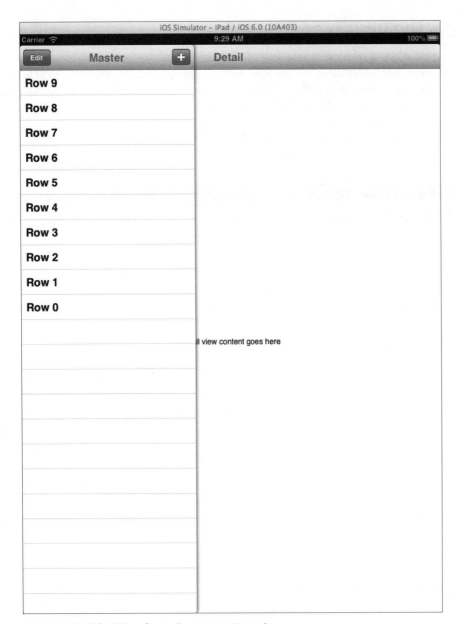

FIGURE 4-6: UISplitViewController in portrait mode

The UISplitViewController does not do anything to support communication between its child view controllers. That code is your responsibility. In the template code when you start a new Master-Detail Application project, the MasterViewController maintains a reference to the

DetailViewController, which is set in the MasterViewController's viewDidLoad method:

```
self.detailViewController = (DetailViewController *)
        [[self.splitViewController.viewControllers lastObject] topViewController];
```

Keep in mind that this is only the default implementation, and you are free to delete this implementation and build the communication between the two views in any way that you choose.

The UISplitViewControllerDelegate Protocol

When the orientation of the device changes, the UISplitViewController calls its delegate methods. The UISplitViewControllerDelegate protocol defines these methods.

The split view controller calls the splitViewController:popoverController:willPresent ViewController: method when the popover containing the root view controller should appear. This happens when the user taps the button in the toolbar while the device is in the portrait orientation. If you are using any other popover controls in your application, make sure that you dismiss them in this delegate method. It is a violation of the Apple Human Interface Guidelines to display more than one popover controller at a time. If you do, Apple will reject your application during the review process.

The split view controller calls the splitViewController:willHideViewController:withBar ButtonItem:forPopoverController: method when it is about to hide the view controller passed into the method. This occurs when the user rotates the device from landscape to portrait orientation. In this method, you need to add the button that will call the popover controller to the toolbar. The application template code implements this method for you.

The split view controller calls the splitViewController:willShowViewController: invalidatingBarButtonItem: method when the user rotates the device from portrait orientation back to landscape orientation. This indicates that the split view controller is about to display the left view controller again. The code in this method should remove the toolbar button from the toolbar that the interface uses in portrait mode to display the popover. Again, the template implements this if you start your project by using the Split View–based Application template.

Finally, the split view controller calls the splitViewController:shouldHideViewController: inOrientation: method for its first child view controller. The return value determines if you display the first view controller in the given orientation. If you implement this method, you should return YES if you would like to hide the first view controller for the specified orientation or NO if you would like the first view controller to remain visible. The default implementation of this method returns YES for portrait orientation and NO for landscape orientation.

Starting the Split View Sample Application

In this chapter, you build a sample application that implements some basic survey features. Survey takers that are out in the field collecting data could use an application like this. The application will use a storyboard and a UISplitViewController to display the names of the people that the user has surveyed on the left side as the master data. The right side will display the actual survey data that the user entered as the child data. Figure 4-7 shows the completed application in landscape mode.

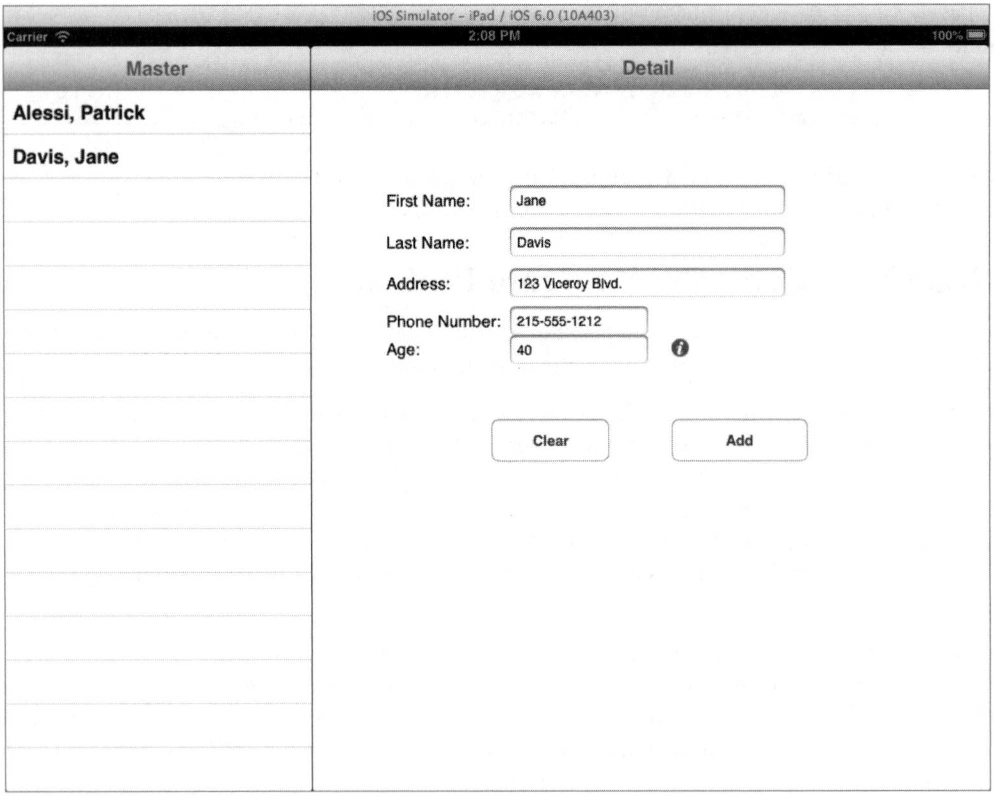

FIGURE 4-7: Completed survey application

The application will allow the user to add new survey responses to the data set and view existing responses. To keep the application focused on demonstrating the user interface features that are unique to the iPad, you will not be implementing every feature that would be required for a complete application. For instance, I won't cover adding the code to modify existing surveys or to delete surveys.

To begin the Survey application, open Xcode and create a new project. Choose to use the Master-Detail Application template for the new project. Make sure that you leave the Use Core Data for Storage checkbox unchecked. You will learn about Core Data in the next section of the book. Check the Use Storyboards checkbox. Select iPad in the Devices drop-down, because you will be developing this application for the iPad. Call your new application **Survey**.

Open the `MainStoryboard.storyboard` storyboard file; it should look like Figure 4-8.

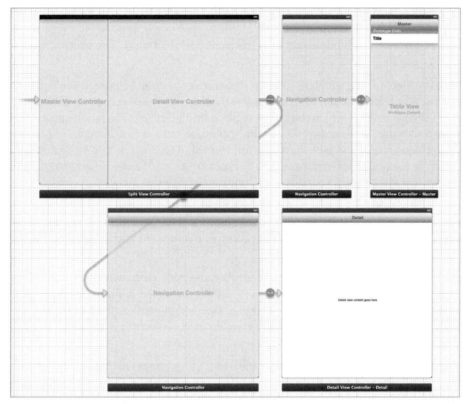

FIGURE 4-8: iPad Master-Detail storyboard

You can see in the storyboard that the root of the application is the Split view controller. The Split view controller houses the Master view controller on the left and the Detail view controller on the right. Next in the hierarchy for both the Master and Detail view controllers is a navigation controller. Finally, you can see the Master and Detail view controllers themselves. The storyboard provides a convenient way for you to visualize the entirety of the application's user interface.

Just to see the basic functionality that you get from the template code, build and run the application. When the iPad simulator starts, you will see the simulated iPad in portrait mode. Notice how the detail view takes up the whole screen. Click on the Master button, and you will see the Master view controller with the options to edit data and add new rows slide in, as you saw in Figure 4-6.

Press Command+left arrow to rotate the iPad in the simulator. You will see the split view change to show the detail in the right pane and the master list in the left pane, as shown in Figure 4-5.

Now you will take a brief look at the code and storyboard that the template provides. First, open the `MainStoryboard.storyboard` file. In the storyboard main window, click the Split view controller. If you look at the Connections Inspector, you should see that the Split view controller maps its Master view controller segue to the Master view controller's navigation controller and its detail view controller segue to the Detail view controller's navigation controller. The thing to notice here is that the Split view controller does not actually do anything on its own. It is simply a container for the Root view controller, which implements the left pane, and the Detail view controller, which implements the right pane.

Now you'll take a brief look at the template code for the `MasterViewController` in the `MasterViewController.h` file. The template configures the `MasterViewController` to be a subclass of `UITableViewController`, which the template places in the left pane in landscape mode and the popover in portrait mode. The template code implementation in `MasterViewController.m` is a straightforward implementation of a table, just like you learned in Chapter 3. You will find the typical table view delegate methods `numberOfSectionsInTableView:`, `tableView:numberOfRowsInSection:`, and `tableView:cellForRowAtIndexPath:` implemented in this class.

The `DetailViewController` is a `UIViewController` subclass, as you can see in `DetailViewController.h`. By default, the storyboard scene for the Detail view controller contains only a single label. In the sample, you will add other controls to allow the user to enter and view survey data.

When the user selects an item in the Master view controller, the table view calls the `tableView:didSelectRowAtIndexPath:` method. The default implementation of this method sets the `detailItem` property of the `DetailViewController`, which, by default, is of type `id`. This is the mechanism for passing data between the `MasterViewController` and the `DetailViewController`.

Instead of relying on the default implementation of the `detailItem` property in the `DetailViewController`, there is code that implements the setter. This is a departure from most of the properties that you have seen so far. The setter is explicitly coded because you need to do some additional processing aside from simply setting the associated instance variable. The method sets the `_detailItem` instance variable and then calls the `configureView` method. The `configureView` method updates the display to show the new `detailItem` data. Then the setter dismisses the popover if it is visible.

Building the Detail Interface

Now you are ready to start working on the detail view interface. First, however, you need to make a couple of changes to the `DetailViewController` header file in preparation for the changes that you will make to the view in the storyboard.

In the `DetailViewController.h` header file, change the type of the `detailItem` in the property declaration for the `detailItem` property to `NSDictionary*`:

```
@property (strong, nonatomic) NSDictionary* detailItem;
```

Next, add outlet properties for the `UITextFields` that you will use in the storyboard to collect the survey data. In the `@interface` section, add the following properties:

```
@property (nonatomic, weak) IBOutlet UITextField* firstNameTextField;
@property (nonatomic, weak) IBOutlet UITextField* lastNameTextField;
@property (nonatomic, weak) IBOutlet UITextField* addressTextField;
@property (nonatomic, weak) IBOutlet UITextField* phoneTextField;
@property (nonatomic, weak) IBOutlet UITextField* ageTextField;
```

Next, add the `clearSurvey` and `addSurvey` `IBAction` methods that will execute when the user taps on the Clear or Add button in the interface:

```
-(IBAction)clearSurvey:(id)sender;
-(IBAction)addSurvey:(id)sender;
```

Because you will not use the `detailDescriptionLabel`, delete the `detailDescriptionLabel` outlet property.

Now you are ready to move on to building the user interface in the storyboard. Select the `MainStoryboard.storyboard` file in the Project Navigator to open the storyboard. Delete the `UILabel` that is in the Detail view controller by default.

You will be building an interface like the one in Figure 4-9. Add a `UILabel` for each field in the interface. Change the text to match the text in Figure 4-9. Then add a `UITextField` next to each of the labels that you just created. Finally, add two `UIButtons` at the bottom of the form and change their text to read **Clear** and **Add**.

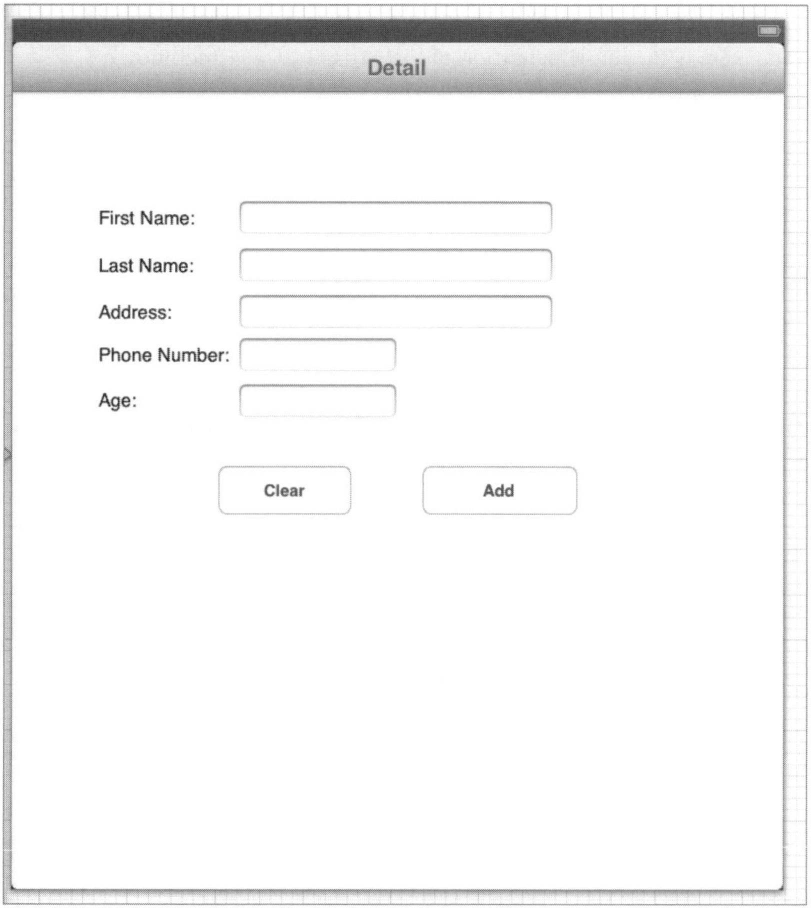

FIGURE 4-9: DetailViewController interface

Now you need to connect each UITextField in the storyboard to the appropriate outlet in the DetailViewController. This will enable you to retrieve the data from these controls or populate the controls with data. Finally, connect the Touch Up Inside event of the Clear button to the clearSurvey: method in the DetailViewController. Likewise, connect the Touch Up Inside event of the Add button to the addSurvey: method in the DetailViewController.

Adding Surveys with the Master/Detail View

In this section, you implement the basic functionality of the application that demonstrates using the split view to show master/detail view relationships.

Setting Up the DetailViewController

First, you will implement stubs for the clearSurvey: and addSurvey: methods in the DetailViewController. These methods will create a log entry in the console when they execute. This will allow you to verify that you have correctly linked the buttons in the user interface to the source code.

The clearSurvey: method should log that the user has invoked the method. Then it should clear all the user interface elements. Here is the implementation of the clearSurvey: method:

```
-(IBAction)clearSurvey:(id)sender
{
    NSLog (@"clearSurvey");
    // Update the user interface for the detail item.
    self.firstNameTextField.text = @"";
    self.lastNameTextField.text = @"";
    self.addressTextField.text = @"";
    self.phoneTextField.text = @"";
    self.ageTextField.text = @"";
}
```

You will eventually code the addSurvey: method to save the survey data. Because you are not quite ready to do that yet, simply implement the method to log that the user has invoked it by tapping the Add button. Here is the implementation:

```
-(IBAction)addSurvey:(id)sender
{
    NSLog (@"addSurvey");
}
```

Before you can run the application, you need to remove the reference to the detailDescription-Label from the configureView method because you deleted the detail description label. The configureView method should look like this:

```
- (void)configureView
{
    // Update the user interface for the detail item.

    if (self.detailItem) {

    }
}
```

Build and run your application. When the application starts in the iPad simulator, click each button and verify that you see the correct log statement in the console. This will prove that you have properly connected the buttons to the code.

Now you are ready to modify the `configureView` method in the `DetailViewController` to take the data from the `detailItem` model object and populate the `UITextField`s that display the data in the user interface. Here is the new implementation of the `configureView` method:

```
- (void)configureView
{
    // Update the user interface for the detail item.

    if (self.detailItem) {
        // Update the user interface for the detail item.
        self.firstNameTextField.text = [self.detailItem
                                objectForKey:@"firstName"];
        self.lastNameTextField.text = [self.detailItem
                                objectForKey:@"lastName"];
        self.addressTextField.text = [self.detailItem
                                objectForKey:@"address"];
        self.phoneTextField.text = [self.detailItem
                                objectForKey:@"phone"];
        self.ageTextField.text = [[self.detailItem
                                objectForKey:@"age"] stringValue];
    }
}
```

Each survey is stored in an `NSDictionary`. If you are not familiar with this class, you can use an `NSDictionary` to store a set of key-value pairs, as long as each key is unique. This method simply calls the `objectForKey:` method on the `detailItem` dictionary to obtain the value that you will display in the text field. The only wrinkle is that the age field is stored as an `NSNumber`, so you need to convert the number to a string by calling the `stringValue` method.

Changes to the MasterViewController

Now you need to move on to the `MasterViewController`. Here, you will add an `NSMutableArray*` to hold the collection of surveys. You cannot simply use an `NSArray` because you need to be able to add surveys to the collection on the fly. Remember, `NSArray` is immutable, meaning that once you have created it, you cannot modify it.

In the `MasterViewController.h` header file, add a property for your new `surveyDataArray`:

```
@property (strong, nonatomic) NSMutableArray* surveyDataArray;
```

Finally, modify the `viewDidLoad` method to remove the Edit and Add buttons and create and initialize the `NSMutableArray`:

```
- (void)viewDidLoad
{
    [super viewDidLoad];
    // Do any additional setup after loading the view, typically from a nib.
    self.detailViewController = (DetailViewController *)
        [[self.splitViewController.viewControllers lastObject]
```

```
        topViewController];

    self.surveyDataArray = [[NSMutableArray alloc] init];

}
```

Modify the TableView Methods

The next step is to modify the table view datasource methods to use the surveyData array as the UITableView's datasource. First, you need to update the tableView:numberOfRowsInSection: method to return the number of items in the array, like this:

```
- (NSInteger)tableView:(UITableView *)tableView
    numberOfRowsInSection:(NSInteger)section
{
    // Return the number of rows in the section.
    return [self.surveyDataArray count];
}
```

Then you should change the tableView:cellForRowAtIndexPath: method to get data from the surveyDataArray to use as the text in the table cells:

```
- (UITableViewCell *)tableView:(UITableView *)tableView
        cellForRowAtIndexPath:(NSIndexPath *)indexPath
{
    UITableViewCell *cell =
        [tableView dequeueReusableCellWithIdentifier:@"Cell"
                                        forIndexPath:indexPath];

    // Configure the cell.
    NSDictionary* sd = [self.surveyDataArray objectAtIndex:indexPath.row];

    cell.textLabel.text = [NSString stringWithFormat:@"%@, %@",
                            [sd objectForKey:@"lastName"],
                            [sd objectForKey:@"firstName"]];

    return cell;
}
```

In this method, you get an NSDictionary object from the surveyDataArray with an index based on the row that the table has requested. Then you get the lastName and firstName strings from the dictionary and display them in the cell's textLabel.

The last thing that you need to do in the table view methods is to update the tableView:didSelectRowAtIndexPath: method. In this method, you need to set the detailItem in the detailViewController to the NSDictionary that you retrieve from the surveyDataArray. This passes the data that you want to display, the survey that the user has chosen, to the DetailViewController. Remember that the setter for the detailItem property contains code; it is not just a synthesized property. This code calls the configureView method that updates the view to display the record that the user has chosen. Here is the code for the tableView:didSelectRowAtIndexPath: method:

```
- (void)tableView:(UITableView *)tableView
    didSelectRowAtIndexPath:(NSIndexPath *)indexPath
{

    /*
    When a row is selected, set the Detail View Controller's detail item to the
    item associated with the selected row.
    */
    [tableView deselectRowAtIndexPath:indexPath animated:NO];

    NSDictionary* sd = [self.surveyDataArray objectAtIndex:indexPath.row];
    self.detailViewController.detailItem = sd;


}
```

Adding Surveys

To complete this example, you will add code to the project to enable the user to add surveys to the application. In the MasterViewController header, you need to declare a method to add a survey. You should call this method addSurveyToDataArray, and the signature should look like this:

```
-(void) addSurveyToDataArray: (NSDictionary*) sd;
```

Recall that you are using an NSDictionary to hold the data for each survey. Therefore, the addSurveyToDataArray method accepts an NSDictionary* that holds the survey data that you want to add to the array of completed surveys.

Next, switch over to the MasterViewController implementation. You should implement the addSurveyToDataArray function as follows:

```
-(void) addSurveyToDataArray: (NSDictionary*) sd
{
    NSLog (@"addSurveyToDataArray");

    // Add the survey to the results array.
    [self.surveyDataArray addObject:sd];

    // Refresh the tableview.
    [self.tableView reloadData];
}
```

This method simply adds the dictionary object that it receives to the surveyDataArray. Then, because the user has modified the data for the table view, you need to tell the table view to reload its data to refresh the display and show the new survey.

You need to move over to the DetailViewController to implement the addSurvey method. This method runs when the user taps the Add button in the user interface. First, however, you need to add an #import statement to the DetailViewController header to import the MasterViewController.h header:

```
#import "MasterViewController.h"
```

Now you can move into the DetailViewController implementation to implement the addSurvey method:

```
-(IBAction)addSurvey:(id)sender
{
    NSLog (@"addSurvey");

    // Create a new NSDictionary object to add to the results array of the Root
    // View Controller.

    // Set the values for the fields in the new object from the text fields of
    // the form.

    NSArray *keys = [NSArray arrayWithObjects:@"firstName", @"lastName",
                     @"address", @"phone", @"age", nil];
    NSArray *objects = [NSArray arrayWithObjects:self.firstNameTextField.text,
                        self.lastNameTextField.text,
                        self.addressTextField.text,
                        self.phoneTextField.text,
                        [NSNumber
                         numberWithInteger:[ self.ageTextField.text intValue]],
                        nil];

    NSDictionary* sData = [[NSDictionary alloc]
                            initWithObjects:objects forKeys:keys];

    // Get a reference to the first navigation controller in the split view.
    UINavigationController* nav = [self.splitViewController.viewControllers
                                   objectAtIndex:0];

    // Use this to get a reference to the MasterViewController.
    MasterViewController* rvc = (MasterViewController*) nav.topViewController ;

    // Call the addSurveyToDataArray method on the MasterViewController to
    // add the survey data to the list.
    [rvc addSurveyToDataArray:sData];

}
```

In this method, you need to build an NSDictionary that you will pass to the MasterView Controller to add to the surveyDataArray. To create the dictionary, you first create two NSArrays: one for the keys of the dictionary and one for the related objects. The keys can be any arbitrary NSStrings. You obtain the objects for the dictionary from the UITextField objects that you added in the storyboard. Once you have built your arrays, you create an NSDictionary by passing in the objects array and the keys array.

Next, you need to call the addSurveyToDataArray method on the MasterViewController. If you remember, the MasterViewController holds a reference to the DetailViewController. However, the DetailViewController does not hold a reference to the MasterViewController. There are a couple of ways that you can remedy this. For this example, I have chosen to get a reference to the

`MasterViewController` by navigating the view hierarchy starting at the split view controller. Since the `DetailViewController` is a `ViewController`, it has a reference to its split view controller. You can get this reference using the `splitViewController` property. From there, you know by looking at the storyboard that the first controller in the split view controller's `viewControllers` array is the navigation controller for the `MasterViewController`. Therefore, you assign that navigation controller to the `nav` variable. Then you can get the `topViewController` from the navigation controller, which is the `MasterViewController`. Finally, you call the `addSurveyToDataArray` method on the `MasterViewController` to add the newly created survey dictionary to the array.

You are now ready to build and run the application. You should be able to add new surveys and see them appear in the left pane in portrait mode. Select an item in the list, and you will see the display in the right pane change to the item you selected. Rotate the device to see how the `UISplitViewController` behaves in both landscape and portrait modes.

DISPLAYING DATA IN A POPOVER

Another user interface element that is unique to the iPad is the `UIPopoverController`. You can use this controller to display information on top of the current view. This allows you to provide context-sensitive information on top of the main application data without swapping views as would be required in an iOS application. The `UISplitViewController` uses a `UIPopoverController` to display the master data list when the device is in portrait orientation and the user taps the button to disclose the master list. For example, when your Survey application is in portrait orientation and the user taps the Master button, iOS displays the `MasterViewController` in a `UIPopover Controller`.

Another interesting feature of the popover is that the user can dismiss it by simply tapping outside its bounds. Therefore, you can use this controller to display information that might not necessarily require user action. In other words, the user does not have to implicitly accept or cancel any action to dismiss the popover.

The `UIPopoverController` displays a `UIViewController` as its content. You can build the content view in any way that you want. However, you should consider the size of the popover as you are building the view that it will contain. You should also consider the position in which you want to show the popover. You should display a popover next to the user interface element that displayed it. When presenting a popover, you can either attach it to a toolbar button or provide a `CGRect` structure to give the popover a reference location. Finally, you can specify the acceptable directions for the arrow that points from the popover to the reference location. You should generally permit UIKit to control the location of the popover by specifying `UIPopoverArrowDirectionAny` as the permitted direction for the arrow.

In this section, you will create a `UIPopoverController` and display it in the Survey application. The popover will simply display a new `UIViewController` that will show the current date and time, as you can see in Figure 4-10.

FIGURE 4-10: The Survey application informational popover

Building the InfoViewController

The `UIPopoverController` is a container that you can use to display another view controller anywhere on the screen on top of another view. Therefore, the first thing that you need to do when you want to display content in the popover is build the view controller that you want to display. For the Survey application, you will create a new class called `InfoViewController`. Then you will display this class in a `UIPopoverController` when the user taps an informational button.

The first step is to create your new class. Add to your project a new `UIViewController` subclass called `InfoViewController`. As you add the class, make sure that you have the Targeted for iPad checkbox in the New File dialog box checked.

Open your new `InfoViewController` header file. Add a `UILabel*` `IBOutlet` property called `infoLabel` that you can use to set the text that you will display in the popover. Next, add an `NSString*` property called `displayText`. You will use the `displayText` property to pass the data that you want to display from the detail view controller to the popover. The header file for the `InfoViewController` should look like this:

```objc
#import <UIKit/UIKit.h>

@interface InfoViewController : UIViewController

@property (nonatomic, weak) IBOutlet UILabel* infoLabel;
@property (nonatomic, strong) NSString* displayText;

@end
```

Next, open the storyboard to add the new view controller to the storyboard and build the user interface. For this application, the user interface will be extremely simple — just a lone UILabel. However, you can build views that are as complex as you want in the storyboard and use the methodology outlined here to display those interfaces using popovers.

Drag a new view controller instance from the Object library and drop it on the storyboard. Open the Identity Inspector and set the class of the new view controller to your new InfoViewController class.

Now that you have the view configured correctly, add a UILabel control and position it in the top-left portion of the view. The exact size and position are not particularly important for this example. I made my label 345 × 70.

Next, connect the new UILabel to the infoLabel property of the InfoViewController class. This connects your code to the interface that you built in the storyboard.

Now you need to add some logic to the InfoViewController implementation file. First, you should add code to the viewDidUnload method to clean up the properties of the class:

```objc
- (void)viewDidUnload {
    [super viewDidUnload];

    self.infoLabel = nil;
    self.displayText = nil;

}
```

The next step is to implement the viewDidLoad method. In this method, you will set the size of the view controller to display in the popover. Here is the code:

```objc
- (void)viewDidLoad
{
    [super viewDidLoad];

    CGSize size;
    size.width=420;
    size.height = 175;
    self.contentSizeForViewInPopover = size;

    self.infoLabel.text=self.displayText;

}
```

The original size of the popover comes from the view controller's `contentSizeForViewInPopover` property. The default size for a `UIPopoverController` is the default value of the current view controller. You can change the size of the popover in two ways. First, you can set the size in the view controller that the popover will hold by setting the view controller's size using the `contentSize ForViewInPopover` property. Alternatively, you can set the size of the `popoverContentSize` property of the popover controller. Keep in mind that if you use this method and change the view controller that you are displaying in the popover, the popover automatically resizes to the dimension of the new view controller. The custom size that you set in the `popoverContentSize` property is lost.

In this example, you created a `CGSize` struct to define the size of the popover in the view controller. You set the size to 420 points wide by 175 points high. Then you set the `contentSizeForView InPopover` property on the view controller.

Finally, you set the text of the `UILabel` to the string that you will pass in from the `DetailViewController`:

```
self.infoLabel.text=self.displayText;
```

Displaying the UIPopoverController

Now that you have a view controller, you need to display it in a popover. You will display the popover when the user taps a button in the `DetailViewController`.

First, you need to add the Info button to the user interface in the storyboard. Open the storyboard and a new `UIButton` next to the age `UITextField`. In the Attributes Inspector for the button, change the type of the button to Info Dark. This will change the button from a rounded rectangle to a gray circle with a white letter *i* inside.

Next, you will create a popover segue from the Info button to the Info view controller. Right-drag, or Control-drag if you are using a trackpad, from the Info button to the Info view controller. When you let go of the button, select popover from the pop-up menu.

Now you need to set an identifier for the segue because you will reference the segue in code to get a pointer to the Info view controller. Select the segue in the storyboard. Then, using the Attributes Inspector, set the Identifier for the segue to `InfoViewControllerSegue`.

You are now finished with the interface, so save the storyboard.

The next step is to make some changes to the `DetailViewController` header file. First, since you will be sending data to the `InfoViewController` using a property, you need to add a `#import` statement for the `InfoViewController.h` header file:

```
#import "InfoViewController.h"
```

Now you need to move over to the `DetailViewController` implementation file.

When you want to send data from one view controller to another via a segue, you can use the `prepareForSegue:sender:` method. The framework calls this method when your application is about to use a segue to move from one view controller to another. Here is the implementation:

```
- (void) prepareForSegue:(UIStoryboardSegue *)segue sender:(id)sender
{
    if ([[segue identifier] isEqualToString:@"InfoViewControllerSegue"])
    {
        InfoViewController *ivc = segue.destinationViewController;

        ivc.displayText= [NSString stringWithFormat:@"It is now: %@",[NSDate date]];

    }
}
```

The first thing that you do in this method is test to see if the segue that you are starting is the segue that you are interested in handling. Therefore, you test to see if the segue identifier is `InfoViewControllerSegue`.

Next, you get a reference to the target view controller using the segue's `destination ViewController` property. Then you use that reference to set the `displayText` property of the `InfoViewController` to pass the text to the popover that you will display inside the popover.

Build and run the application. When the interface appears, tap the new Info button. You should see the message with the current date and time appear in a popover next to the Info button.

GESTURE RECOGNIZERS

The basic UIKit controls such as the `UIButton` can detect simple user interactions such as pressing down on the button and lifting a finger. You can see these events in Interface Builder by selecting a `UIButton` and opening the Connections Inspector.

To assist developers in implementing more complex behaviors such as recognizing swipe or pinch gestures, Apple introduced the concept of Gesture Recognizers. You can use gesture recognizers on both the iPhone and the iPad.

The UIGestureRecognizer Class

The `UIGestureRecognizer` class is an abstract base class that defines what gesture recognizer classes must do and how they should operate. Apple has provided the concrete subclasses `UIPinchGestureRecognizer`, `UIPanGestureRecognizer`, `UITapGestureRecognizer`, `UIRotationGestureRecognizer`, `UILongPressGestureRecognizer`, and `UISwipeGesture Recogsnizer` that you can use in your applications to recognize the corresponding gestures. This saves you from having to write the significant amount of code required to interpret a series of touches as one of these common gestures. However, if your application requires gestures that the framework does not support, you can implement your own custom gesture recognizer as a `UIGestureRecognizer` subclass to define any gesture that your application may need.

To use a gesture recognizer, you must attach the gesture recognizer to a view. When you attach a gesture recognizer to a view, the framework routes touches in the application to the gesture recognizer before sending them to the view. This gives the gesture recognizer the chance to evaluate the touches to see if they qualify as a gesture. If the touches meet the requirements of a gesture, the framework cancels the touch messages and sends a gesture message instead of sending the touches to the view. If the touches do not qualify as a gesture, the framework sends the touches to the view.

There are two different types of gestures: discrete and continuous. A *discrete gesture*, such as a tap, causes the gesture recognizer to simply send one action message when the action is complete. A *continuous gesture*, like a pinch, results in the gesture recognizer sending the action message multiple times until the continuous action is completed.

You implement a gesture recognizer in your code by instantiating a gesture recognizer concrete class. This can be one of the Apple-provided classes mentioned above, or your own custom subclass of `UIGestureRecognizer`. Then you assign a target and an action to the recognizer. The target is the class that will receive the action, and the action is the method that the gesture recognizer will call when a gesture is recognized. Finally, you attach the gesture recognizer to the view where you want gestures recognized.

In this section, you will add gesture recognizers to your Survey application. You will use a `UISwipeGestureRecognizer` to determine if the user has swiped across the `DetailViewController` screen. If he has, you will navigate either forward or backward in the survey list, depending on the direction of the swipe, and display the appropriate record.

Using Gesture Recognizers

The first step in using a gesture recognizer is to create an instance of the recognizer that you want to use and attach it to a view. You can do this in the storyboard using Interface Builder. Open the storyboard for the project and select the Detail view controller. Drag a swipe gesture recognizer from the Object Library and drop it on to the Detail view controller's view. While you will not see visual feedback that you were successful on the view controller, you should see a swipe gesture recognizer appear in the Detail view controller section of the document outline. Repeat the process to add a second gesture recognizer to the Detail view controller. The interface should look like Figure 4-11.

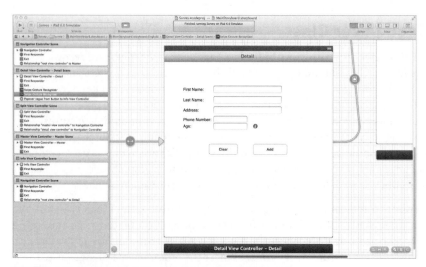

FIGURE 4-11: Adding gesture recognizers in a storyboard

Next, you need to configure one of the swipe gesture recognizers to recognize a left swipe. By default, Interface Builder configures the swipe gesture recognizer to handle a right swipe. In the document outline, select one of the gesture recognizers and change its swipe type to Left in the Attributes Inspector.

Now you need to connect the gesture recognizers in the storyboard to the code. Show the Assistant editor so that you can connect the gesture recognizers to the DetailViewController.h header. Right-drag the left swipe gesture recognizer and drop it onto the Detail view controller header. In the pop-up that appears, change the connection type to Action and name the action method **handleSwipeLeft**. Then right-drag the right swipe gesture recognizer and drop it onto the Detail view controller header. In the pop-up that appears, change the connection type to Action and name the action method **handleSwipeRight**. You should see two new methods declared in the header:

```
- (IBAction)handleSwipeRight:(id)sender;
- (IBAction)handleSwipeLeft:(id)sender;
```

To be able to implement the functionality to navigate forward and backward in the survey array using gestures, you have to add a variable and a couple of methods to the MasterViewController. In the MasterViewController.h header file, add an instance variable of type int called currentIndex. You will use this variable to maintain the index of the record that you are displaying in the DetailViewController. Here is the declaration:

```
int currentIndex;
```

You also need to add declarations for two new methods: moveNext and movePrevious. The gesture recognizer action methods will call these methods on the MasterViewController to tell the MasterViewController to navigate to the next or previous record. Here are the declarations for the moveNext and movePrevious methods:

```
-(void) moveNext;
-(void) movePrevious;
```

The MasterViewController.h header should look like this:

```
#import <UIKit/UIKit.h>

@class DetailViewController;

@interface MasterViewController : UITableViewController
{
    int currentIndex;

}
@property (strong, nonatomic) DetailViewController *detailViewController;
@property (strong, nonatomic) NSMutableArray* surveyDataArray;

-(void) addSurveyToDataArray: (NSDictionary*) sd;

-(void) moveNext;
-(void) movePrevious;

@end
```

In the `MasterViewController` implementation, you need to add code to the `viewDidLoad` method to initialize the `currentIndex` instance variable:

```
- (void)viewDidLoad
{
    [super viewDidLoad];
    // Do any additional setup after loading the view, typically from a nib.
    self.detailViewController = (DetailViewController *)
        [[self.splitViewController.viewControllers lastObject]
        topViewController];

    self.surveyDataArray = [[NSMutableArray alloc] init];

    // Initialize the current index.
    currentIndex = 0;

}
```

Next, modify the `tableView:didSelectRowAtIndexPath:` method to set the `currentIndex` instance variable to the row that the user has selected in the table:

```
- (void)tableView:(UITableView *)tableView
    didSelectRowAtIndexPath:(NSIndexPath *)indexPath
{

    /*
     When a row is selected, set the detail View Controller's detail item to the
     item associated with the selected row.
     */
    [tableView deselectRowAtIndexPath:indexPath animated:NO];

    NSDictionary* sd = [self.surveyDataArray objectAtIndex:indexPath.row];
    self.detailViewController.detailItem = sd;

    // Set the currentIndex.
    currentIndex = indexPath.row;

}
```

Finally, implement the `moveNext` and `movePrevious` methods:

```
-(void) moveNext
{
    NSLog (@"moveNext");
    // Check to make sure that there is a next item to move to.
    if (currentIndex < (int)[self.surveyDataArray count] -1)
    {
        NSDictionary* sd = [self.surveyDataArray objectAtIndex:++currentIndex];
        self.detailViewController.detailItem = sd;
    }
}

-(void) movePrevious
{
    NSLog (@"movePrevious");
```

```
    // Check to make sure that there is a previous item to move to.
    if (currentIndex > 0)
    {

        NSDictionary* sd = [self.surveyDataArray objectAtIndex:--currentIndex];
        self.detailViewController.detailItem = sd;
    }

}
```

In the moveNext method, first check to make sure that the next record exists. If it does, you increment the currentIndex, get the object at the new index from the surveyDataArray, and set the detailItem of the DetailViewController to the corresponding NSDictionary.

The movePrevious method is the same with one minor exception. You need to test to make sure that the user is not trying to navigate backward if the current index is already 0.

Back in the DetailViewController implementation, you are ready to implement the handleSwipeRight and handleSwipeLeft methods:

```
- (IBAction)handleSwipeRight:(id)sender
{
    NSLog (@"handleSwipeRight");

    // Get a reference to the first navigation controller in the split view.
    UINavigationController* nav = [self.splitViewController.viewControllers
                                    objectAtIndex:0];

    // Use this to get a reference to the MasterViewController.
    MasterViewController* rvc = (MasterViewController*) nav.topViewController ;


    // Call the movePrevious method on the MasterViewController to move to the
    // previous survey in the list.
    [rvc moveNext];
}

- (IBAction)handleSwipeLeft:(id)sender
{
    NSLog (@"handleSwipeLeft");

    // Get a reference to the first navigation controller in the split view.
    UINavigationController* nav = [self.splitViewController.viewControllers
                                    objectAtIndex:0];

    // Use this to get a reference to the MasterViewController.
    MasterViewController* rvc = (MasterViewController*) nav.topViewController ;


    // Call the moveNext method on the MasterViewController to move to the
    // next survey in the list.
    [rvc movePrevious];
}
```

In the `handleSwipeRight` and `handleSwipeLeft` methods, you do almost the same thing. First, you get a reference to the `MasterViewController`. Then you call the appropriate method — either `moveNext` or `movePrevious` — on the `MasterViewController`.

Build and run the application. You should be able to add new surveys to the application. Then select a row, or just start with the first row. Swipe right in the `DetailViewController`, and the application should display the data in the `DetailViewController` for the next entry in the completed survey list. Swiping to the left should display the detail information for the previous entry in the list.

FILE SHARING SUPPORT

Sometimes, when building applications, you will create data on the device that you want to share with the desktop or vice versa. Apple provides the capability of sharing files between the desktop and the device through iTunes. If you have purchased the Pages, Numbers, or Keynote application for the iPad, you have seen that you can create documents on your computer and make them available on the iPad. Conversely, you can create new documents on the iPad that are available in iTunes to move onto the computer.

Using the file-sharing support, developers can make the contents of the application's `/Documents` directory available to the user on the computer. Keep in mind that file-sharing support does not enable sharing of documents between applications on the device.

Enabling file sharing is simple. You need only make a change to the `Info.plist` file that you deploy with your application. In this section, you will add code to the Survey application that will store the completed surveys as an XML file. Then, using file sharing, you will see that you can access this file on the computer after syncing through iTunes.

Enable File Sharing in the Sample Application

First, you need to add a new key, `UIFileSharingEnabled`, to the `Survey-Info.plist` file. This file is located in the `Supporting Files` folder of your Xcode project. You can add this key inside of Xcode by first selecting the `Survey-Info.plist` file in the Project Navigator. You should see the plist file displayed in the right pane in Xcode. Click the plus sign next to the entry Information Property List to add a new entry to the plist. In the drop-down list that appears, select Application Supports iTunes File Sharing. To the right of the key, you will then see that the default value for this property is `NO`. Change this value to `YES`.

That is all that you need to do to enable file sharing.

Serializing the Survey Data Array

Next, you add code to serialize the `surveyDataArray` and store the serialized file in the `/Documents` folder for the application.

When the user installs an application on an iOS device, the installation process creates a home directory for that application. Each application has its own home directory. You should write your application data files to the /Documents directory. Additionally, iTunes backs up this directory when the user syncs the device with a computer.

Now that you understand where to save the application data, you will add code to the applicationDidEnterBackground method in the AppDelegate to serialize the array and save it to a file when the application enters the background state. The application enters this state when the user presses the Home button or switches to another application.

First, you need to add a #import statement to the AppDelegate.h header file so that you can reference the MasterViewController:

```
#import "MasterViewController.h"
```

Serialization simply takes a data structure that is stored in memory, in this case an array, and converts it to a format that can be saved to a file or sent over a network. Here is the implementation of the applicationWillTerminate method in the AppDelegate:

```
- (void)applicationDidEnterBackground:(UIApplication *)application
{
    // Use this method to release shared resources, save user data, invalidate
    // timers, and store enough application state information to restore your
    // application to its current state in case it is terminated later.
    // If your application supports background execution, this method is called
    // instead of applicationWillTerminate: when the user quits.
    NSData *serializedData;
    NSString *error;

    // Get a reference to the first navigation controller in the split view
    UISplitViewController *splitViewController =
    (UISplitViewController *)self.window.rootViewController;
    UINavigationController* nav = [splitViewController.viewControllers
                            objectAtIndex:0];

    // Use this to get a reference to the MasterViewController.
    MasterViewController* rvc = (MasterViewController*) nav.topViewController ;

    serializedData = [NSPropertyListSerialization
                    dataFromPropertyList:rvc.surveyDataArray
                    format:NSPropertyListXMLFormat_v1_0
                    errorDescription:&error];

    if (serializedData)
    {
        // Serialization was successful. Write the data to the file system.
        // Get an array of paths.
        // (This function is carried over from the desktop.)
        NSArray *documentDirectoryPath =
        NSSearchPathForDirectoriesInDomains(NSDocumentDirectory,
                                    NSUserDomainMask, YES);
        NSString *docDir = [NSString stringWithFormat:@"%@/serialized.xml",
                        [documentDirectoryPath objectAtIndex:0]];
```

```
        [serializedData writeToFile:docDir atomically:YES];
    }
    else
    {
        // An error has occurred. Log it.
        NSLog(@"Error: %@",error);
    }
}
```

First, you get a reference to the `MasterViewController` by navigating the view hierarchy from the split view controller to the navigation controller, finally arriving at the Master View Controller.

Next, serialize the data in the `surveyData` array by using the `NSPropertyListSerialization` class. This class provides methods that convert the types of objects that you can use in a property list (`NSData`, `NSString`, `NSArray`, `NSDictionary`, `NSDate`, and `NSNumber`) into different serialized forms. In this case, you will convert an `NSArray` into XML format. I chose XML for this example so that you could open the file on your computer after syncing with iTunes and verify that the data in the file is the same as the data that is contained in the application. For production applications, it is generally more efficient to use the binary format.

After serializing the array to XML, the code obtains the path to the /`Documents` directory for the application. Here, you use the `NSSearchPathForDirectoriesInDomains` function to obtain the path to the /`Documents` directory by passing in the `NSDocumentDirectory` constant as the directory parameter. The `NSSearchPathDirectory` enumeration provides several predefined constants that you can use to help you navigate to specific directories.

Next, you use the path to the /`Documents` directory to build a string that represents the file that you want to save. Finally, you call the `writeToFile` method of the `serializedData` object to write the XML to a file.

Deserializing and Loading the Survey Data Array

Now that you have written code to save the survey data array to disk, you need to add code to load the array from disk when the application starts. *Deserialization* is the process of taking the data from its on-disk format and turning it back into an object. You will do that in the `MasterViewController`'s `viewDidLoad` method. Modify the `viewDidLoad` method to use the data from the plist, if it exists, like this:

```
- (void)viewDidLoad
{
    [super viewDidLoad];
    // Do any additional setup after loading the view, typically from a nib.
    self.detailViewController = (DetailViewController *)
        [[self.splitViewController.viewControllers lastObject]
         topViewController];


    // Get an array of paths. (This function is carried over from the desktop.)
    NSArray *documentDirectoryPath =
    NSSearchPathForDirectoriesInDomains(NSDocumentDirectory,
```

```
                                    NSUserDomainMask, YES);
    NSString *docDir = [NSString stringWithFormat:@"%@/serialized.xml",
                      [documentDirectoryPath objectAtIndex:0]];
    NSData* serializedData = [NSData dataWithContentsOfFile:docDir];

    // If serializedData is nil, the file doesn't exist yet.
    if (serializedData == nil)
    {
        self.surveyDataArray = [[NSMutableArray alloc] init];

    }
    else
    {
        // Read data from the file.
        NSString *error;

        self.surveyDataArray =
        (NSMutableArray *)[NSPropertyListSerialization
                      propertyListFromData:serializedData
                      mutabilityOption:kCFPropertyListMutableContainers
                      format:NULL errorDescription:&error];
    }

    // Initialize the current index.
    currentIndex = 0;

}
```

This code is the opposite of the code that you wrote in the previous section. First, you create the filename the same way that you did before using the NSSearchPathForDirectoriesInDomains function. Then you create an NSData object from the serialized file by calling the dataWithContentsOfFile method.

Next, you need to check whether the serialized data exists. If there is no data, you need to create a new NSMutableArray* to hold the completed surveys. If there was data, you populate the surveyDataArray from the NSData object by calling the propertyListFromData:mutabilityOption: format:errorDescription: method of the NSPropertyListSerialization class.

Sharing the Data

Now you are ready to build and run the application on an iPad device. Add some survey data, and then quit the application.

To retrieve the data from the iPad, hook up your iPad to your computer and sync it with iTunes. Click on the iPad under Devices in iTunes and select the Apps tab. If you scroll to the bottom, you should see Survey listed as one of the applications in the Apps box, as in Figure 4-12. Click Survey, and you should see serialized.xml in the Survey Documents window. Click serialized.xml and click the Save To button. Save the file to your desktop or some other convenient location.

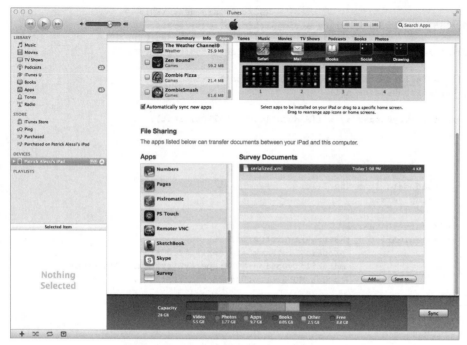

FIGURE 4-12: Survey application and data in iTunes

You should be able to navigate to that XML file using the Finder. If you open the XML file, you should see an XML representation of your data. The XML for the sample data looks like this:

```
<?xml version="1.0" encoding="UTF-8"?>
<!DOCTYPE plist PUBLIC "-//Apple//DTD PLIST 1.0//EN"
"http://www.apple.com/DTDs/PropertyList-1.0.dtd">
<plist version="1.0">
<array>
    <dict>
        <key>address</key>
        <string>123 Any St.</string>
        <key>age</key>
        <integer>20</integer>
        <key>firstName</key>
        <string>John</string>
        <key>lastName</key>
        <string>Smith</string>
        <key>phone</key>
        <string>555-1234</string>
    </dict>
    <dict>
        <key>address</key>
        <string>789 Town St.</string>
        <key>age</key>
        <integer>40</integer>
```

```
            <key>firstName</key>
            <string>Doris</string>
            <key>lastName</key>
            <string>Jones</string>
            <key>phone</key>
            <string>555-1234</string>
        </dict>
    </array>
</plist>
```

MOVING FORWARD

In this chapter, you learned about some interesting user interface elements and other features of iOS that can help you build better data-driven applications.

First, you learned how to design and build the user interface for your applications using storyboards. Then you explored using the `UISplitViewController` to build master/detail displays to take advantage of the screen real estate of the iPad. After that, you learned how to display a popover view on top of another view using the `UIPopoverController`. Next, you discovered how to use gesture recognizers to handle complex user interactions. Finally, you found out how to share data between the device and the computer by using file-sharing support.

This concludes Part I, where you learned how to build a simple data-based application, how to get data onto the device and store it using SQLite, how to display data and customize the display of data using the `UITableView`, and how to extend your applications and interfaces with some additional user interface elements like the `UISplitViewController` and the `UIPopoverController`.

In Part II, you will learn about the Core Data framework. Core Data is a powerful library that you can use to create and manage data on iOS. Core Data comes with a powerful modeling tool that you will use to help you define the data model for your applications.

PART II
Managing Your Data with Core Data

5

Introducing Core Data

WHAT'S IN THIS CHAPTER?

➤ Describing what the Core Data API can do for you

➤ Understanding the various objects that make up the Core Data API

➤ Designing for iCloud Integration

➤ Securing your data with data protection

➤ Understanding how the template code works to configure your application to use Core Data

➤ Creating a simple application that uses Core Data to maintain application state

WROX.COM CODE DOWNLOADS FOR THIS CHAPTER

The wrox.com code downloads for this chapter are found at www.wrox.com/remtitle .cgi?isbn=1118391845 on the Download Code tab. The code is in the Chapter 5 download and individually named according to the names throughout the chapter.

Now that you have completed the first part of the book, you should be comfortable using an SQLite database and implementing views into your data with the UITableView control. You have learned to build data-driven applications for iOS that can efficiently access large amounts of data stored in an SQLite database and display that data with your own highly customized tables.

Up until this point, you have not looked at how to store the data that users create on the device. For instance, if you wanted to create a task manager, you would need to be able to save the user-created tasks. You could use SQLite to INSERT the data, now that you know how to execute arbitrary SQL statements against the database. However, there is an API designed specifically for storing the objects in your application model: Core Data.

In this chapter, you will learn about the architecture of the Core Data API and the classes for building a Core Data application. You will get an introduction to how Core Data and iCloud work together to provide you with an infrastructure that you can use to synchronize data across devices. You will also see how to use the data protection API to add security to your data. Then you will walk through a Core Data template application to learn how to implement the architecture in code. Finally, you will build a simple application that uses Core Data for storage.

This chapter prepares you for the next few chapters where you dive deeply into the Core Data tools and API.

THE BASICS OF CORE DATA

Core Data is a set of APIs designed to simplify the persistence of data objects. Sometimes you will hear people refer to Core Data as an object persistence framework or an object graph manager. Core Data provides a framework for saving your model objects and retrieving them later. Core Data also manages changes to your object model, provides undo support, and ensures the consistency of relationships between your model objects. All of these features help to free you from having to write the code to implement this functionality. In essence, Core Data simplifies the creation of the Model part of the Model-View-Controller (MVC) architecture.

The foundation of the Core Data toolset is a code-based API that you use to manipulate your data objects in code. However, the toolset also includes a graphical data modeler that you can use to define your model objects. The modeler allows you to define your data objects, their attributes, and their relationships with the other objects in your application. You can even specify constraints and simple validation rules inside the graphical tool. You explore the data modeling tool and all of its uses in the next chapter.

The graphical modeler simplifies creation of the model in the same way that Interface Builder and Storyboards simplify the creation of the view. Using Core Data and Interface Builder, you can quickly build the Model and View components of the MVC architecture, leaving only the controller business logic to code. This can significantly reduce the development time of your projects.

In addition to its ease of use, Core Data provides some important performance enhancements. Core Data can use SQLite as its backing data store. This provides Core Data with a high-performance query engine. Compared to searching and sorting through flat data files or plists, Core Data is the clear choice for speed. Additionally, the API is able to conserve memory by retrieving only the data that you need at any specific time. For example, if you have two related entities, Core Data will not retrieve the child entities until you ask for them. This conserves memory, which is a scarce resource on mobile devices. You learn more about this functionality, called *faulting*, in the chapters to come.

Core Data provides many of the functions that you would expect to find when dealing with data objects. Specifically, you can filter your data using predicates with the `NSPredicate` class and sort your data using the `NSSortDescriptor` class. I touch on these classes here and get into much finer detail in Chapter 8.

THE CORE DATA ARCHITECTURE

To use Core Data, it helps to have an understanding of the underlying architecture. While you will not be accessing most of the objects contained in the API directly, you will be much more proficient if you understand how Core Data works.

The Core Data Stack

You can see an overview of the design of the Core Data stack in Figure 5-1. The key components are the data store, the Persistent Store Coordinator, the Managed Object Model, and the Managed Object Context. While it is important to understand what is going on behind the scenes, try not to get confused by the terminology introduced in this section. It may seem overwhelming now, but as you work through the template and the sample in this chapter, the details of how you use Core Data should become clear.

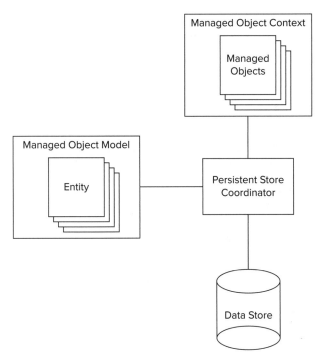

FIGURE 5-1: The Core Data stack

The Data Store

The *data store* is the file or group of files that hold your data. This is the actual file written to the disk when the save message is sent to Core Data. Typically, in a mobile application, only one data store file is used. However, it is possible to use a group of files as the data store.

The data store can be a binary data file, an SQLite database, or an in-memory data file, depending on the parameters used when creating the data store. You will see how to specify the storage type for your data in the example at the end of the chapter.

As the developer, you will never directly access the data store. The Persistent Store Coordinator abstracts away access to the data file. In addition, you do not need to concern yourself with the data store implementation. Simply consider it a file that holds all your data.

The Persistent Store Coordinator

This *Persistent Store Coordinator* acts as a mediator between the Managed Object Context and the data store. The coordinator takes requests for data from the context and forwards them to the appropriate data store. The coordinator also allows the context to access one or more data stores as if they were one. Finally, the coordinator associates a data store with a Managed Object Model. The Persistent Store Coordinator is an instance of the `NSPersistentStoreCoordinator` class.

You need to be aware that the `NSPersistentStoreCoordinator` class is not thread safe. Therefore, if you plan to access a data store simultaneously across multiple threads, you have to either create a coordinator for each thread or lock and unlock the single coordinator manually.

The Managed Object Model

The *Managed Object Model* represents the data model schema. In code, the Managed Object Model is an instance of the `NSManagedObjectModel` class.

The model consists of a set of entities that define the data objects in your application. When designing your model, you specify the data entities that your application will deal with. You can specify attributes for these entities and define the relationships between them.

You typically create the model graphically using the Xcode data-modeling tool, although it is possible to define the model in code. You can think of the Managed Object Model like the Entity-Relationship diagram that you would create when designing a database.

The data model should define each data object used in your application. The Persistent Store Coordinator uses the model to create Managed Objects according to conventions from the entities defined in the model. The coordinator also maps the entities in the model into the physical data store file that Core Data writes to disk.

You will rarely access the object model through your code. If the need arises, you can use the `NSManagedObjectModel` class. You access the Managed Objects created from the model entities using the Managed Object Context.

The Managed Object Context

The *Managed Object Context*, also referred to simply as the *context*, provides the main interface that you will use to access your managed data objects. The Managed Object Context is an instance of the `NSManagedObjectContext` class.

You use the context to hold all your managed data objects. Your managed data objects are either instances or subclasses of the `NSManagedObject` class. The name Managed Object makes sense because the Managed Object Context manages all these objects.

You can think of the context as the sandbox that holds all your application data. You can add objects to the context, delete them, and modify them in memory. Then, when you are ready, you can tell the context to commit its current state to disk. Behind the scenes, the context uses the Persistent Store Coordinator to write your data to the data store on disk. The context uses the object model to ensure that your data is in a consistent state with respect to your defined relationships, constraints, and validation rules before committing it to disk.

You make fetch requests against the context to fetch data from the data store back into the context. You fetch data into Managed Objects that you use to manipulate and display your data. Fetch requests are similar to SQL SELECT statements. When creating a fetch request, you can provide a predicate to filter your data as you would do in SQL with a WHERE clause. You can also provide a sort array that functions like the SQL ORDER BY clause.

SQLite and Core Data

In Chapter 2, you learned how to use SQLite as the database engine for your application. Now that you have learned about Core Data, you may be wondering how the two are related.

SQLite is a library that provides a relational database implementation used on iOS. Core Data can use SQLite as the on-disk data store to persist your data. Core Data can also use a proprietary binary data file for the data store. However, I would not generally recommend this because the binary format requires that your entire object graph be loaded into memory as opposed to using the SQLite format, which allows parts of the object graph to be loaded as needed.

While you learned how to view and modify the schema and data in an SQLite database, you should never attempt to manually modify the schema or data in a Core Data SQLite data store. Core Data requires that the data in the database be stored in a specific way to function. Feel free to browse the schema and data, but don't attempt to modify either.

CORE DATA AND ICLOUD

iCloud is a free service provided by Apple that allows app users to automatically synchronize their data between different devices. The service includes the server infrastructure, a backup system, and user account management. Implementing iCloud in your applications gives you the benefit of cloud-based data synchronization without the expense and effort of implementing the back-end functionality yourself.

iCloud provides three different types of storage solutions: key-value storage, document storage, and Core Data storage. You should use key-value storage to store individual key-value pairs. This is useful for small bits of data like user preferences, game scores, and application settings. Document storage is useful for storing file-based content like spreadsheets, text documents, and drawings. Core Data storage allows you to synchronize Core Data applications across multiple devices.

When you build a Core Data application, you build a Managed Object Model and work with Managed Objects as you learned earlier in this chapter. The most important thing to remember about working with iCloud and Core Data is that Core Data only sends incremental changes to iCloud. Each iCloud-enabled instance of your application maintains its own local data store. Core Data never synchronizes its entire database with iCloud. When you make changes to managed objects, Core Data logs these changes to a file that it synchronizes with iCloud. Then Core Data uses this file to propagate the changes to the managed objects to the local instance of the data store.

If you decide to include iCloud synchronization with your application, you need to pay particular attention to some specific areas in your app. First, you need to present the option to use iCloud to the user. Not all users will want to use iCloud, and you need to handle both the case when the user wants to use iCloud and the case where he does not.

As the application designer, you also need to think about how you will handle situations when iCloud is not available. For instance, allowing a user to edit existing records when iCloud is not available will result in extra processing to handle reconciliation of the changes.

A complete discussion of using iCloud is beyond the scope of this book. If you need to include iCloud integration with your Core Data application, I would recommend reading the "iCloud Design Guide" and "Using Core Data with iCloud" Release Notes that Apple provides as part of the Xcode documentation.

DATA PROTECTION

If you are building an application that will house sensitive data, security should be a major concern. Apple includes a data protection API that enables you to securely encrypt your application data. In general, you can configure when you protect your data files by setting an attribute on the file using the NSFileManager object with the setAttributes:ofItemAtPath:error: method.

The API allows you to set the file protection key to different values to give you some options concerning when the protected data is in its encrypted or decrypted state:

➤ NSFileProtectionNone: The file is not encrypted. The application can write to and read from the file at any time.

➤ NSFileProtectionComplete: The file is in an encrypted state any time that the device is locked or when the device is booting. Your application cannot write to or read from the file when it is in this state.

➤ NSFileProtectionCompleteUnlessOpen: The file is encrypted until it is opened with the device unlocked. Once the file is open, your application can write to and read from the file at any time, even if the device is locked.

➤ NSFileProtectionCompleteUntilFirstUserAuthentication: The file is encrypted while the device is booting and remains locked until the user unlocks the device for the first time. Once the user has unlocked the device for the first time, your application can write to and read from the file.

When you are working in Core Data using an SQLite data store, your data is stored in an SQLite database on the device. The default file protection for the data store is NSFileProtection CompleteUntilFirstUserAuthentication. However, it is possible to change the data protection level when you create the data store for the first time by modifying the code in the App Delegate that creates the database file. In the `persistentStoreCoordinator` method, you first need to create an `NSDictionary` that contains the file protection level that you want, in this case `NSFileProtectionComplete`:

```
NSDictionary *optionsDictionary =
    [NSDictionary dictionaryWithObject:NSFileProtectionComplete
                               forKey:NSFileProtectionKey];
```

Then modify the call to `addPersistentStoreWithType:configuration:URL:options:error:` to use your options dictionary:

```
if (![_persistentStoreCoordinator addPersistentStoreWithType:NSSQLiteStoreType
    configuration:nil URL:storeURL options:optionsDictionary error:&error]) {
```

Now when your application creates the SQLite database for the first time, Core Data will configure it to leave your database in an encrypted state any time the user locks the device or when the device is booting. Keep in mind that if you set this encryption level, your application will not be able to access the database in the background while the user has the device locked. If you need to support more stringent encryption than the default along with background processing, use `NSFileProtectionCompleteUnlessOpen`.

USING CORE DATA: A SIMPLE TASK MANAGER

Now that you are familiar with the terminology and the Core Data API architecture, I am going to walk through a simple example application so that you can get your feet wet with using Core Data. You will first take a look at everything that you get "for free" when you start a new application and tell Xcode that you want to use Core Data as the backing data store. Then you will customize the template-generated code to create an application to keep track of a simple task list.

You may feel overwhelmed by all the information that you learned in the previous sections. You should take two things away from what you have learned about Core Data so far. First is that most, if not all, of your interaction with Core Data in your code will be through the Managed Object Context and Managed Objects. The other is that you will define your data model graphically using the tool provided in Xcode.

Creating the Project

The application that you are going to create is a simple task manager that will allow you to enter new tasks and remove completed tasks. When you create a task, it will be timestamped. The application will sort the tasks based on the timestamp with the newest tasks at the top of the list. Figure 5-2 shows the application in action.

FIGURE 5-2: The completed Tasks application

To start the project, open Xcode and create a new Master-Detail Application from the new project template. Make sure that you check the option to use Core Data in the new project window. Set the device to iPhone and call the new project Tasks.

After you have created the project, build and run it. You will see that you get quite a bit of functionality from the template without adding any code.

If you click on the plus button in the upper-right corner, timestamp entries are added to your table view. You can swipe across an entry and click the Delete button to delete individual timestamps. You can also click the Edit button to go into editing mode where you can delete entries by clicking the icon to the left of a timestamp and then clicking the Delete button.

If you click the Home button in the iPhone simulator and then click the icon on the home screen for your Tasks application, you will see that any timestamps that you did not delete are still there. Your application already includes the code required to persist your data.

Examining the Template Code

Before you get into modifying the code to create and display tasks, let's take a walk through the template code. This should provide you with some insight into how the application works and show you how to implement the Core Data architecture in code. Keep in mind that all this code is auto-generated when you select the Master-Detail Application template and opt to use Core Data for storage.

The template creates three classes: `MasterViewController`, `DetailViewController`, and `AppDelegate`. You create these same classes in any typical Master-Detail application. Additionally, you will see a data model file that the template auto-generates called `Tasks.xcdatamodeld`. Let's look at each of these files.

Tasks AppDelegate

While you won't be modifying any of the code in the App Delegate, it is instructive to look at the code. The code in the App Delegate sets up the Core Data stack. Therefore, as you might imagine, there is code to create a Persistent Store Coordinator, Managed Object Model, and Managed Object Context.

The `persistentStoreCoordinator` getter method returns the Persistent Store Coordinator for the application. Here is the code:

```
- (NSPersistentStoreCoordinator *)persistentStoreCoordinator
{
    if (_persistentStoreCoordinator != nil) {
        return _persistentStoreCoordinator;
    }

    NSURL *storeURL = [[self applicationDocumentsDirectory]
                    URLByAppendingPathComponent:@"Tasks.sqlite"];

    NSError *error = nil;
    _persistentStoreCoordinator = [[NSPersistentStoreCoordinator alloc]
        initWithManagedObjectModel:[self managedObjectModel]];
```

```
     if (![_persistentStoreCoordinator
           addPersistentStoreWithType:NSSQLiteStoreType
           configuration:nil
           URL:storeURL
           options:nil
           error:&error]) {
       /*
       Replace this implementation with code to handle the error
       appropriately.

       abort() causes the application to generate a crash log and terminate.
       You should not use this function in a shipping application, although it
       may be useful during development.

       Typical reasons for an error here include:
       * The persistent store is not accessible;
       * The schema for the persistent store is incompatible with current
       managed object model.
       Check the error message to determine what the actual problem was.


       If the persistent store is not accessible, there is typically something
       wrong with the file path. Often, a file URL is pointing into the
       application's resources directory instead of a writeable directory.

       If you encounter schema incompatibility errors during development, you
       can reduce their frequency by:
       * Simply deleting the existing store:
       [[NSFileManager defaultManager] removeItemAtURL:storeURL error:nil]

       * Performing automatic lightweight migration by passing the following
       dictionary as the options parameter:
       @{NSMigratePersistentStoresAutomaticallyOption:@YES,
       NSInferMappingModelAutomaticallyOption:@YES}

       Lightweight migration will only work for a limited set of schema
       changes; consult "Core Data Model Versioning and Data Migration
       Programming Guide" for details.

       */
       NSLog(@"Unresolved error %@, %@", error, [error userInfo]);
       abort();
     }

     return _persistentStoreCoordinator;
   }
```

The code first determines if the Persistent Store Coordinator already exists. If it exists, the method returns it to you.

If the coordinator does not exist, the code must create it. To create the coordinator, you need to pass in a URL that points to the data store. The template gets the URL for the documents directory for your application; then it appends the name of your data store file and creates a new URL using the `URLByAppendingPathComponent:` method. You can see that the store name will be `Tasks.sqlite`.

Next, the code allocates an NSError object to hold any error data that the Persistent Store Coordinator generates if there is a problem configuring the coordinator.

The next line allocates and initializes the coordinator using the Managed Object Model. You will look at the managedObjectModel getter method in a moment. Remember that you use the Persistent Store Coordinator to mediate between the Managed Object Context, the Managed Object Model, and the data store. Therefore, it makes sense that the coordinator would need to have a reference to the model.

Now that the coordinator knows about the model, the code goes on to tell it about the data store. The next line of code adds the data store to the coordinator. You will notice that the type of the data store is NSSQLiteStoreType. This indicates that the template uses the SQLite backing data store. If you wanted to use the binary store, you would change this enumeration value to NSBinaryStoreType, and if you wanted to use the in-memory store, you would set the value to NSInMemoryStoreType. Remember that most often you will be using the SQLite backing store.

If you need to include advanced file protection features on your data store as you learned about earlier in this chapter, you would add code here to create an NSDictionary to hold your additional configuration options. Specifically, you would add the NSFileProtectionKey key and one of the NSFileProtection enumeration values to the dictionary. Then you would pass the dictionary into the addPersistentStoreWithType:configuration:URL:options:error: call as the options: parameter.

The rest of the code logs an error if there was a problem adding the SQLite store to the coordinator. If there was no error, the method returns the coordinator.

The getter function to return the Managed Object Model is straightforward:

```
- (NSManagedObjectModel *)managedObjectModel
{
    if (_managedObjectModel != nil) {
        return _managedObjectModel;
    }
    NSURL *modelURL = [[NSBundle mainBundle] URLForResource:@"Tasks"
                                        withExtension:@"momd"];
    _managedObjectModel = [[NSManagedObjectModel alloc]
                        initWithContentsOfURL:modelURL];
    return _managedObjectModel;
}
```

If the model already exists, the getter method returns it. If not, the code creates a new Managed Object Model from the model files contained in the application bundle. In this case, the Tasks.xcdatamodeld file contains the object model. Behind the scenes, Xcode compiles the xcdatamodeld file into an momd file. The momd file is the file that is deployed to the device. This file is included with the application bundle, so this method takes that file and uses it to create the NSManagedObjectModel object.

The last bit of interesting code in the App Delegate is the managedObjectContext getter method:

```
- (NSManagedObjectContext *)managedObjectContext
{
    if (_managedObjectContext != nil) {
```

```
        return _managedObjectContext;
    }

    NSPersistentStoreCoordinator *coordinator =
        [self persistentStoreCoordinator];
    if (coordinator != nil) {
        _managedObjectContext = [[NSManagedObjectContext alloc] init];
        [_managedObjectContext setPersistentStoreCoordinator:coordinator];
    }
    return _managedObjectContext;
}
```

This method works similarly to the previous two. The first thing it does is check to see if the context already exists. If the context exists, the method returns it.

Next, the code gets a reference to the `persistentStoreCoordinator`. If you refer back to Figure 5-1, you will see that the Managed Object Context needs only a reference to the Persistent Store Coordinator.

If the code successfully gets a reference to the coordinator, it goes on to create the context. Then the code sets the coordinator for the context and returns the context.

I hope that the way in which all the objects in the Core Data stack fit together is becoming a bit clearer. Remember that you did not have to write code to create the data store, the Persistent Store Coordinator, the Managed Object Model, or the Managed Object Context. The template code takes care of all this for you automatically. The only interface you need to deal with is that of the Managed Object Context.

The Data Model

Before you examine the `MasterViewController` and how to use it to create your table view using Core Data, you'll look at the template Managed Object Model. You can look at your model in two ways: Table Editor Style or Graph Editor Style. If you open the `Tasks.xcdatamodeld` file, you should see something similar to the Table Editor Style in Figure 5-3.

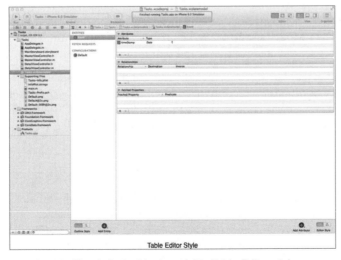

FIGURE 5-3: The default object model in Table Editor style

You can use the buttons at the bottom right of the Xcode interface to switch between Table and Graph editor styles. The code template creates a default entity called Event. If you switch to the Graph editor style, the blue highlighting and resize handles indicate that you have selected the Event entity. You can see the Graph editor style in Figure 5-4. Click anywhere else in the diagram to deselect the Event entity, and it will turn pink to indicate that it is no longer selected. Click on the Event entity again to select it.

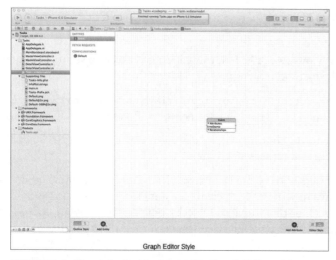

Graph Editor Style

FIGURE 5-4: The default object model in Graph Editor style

If you switch to the Table editor style, you will see two panes in the data-modeling tool. The left pane shows an outline of all your data entities. The right pane shows information about the selected entity.

You can see in Figure 5-3 that the Event entity has an attribute called `timeStamp`. If you select the Event entity and then select the `timeStamp` attribute in the Attributes pane, you can see the details of the `timeStamp` attribute in the Data Model inspector in the Utility view on the right side of the Xcode interface. If you don't see the Data Model inspector, make sure you have the Utility view open. You should see that the `timeStamp` attribute is optional and that it is a `Date` type.

Your Managed Object Context will manage the objects defined by the Event entity. Remember that when you created the Persistent Store Coordinator, you initialized it with all the Managed Object Models in the bundle. Then when you created the context, it used the Persistent Store Coordinator. Next, you will see how to use the Event entity to create and manage Core Data Managed Objects in code.

MasterViewController

The `MasterViewController` is a subclass of `UITableViewController` that contains the table view that you will use to display your data. This class has a property that holds the context, which the Application Delegate sets when it creates the `MasterViewController` instance. The `MasterViewController` also has a property that holds an `NSFetchedResultsController`.

The NSFetchedResultsController class is the glue that binds the results of a fetch request against your datasource to a table view. You will look at the NSFetchedResultsController class in more detail in Chapter 7.

Figure 5-5 shows a high-level view of how the NSFetchedResultsController class works. The class takes a fetch request and a context as its inputs and calls delegate methods when the data in the fetch request changes. The controller applies methods that you use when implementing the table view delegate methods that you are familiar with from Chapter 3.

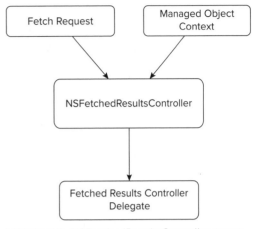

FIGURE 5-5: NSFetchedResultsController usage

The first thing to notice is that the Master ViewController implements the NSFetched ResultsControllerDelegate protocol. You can see this in the MasterViewController.h header file. Declaring that you implement a protocol is a contract committing you to implementation of certain methods. Classes that do not implement this protocol cannot be delegates for an NSFetchedResultsController.

The following is the code for the getter method for the fetchedResultsController property:

```objc
- (NSFetchedResultsController *)fetchedResultsController
{
    if (_fetchedResultsController != nil) {
        return _fetchedResultsController;
    }

    NSFetchRequest *fetchRequest = [[NSFetchRequest alloc] init];
    // Edit the entity name as appropriate.
    NSEntityDescription *entity =
    [NSEntityDescription
        entityForName:@"Event"
        inManagedObjectContext:self.managedObjectContext];
    [fetchRequest setEntity:entity];

    // Set the batch size to a suitable number.
    [fetchRequest setFetchBatchSize:20];

    // Edit the sort key as appropriate.
    NSSortDescriptor *sortDescriptor = [[NSSortDescriptor alloc]
                                        initWithKey:@"timeStamp" ascending:NO];
    NSArray *sortDescriptors = @[sortDescriptor];

    [fetchRequest setSortDescriptors:sortDescriptors];

    // Edit the section name key path and cache name if appropriate.
    // nil for section name key path means "no sections."
    NSFetchedResultsController *aFetchedResultsController =
        [[NSFetchedResultsController alloc]
        initWithFetchRequest:fetchRequest
```

```
            managedObjectContext:self.managedObjectContext
            sectionNameKeyPath:nil cacheName:@"Master"];
    aFetchedResultsController.delegate = self;
    self.fetchedResultsController = aFetchedResultsController;

    NSError *error = nil;
    if (![self.fetchedResultsController performFetch:&error]) {
        // Replace this implementation with code to handle the error
        // appropriately.
        // abort() causes the application to generate a crash log and
        // terminate. You should not use this function in a shipping
        // application, although it may be useful during development.
        NSLog(@"Unresolved error %@, %@", error, [error userInfo]);
        abort();
    }

    return _fetchedResultsController;
}
```

The first part of the code should be familiar. It checks to see if you have already created the fetchedResultsController. If it already exists, the method returns the controller. If not, the code goes on to create it.

The next section of code creates and configures the objects needed by the fetchedResults Controller. As you can see from Figure 5-5, you need a fetch request and a context to be able to use the fetchedResultsController. Because you already have a context in the managedObjectContext property, the code only needs to create a fetch request.

You can think of a fetch request as an SQL SELECT statement. The code creates an NSFetchRequest object, creates an entity based on the Event entity in the context, and then sets the entity used by the fetchRequest. Next, the code sets the batch size of the fetchRequest to a reasonable number of records to receive at a time.

The next bit of code creates an NSSortDescriptor. You use the NSSortDescriptor to sort the results in the fetchRequest. You can think of the NSSortDescriptor as an SQL ORDER BY clause. Here, you order the result set based on the timeStamp field in descending order. The NSSortDescriptor then sets the sort descriptor used by the fetch request.

Finally, calling the initWithFetchRequest:managedObjectContext:sectionNameKeyPath:cache Name: method creates and initializes fetchedResultsController. The template then sets the delegate to self and assigns the fetchedResultsController property.

The template has basic implementations for the four change methods from the NSFetchedResultsControllerDelegate protocol:

➤ controllerWillChangeContent:

➤ controller:didChangeObject:atIndexPath:forChangeType:newIndexPath:

➤ controller:didChangeSection:atIndex:forChangeType:

➤ controllerDidChangeContent:

The implementations for controllerWillChangeContent: and controllerDidChangeContent: are straightforward:

```
- (void)controllerWillChangeContent:(NSFetchedResultsController *)controller
{
    [self.tableView beginUpdates];
}

- (void)controllerDidChangeContent:(NSFetchedResultsController *)controller
{
    [self.tableView endUpdates];
}
```

The `controllerWillChangeContent:` method notifies you that the fetched results controller will change content. So the template tells the table that updates are incoming by calling the `beginUpdates` method on the table view.

Similarly, the `controllerDidChangeContent:` method tells you that the fetched results controller has finished its changes. Here, the template tells the table view that updates are complete by calling the `endUpdates` method.

The `controller:didChangeSection:atIndex:forChangeType:` method lets you handle cases where sections change. The template code will insert a new section if the change type is `NSFetchedResults ChangeInsert` and will delete a section if the change type is `NSFetchedResultsChangeDelete`. Here is the code from the template:

```
- (void)controller:(NSFetchedResultsController *)controller
    didChangeSection:(id <NSFetchedResultsSectionInfo>)sectionInfo
           atIndex:(NSUInteger)sectionIndex
     forChangeType:(NSFetchedResultsChangeType)type
{
    switch(type) {
        case NSFetchedResultsChangeInsert:
            [self.tableView
             insertSections:[NSIndexSet indexSetWithIndex:sectionIndex]
             withRowAnimation:UITableViewRowAnimationFade];
            break;

        case NSFetchedResultsChangeDelete:
            [self.tableView
             deleteSections:[NSIndexSet indexSetWithIndex:sectionIndex]
             withRowAnimation:UITableViewRowAnimationFade];
            break;
    }
}
```

Finally, the `controller:didChangeObject:atIndexPath:forChangeType:newIndexPath:` method notifies you that an object in the fetch results has been added, removed, moved, or updated. The template code handles each case individually by updating the table view accordingly:

```
- (void)controller:(NSFetchedResultsController *)controller
        didChangeObject:(id)anObject
        atIndexPath:(NSIndexPath *)indexPath
        forChangeType:(NSFetchedResultsChangeType)type
        newIndexPath:(NSIndexPath *)newIndexPath
{
    UITableView *tableView = self.tableView;
```

```
switch(type) {
    case NSFetchedResultsChangeInsert:
        [tableView insertRowsAtIndexPaths:@[newIndexPath]
                        withRowAnimation:UITableViewRowAnimationFade];
        break;

    case NSFetchedResultsChangeDelete:
        [tableView deleteRowsAtIndexPaths:@[indexPath]
                        withRowAnimation:UITableViewRowAnimationFade];
        break;

    case NSFetchedResultsChangeUpdate:
        [self configureCell:[tableView cellForRowAtIndexPath:indexPath]
                atIndexPath:indexPath];
        break;

    case NSFetchedResultsChangeMove:
        [tableView deleteRowsAtIndexPaths:@[indexPath]
                        withRowAnimation:UITableViewRowAnimationFade];
        [tableView insertRowsAtIndexPaths:@[newIndexPath]
                        withRowAnimation:UITableViewRowAnimationFade];
        break;
    }
}
```

Now that you have seen how to create and configure the fetchedResultsController, you'll look at how to configure the MasterViewController at startup. You do this in the viewDidLoad method:

```
- (void)viewDidLoad
{
    [super viewDidLoad];
    // Do any additional setup after loading the view, typically from a nib.
    self.navigationItem.leftBarButtonItem = self.editButtonItem;

    UIBarButtonItem *addButton = [[UIBarButtonItem alloc]
            initWithBarButtonSystemItem:UIBarButtonSystemItemAdd
                                 target:self
                                 action:@selector(insertNewObject:)];
    self.navigationItem.rightBarButtonItem = addButton;
}
```

The method first calls the superclass version of viewDidLoad to ensure that you perform any initialization that the superclass requires.

Next, the code configures the Edit button, creates the Add button, and adds the buttons to the navigation at the top of the screen. You can see in the initialization of the addButton that the insertNewObject method will be called when someone taps the Add button.

Now you will look at how to use the table view delegate methods to display your data. These should be familiar to you from Chapter 3.

The first method is `numberOfSectionsInTableView`:

```
- (NSInteger)numberOfSectionsInTableView:(UITableView *)tableView
{
    return [[self.fetchedResultsController sections] count];
}
```

As you may recall, the table view calls this method when it needs to know how many sections to display. Here, the code simply asks the `fetchedResultsController` for the number of sections.

The next table view delegate method is `numberOfRowsInSection`:

```
- (NSInteger)tableView:(UITableView *)tableView
    numberOfRowsInSection:(NSInteger)section
{
    id <NSFetchedResultsSectionInfo> sectionInfo =
        [self.fetchedResultsController sections][section];
    return [sectionInfo numberOfObjects];
}
```

Again, you call upon the `fetchedResultsController` to return the number of rows to display.

You configure the cell in the `tableView:cellForRowAtIndexPath:` and `configureCell` methods:

```
- (UITableViewCell *)tableView:(UITableView *)tableView
        cellForRowAtIndexPath:(NSIndexPath *)indexPath
{
    UITableViewCell *cell =
        [tableView dequeueReusableCellWithIdentifier:@"Cell"
                                        forIndexPath:indexPath];
    [self configureCell:cell atIndexPath:indexPath];
    return cell;
}
- (void)configureCell:(UITableViewCell *)cell atIndexPath:(NSIndexPath *)indexPath
{
    NSManagedObject *object =
        [self.fetchedResultsController objectAtIndexPath:indexPath];
    cell.textLabel.text = [[object valueForKey:@"timeStamp"] description];
}
```

This code should be familiar down to the point where it retrieves the Managed Object. Again, the code asks `fetchedResultsController` for the object that the index path points to. Once it obtains this object, the code uses key-value coding to get the value for the `timeStamp` property. You learn more about key-value coding in Chapter 8.

The `commitEditingStyle:forRowAtIndexPath:` method contains the code to handle editing rows in the table view. The table view calls this method when editing of the table view will cause a change to the underlying data. In this case, deleting an object in the table view should delete the object from the context:

```
- (void)tableView:(UITableView *)tableView
    commitEditingStyle:(UITableViewCellEditingStyle)editingStyle
    forRowAtIndexPath:(NSIndexPath *)indexPath
{
```

```
    if (editingStyle == UITableViewCellEditingStyleDelete) {
        NSManagedObjectContext *context =
            [self.fetchedResultsController managedObjectContext];
        [context deleteObject:[self.fetchedResultsController
                                 objectAtIndexPath:indexPath]];

        NSError *error = nil;
        if (![context save:&error]) {
            // Replace this implementation with code to handle the error
            // appropriately.
            // abort() causes the application to generate a crash log and
            // terminate. You should not use this function in a shipping
            // application, although it may be useful during development.
            NSLog(@"Unresolved error %@, %@", error, [error userInfo]);
            abort();
        }
    }
}
```

The code first determines if the user has deleted a cell. Then it gets a reference to the context and tells the context to delete the object that the user deleted from the table view. Last, the context changes are committed to disk by calling the `save:` method.

Another interesting bit of code in the `MasterViewController` is the `insertNewObject:` method. Recall that this is the method you call when a user taps the Add button at the top of the screen:

```
- (void)insertNewObject:(id)sender
{
    NSManagedObjectContext *context =
        [self.fetchedResultsController managedObjectContext];
    NSEntityDescription *entity =
        [[self.fetchedResultsController fetchRequest] entity];
    NSManagedObject *newManagedObject =
        [NSEntityDescription insertNewObjectForEntityForName:[entity name]
                                      inManagedObjectContext:context];

    // If appropriate, configure the new Managed Object.
    // Normally you should use accessor methods, but using KVC here avoids the
    // need to add a custom class to the template.
    [newManagedObject setValue:[NSDate date] forKey:@"timeStamp"];

    // Save the context.
    NSError *error = nil;
    if (![context save:&error]) {
        // Replace this implementation with code to handle the error
        // appropriately.
        // abort() causes the application to generate a crash log and
        // terminate. You should not use this function in a shipping
        // application, although it may be useful during development.
        NSLog(@"Unresolved error %@, %@", error, [error userInfo]);
        abort();
    }
}
```

Like the `commitEditingStyle:forRowAtIndexPath:` method, this code first gets a reference to the context. Next, the code creates a new entity based on the entity that the `fetchedResults Controller` uses. The code then creates a new Managed Object based on that entity and inserts it into the context. Next, the code configures the Managed Object with the appropriate data — in this case, a timestamp. Finally, the context is committed to disk with the `save:` method.

The last method that you should review is `prepareForSegue:sender:`. This method tells you that the view controller is about to execute a segue. In this method, the template gets the Managed Object that corresponds to the row the user tapped and passes it to the `DetailViewController` by calling its `setDetailItem:` method. Here is the code for `prepareForSegue:sender:`.

```
- (void)prepareForSegue:(UIStoryboardSegue *)segue sender:(id)sender
{
    if ([[segue identifier] isEqualToString:@"showDetail"]) {
        NSIndexPath *indexPath = [self.tableView indexPathForSelectedRow];
        NSManagedObject *object = [[self fetchedResultsController]
                                   objectAtIndexPath:indexPath];
        [[segue destinationViewController] setDetailItem:object];
    }
}
```

DetailViewController

The template application uses the `DetailViewController` to display details about a selected row. Tapping a row pushes the `DetailViewController` onto the navigation stack using a segue and shows the event timestamp. The `MasterViewController` passes the Managed Object that contains the data that will be displayed in the `DetailViewController` by calling the `DetailViewController`'s `setDetailItem` method:

```
- (void)setDetailItem:(id)newDetailItem
{
    if (_detailItem != newDetailItem) {
        _detailItem = newDetailItem;

        // Update the view.
        [self configureView];
    }
}
```

This method accepts the detail item and then calls an internal method, `configureView`, to display the information in the detail item:

```
- (void)configureView
{
    // Update the user interface for the detail item.

    if (self.detailItem) {
        self.detailDescriptionLabel.text =
        [[self.detailItem valueForKey:@"timeStamp"] description];
    }
}
```

Modifying the Template Code

Now that you are familiar with how the template code works, you will modify it to create tasks instead of timestamps. To build the Task application, you will modify the data model by creating a Task entity, create a new view controller that you will use to create tasks, and update the `MasterViewController` to use the new Task entity.

The first thing that you will do is to modify the data model by changing the existing Event entity to make it a Task entity. If you make a change to the data model and attempt to run your application, you will get an error that looks something like this:

```
2012-10-16 18:40:02.631 Tasks[49165:c07] Unresolved error
Error Domain=NSCocoaErrorDomain Code=134100 "The operation couldn't be completed.
(Cocoa error 134100.)" UserInfo=0x855d4a0 {metadata={
    NSPersistenceFrameworkVersion = 419;
    NSStoreModelVersionHashes =        {
        Event = <5431c046 d30e7f32 c2cc8099 58add1e7 579ad104 a3aa8fc4 846e97d7
                af01cc79>;
    };
    NSStoreModelVersionHashesVersion = 3;
    NSStoreModelVersionIdentifiers =        (
        ""
    );
    NSStoreType = SQLite;
    NSStoreUUID = "BD0F513A-E9E9-4A7C-8746-3B40EC06CD58";
    "_NSAutoVacuumLevel" = 2;
}, reason=The model used to open the store is incompatible with the one
        used to create the store}, {
    metadata =      {
        NSPersistenceFrameworkVersion = 419;
        NSStoreModelVersionHashes =           {
            Event = <5431c046 d30e7f32 c2cc8099 58add1e7 579ad104 a3aa8fc4
                846e97d7 af01cc79>;
        };
        NSStoreModelVersionHashesVersion = 3;
        NSStoreModelVersionIdentifiers =           (
            ""
        );
        NSStoreType = SQLite;
        NSStoreUUID = "BD0F513A-E9E9-4A7C-8746-3B40EC06CD58";
        "_NSAutoVacuumLevel" = 2;
    };
    reason = "The model used to open the store is incompatible with the one
            used to create the store";
}
```

This error says that, "The model used to open the store is incompatible with the one used to create the store." This means exactly what it sounds like: the data store on the device is not compatible with your revised data model, so Core Data cannot open it. When you encounter this situation, you need to use Core Data migration to move your data from one data model to another. Core Data migration is covered in detail in Chapter 9. For now, simply delete the existing application from the simulator or device before trying to run it again. This forces Core Data to build a new data sto that is compatible with the data model.

Open the `Tasks.xcdatamodeld` file, and then select the Event entity. Change the name of the entit to **Task**. Using the table editor style, add a new attribute to the Task entity by clicking the plus icon below the Attributes area. Call the attribute `taskText` and set its type to `String`. You will use the new attribute to store the text for your tasks. Your data model should look like Figure 5-6.

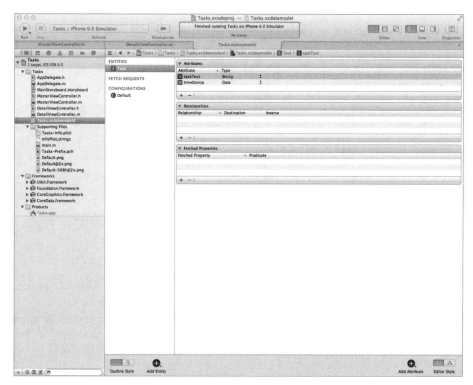

FIGURE 5-6: Revised Tasks data model

Next, you need to build a new screen for entering the Task text. In a production application, you would probably want to use Interface Builder to build a nice user interface for this screen. However, to keep this example simple, you will just build a simple interface in code.

Add a new `UIViewController` subclass to your project. Make sure you clear the checkboxes for Targeted for iPad and With XIB for User Interface. Call your new class **TaskEntryViewController**.

Modify the `TaskEntryViewController.h` header to include properties for a `UITextField` and the Managed Object Context. When the `MasterViewController` calls up the `TaskEntryViewController`, it will set the reference to the context. Finally, modify the interface definition to indicate that you will be implementing the `UITextFieldDelegate` protocol. You use this protocol to receive messages from the `UITextField`. Specifically, you will be implementing the `textFieldShouldReturn:` method that runs when the Return button is pressed in a text field.

.cryViewController.h header should look like this:

```
_c/UIKit.h>

_ace TaskEntryViewController : UIViewController <UITextFieldDelegate>

property (strong, nonatomic) UITextField *tf;
@property (strong, nonatomic) NSManagedObjectContext *managedObjectContext;

@end
```

Now you will implement the `TaskEntryViewController`. First, you need to add code to
`TaskEntryViewController.m` to programmatically create the UI in the `loadView` method:

```
- (void)loadView {
    [super loadView];

    self.tf = [[UITextField alloc] initWithFrame:CGRectMake(65, 20, 200, 20)];
    [self.tf setBackgroundColor:[UIColor lightGrayColor]];
    [self.tf setDelegate:self];
    [self.view addSubview:self.tf];

    UILabel *lbl = [[UILabel alloc] initWithFrame:CGRectMake(5, 20, 60, 20)];

    [lbl setText:@"Task:"];

    [self.view addSubview:lbl];

}
```

The code creates a `UITextField` object with the specified screen coordinates. Then it sets the background color so it is easy to see. The delegate is then set, and the code adds the control to the main view. The code also creates a `UILabel` so that users will know what the text field represents. Remember that when you are creating a production application, you will not need this code. You will most likely use Interface Builder to build a nicer interface than a plaintext label and a gray text entry field.

The next step is to add the `textFieldShouldReturn:` method to `TaskEntryViewController.m`. The framework calls this `UITextFieldDelegate` method when Return is pressed. The code inserts a new Task object into the context:

```
- (BOOL)textFieldShouldReturn:(UITextField *)textField
{
    // Create a new instance of the entity managed by the fetched results
    // controller.
    NSManagedObjectContext *context = self.managedObjectContext;

    NSEntityDescription *entity = [NSEntityDescription
                                   entityForName:@"Task"
                                   inManagedObjectContext:conte

    NSManagedObject *newManagedObject =
    [NSEntityDescription insertNewObjectForEntityForName:[entity
                                   inManagedObjectContext:context]

    // If appropriate, configure the new Managed Object.
```

```
[newManagedObject setValue:[NSDate date] forKey:@"timeStamp"];
[newManagedObject setValue:[self.tf text] forKey:@"taskText"];

// Save the context.
NSError *error = nil;
if (![context save:&error]) {
    /*
     Replace this implementation with code to handle the error
     appropriately.

     */
    NSLog(@"Unresolved error %@, %@", error, [error userInfo]);
    abort();
}

[self dismissViewControllerAnimated:YES completion:nil];
return YES;
}
```

First, this code gets a pointer to the context. Then you define a new `Task` entity from the context. Next, the code inserts a Managed Object into the context. After that, the code configures the Managed Object using a timestamp and the text entered in the text field. The context is then committed to disk, and you dismiss the view controller. The interface will look like Figure 5-7.

The last thing to do is modify the `MasterViewController` to use the new Task entity and to call up the Text Entry interface when a user clicks the plus button to enter a new task.

Because you will be referencing the `TaskEntryViewController`, you need to add an `import` statement to `MasterViewController.m` for `TaskEntryViewController.h`:

```
#import "TaskEntryViewController.h"
```

FIGURE 5-7: Text entry interface

Next, you need to modify the `fetchedResultsController` getter method to use the Task entity instead of the Event entity. I have presented the modified code in bold:

```
- (NSFetchedResultsController *)fetchedResultsController
{
    if (_fetchedResultsController != nil) {
        return _fetchedResultsController;
    }

    NSFetchRequest *fetchRequest = [[NSFetchRequest alloc] init];
    // Edit the entity name as appropriate.
    NSEntityDescription *entity =
    [NSEntityDescription
        entityForName:@"Task"
        inManagedObjectContext:self.managedObjectContext];
    [fetchRequest setEntity:entity];

    ...
```

Now delete the old `insertNewObject` method. You need to recode this method to present the `TaskEntryViewController` like this:

```
- (void)insertNewObject:(id)sender {

    //  Ask for text from TaskEntryViewController.
    TaskEntryViewController *tevc = [[TaskEntryViewController alloc] init];

    tevc.managedObjectContext = self.managedObjectContext;

    [self presentViewController:tevc animated:YES completion:nil];

}
```

This code simply creates a `TaskEntryViewController`, sets the context, and presents it.

Next, you want to change the style of cell that you will display in your table view. You can do this by opening the main storyboard for your project. Once you have the storyboard open, navigate over to the master view controller and select the prototype cell. The prototype cell should contain the text Title. Open the Utilities pane, navigate to the Attributes inspector, and set the Style of the cell to Subtitle. You should see the prototype cell change. It will now show a title and subtitle, as you can see in Figure 5-8.

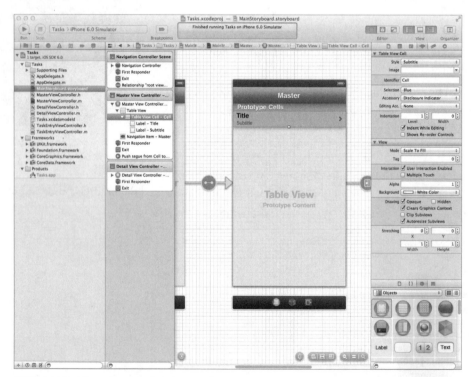

FIGURE 5-8: Changing the prototype cell

The final step is to modify the `configureCell:atIndexPath:` method to use the `taskText` attribute for the main text and the `timeStamp` attribute for the detail text:

```
- (void)configureCell:(UITableViewCell *)cell
        atIndexPath:(NSIndexPath *)indexPath
{
    NSManagedObject *object =
        [self.fetchedResultsController objectAtIndexPath:indexPath];
    cell.textLabel.text = [[object valueForKey:@"taskText"] description];
    cell.detailTextLabel.text =[[object valueForKey:@"timeStamp"] description];
}
```

First, the code retrieves that Managed Object for the cell using the fetched results controller. Then the code sets the cell's `textLabel.text` property to the string contained in the `taskText` attribute of the Managed Object and sets the `detailTextLabel.text` property to the `timeStamp` attribute.

You should now be able to build and run the application. Try clicking the plus icon to add new tasks. After typing in the text and pressing Return, you should see your task listed in the table view. Try adding a few more tasks and then swiping across a task in the table view. You should see a Delete button, which will allow you to delete the task. Tap the Edit button, and notice that you go into edit mode. If you tap a red circle icon in edit mode, you see a Delete button, which allows you to delete the row. Since you have not modified the `DetailViewController`, tapping a task will display the timestamp for the task. Feel free to modify the `DetailViewController` to display both the task text and the timestamp for the task. The completed application should look like Figure 5-2.

MOVING FORWARD

In this chapter, you learned about the basics of Core Data. You examined the Core Data architecture and learned the basic terminology necessary to understand the Core Data API stack. Next, you discovered how Core Data and iCloud work together to provide an infrastructure that you can use to synchronize data across devices. You also learned how to use the data protection API to add security to your data. Then you explored the template code to understand how to implement the Core Data architecture. Finally, you modified the template application to produce a functional task manager application.

In the next few chapters, your knowledge of Core Data will go from cursory to detailed. In the next chapter, you learn to use the Xcode data modeler to develop a model that incorporates many of the features of Core Data. Then in Chapter 7 you learn how to bring that model to life through code.

Modeling Data in Xcode

WHAT'S IN THIS CHAPTER?

- ➤ Defining entities and their attributes
- ➤ Expressing the relationships between entities
- ➤ Creating fetched properties and fetch requests using the predicate builder
- ➤ Generating custom subclasses of NSManagedObject from your model

WROX.COM CODE DOWNLOADS FOR THIS CHAPTER

The wrox.com code downloads for this chapter are found at www.wrox.com/remtitle .cgi?isbn=1118391845 on the Download Code tab. The code is in the Chapter 6 download and individually named according to the names throughout the chapter.

In the previous chapter, you learned the fundamentals of working with Core Data. In this chapter, you explore the Xcode data modeling tool and discover how to create data models.

In this chapter, you learn how to use the Xcode data modeling tool to create your Core Data model. The tool is easy to use and can dramatically speed the development time of your next data-driven application. Think of the data modeling tool as Interface Builder for your data.

You can use the tool to model the entities and attributes that you will use in your application. You can also use the tool to define relationships between entities, create fetched properties, and even build fetch requests.

MODELING YOUR DATA

In Chapter 2, you learned about the importance of modeling your data before you begin work on your application. You saw how to use OmniGraffle to create Entity-Relationship Diagrams (ERDs). Then you explored how to turn those diagrams into an SQLite database. In this chapter, you learn how to use the Xcode modeling tool to model your data and turn the model into Core Data objects.

The Xcode modeling tool gives you two different styles that you can use to look at your model. The default style is the Table style that you can see in Figure 6-1. This figure shows the Utilities view opened on the right side with the Data Model Inspector selected.

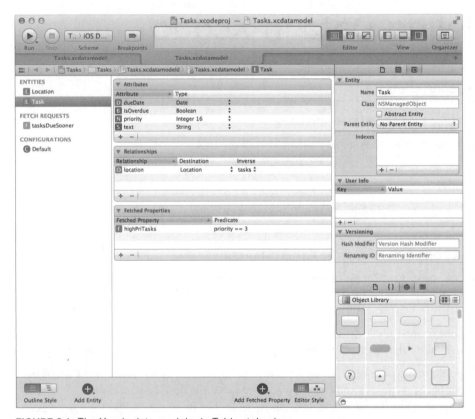

FIGURE 6-1: The Xcode data modeler in Table style view

Looking at Figure 6-1, you can see three areas where you will do your data modeling. On the left side is the model outline. This pane shows an outline of your data model, including all entities, fetch requests, and configurations.

The middle area of the screen shows information on the item that you have selected in the outline. In the case of Figure 6-1, since I have selected the Task entity, you can see its attributes, relationships, and fetched properties.

The right side of the screen displays more detailed information on the item that you have selected in either the outline, attributes, relationships, or fetched properties areas. In Figure 6-1, you can see more details about the Task entity.

Alternatively, if you prefer to view your model graphically, you can switch to the Graph editor style, as you can see in Figure 6-2. Here you still see the outline on the left and the Utilities view on the right, but the Table style editor is replaced with a graphical representation of the data model.

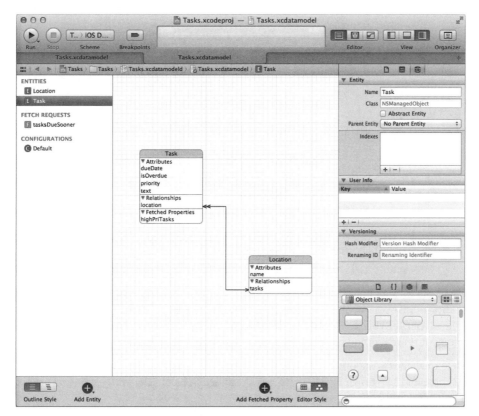

FIGURE 6-2: The Xcode data modeler in Graph style view

You can freely switch between the Table and Graph styles by clicking the Editor Style icons from the toolbar at the bottom of the screen.

Defining Entities and Their Attributes

To show all the features of the data modeler, I will walk you through the creation of a data model for a catalog application like the one you created in Chapters 1 through 3. Then, at the end of the chapter, you will create an extended version of the Task data model from Chapter 5, which you will use in the example code in Chapter 7.

Figure 6-3 shows the Entity-Relationship Diagram that you developed in Chapter 2. If you recall, this diagram represents the data that you needed to build a catalog application. The application presented a company's product catalog and contained information about the products, manufacturers, and countries of origin of the products. This chapter presents the creation of the catalog data model as a tutorial, but you do not necessarily need to follow along — you will not be using it in code. I am just walking you through the process to demonstrate the capabilities of the data-modeling tool. At the end of this chapter, you will create another data model for a task application that you will use going forward into Chapter 7.

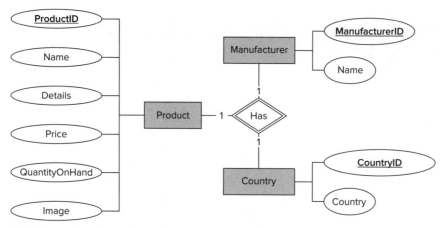

FIGURE 6-3: Catalog database Entity-Relationship Diagram

The main entity in the catalog application is the Product. So, let's create a Product entity in the tool. You can create entities in a couple of ways. You can click the Add Entity button in the toolbar at the bottom of the screen, or you can create an entity from the menu bar by selecting Editor ⇨ Add Entity. Choose one of these methods and create a new entity called Product.

After you create a new entity, the outline shows the entity as selected. In the Graph editor style, a selected entity is blue and has resize handles. Because you have selected the entity, you can see its details in the Data Model Inspector.

Entity Details

You can view the details for a specific entity by selecting the entity in either the outline or the Graph style view. Xcode displays the entity details in the Data Model Inspector. You need to have the Utilities view open to see the Data Model Inspector.

In the Data Model Inspector, the Entity area contains general information about the selected entity. In the Name field, you can change the name of your entity. Change the name of this entity from Entity to Product.

The Class field displays the name of the class that represents the entity in code. The tool sets the class field to NSManagedObject by default. Later in the chapter, when you create custom subclasses of NSManagedObject, you will see the name change to the name of the custom subclass.

Using the Parent Entity field, you can implement an inheritance hierarchy in your model between entities like those that you would implement between classes in code. Suppose that all your products shared common attributes such as Name, Price, and Quantity, but each category of product had different subattributes. You could design your model such that different data entities would represent different categories. For example, if your company was selling screws, a screw entity might have attributes such as head type, thread pitch, and length. An entity to model hammers would not need the attributes of screws, but it might need attributes such as weight and claw length. You could define the hammer and screw as entities in your model with a parent type of Product. That way, both the hammer and screw classes would inherit all the attributes and relationships of the parent class, Product, while still being able to define their own unique relationships and attributes.

You can tell Core Data that an entity is abstract by selecting the Abstract Entity checkbox. You cannot instantiate abstract entities and can use them only as the base for another entity.

Create two new entities in the model and call them Hammer and Screw. For each of these new entities, set the Parent Entity in the Entity area of the Data Model Inspector to Product. You will see an inheritance arrow drawn from the subclasses to the superclass, as in Figure 6-4.

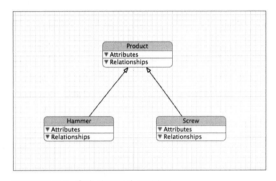

FIGURE 6-4: Subclassed entities

The next area of the Data Model Inspector displays User Info. The NSManagedObject class that you create to represent your Core Data entity in code has a property called entity that returns an NSEntityDescription. The NSEntityDescription has a userInfo property that returns an NSDictionary containing user-defined key-value pairs. The User Info area allows you to create key-value pairs and associate them with the current entity. At runtime, you can access these values using the userInfo property of the NSEntityDescription. Use the plus at the bottom of the window to add a new key-value pair to the entity, and use the minus to remove the selected pair.

In the outline pane on the left side of the Xcode window, below the Entities and Fetch Requests sections, you will find the Configurations section. Configurations enable you to name various groups of entities in your data model. You create a configuration using the plus button at the bottom left of the Xcode window. By default, this button says Add Entity, but if you hold down the mouse button, you will see options for adding Fetch Requests and Configurations as well. Once you create a configuration, that configuration is available for all entities. Then you can go through each entity individually and assign it to one or more configurations. At runtime, you can retrieve the entities in a configuration using the entitiesForConfiguration method on the NSManagedObjectModel class. This method will return an NSArray of entities in the chosen configuration. You use configurations to split the entities in a model across multiple data stores. When developing applications for iOS, you will generally use only one data store, so you may not have much use for configurations. However, it is useful to know that you can group entities in the modeler and retrieve your groups at runtime.

Adding Attributes

Now that you have created the Product entity, you need to add attributes to it. The Product should have the attributes defined in the Entity-Relationship Diagram, as shown previously in Figure 6-3.

Select the Product entity in the data model. With the entity selected, click the Add Attribute plus icon at the bottom right of the Editor pane. The button may also say Add Relationship or Add Fetched Property. You should see a new attribute appear in the Attributes section of the Table editor. If you are using the Graph editor style, you will see the new attribute appear in the Attributes section of the Product entity.

When you select an attribute, the information in the Data Model Inspector is slightly different from the options available when you select an entity, as you can see in Figure 6-5.

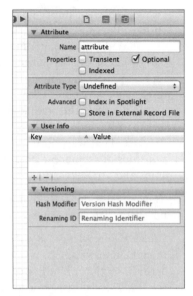

FIGURE 6-5: Data Model Inspector for attributes

The Attribute area in the Data Model Inspector allows you to define the name and type of your attribute. Change the name of the attribute that you just added to **name**. You will store the name of the product in this attribute. Change the type of the name attribute to String.

Depending on the data type that you select for your attribute, the Attribute area will display different fields that allow you to set additional options for the attribute.

For the numeric types Integer 16, Integer 32, Integer 64, Decimal, Double, Float, and Date, the area allows you to enter minimum and maximum values to use for validation. If the user attempts to save an entity with a value that is outside the specified range, Core Data raises an error to notify you that a validation rule has been broken. You can also enter a default value for any of the numeric types.

For a String, the area presents you with minimum and maximum length constraints. Again, if the user attempts to save an entity with a string that violates either the minimum or the maximum length, Core Data raises an error to notify you that a validation rule has been broken. There is also a field for entering a default string value.

In addition, there is a field that allows you to build a regular expression that the framework will use to validate the String. Regular expressions are special strings that define a set of rules. For example, you can write a regular expression that constrains the String to be all capital letters or to allow only certain characters. The framework compares the String that the user enters for the attribute at runtime with the regular expression. If the String fails the comparison, meaning that it does not conform to the rules defined by the regular expression, Core Data raises an error indicating that a validation rule has failed. A detailed look at regular expressions is beyond the scope of this book. If you are interested in further exploration of regular expressions, I recommend that you start at: http://www.regular-expressions.info/. This website has a good regular expression tutorial and features a regular expression reference as well.

For `Boolean` attributes, the only option you will see in the pane is for the default value. Your options here are `YES`, `NO`, or `None`.

The `Binary` data type has an option called Allows External Storage. Use this type if you plan to store binary data such as an image in the attribute. The Allows External Storage flag notifies Core Data that the data in the attribute can be stored outside the persistent store. This could be useful if you are building an application to store images and you want to leave the images in their native format, intact in the filesystem, instead of putting them into the SQLite data store.

The final data type is `Transformable`. `Transformable` attributes enable you to store nonstandard data types such as your own custom classes or C structs. Behind the scenes, Core Data converts the attribute into an `NSData` object using the `NSValueTransformer` class. This binary data is then stored in the persistent store.

The name of your attribute has three checkboxes beneath it. The Optional checkbox allows you to indicate if the attribute is optional or required. If the attribute is not optional, you should provide a default value. If you attempt to save an entity with a nonoptional field that is blank, Core Data raises an error indicating that a validation rule has failed.

You use the Transient checkbox to indicate that you do not want the attribute saved in the persistent store. You use this to retain data in memory that will not be necessary to restore later or data that you compute dynamically at runtime.

The Indexed checkbox sets whether or not the attribute should be indexed in the persistent store. This is particularly important when your backing store is the SQLite database. Selecting this box causes Core Data to create a database index on the attribute. Proper use of indexes can greatly speed up queries that filter or sort on the indexed attribute. You need to be aware, however, that creating too many indices can reduce performance. You should carefully consider which fields you need indexed. Generally, if you are searching or sorting based on an attribute, you should index on the attribute.

Now that you know how to create attributes, go ahead and create the remaining attributes for the Product entity.

Adding Relationships Between Entities

Now that you have modeled the Product entity, it is time to add the related entities. Create two new entities named Manufacturer and Country. Feel free to add any attributes that make sense for the two new entities. I have added attributes for the name, address, and preferred provider status for the Manufacturer. I have also added attributes for name and region to the Country entity.

If you examine the Entity-Relationship Diagram in Figure 6-3, you will notice that the Product entity and Manufacturer entity are related. Each Product has a Manufacturer. A Manufacturer can have many Products. You need to express this relationship in your Core Data model. Including this information in the model allows Core Data to enforce the relationship and provides additional functionality when you go to build an application that uses the model. It is important to include as much information as you can when building your model. Core Data uses all this information at runtime to ensure that the data in your application is consistent with the design expressed in the model.

Select the Product entity. In the Relationships section in the Table editor, click the plus icon. This adds a new relationship to the Product entity. The Data Model Inspector now displays options related to the relationship, as you can see in Figure 6-6. In the Name field, change the name of the relationship to **manufacturer**.

The Destination drop-down allows you to select the entity on the receiving end of the relationship. In this case, the manufacturer relationship should point to the Manufacturer entity. So in the Destination drop-down, select Manufacturer. Once you set the Destination, you will notice that the tool draws a line between the Product and Manufacturer entities in the Graph editor. The arrowhead on the line points to the destination entity.

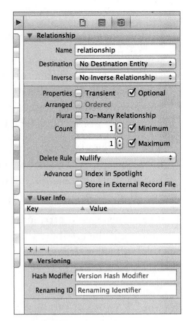

FIGURE 6-6: Data Model Inspector for a relationship

You use the Inverse drop-down to set an inverse relationship. In your case, you want to create an inverse relationship between manufacturers and products. To specify this relationship, you must first define a relationship for the Manufacturer entity. In the Manufacturer entity, add a new relationship called products. Make the Destination for this new relationship Product. You will see that there is now a line in the Graph editor pointing from Manufacturer to Product. Select the Product entity and change the Inverse drop-down from No Inverse Relationship to Products.

The two lines that were in the diagram change to one line with arrowheads on each end. If you select the products relationship in the Manufacturer entity, you can see that the tool has automatically set its Inverse to Manufacturer. You have established a two-way relationship between these entities.

The Optional and Transient checkboxes have the same functionality as for attributes.

The Arranged checkbox was added in iOS 5. Checking this box indicates that the relationship is ordered. This prompts Xcode to generate additional methods that help you to insert data objects in a location that you specify in the underlying NSOrderedSet data structure.

Selecting the To-Many Relationship checkbox defines the relationship as a To-Many Relationship. Let's assume that only one manufacturer makes a specific product, but a manufacturer can make many different products. In the Product entity, you should leave the To-Many Relationship checkbox unchecked for the manufacturer relationship because there is only a single manufacturer for a given product. However, you should check the checkbox for the products relationship in the Manufacturer entity because one manufacturer can build many products. Select the Manufacturer entity and then the products relationship. Then select the To-Many Relationship checkbox. You will see that the arrow that points to the Product entity now has two arrowheads, indicating that the Product entity is the destination of a To-Many relationship. Your diagram should now look like Figure 6-7.

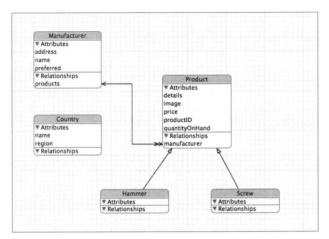

FIGURE 6-7: Relationships in the Graph editor

The next two fields in the Data Model Inspector, the Count fields, allow you to optionally set the minimum and maximum number of entities contained in the relationship. For the manufacturer relationship, these fields are both set to 1 because the relationship of manufacturers to products is 1 to 1. You cannot change these fields unless you have declared a To-Many relationship. If you select the products relationship in the Manufacturer entity, these fields are empty. This means the number of products that can be associated with a manufacturer is unlimited.

The final field is the Delete Rule drop-down. You use this to specify what happens when you try to delete the source object in a relationship. The options are No Action, Nullify, Cascade, and Deny.

No Action means that the framework does nothing to the destination object in the relationship. Using No Action is discouraged because this option leaves maintenance of the integrity of the model to you. Part of the power of Core Data is its ability to manage the integrity of the data model. In the example in this chapter, imagine that you set the manufacturer relationship in the Product entity to No Action. Now, if you deleted a Product entity, its related Manufacturer object would still appear related to the now nonexistent product. It would be up to you to remove the now-defunct product from the Manufacturer entity. This functionality is automatic when you choose one of the other Delete Rule options.

The Nullify option is the default. It nulls out the inverse relationship for you automatically. This only works for relationships in which the inverse relationship is optional. Consider the previous example with the Delete Rule changed from No Action to Nullify. In this case, if you delete a product, that product will no longer appear in the Manufacturer's products relationship.

The Cascade option cascades deletions from the source to the destination of the relationship. In this case, you examine the products relationship of the Manufacturer object. If this relationship had its Delete Rule set to Cascade, deleting a manufacturer would delete all the products made by that manufacturer.

Finally, the Deny option prevents the deletion of source objects if there are objects at the destination. In the case of the products relationship of the Manufacturer object, if you attempted to delete a manufacturer that still had products, Core Data would raise a validation error. In this case, you would have to manually delete all products associated with a manufacturer before you could delete the manufacturer.

The last aspect of relationships that you will look at is the many-to-many relationship. Imagine that many different countries produce a product and that a country could make many different products. Create a countries relationship in the Product entity and point it to the Country entity. Mark this new relationship as a To-Many relationship. Then create a products relationship in the Country entity, mark it as a To-Many relationship, and point it to the Product entity. Now set the inverse relation to products. This may cause you some concern if you are an experienced database developer, because in an SQL database, you would have to create a join table to implement this design. Core Data automatically creates the join table behind the scenes in the SQLite database so that you don't need to worry about creating it in your model. You can simply create a many-to-many relationship and let Core Data handle the implementation details for you.

You can also express reflexive relationships in Core Data. A *reflexive relationship* is a relationship where the source and destination entities are the same. For instance, suppose that you want to keep track of all the other Product entities related to a specific Product entity. You could create a related-Products relationship in the Product entity that has a destination of Product since both the source and destination entities in the relationship are Product entities. For example, suppose that you have a Screw entity and wanted to create a relationship that maps a particular screw to all other screws of the same type. You could create a relatedScrews relationship that has a Screw entity as both its source and destination. You will see the arrow coming out of the Product entity and then circle around and point right back to itself.

Creating Fetched Properties and Fetch Request Templates

In the previous section, you learned how to create relationships between your entities. Fetched properties work similarly to relationships. An important difference is that you can apply predicates to filter the entities returned by a fetched property. For instance, the Product entity has a manufacturer relationship. You must add a Manufacturer to a Product for the relationship to have any meaning. Core Data can calculate a fetched property without your having to specify which entities meet the criteria. You can use fetch request templates to prepare a fetch request in your model and include variables for resolution at runtime. You can think of fetch request templates like stored queries.

Fetched Properties

Suppose that you wanted to always be able to find a list of cheap products, say products that sold for less than $1. You can use a fetched property to add a property called `cheapProducts` to the Product entity. You then specify a predicate that the framework applies to filter your search results. Select the Product entity. Then, click the plus button below the Fetched Properties section in the table editor to add a fetched property to the Product entity. Call the new Fetched Property **cheapProducts**. Set the destination entity to Product because the fetched property should query all the Product entities.

Since you want to find all products where the price is less than $1.00, enter the predicate `price < 1.00` into the Predicate text box in the Data Model Inspector as you can see in Figure 6-8. In your code, when you have a Product and retrieve the `cheapProducts` property, you will get back an `NSArray` of products that cost less than $1.00.

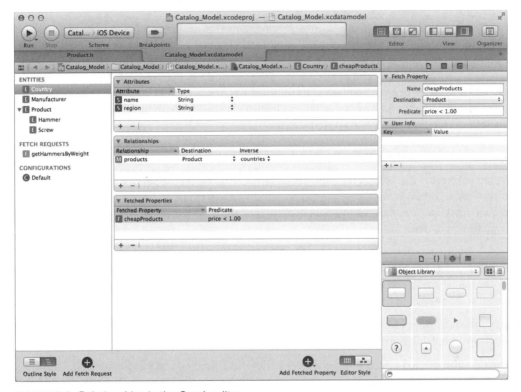

FIGURE 6-8: Relationships in the Graph editor

This predicate works fine for a constant value such as $1.00. However, suppose that you wanted to be able to get back a list of products that are cheaper than the current product. You can accomplish this by using a variable in your predicate.

Core Data has a special variable called `$FETCH_SOURCE`. This variable is a reference to the object executing the fetched property — in this case, the Product object. Your predicate should compare the price of the object under consideration to the price of the object executing the property.

Change the name of the fetched property that you just created to **cheaperProducts**. The predicate is currently defined to return any Products that have a price less than 1.00. However, you do not want to compare to a constant $1.00 price; you want to compare to the price of the current entity and find all products that are cheaper. To do this, you need to compare the price to the `$FETCH_SOURCE.price`. So, your predicate should be `price < $FETCH_SOURCE.price`.

Predicates are not limited to only simple, one-line filters. You can use boolean operators such as AND and OR to combine criteria and generate complex predicates. It doesn't make much sense, but as an example, suppose that you wanted midpriced products made in China by Manufacturer A or Manufacturer B. You would construct this predicate like this:

```
((price < 5 AND price > 1) AND ANY countries.name == "China") AND
(manufacturer.name ==
"Manufacturer A" OR manufacturer.name == "Manufacturer B").
```

You can also use predefined expressions in your predicate. For instance, you can use the `@avg` expression to determine the average of a series of numbers or `@sum` to calculate the sum. You use the expression in the key path of the object that you want to use for your calculation. So, a fetched property to return products with below-average prices would use the predicate `price < $FETCH_SOURCE.@avg.price`. You will learn more about key paths in Chapter 8 when you learn about Key-Value Coding and Key-Value Observing. In general, you can use a key path to traverse a set of nested objects using a dot-separated string.

Fetch Request Templates

If you plan to execute the same fetch repeatedly, only changing the value of a variable, you can predefine a fetch request template in the data model. You can think of a fetch request template as a stored query or view. You can pass variable values into the template at runtime that the framework applies in the predicate.

To create a fetch request template, click and hold on the plus icon at the bottom left of the Xcode window and select Add Fetch Request. The editor pane will change to show you the predicate builder for the new fetch request that you just created. You can use the predicate builder as an easy way to build the predicate that Core Data will use to filter items to return in the fetch request.

In the Data Model Inspector pane, you will see the name of your new fetch request along with the entity, result type, fetch limit, and batch size that define the fetch.

Suppose that you needed a screen in your application that allowed the user to specify a certain weight and then you wanted to display all hammers of that weight. You could build this screen by fetching all the hammers and then filtering the ones that didn't meet your criteria as you create your table cells. However, this would waste memory, because you would be bringing objects into memory that you aren't going to use. Another option would be to define your predicate in code and apply that to the fetch request. That is a perfectly viable option; in fact, that is what a stored fetch request does. Using a stored fetch request can simplify your code because you can define the fetch request in the model instead of having to do it in code.

First, you need to add a weight attribute to the Hammer entity. Click the Hammer entity, and then click the plus sign in the Attributes area of the editor pane. Call the attribute **weight** and set its type to Decimal.

To add a fetch request related to your Hammer entity, select the Hammer entity and then click the plus icon that says Add Fetch Request at the bottom left of the Xcode window pane. If the plus icon does not say Add Fetch Request, just hold down the mouse button, and the option to add a fetch request should appear.

In the Data Model Inspector, change the name of the fetch request to **getHammersByWeight**. Next, you will use the predicate builder to edit the predicate and create the criteria for the fetch request. Xcode should look like Figure 6-9.

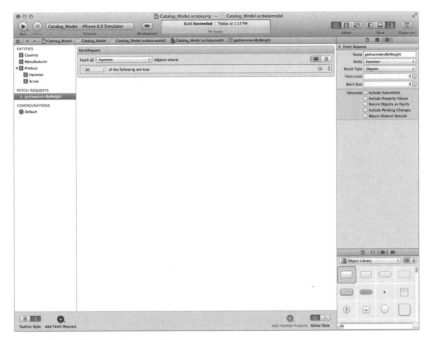

FIGURE 6-9: The predicate editor

Click the plus button on the right side of the first row in the predicate editor to add a criterion. In the first drop-down, select Expression. In the text box, enter **weight == $WEIGHT**.

In your code, you will retrieve the fetch request using the `fetchRequestFromTemplateWithName: substitutionVariables:` method of the `NSManagedObjectModel` object. This method accepts the name of your fetch request template and an `NSDictionary` of key-value pairs used to substitute for the variables in your template.

CREATING CUSTOM NSMANAGEDOBJECT SUBCLASSES

In Chapter 5, you learned how to get data out of an entity retrieved by Core Data using the `NSManagedObject` class. All instances of entities returned by a fetch request are instances of `NSManagedObject`. If you remember, you accessed the data inside of your managed object by using key-value coding. Therefore, to access the `name` field in a `Product` entity, you would use the `valueForKey:` method on the `NSManagedObject` instance that you got back from your fetch request. This method is perfectly fine, but a problem occurs if you incorrectly type the name of the key. At runtime, Core Data would not be able to find the key that you specified, and an error would occur. It would be nice if you could have a compile-time check of your field names. This is possible by subclassing `NSManagedObject`.

Creating custom subclasses of `NSManagedObject` to represent your data objects has several advantages. The first is that the subclass provides access to your data fields using properties. If you use the properties to access your data instead of key-value coding, the compiler can verify that the properties exist at compile time. Xcode will also provide code completion help by displaying a list of the properties for an object after you type the period key.

Another advantage to creating a subclass is that you can extend the functionality of your data object beyond simply providing access to your data. Your data objects can implement complex validation rules for single or multiple fields. You can also implement intelligent default values that you cannot express by specifying a default string or number in the data modeler. In addition, you can define calculated fields that are not stored in the data store. You would then write code to calculate the values for these fields at runtime in your custom subclass.

Creating a custom subclass of NSManagedObject for an entity in your model is simple. In your object model, select the entity for which you want to generate a custom subclass. Next, from the Xcode drop-down menu, choose File ⇨ New ⇨ File, just as you would when creating a new class file. In the New File dialog, select Core Data in the left pane. You should notice that there is a new option called NSManagedObject subclass. Select this option and click Next. The next dialog asks where you want to save your new class, the project to add it to, and the build target that should include the file. Accept the default values and click Create.

If you look in the Xcode Project Navigator, you will see two new files in your project: Product.h and Product.m. The managed object class generation tool generated these classes for the Product entity based on your data model.

The following is the header code for the Product entity class. Note that the order of the properties in your header may differ from what's shown here:

```
#import <Foundation/Foundation.h>
#import <CoreData/CoreData.h>


@interface Product : NSManagedObject

@property (nonatomic, retain) NSString * details;
@property (nonatomic, retain) NSData * image;
@property (nonatomic, retain) NSDecimalNumber * price;
@property (nonatomic, retain) id productID;
@property (nonatomic, retain) NSNumber * quantityOnHand;
@property (nonatomic, retain) NSSet *countries;
@property (nonatomic, retain) NSManagedObject *manufacturer;
@end

@interface Product (CoreDataGeneratedAccessors)

- (void)addCountriesObject:(NSManagedObject *)value;
- (void)removeCountriesObject:(NSManagedObject *)value;
- (void)addCountries:(NSSet *)values;
- (void)removeCountries:(NSSet *)values;

@end
```

You can see from the header that the tool defines properties to implement all the attributes in your model entity. Notice that the relationships return instances of NSSet, so the entities returned from a relationship are unordered. You can also see that the tool generated interface methods to allow you to add and remove entities from the countries relationship.

The following is the code for the Product implementation:

```
#import "Product.h"


@implementation Product

@dynamic details;
@dynamic image;
@dynamic price;
@dynamic productID;
@dynamic quantityOnHand;
@dynamic countries;
@dynamic manufacturer;

@end
```

The tool uses the @dynamic keyword instead of @synthesize to define properties. @synthesize instructs the compiler to create the getter and setter methods for you, whereas @dynamic tells the compiler that you will create the getter and setters. You don't use @synthesize here because you don't want the compiler to generate these methods for you at compile time; Core Data takes care of generating the getters and setters for you at runtime.

Implementing Validation Rules

Aside from exposing your entity's attributes as properties, another benefit to creating subclasses of NSManagedObject is the ability to add complex custom validation rules. Earlier in the chapter, I covered how to add a simple validation range to an attribute using the modeler. Most data types allow you to set simple validation rules in the Data Model Inspector. These rules are limited to min/max values for number and date types, and min/max length or a regular expression for a string type. These options are adequate for general use, but they do not give you much flexibility when trying to express complex business logic.

Suppose that your application allowed you to create new products on the device. You might want to be able to prevent the user from entering certain words as part of the name of the product, to avoid embarrassment when showing the catalog to a client. You could implement a custom validation function that checks the input against a list of inappropriate words before insertion into the database.

The implementation of validation rules for a single field is straightforward. Core Data will automatically call a method validateNnnn:error:, where Nnnn is the name of your attribute, for every attribute in your class. If the method does not exist, it is not a problem. You are free to implement as many or as few of these methods as you want. The method should return a BOOL with a value of YES if the validation is successful and NO if it fails. If the validation fails, it is common practice to return an NSError object to provide further information about why the validation failed.

In the case described, you would implement the function -(BOOL)validateName:(id *)ioValue error:(NSError **)outError. You should notice a couple of things in this method signature. First, it accepts the input parameter as an id pointer. Because you are receiving a pointer to the input, you could conceivably change the value that you received. You should avoid this, because it is bad design and introduces a side effect to validating a piece of data. Additionally, changing the value within the validation method will cause Core Data to try to validate the value again, possibly causing an infinite loop.

The NSError object that you return is a pointer to a pointer. This is a consequence of the fact that Objective-C passes all objects by value. If you passed the NSError pointer as a regular pointer, you would only be able to modify the NSError that you passed into the method. Accepting a pointer to a pointer allows you to pass back a completely different NSError object than the one that you passed into the method. Therefore, instead of changing the values in the object that you passed in, you can create a new NSError with your own values to return.

Implementing validateNnnn:error: methods work when you are trying to validate the value for one field. Suppose, however, that you need to validate multiple fields simultaneously because they depend on each other's value. Imagine that you wanted to make the details attribute required only when the price of a product is greater than $1.00.

The framework calls two methods after all the single-field validation methods are completed. These are validateForInsert: for inserting new objects and validateForUpdate: for updates. As in the single field validation, these functions return a BOOL indicating whether validation is successful. You could write a function to check the price field and return NO if the price is greater than $1.00 and the details field is empty. Then you could put a call to this function in the validateForInsert: and validateForUpdate: methods so that the rule runs anytime a new object is inserted into Core Data or when an existing object is modified.

Implementing Default Values

As you have seen with custom validation rules, it is possible to code rules that are more complex than what you can create in the modeling tool. You can apply the same principle to implementing default values for the attributes of your entity.

Most of the data types allow you to hard-code a default value in the modeling tool. However, suppose that you want to dynamically determine the default value at runtime. You could also use this technique to set the default value for transformable objects because the tool does not allow you to specify a default transformable object.

To implement custom default values, you override the awakeFromInsert method. The framework calls this method after code inserts the object into the context but before the object becomes available for use. You could use this method to set the current date as the default in date fields or for any other purpose where you need to determine your default value at runtime.

CREATING THE TASKS MODEL

Now that you are familiar with Core Data and using the modeler to create a data model, you will build the model for the application that you will code in the next chapter. The application will be a task manager like the one that you built in the previous chapter, but it will have more features to demonstrate some of the functionality of Core Data that you learned about in this chapter.

The Tasks application will implement a feature where you will be able to assign locations to your tasks so that you know what you have to do when you are in a specific location. Tasks will also have due dates that you can use to indicate if a task is overdue. You will also give the task a priority attribute so that you can mark and filter tasks based on priority.

To begin, start a new Xcode Master-Detail Application project called Tasks. Ensure that you select the Use Storyboards, Use Core Data, and Use Automatic Reference Counting checkboxes. Set the Device to iPhone. This will generate your template application and the associated data model.

Open the `Tasks.xcdatamodeld` file to begin editing the data model. Delete the `Event` entity because you won't be using it in this example. You will be creating your entities from scratch.

Click the plus icon labeled Add Entity at the bottom left of the Editor pane to create a new entity. Rename the new entity **Task**.

Next, you will add the attributes for your Task entity. Create a `dueDate` attribute using the `Date` data type. You can leave the `dueDate` marked as optional. To go along with the `dueDate`, create a `Boolean isOverdue` attribute. Mark this attribute as Transient because you will dynamically compute its value at runtime, and it won't be stored in the data store.

Now add a required `priority` attribute of type `Integer 16`. You will use this attribute to store the priority of the task. Set the minimum value to 0, which you will use to indicate that there is no priority set, and the maximum to 3, indicating high priority. Set the default value to 0.

Last, add a `String` attribute called `text` that you will use to store the text of the task. Clear the Optional checkbox and set the Default Value to Text. Remember that it is wise to specify a default value when defining required attributes.

The next item that you will add to the Task entity is a `highPriTasks` fetched property. You will use this property in the application to get a list of all tasks that are marked as high priority. So, add a new fetched property to the Task entity called `highPriTasks`. Set the destination entity to Task. Edit the predicate so that your filter criteria is `priority == 3`. Your Task entity should look like Figure 6-10.

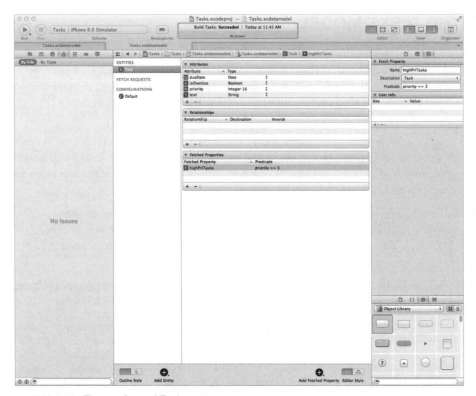

FIGURE 6-10: The configured Task entity

You now need to add a new entity to store the locations where you will perform the task. Add a new entity called Location. Add a String attribute to the Location entity called name. Clear the Optional checkbox because a location without a name would be useless in the application. Set the default value to Location.

Now you will add a relationship to the Task entity to store the location where the user will perform a task. Select the Task entity, and click the plus button below the Relationships table using the table editor style. Set the relationship name to location. Set the Destination to Location.

Next, you will create an inverse relationship in the Location entity to hold a list of tasks for a particular location. Select the Location entity, and add a new relationship called tasks. Set the Destination for this relationship to Task, and set the Inverse relationship to Location. Also, check the To-Many Relationship checkbox because one location could have many tasks assigned to it.

The last thing that you will do is add a fetch request template to the Task entity to retrieve the list of tasks due sooner than the selected task. Select the Task entity and create a new fetch request using the plus icon at the bottom left of the editor pane. Call the fetch request tasksDueSooner. Click the fetch request to define the predicate that you will use. Click the plus (+) on the line that says "All of the following are true" to add your first criterion. Select Expression from the first drop-down list. You want to be able to pass in the due date at runtime and return the tasks that occur before that date. Set your expression to `dueDate < $DUE_DATE`. `DUE_DATE` is the name that you will use in code to replace the variable in the model with an actual location name.

You are finished editing the model. The model should look like Figure 6-11. You can now save the model and quit Xcode.

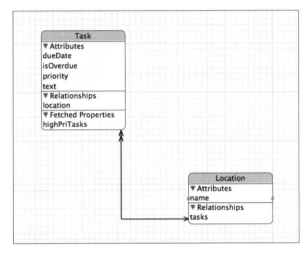

FIGURE 6-11: Tasks data model

MOVING FORWARD

In this chapter, you learned how to express your application's data model graphically using the Xcode data modeling tool. You also laid the framework for building a complete task management application.

By creating custom subclasses of `NSManagedObject` from your model, you now have the ability to access the data in your object model as properties of an Objective-C class. You also now know how to use the Predicate Builder to easily generate complex queries on the data in your model.

You are now ready to combine the knowledge that you learned from the previous chapter on the Core Data architecture with what you learned in this chapter about defining your data model to build a fully featured Core Data application. You will write the code to implement your Task model in the next chapter.

Building a Core Data Application

WHAT'S IN THIS CHAPTER?

➤ Fetching data using the NSFetchedResultsController

➤ Filtering and sorting your data using NSPredicate and NSSortOrdering

➤ Displaying related data using the UITableView

➤ Implementing complex validation and default values using custom subclasses of NSManagedObject

WROX.COM CODE DOWNLOADS FOR THIS CHAPTER

The wrox.com code downloads for this chapter are found at www.wrox.com/remtitle .cgi?isbn=1118391845 on the Download Code tab. The code is in the Chapter 7 download and individually named according to the names throughout the chapter.

In the previous chapter, you explored the Xcode Data Modeling tool and learned how to graphically create a data model. In this chapter, you discover how to build a complete data-driven application using Core Data. You learn how to fetch, filter, and sort your data and display it in a UITableView using the NSFetchedResultsController. You also discover how to modify and delete existing data and take advantage of the relationships that you have defined between your data entities. Finally, you learn how to implement complex validation rules and default values using custom subclasses of NSManagedObject.

I introduced these topics in the Chapter 6. In this chapter, you build a fully functional task manager application while putting the concepts that you learned in the previous chapter into action.

THE TASKS APPLICATION ARCHITECTURE

Before you sit down to start coding a new application, it is good to have an idea of what the application will do and how the application will do it. The client on the project typically determines what the application must do. The client should communicate the desired functionality in the form of user requirements or specifications. Usually, you, as the developer, determine how the software will fulfill these requirements.

The application that you build in this chapter will be a task manager like the one you built in Chapter 4. You will add more functionality to help demonstrate some of the features of Core Data that you learned about in Chapter 5. In this more advanced tasks application, the user should be able to do the following:

➤ Create, edit, and delete tasks

➤ View overdue tasks in red, sort tasks alphabetically in ascending and descending order, and filter the data to view only high-priority tasks

➤ Create task locations, assign a location to a task, and view tasks grouped by their location

➤ Display a list of tasks due sooner than another

The Data Model

The first piece of the application is the data model. You need to design a data model that has the entities and attributes needed to implement the functions that I laid out in the previous section. Fortunately, you already did that in Chapter 6. Figure 7-1 shows the data model you built.

The main entity in this application is the task. Tasks have attributes for due date, priority, and text. There is a transient property, calculated at runtime, that indicates whether a task is overdue. You have also included a fetched property that lists all high-priority tasks. In addition, you have created a relationship to relate a location to a task. Finally, you have added a fetch request to determine tasks that take priority over the selected task.

The other entity is the location. A user can optionally mark a task with a location. Locations have only a name attribute and the task's inverse relationship.

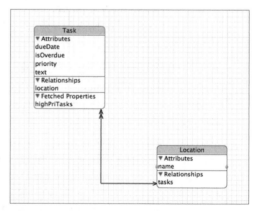

FIGURE 7-1: Tasks application data model

The Class Model

Now that you have a data model, you need to think about how you will design the architecture for the application. The Tasks application that you will build in this chapter consists of a series of table view controllers and regular view controllers that a user will use to view, create, and edit tasks. There will also be custom `NSManagedObject` subclasses that you will use to implement defaulting and data validation.

In Figure 7-2, you can see the class model for the completed Tasks application. The diagram shows that most of the screens for editing individual pieces of data inherit from UITableViewController. The only exception is the EditDateController. I wanted the UIDatePicker to be at the bottom of the screen and not be part of a table. Every other edit screen consists of a table that you use to display the data to be edited or a list of values that the user can choose for fields such as Location and Priority. Editing data in the form of a table should be familiar to you if you have used the Contacts application that comes with the iPhone.

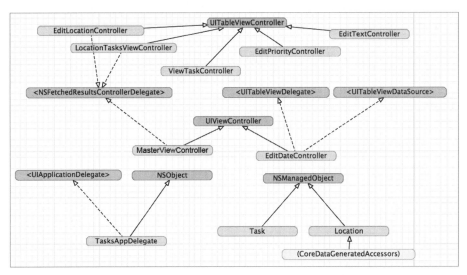

FIGURE 7-2: Tasks application class model

You may have noticed that the MasterViewController is not a UITableViewController. It is a subclass of UIViewController. I did this so that I could embed a UIToolbar at the bottom of the screen for filtering and sorting the data in the table. In summary, any screens that consist solely of a table are subclasses of UITableViewController, and screens that contain other controls in addition to the table are subclasses of UIViewController.

Finally, the Location and Task objects are subclasses of NSManagedObject. You will generate these classes from the data model that you built in Chapter 6. Then you will implement custom functionality in the Task class to create default due dates at runtime and perform single field and multi-field validation.

The User Interface

Now that you have seen the data model and class model for the Tasks application, it is time to look at the user interface. Keep in mind that I designed the interface to provide an example of using Core Data. It is not a model of the most beautiful iOS application ever built, but it demonstrates most of the features of Core Data that you will likely use in your own applications.

Figure 7-3 shows the UI and the process flow of the application on the storyboard. The MasterViewController is the main Tasks screen. This screen displays all the user's tasks. It also provides a toolbar to perform sorting and filtering of high-priority tasks. Finally, there is a button that brings the user to the `LocationTasksViewController`, which displays a list of tasks grouped by location.

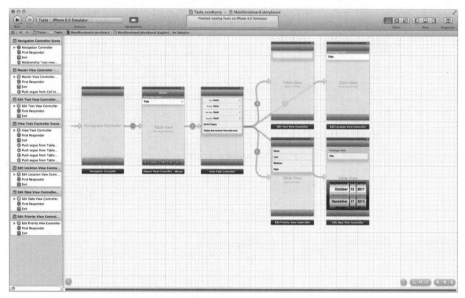

FIGURE 7-3: Tasks application user interface

Tapping the plus button on top of the `MasterViewController` adds a new task and takes the user to the `ViewTaskController`. Likewise, tapping on an existing task takes the user to the `ViewTaskController`. This screen shows the details of the chosen task or the new task. There are also options on this screen to see all high-priority tasks and to see a list of tasks that are due sooner than the currently selected task.

Tapping a row on the `ViewTaskController` takes the user to the appropriate editing screen. Aside from allowing the user to select a location for a task, the location selection screen can create new locations or delete existing locations. You will see each of these screens in full detail as you build the application.

CODING THE APPLICATION

Now that you are familiar with the basic concepts behind the application, it is time to start writing some code.

To complete this application, you need to do the following:

1. Build the `MasterViewController` and its interface using Interface Builder.

2. Generate the `NSManagedObject` subclasses for use with Core Data.

3. Implement the `ViewTaskController` to allow users to create and edit tasks.

4. Build the subscreens used to edit the individual task fields.

5. Implement the filtering and sorting buttons on the toolbar of the `MasterViewController` and the `LocationTasksViewController` used to view tasks grouped by location.

6. Implement the advanced features of custom `NSManagedObjects` in the `Task` object.

When you are finished, you should have a detailed understanding of how to implement many of the most important features of Core Data. In addition, you will have a fully featured Core Data–based task management application that you can use to continue experimenting with the features of Core Data.

MASTERVIEWCONTROLLER AND THE BASIC UI

The first step in creating the Tasks application is to build the `MasterViewController` screen, as shown in Figure 7-4. This is the first screen that the user sees and should contain a list of all the current tasks. There will be a plus button in the navigation bar used to create new tasks. In addition, you need a toolbar at the bottom of the screen to allow the user to filter and sort the tasks, along with a button to allow the user to bring up the group by location view.

Open the Tasks project that you created in the previous chapter. Next, click the `MainStoryboard.storyboard` file to open it with Interface Builder.

You worked with storyboards earlier in the book, so I won't explain them here. Also, this book assumes that you already know how to use Interface Builder to create and edit user interfaces for your iOS applications. If you need a refresher on using Interface Builder, I recommend reading the Xcode 4 User Guide, which you can find at https://developer.apple.com/library/ios/documentation/ ToolsLanguages/Conceptual/Xcode4UserGuide/Xcode4UserGuide.pdf.

FIGURE 7-4: MasterView Controller screen

You now need to add a toolbar and its buttons to the interface. Fortunately, the navigation controller already has a toolbar associated with it; you just need to turn it on. In Interface Builder, click the navigation controller in the Navigation Controller Scene to select it. With the Utilities View open on the left side of Xcode, select the Attributes Inspector. In the Attributes Inspector, find the Shows Toolbar checkbox in the Navigation Controller section, and select it. This shows the toolbar in any views that the navigation controller controls.

Because you do not want to see the toolbar on the detail view, select the detail view controller to remove the toolbar. Once you have the detail view controller selected, use the Attributes Inspector to set the Bottom Bar to None. That removes the toolbar from the detail view.

Next, add five `UIBarButtonItem` objects to the toolbar in the master view controller by dragging them from the object library in the bottom-right corner of the Xcode window and dropping them onto the toolbar. The toolbar should now contain the five buttons. Set the title of each `UIBarButtonItem` to one of the following: All, Location, Hi-Pri, Asc, or Dsc.

The look of the interface is now complete. The next thing you need to do is add appropriate action methods to the `MasterViewController.h` header file. Using the Assistant Editor, open `MasterViewController.h` in the assistant pane next to the storyboard.

When a user clicks one of the buttons in the toolbar, you need to invoke a method in your code. Therefore, the next step is to add the action methods called when the user clicks on the toolbar buttons. You do this by Ctrl-dragging the toolbar buttons from the storyboard and dropping them into the `MasterViewController.h` header file.

Ctrl-drag the All button from the storyboard and drop it into the master view controller header. You should see a pop-up that allows you to connect the button to your code. Change the Connection type to Action. Then set the name to `toolbarFilterAll` and click Connect.

Do the same for the Location and Hi-Pri buttons, and call their action methods `locationButtonPressed` and `toolbarFilterHiPri`, respectively.

Finally, Ctrl-drag the Asc button from the storyboard and drop it into the master view controller header. Change the Connection type to Action, set the name to `toolbarSortOrderChanged`, and click Connect. Do the same for the Dsc button. This connects both sort buttons to the same method to control the sort order.

The `MasterViewController` header file should look like this:

```
#import <UIKit/UIKit.h>

#import <CoreData/CoreData.h>

@interface MasterViewController : UITableViewController
<NSFetchedResultsControllerDelegate>


@property (strong, nonatomic) NSFetchedResultsController *fetchedResultsController;
@property (strong, nonatomic) NSManagedObjectContext *managedObjectContext;

- (IBAction)toolbarFilterHiPri:(id)sender;
- (IBAction)toolbarFilterAll:(id)sender;
- (IBAction)locationButtonPressed:(id)sender;
- (IBAction)toolbarSortOrderChanged:(id)sender;

@end
```

Now that the interface and header are ready, you need to get in and modify the `MasterView Controller.m` implementation file. Although you are not ready to implement the full functionality, you should add stub implementations of the action methods that you declared in the header file. The stubs use the `NSLog` function to log a message when the user presses a button. This is helpful in debugging issues with Interface Builder because it proves that you have correctly linked the buttons in Interface Builder to their action methods in code. On more than one occasion, I have found myself searching for an elusive bug only to realize that I did not correctly hook up the control to the action method. Using this easy method, you can see a message in the console any time a button is pressed. The stub code should look like this:

```objc
- (IBAction)toolbarFilterHiPri:(id)sender {
    NSLog(@"toolbarFilterHiPri");
}

- (IBAction)toolbarFilterAll:(id)sender {
    NSLog(@"toolbarFilterAll");
}

- (IBAction)locationButtonPressed:(id)sender {
    NSLog(@"locationButtonPressed");
}

- (IBAction)toolbarSortOrderChanged:(id)sender {
    NSLog(@"toolbarSortOrderChanged");
}
```

The `MasterViewController` will display data from the `Task` entity. Therefore, you need to modify the `fetchedResultsController` accessor method to use the `Task` entity instead of the default `Event` entity:

```objc
// Edit the entity name as appropriate.
NSEntityDescription *entity =
    [NSEntityDescription entityForName:@"Task"
                inManagedObjectContext:self.managedObjectContext];
```

You also need to change the sort descriptor to use the `Task` entity's `text` attribute instead of `timestamp`:

```objc
// Edit the sort key as appropriate.
NSSortDescriptor *sortDescriptor =
    [[NSSortDescriptor alloc] initWithKey:@"text" ascending:NO];
```

The finished `fetchedResultsController` accessor method should look like this:

```objc
- (NSFetchedResultsController *)fetchedResultsController
{
    if (_fetchedResultsController != nil) {
        return _fetchedResultsController;
    }

    NSFetchRequest *fetchRequest = [[NSFetchRequest alloc] init];
    // Edit the entity name as appropriate.
    NSEntityDescription *entity =
        [NSEntityDescription entityForName:@"Task"
                    inManagedObjectContext:self.managedObjectContext];
    [fetchRequest setEntity:entity];

    // Set the batch size to a suitable number.
    [fetchRequest setFetchBatchSize:20];

    // Edit the sort key as appropriate.
    NSSortDescriptor *sortDescriptor =
        [[NSSortDescriptor alloc] initWithKey:@"text" ascending:NO];
```

```
        NSArray *sortDescriptors = @[sortDescriptor];

        [fetchRequest setSortDescriptors:sortDescriptors];

        // Edit the section name key path and cache name if appropriate.
        // nil for section name key path means "no sections".
        NSFetchedResultsController *aFetchedResultsController =
            [[NSFetchedResultsController alloc]
             initWithFetchRequest:fetchRequest
             managedObjectContext:self.managedObjectContext
             sectionNameKeyPath:nil cacheName:@"Master"];
        aFetchedResultsController.delegate = self;
        self.fetchedResultsController = aFetchedResultsController;

        NSError *error = nil;
        if (![self.fetchedResultsController performFetch:&error]) {
            // Replace this implementation with code to handle the error
            // appropriately.
            // abort() causes the application to generate a crash log and
            // terminate. You should not use this function in a shipping
            // application, although it may be useful during development.
            NSLog(@"Unresolved error %@, %@", error, [error userInfo]);
            abort();
        }

        return _fetchedResultsController;
    }
```

You are finished with the `MasterViewController` for now. You should be able to build and run the application. Verify that you receive no errors or warnings during the build process. Once the application comes up in the simulator, click all the toolbar buttons at the bottom of the screen. Because you added those stub action methods with the `NSLog` statement, you should be able to quickly verify that you have hooked up the buttons properly in Interface Builder by examining the Xcode console. Each time you press a button, the appropriate log message should print.

GENERATING THE MANAGED OBJECT SUBCLASSES

Now that you have built the `MasterViewController`, the next task is to generate your custom `NSManagedObject` subclasses from the data model. Open the `Tasks.xcdatamodel` file.

Select File ⇨ New ⇨ File. In the New File dialog box, you should see an option that is not usually there to create an `NSManagedObject` subclass. Xcode shows this option only when you open this dialog while using the data modeler. After selecting the `NSManagedObject` subclass, click Next. If you didn't have any entities selected in the model, you will see a screen that lets you pick the data model entities for which you want to generate code. Select the Location entity and click Next. In the final dialog, click Create.

Repeat the process to create the `Task` object. You would think that you could just check both the `Task` and `Location` entities the first time through to generate classes for both entities. Generally, you would be correct. However, because the `Task` and `Location` objects depend on one another, if you generate both classes at the same time and Xcode generates the `Task` class first, the tool does not create the correct reference in the Task header for the type (Location*) of the location property. This appears to be a bug in the tool.

When you have finished generating the classes, go back into Xcode. In the left pane, create a new group under Tasks called Managed Objects. Groups are like folders and can help you keep your project organized. Move the Task.m, Task.h, Location.m, and Location.h files into the new Managed Objects group.

Open the header for the Task class, Task.h. Add a property for the highPriTasks fetched property:

```
@property (nonatomic,retain) NSArray* highPriTasks;
```

Finally, in Task.m, add an @dynamic statement for the highPriTasks fetched property to tell the compiler that the framework will dynamically generate this property at runtime:

```
@dynamic highPriTasks;
```

Add a method stub for the isOverdue getter function to return NO. You will implement the actual function later on in the chapter:

```
- (NSNumber*) isOverdue
{
    BOOL isTaskOverdue = NO;

    return [NSNumber numberWithBool:isTaskOverdue];
}
```

ADDING AND VIEWING TASKS

Now that you have built the main screen where a user can add and select tasks, you need to build a way for your users to view and edit tasks. You will implement this functionality with the ViewTaskController. You can see the interface for the ViewTaskController in Figure 7-5.

Building the ViewTaskController

In Xcode, create a new Objective-C class that is a subclass of UITableViewController and call it ViewTaskController. Make sure that "Targeted for iPad" and "With XIB for user interface" are not selected.

In the ViewTaskController.h header file, add #import statements for the Task.h and Location.h headers:

FIGURE 7-5: The ViewTaskController

```
#import "Task.h"
#import "Location.h"
```

In the interface section, add a property variable to hold an instance of the managed object context. Add another property to hold a Task object:

```
@property (nonatomic, retain) NSManagedObjectContext *managedObjectContext;
@property (nonatomic, retain) Task* managedTaskObject;
```

The completed header should look like this:

```
#import <UIKit/UIKit.h>
#import "Task.h"
#import "Location.h"

@interface ViewTaskController : UITableViewController

@property (nonatomic, retain) NSManagedObjectContext *managedObjectContext;
@property (nonatomic, retain) Task* managedTaskObject;


@end
```

You add code to the `MasterViewController` to create an instance of the `ViewTaskController` when a user selects a row in the table or when a user clicks the plus sign to add a new task. You then populate the `ViewTaskController` properties with a pointer to the managed object context and a pointer to the `Task` object that the `ViewTaskController` displays.

This design prevents the `ViewTaskController` from having to know anything about the class that is calling it. The `ViewTaskController` doesn't need to know how to find the `Task` object that it will display. This prevents the `ViewTaskController` from needing a reference to the context. In general, it is a good practice to pass in all the data that an object needs to function. This loosely couples the class to other classes in the application.

Sure, the `ViewTaskController` could have obtained a pointer to the managed object context from the app delegate, but that would tightly couple it to this application. A more generic and reusable design is to build the controller such that it has all the information that it needs to operate without having to look outside the class.

Now that you have created the `ViewTaskController`, you need to add it to the storyboard. You will replace the default detail view controller with your new `ViewTaskController`.

Open the `MainStoryboard.storyboard` storyboard. Drag a new `UITableViewController` from the Objects palette and drop it onto the storyboard. Using the Identity Inspector, change the class of the new table view controller to `ViewTaskController`. Then set the Storyboard ID to `ViewTaskController`. You will use the Storyboard ID to programmatically create an instance of the `ViewTaskController` when the user adds a new task.

Next, delete the detail view controller from the storyboard. You can also remove the `DetailViewController.m` and `DetailViewController.h` files from your project.

The next task that you need to do is to build your view task user interface in the storyboard. First, you will work on the default table view in the View Task Controller Scene. Select the table view in the view task controller. Then use the Attributes Inspector to change the content type to Static Cells. You will use static cells because you know that you will fix the size of this table at six rows. While you are in the Attributes Inspector, change the table style to Grouped.

Next, you will add more rows to the table. You can do this by selecting the table view section from the outline or clicking in the table again in the Interface Builder window. Use the Attributes Inspector to set the number of rows to six.

You now need to change the style of the individual cells. Select the first four rows in the table view and use the Attributes Inspector to set the style to Left Detail. Then select the final two rows and set the style to Basic.

You need to set the Title labels on the left side of each cell to something meaningful. You can either use the outline to select the labels or click the labels in the table view. Set the labels to Text, Priority, Due Date, and Location, as in Figure 7-5. In the bottom two rows, set the cell labels to Hi-Pri Tasks and Tasks due sooner than this one.

You need to create outlets from the text labels in Interface Builder to your `ViewTaskController.h` header file. This allows you to programmatically change the values of the labels at runtime. Use the Assistant editor to open the `ViewTaskController.h` header file in the pane next to Interface Builder. Create outlets for the Text, Priority, Due Date, and Location detail fields by Ctrl-dragging each label and dropping it into the `ViewTaskController.h` header. Name the outlets **taskText**, **taskPriority**, **taskDueDate**, and **taskLocation**, respectively.

Now you need to set up the navigation from the cells in the master view controller to the view task controller. When a user taps a cell in the master view controller, you want to segue to the view task controller with a push segue. So, Ctrl-drag from the prototype cell in the master view controller to the view task controller. Select Push from the pop-up menu to configure the push segue. The last thing that you need to do is set the identifier for your new segue. Click the segue and use the Attributes Inspector to set the identifier to `showViewTaskController`. Your storyboard should look like Figure 7-6.

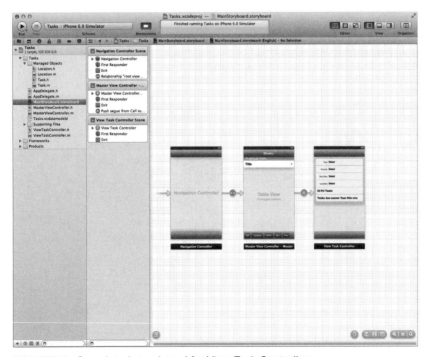

FIGURE 7-6: Completed storyboard for View Task Controller

You are finished working with the `ViewTaskController` in the storyboard, so you can move on to the implementation. Open the `ViewTaskController.m` implementation file. Add a line of code to the `viewDidLoad` method to set the title of the screen. The Nav Bar control displays this title at the top of the screen as well as in the Back button on subsequent screens. The `viewDidLoad` method should look like this:

```
- (void)viewDidLoad
{
    [super viewDidLoad];

    self.navigationItem.title = @"Task Detail";

}
```

Now implement the `viewWillAppear` method and call `[self configureView];` to refresh the data in the table view. The `viewWillAppear` method should look like this:

```
- (void)viewWillAppear:(BOOL)animated {
    [super viewWillAppear:animated];

    // Reload the data for the table to refresh from the context
    [self configureView];

}
```

Because the table contains a static cell layout, you can delete the default implementation of the table view delegate methods `numberOfSectionsInTableView:`, `tableView:numberOfRowsInSection:`, and `tableView:cellForRowAtIndexPath:`.

Finally, you need to implement the `configureView` method. This method, as you can probably guess, will configure the view. It is in this method where you will take the data from the `Task` object and use the outlets to populate the label controls in the table view. Implement the `configureView` method like this:

```
- (void)configureView
{
    if (self.managedTaskObject) {
        // Refresh the context
        [self.managedObjectContext refreshObject:self.managedTaskObject
                                    mergeChanges:YES];
        // Set Task Text
        self.taskText.text = self.managedTaskObject.text;

        // Set Priority Text
        // Get the priority number and convert it to a string
        NSString* priorityString=nil;

        switch ([self.managedTaskObject.priority intValue]) {
            case 0:
                priorityString = @"None";
                break;
            case 1:
                priorityString = @"Low";
```

```
                    break;
            case 2:
                priorityString = @"Medium";
                break;
            case 3:
                priorityString = @"High";
                break;
            default:
                break;
        }
        self.taskPriority.text = priorityString;

        // Set Due Date text
        // Create a date formatter to format the date from the picker
        NSDateFormatter* df = [[NSDateFormatter alloc] init];
        [df setDateStyle:NSDateFormatterLongStyle];
        self.taskDueDate.text = [df stringFromDate:self.managedTaskObject.dueDate ];

        // Set Location text
        Location* locationObject = self.managedTaskObject.location;
        if (locationObject!=nil)
        {
            self.taskLocation.text = locationObject.name;
        }
        else {
            self.taskLocation.text = @"Not Set";

        }
    }
}
```

The code first checks to make sure that you have a `Task` object from which you will get the data that you need to populate the labels. Next, the code calls the `refreshObject:mergeChanges:` method. This method updates the properties of the managed object from the latest values in the persistent store. By default, Core Data will cache the managed object. So, if the managed object gets modified somewhere else, this cache could be outdated. You can call `refreshObject:mergeChanges:` to ensure that you are using the most up-to-date version of the managed object.

Then the code gets the `text` property from the managed `Task` object and uses it to set the text of the `taskText` label.

The next block of code converts the integer priority from the `Task` object into a priority string that you display in the table view.

Next, the code builds the Due Date value. The code uses an `NSDateFormatter` to convert the `NSDate` object stored in the managed object into a string. You can use one of the predefined formats or define your own. For more information on using `NSDateFormatter`, look at the Xcode SDK documentation or go to `http://developer.apple.com/iphone/library/documentation/Cocoa/Reference/Foundation/Classes/NSDateFormatter_Class/Reference/Reference.html`.

The final bit of code builds the Location label. The code tries to get a `Location` object from the `Task`'s `location` property. The code displays the name property of the `Location` object, if it exists. If not, the code displays "Not Set."

Changes to the MasterViewController

Now that you have built the `ViewTaskController`, you need to make some changes to the `MasterViewController` to access the new screen.

First, you will configure the `MasterViewController` navigation bar. In the `viewDidLoad` method of the `MasterViewController.m` implementation file, remove the line:

```
self.navigationItem.leftBarButtonItem = self.editButtonItem;
```

This screen will not be using the Edit button.

At the end of `viewDidLoad`, add the following line of code to set the title of the screen in the navigation bar:

```
self.title = @"Tasks";
```

You also need to add `#import` statements to import the headers for the `Location` and `Task` objects as well as the `ViewTaskController`. Add the following `#import` statements to the top of the `MasterViewController` implementation file:

```
#import "ViewTaskController.h"
#import "Location.h"
#import "Task.h"
```

Also, remove the `#import` for the `DetailViewController.h` because you have removed the `DetailViewController` from your project.

Next, you need to implement the `insertNewObject` method. This method creates a new `Task` object and then passes control off to the `ViewTaskController` to edit the new task. Tapping the plus button in the navigation bar calls the `insertNewObject` method. Here is the `insertNewObject` method:

```
- (void)insertNewObject:(id)sender {

    NSManagedObjectContext *context =
        [self.fetchedResultsController managedObjectContext];


    NSEntityDescription *entity =
        [[self.fetchedResultsController fetchRequest] entity];
    Task *newTask =
        [NSEntityDescription insertNewObjectForEntityForName:[entity name]
                                      inManagedObjectContext:context];

    // Save the context.
    NSError *error = nil;
    if (![context save:&error]) {
        // Replace this implementation with code to handle the error
        // appropriately.
        // abort() causes the application to generate a crash log and terminate.
        // You should not use this function in a shipping application, although
        // it may be useful during development.
        NSLog(@"Unresolved error %@, %@", error, [error userInfo]);
```

```
        abort();
    }


    ViewTaskController* taskController =
        [[ViewTaskController alloc] initWithStyle:UITableViewStyleGrouped];
    taskController.managedTaskObject=newTask;
    taskController.managedObjectContext = context;


    [self.navigationController pushViewController:taskController animated:YES];


}
```

This method is straightforward. First, you obtain a reference to the `managedObjectContext` from the `fetchedResultsController`. Then you get the entity description for the entity from the fetch request. Next, you use the entity and the context to create an instance of the managed `Task` object.

After you create your new `Task` object, you save the context.

Once you save the context, you create an instance of the `ViewTaskController` and populate its `managedTaskObject` and `managedObjectContext` properties. Last, you push the new `ViewTaskController` onto the navigation stack for display.

The last change in the `MasterViewController` is to implement the table view methods. You can leave the default `numberOfSectionsInTableView:`, `tableView:numberOfRowsInSection:`, `tableView:commitEditingStyle:forRowAtIndexPath:`, and `tableView:canMoveRowAtIndexPath:` methods.

You do need to modify the implementation of the `configureCell:atIndexPath:` method to display the text property of the `Task` object for the row. You will also add some code to check the `isOverdue` transient property and display overdue tasks in red. Here is the code for `configureCell:atIndexPath:`:

```
- (UITableViewCell *)tableView:(UITableView *)tableView
        cellForRowAtIndexPath:(NSIndexPath *)indexPath {

    UITableViewCell *cell =
        [tableView dequeueReusableCellWithIdentifier:@"Cell"
                                      forIndexPath:indexPath];

    [self configureCell:cell atIndexPath:indexPath];

    return cell;
}
- (void)configureCell:(UITableViewCell *)cell atIndexPath:(NSIndexPath *)indexPath
{

    // Configure the cell.
    Task *managedTaskObject =
        [self.fetchedResultsController objectAtIndexPath:indexPath];

    cell.textLabel.text = managedTaskObject.text;

    // Change the text color if the task is overdue.
```

```
        if (managedTaskObject.isOverdue==[NSNumber numberWithBool: YES])
        {
            cell.textLabel.textColor = [UIColor redColor];
        }
        else {
            cell.textLabel.textColor = [UIColor blackColor];
        }

    }
```

You should be familiar with how this code works. The beginning of the `tableView:
cellForRowAtIndexPath:` method tries to dequeue a cell, and if it cannot, it creates a new one.
Next, the code calls `configureCell:atIndexPath:`. This method gets the `Task` object from the
`fetchedResultsController` that corresponds to the requested cell. Then the cell's `textLabel` is set
with the text from the `Task` object. Finally, you use the value of the `Task`'s `isOverdue` property to
determine the color of the text.

The final task is to modify the `prepareForSegue:sender:` method to pass the correct data to the
`ViewTaskController` in the segue. Implement the `prepareForSegue:sender:` like this:

```
- (void)prepareForSegue:(UIStoryboardSegue *)segue sender:(id)sender
{
    if ([[segue identifier] isEqualToString:@"showViewTaskController"]) {
        NSIndexPath *indexPath = [self.tableView indexPathForSelectedRow];
        Task *taskObject = [[self fetchedResultsController] objectAtIndexPath:indexPath];

        ViewTaskController* viewTaskController = [segue destinationViewController];
        viewTaskController.managedObjectContext = self.managedObjectContext;
        viewTaskController.managedTaskObject=taskObject;
    }
}
```

First, you test to make sure that you are performing the `showViewTaskController` segue. Then you
get the `Task` object that the user wants to view from the fetched results controller. Next, you get a
reference to the view task controller that the segue is going to show. Finally, you set the context and
task properties on the view task controller.

Build and run the application. You should not get errors or warnings. The application should now
allow you to create new default tasks and then navigate to the `ViewTaskController` screen. You
should also be able to select tasks in the `Tasks` screen and view them in the `ViewTaskController`
screen.

BUILDING THE EDITING CONTROLLERS

Your Tasks application now has the capability to create new tasks and view existing tasks. Although
there is some decent functionality there, the application is useless without being able to edit the
contents of your tasks. In this section, you implement the screens shown in Figure 7-7. These screens
allow the user to edit each piece of data in a task. Create a new group under Tasks called Sub
Controllers to hold all your edit controller code.

(a) Text Editing Screen - EditTextController

(b) Priority Selection Screen - EditPriorityController

(c) Location Selection Screen - EditLocationController

(d) Date Editing Screen - EditDateController

FIGURE 7-7: Tasks data editing screens

Editing Text with the EditTextViewController

The EditTextViewController screen, as you can see in Figure 7-8, allows the user to edit the text used in the Task and Location objects. The screen consists of a UITableView with one cell. Embedded in that cell is a UITextField. This design is consistent with the behavior of the text-editing screens in the stock iOS applications such as Contacts.

In the new Sub Controllers group, create a new UITableViewController without XIB called EditTextViewController. Open the

FIGURE 7-8: EditText-
ViewController screen

`EditTextViewController.h` header file and add properties for an `NSManagedObject` and `NSManagedObjectContext`:

```
@property (nonatomic, retain) NSManagedObjectContext* managedObjectContext;
@property (nonatomic, retain) NSManagedObject* managedObject;
```

The parent screen sets the managed object, and the context before it segues to the `EditTextViewController`.

You also need to add a property to hold an `NSString*` called `keyString`. Because this screen supports editing both the text property of the `Task` object and the name property of the `Location` object, you will use key-value coding (KVC) to take the text entered on the screen and update the managed object. This is also the reason that the screen accepts an `NSManagedObject` instead of one of your custom subclasses like `Task` or `Location`. That way, the screen is generic enough to edit text fields on any managed object and is not limited to editing only `Task` or `Location` objects.

Finally, add an outlet property for the `UITextField` that you will embed in the table view:

```
@property (weak, nonatomic) IBOutlet UITextField *textField;
```

Your finished header file should look like this:

```
#import <UIKit/UIKit.h>

@interface EditTextViewController : UITableViewController

@property (nonatomic, strong) NSManagedObjectContext *managedObjectContext;
@property (nonatomic, strong) NSManagedObject* managedObject;
@property (nonatomic, strong) NSString* keyString;

@property (weak, nonatomic) IBOutlet UITextField *textField;


@end
```

Now that you are finished with the header, you are ready to add the `EditTextViewController` to the storyboard. Open the `MainStoryboard.storyboard` storyboard. Drag a new `UITableViewController` from the Objects palette and drop it onto the storyboard. Using the Identity Inspector, change the class of the new table view controller to `EditTextViewController`. Then set the Storyboard ID to `EditTextViewController` as well. You will use this identifier when you need to transition to the edit text view in code.

You now need to add your `UITextField` to the `EditTextViewController` so that a user can use the controller to enter and edit text. Select the table view in the edit text view controller. Then use the Attributes Inspector to change the content type to Static Cells. You will use static cells because you know that this table contains only one row. While you are in the Attributes Inspector, change the table style to Grouped.

Next, you will remove rows from the table. You can do this by selecting the table view section from the outline or clicking in the table again in the Interface Builder window. Use the Attributes Inspector to set the number of rows to 1.

Now you can add the `UITextField` to the `EditTextViewController` by dragging a `UITextField` from the Objects palette and dropping it into the table cell. Resize the text field to fill the entire table cell. You can also use the Attributes Inspector to hide the borders of the text field by selecting the dotted border style.

You need to create an outlet from the text field in Interface Builder to your `EditTextViewController.h` header file. This allows you to programmatically change and read the value of the text box at runtime. Use the Assistant editor to open the `EditTextViewController.h` header file in the pane next to Interface Builder. Connect the text view to the `IBOutlet` in your header by Ctrl-dragging the text field and dropping it into the `EditTextViewController.h` header.

Now you need to set up the navigation from the Text cell in the view task controller to the edit text view controller. When a user taps a text field in the view task controller, you want to segue to the edit text view controller with a push segue. So Ctrl-drag from the Text cell in the view task controller to the edit text view controller. Select Push from the pop-up menu to configure the push segue. You need to set the identifier for this segue. Click the segue and use the Attributes Inspector to set the identifier to `showEditTextViewController`.

You are finished working with the `EditTextViewController` in the storyboard, so it's time to move on to the implementation. Open the `EditTextViewController.m` implementation file. Because the table contains a static cell layout, you can delete the default implementation of the table view delegate methods `numberOfSectionsInTableView:`, `tableView:numberOfRowsInSection:`, and `tableView:cellForRowAtIndexPath:`.

Next, implement the `configureView` method that configures the view with the managed object that the view controller receives from its caller:

```
- (void)configureView
{
    if (self.managedObject) {
        self.textField.text = [self.managedObject valueForKey:self.keyString];
        self.textField.clearsOnBeginEditing=YES;
    }
}
```

You now need to add code to the `viewDidLoad` method to add a Save button to the navigation bar and to call `configureView`:

```
- (void)viewDidLoad
{
    [super viewDidLoad];

    // Add the Save button
    UIBarButtonItem* saveButton =[[UIBarButtonItem alloc]
        initWithBarButtonSystemItem:UIBarButtonSystemItemSave
                            target:self
                            action:@selector (saveButtonPressed:)];

    self.navigationItem.rightBarButtonItem = saveButton;

    [self configureView];

}
```

The first thing you need to do in `viewDidLoad` is call `super viewDidLoad`. In general, you want to call the superclass version of a method before you do anything in your method to ensure that everything in the superclass is set up properly before you begin your work.

Next, you move on to create the Save button and set it as the `rightBarButtonItem` in the navigation bar. Finally, you call the `configureView` method that sets up the view based on the data in the managed object.

The next task is to implement the `saveButtonPressed:` method. Pressing the Save button in the navigation bar calls the `saveButtonPressed:` method. In this method, you will get the text from the text field and use KVC to set the appropriate key in the managed object. Remember that the previous screen set the `keyString` before displaying the `EditTextViewController`. Then you save the context and pop the view controller off the navigation stack. Here is the code:

```
- (void) saveButtonPressed: (id) sender
{

    // Configure the managed object.
    // Notice how you use KVC here because you might get a Task or a Location
    // in this generic text editor.
    [self.managedObject setValue:self.textField.text forKey:self.keyString];

    // Save the context.
    NSError *error = nil;
    if (![self.managedObjectContext save:&error]) {
        NSLog(@"Unresolved error %@, %@", error, [error userInfo]);
        abort();
    }

    // Pop the view.
    [self.navigationController popViewControllerAnimated:YES];

}
```

The final task is to write the `prepareForSegue:sender:` method in the `ViewTaskController`. You will use this method to pass the task text data to the `EditTextViewController` in the segue.

First, you need to add an `#import` directive to import the `EditTextViewController.h` header:

```
#import "EditTextViewController.h"
```

Then you can implement `prepareForSegue:sender:` like this:

```
- (void)prepareForSegue:(UIStoryboardSegue *)segue sender:(id)sender
{
    if ([[segue identifier] isEqualToString:@"showEditTextViewController"]) {
        EditTextViewController* EditTextViewController =
            [segue destinationViewController];
        EditTextViewController.managedObjectContext = self.managedObjectContext;
        EditTextViewController.managedObject=self.managedTaskObject;
        EditTextViewController.keyString=@"text";
    }
}
```

Test to make sure that you are performing the showEditTextViewController segue. Then set the context and set the keyString to specify which field in the managed object the edit text view controller should edit.

Build and run the program. You should now be able to create a task or select an existing task. From the view task screen, you should also be able to tap on the text of a task, navigate to the EditTextViewController, and edit the text of your task. Tapping the Save button should save the edited text and pop the view controller, showing your edited task text on the ViewTaskController.

Setting Priorities with the EditPriorityViewController

The EditPriorityViewController screen, which you can see in Figure 7-9, allows the user to choose the priority for a task. Again, you will implement the screen as a table view. This time, there will be a row for each priority level. In the Sub Controllers group, create a new UITableViewController without a NIB called EditPriorityViewController.

In the header file, you need properties for a Task object and the context. You also need to add an #import directive for the Task.h header file. Your header should look like this:

FIGURE 7-9: The EditPriorityViewController

```
#import <UIKit/UIKit.h>
#import "Task.h"

@interface EditPriorityViewController : UITableViewController

@property (nonatomic, retain) Task* managedTaskObject;
@property (nonatomic, retain) NSManagedObjectContext *managedObjectContext;

@end
```

That's all that you need to do with the header. Now you are ready to add the EditPriorityViewController to the storyboard. Open the MainStoryboard.storyboard storyboard. Drag a new UITableViewController from the Objects palette and drop it onto the storyboard. Using the Identity Inspector, change the class of the new table view controller to EditPriorityViewController.

Select the table view in the edit priority view controller. Then use the Attributes Inspector to change the content type to Static Cells. You will use static cells because you know that this table will always contain four rows. While you are in the Attributes Inspector, change the table style to Grouped.

Next, add an additional row to the table. You can do this by selecting the table view section from the outline or clicking in the table in the Interface Builder window. Use the Attributes Inspector to set the number of rows to 4.

Now you need to set the text in each of the table cells. Select all four cells and use the Attributes Inspector to set the style of the cells to Basic. Then change the title of the label in each cell to None, Low, Medium, and High, as in Figure 7-9.

You need to create outlets from the table view cells in Interface Builder to your EditPriorityViewController.h header file. This allows you to programmatically access the cells to add checkmarks for the selected cell at runtime. Use the Assistant editor to open the EditPriorityViewController.h header file in the pane next to Interface Builder. Create outlets for the None, Low, Medium, and High cells by Ctrl-dragging each cell and dropping it into the EditPriorityViewController.h header. Name the outlets priNone, priLow, priMedium, and priHigh, respectively. The completed EditPriorityViewController header should look like this:

```
#import <UIKit/UIKit.h>
#import "Task.h"

@interface EditPriorityViewController : UITableViewController

@property (nonatomic, retain) Task* managedTaskObject;
@property (nonatomic, retain) NSManagedObjectContext *managedObjectContext;
@property (weak, nonatomic) IBOutlet UITableViewCell *priNone;
@property (weak, nonatomic) IBOutlet UITableViewCell *priLow;
@property (weak, nonatomic) IBOutlet UITableViewCell *priMedium;
@property (weak, nonatomic) IBOutlet UITableViewCell *priHigh;

@end
```

Now you need to set up the navigation from the Priority cell in the view task controller to the edit priority view controller. When a user taps the Priority field in the view task controller, you want to segue to the edit priority view controller with a push segue. So Ctrl-drag from the Priority cell in the view task controller to the edit priority view controller. Select Push from the pop-up menu to configure the push segue. You need to set the identifier for this segue. Click the segue and use the Attributes Inspector to set the identifier to showEditPriorityViewController.

You are finished working with the EditPriorityViewController in the storyboard, so it's time to move on to the implementation. Open the EditPriorityViewController.m implementation file. Because the table contains a static cell layout, you can delete the default implementation of the table view delegate methods numberOfSectionsInTableView:, tableView:numberOfRowsInSection:, and tableView:cellForRowAtIndexPath:.

Next, implement the configureView method that configures the view with the managed object that the view controller receives from its caller:

```
- (void)configureView
{
    if (self.managedTaskObject) {

        switch ([self.managedTaskObject.priority intValue]) {
            case 0:
                self.priNone.accessoryType=UITableViewCellAccessoryCheckmark;
                break;
            case 1:
                self.priLow.accessoryType=UITableViewCellAccessoryCheckmark;
```

```
                    break;
                case 2:
                    self.priMedium.accessoryType=UITableViewCellAccessoryCheckmark;
                    break;
                case 3:
                    self.priHigh.accessoryType=UITableViewCellAccessoryCheckmark;
                    break;
                default:
                    break;

        }
    }
}
```

In the `configureView` method, the code determines which cell to check based on the data in the `Task` object. The code uses the outlets that you created to each cell and sets the cell's `accessoryType` to `UITableViewCellAccessoryCheckmark`, which displays a checkmark next to the currently chosen priority for the task.

You now need to add code to the `viewDidLoad` method to call `configureView`:

```
- (void)viewDidLoad
{
    [super viewDidLoad];

    [self configureView];

}
```

When a user taps a row, you need to save that selection in the `Task` object. You will do that in the `tableView:didSelectRowAtIndexPath:` method:

```
- (void)tableView:(UITableView *)tableView
didSelectRowAtIndexPath:(NSIndexPath *)indexPath {
    // Deselect the currently selected row according to the HIG.
    [tableView deselectRowAtIndexPath:indexPath animated:NO];

    // Configure the managed object
    self.managedTaskObject.priority=[NSNumber numberWithInt:indexPath.row];

    // Save the context.
    NSError *error = nil;
    if (![self.managedObjectContext save:&error]) {
        // There was an error validating the date.
        // Display error information.

        NSLog(@"Unresolved error %@, %@", error, [error userInfo]);

        UIAlertView* alert = [[UIAlertView alloc]
                initWithTitle:@"Invalid Due Date"
                message:[[error userInfo] valueForKey:@"ErrorString"]
                delegate:nil cancelButtonTitle:@"OK" otherButtonTitles:nil ];
        [alert show];

        // Roll back the context to
```

```
        // revert to the old priority.
        [self.managedObjectContext rollback];


    }
    else {
        // Pop the view.
        [self.navigationController popViewControllerAnimated:YES];

    }
}
```

The first thing that this method does is deselect the selected row, as I explained in the previous section.

The next line sets the `Task` object's Priority field to the priority level selected on the screen. Then the code saves the context. Because you are going to add a validation rule that includes the priority and a date, there is a possibility that the new priority could fail the date validation. If the validation fails, the save method will fail also, so you need to roll the context back to its state before the failed save. If the save method fails, you revert the priority to its original state using the `rollback` method of the context. The `rollback` method undoes all changes to the context that have not yet been committed with a successful save call. If an error occurs, such as a validation failure, you show the user an alert to inform him that a problem has occurred. If there is no problem, the code pops the view controller from the stack.

The final task is to modify the `prepareForSegue:sender:` method in the `ViewTaskController`. You will use this method to pass the task text data to the `EditPriorityViewController` in the segue.

First, you will need to add an `#import` directive to import the `EditPriorityViewController.h` header:

```
#import "EditPriorityViewController.h"
```

Then modify the `prepareForSegue:sender:` method to handle the case where you are using the `showEditPriorityViewController` segue like this:

```
- (void)prepareForSegue:(UIStoryboardSegue *)segue sender:(id)sender
{
    if ([[segue identifier] isEqualToString:@"showEditTextViewController"]) {
        EditTextViewController* EditTextViewController =
            [segue destinationViewController];
        EditTextViewController.managedObjectContext = self.managedObjectContext;
        EditTextViewController.managedObject=self.managedTaskObject;
        EditTextViewController.keyString=@"text";
    }
    else if ([[segue identifier] isEqualToString:@"showEditPriorityViewController"]) {
        EditPriorityViewController* editPriorityViewController =
            [segue destinationViewController];
        editPriorityViewController.managedObjectContext = self.managedObjectContext;
        editPriorityViewController.managedTaskObject=self.managedTaskObject;
    }
}
```

Build and run the program. You should now be able to view and modify the priority for your tasks using the `EditPriorityViewController`.

Adding and Editing Locations with the EditLocationViewController

The user navigates to the `EditLocationViewController` by tapping the location cell on the `ViewTaskController`. The `EditLocationViewController`, as shown in Figure 7-10, allows the user to select a location, add new locations, and delete existing locations. To create the `EditLocationViewController`, create a new `UITableViewController` without a NIB called `EditLocationViewController`.

Modify your new header file properties to hold the context and `Task` objects that the parent screen configures. You also need to add a property for the `NSFetchedResultsController` to display your location list. In addition, you need to add `#import` directives for the `Task` and `Location` header files. The completed header file should look like this:

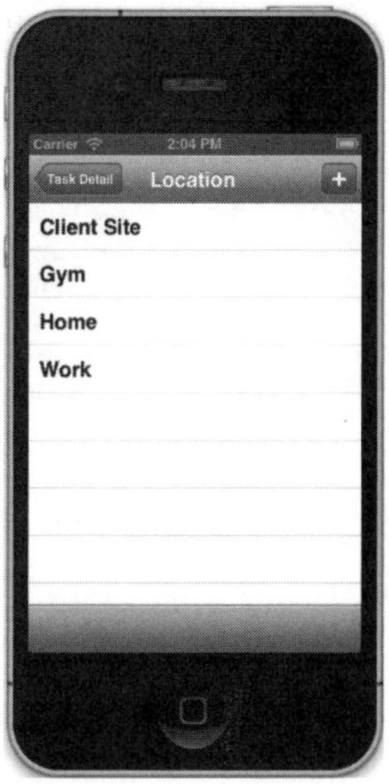

FIGURE 7-10: The EditLocation ViewController

```
#import <UIKit/UIKit.h>
#import "Task.h"
#import "Location.h"

@interface EditLocationViewController : UITableViewController
    <NSFetchedResultsControllerDelegate>

@property (nonatomic, retain) NSFetchedResultsController
    *fetchedResultsController;
@property (nonatomic, retain) NSManagedObjectContext *managedObjectContext;
@property (nonatomic, retain) Task* managedTaskObject;

@end
```

You're finished with the header, so now you need to add the `EditLocationViewController` to the storyboard. Open the `MainStoryboard.storyboard` storyboard. Drag a new `UITableViewController` from the Objects palette and drop it onto the storyboard. Using the Identity Inspector, change the class of the new table view controller to `EditLocationViewController`.

You need to configure the prototype cell so the table view knows how to display cells. Select the prototype cell. Then, using the Attributes Inspector, set the cell style to Basic. Next, set the reuse identifier to Cell.

Now you need to set up the navigation from the Location cell in the view task controller to the edit location view controller. When a user taps the Location field in the view task controller, you want to segue to the edit location view controller with a push segue. So Ctrl-drag from the Location cell in the view task controller to the edit location view controller. Select Push from the pop-up menu to configure the push segue. You need to set the identifier for this segue. Click the segue and use the Attributes Inspector to set the identifier to `showEditLocationViewController`.

Now you are ready to work with the `EditLocationViewController.m` implementation file. First, implement the `viewDidLoad` method:

```
- (void)viewDidLoad {
    [super viewDidLoad];

    // Set up the Add button.
    UIBarButtonItem *addButton = [[UIBarButtonItem alloc]
                        initWithBarButtonSystemItem:UIBarButtonSystemItemAdd
                        target:self action:@selector(insertNewLocation)];

    self.navigationItem.rightBarButtonItem = addButton;

    NSError* error;

    if (![self.fetchedResultsController performFetch:&error]) {
        NSLog(@"Unresolved error %@, %@", error, [error userInfo]);
        abort();
    }

    // Set the title to display in the navigation bar.
    self.title = @"Location";

}
```

This code creates the Add button and sets it to call the `insertNewLocation` method. It then appends the Add button to the navigation bar. Next, you tell the fetched results controller to fetch its data. Finally, you set the title of the screen to Location.

Now you will build the `insertNewLocation` method that runs when the user taps the Add button that you created in `viewDidLoad`. This method adds a new `Location` to the context and pushes the text controller onto the navigation stack to allow the user to edit the location name. Because you will be creating an instance of the `EditTextViewController`, you need to import its header. Add the line to import the header at the top of the implementation file:

```
#import "EditTextViewController.h"
```

Here is the `insertNewLocation` method:

```
- (void)insertNewLocation {

    NSManagedObjectContext *context = self.managedObjectContext;

    Location *newLocation =
    [NSEntityDescription insertNewObjectForEntityForName:@"Location"
                            inManagedObjectContext:context];

    UIStoryboard *sb = [UIStoryboard
                    storyboardWithName:@"MainStoryboard" bundle:nil];

    EditTextViewController* textController =
    [sb instantiateViewControllerWithIdentifier:@"EditTextViewController"];


    textController.managedObject=newLocation;
```

```
textController.managedObjectContext = self.managedObjectContext;
textController.keyString=@"name";

[self.navigationController pushViewController:textController animated:YES];

}
```

This code uses the context to create a new Location object. Then it uses the storyboard to instantiate an EditTextViewController. This bit of code demonstrates how to programmatically create an instance of a view controller that you have built graphically in Interface Builder. Finally, the code configures the edit text view controller and pushes it onto the navigation stack for display.

Next, implement the fetched results controller accessor method to fetch the Location entities and sort them in ascending order by name:

```
- (NSFetchedResultsController *)fetchedResultsController {

    if (_fetchedResultsController != nil) {
        return _fetchedResultsController;
    }

    // Set up the fetched results controller.
    // Create the fetch request for the entity.
    NSFetchRequest *fetchRequest = [[NSFetchRequest alloc] init];
    // Edit the entity name as appropriate.
    NSEntityDescription *entity =
    [NSEntityDescription
     entityForName:@"Location"
     inManagedObjectContext:self.managedObjectContext];
    [fetchRequest setEntity:entity];

    // Edit the sort key as appropriate.
    NSSortDescriptor *sortDescriptor =
    [[NSSortDescriptor alloc]
     initWithKey:@"name"
     ascending:YES];
    NSArray *sortDescriptors = [[NSArray alloc]
                                initWithObjects:sortDescriptor, nil];

    [fetchRequest setSortDescriptors:sortDescriptors];

    // Edit the section name key path and cache name if appropriate.
    // nil for section name key path means "no sections."
    NSFetchedResultsController *aFetchedResultsController =
    [[NSFetchedResultsController alloc]
     initWithFetchRequest:fetchRequest
     managedObjectContext:self.managedObjectContext
     sectionNameKeyPath:nil cacheName:nil];
    aFetchedResultsController.delegate = self;
    _fetchedResultsController = aFetchedResultsController;

    return _fetchedResultsController;
}
```

Implement the `controllerDidChangeContent` delegate method to reload the table data:

```
// NSFetchedResultsControllerDelegate method to notify the delegate
// that all section and object changes have been processed.
- (void)controllerDidChangeContent:(NSFetchedResultsController *)controller {

    [self.tableView reloadData];
}
```

Notice that you need to use the `_fetchedResultsController` instance variable instead of `self.fetchedResultsController` in the accessor method because you are calling the accessor method when you use `self.fetchedResultsController`. If you used `self.fetchedResultsController` in the accessor, you would create an infinite loop.

Change the `numberOfSectionsInTableView` and `tableView:numberOfRowsInSection:` methods to use the `fetchedResultsController`:

```
- (NSInteger)numberOfSectionsInTableView:(UITableView *)tableView {
    return [[self.fetchedResultsController sections] count];
}

// Customize the number of rows in the table view.
- (NSInteger)tableView:(UITableView *)tableView
 numberOfRowsInSection:(NSInteger)section {

    id <NSFetchedResultsSectionInfo> sectionInfo =
    [[self.fetchedResultsController sections] objectAtIndex:section];
    return [sectionInfo numberOfObjects];
}
```

Now implement the `tableView:cellForRowAtIndexPath:` method to show the locations from the fetched results controller:

```
// Customize the appearance of table view cells.
- (UITableViewCell *)tableView:(UITableView *)tableView
        cellForRowAtIndexPath:(NSIndexPath *)indexPath {

    static NSString *CellIdentifier = @"Cell";

    UITableViewCell *cell =
    [tableView dequeueReusableCellWithIdentifier:CellIdentifier];
    if (cell == nil) {
        cell = [[UITableViewCell alloc]
                initWithStyle:UITableViewCellStyleDefault
                reuseIdentifier:CellIdentifier];
    }

    Location *managedLocationObject =
    [self.fetchedResultsController objectAtIndexPath:indexPath];

    // If the location in the task object is the same as the location object
    // draw the checkmark.
    if (self.managedTaskObject.location == managedLocationObject)
    {
```

```
        cell.accessoryType=UITableViewCellAccessoryCheckmark;

    }

    cell.textLabel.text = managedLocationObject.name;

    return cell;
}
```

You can see that the code does the usual cell set up and dequeuing. Then it obtains a `Location` object for the cell from the `fetchedResultsController`. The code then checks to see if the location that it will use is also the location in the `Task`. If it is, the code displays the checkmark accessory for the cell. You use the `name` property of the `Location` object as the cell text.

Next, you need to implement `tableView:didSelectRowAtIndexPath:` to save the selected location:

```
- (void)tableView:(UITableView *)tableView
didSelectRowAtIndexPath:(NSIndexPath *)indexPath {

    // Deselect the currently selected row according to the HIG.
    [tableView deselectRowAtIndexPath:indexPath animated:NO];

    // Set the task's location to the chosen location.
    Location *newLocationObject =
    [self.fetchedResultsController objectAtIndexPath:indexPath];

    self.managedTaskObject.location=newLocationObject;

    // Save the context.
    NSError *error = nil;

    if (![self.managedObjectContext save:&error]) {
        NSLog(@"Unresolved error %@, %@", error, [error userInfo]);
        abort();
    }
    else {

        // Pop the view.
        [self.navigationController popViewControllerAnimated:YES];
    }
}
```

This code gets the selected `Location` object from the `fetchedResultsController`, sets the location in the `Task` object, saves the context, and pops the view from the navigation stack.

To allow the user to delete locations, uncomment and implement the `tableView:commitEditingStyle:` method:

```
// Override to support editing the table view.
- (void)tableView:(UITableView *)tableView
commitEditingStyle:(UITableViewCellEditingStyle)editingStyle
forRowAtIndexPath:(NSIndexPath *)indexPath {

    if (editingStyle == UITableViewCellEditingStyleDelete) {
        // Delete the managed object for the given index path.
```

```
NSManagedObjectContext *context =
[self.fetchedResultsController managedObjectContext];

[context deleteObject:[self.fetchedResultsController
                          objectAtIndexPath:indexPath]];

// Save the context.
NSError *error = nil;
if (![context save:&error]) {
    NSLog(@"Unresolved error %@, %@", error, [error userInfo]);
    abort();
}
        }
    }
}
```

This code enables the delete editing style that displays the Delete button when a user swipes across a row. The code then gets the context, deletes the Location that the user selected, and saves the context.

The final task is to modify the prepareForSegue:sender: method in the ViewTaskController. You will use this method to pass the task data to the EditLocationViewController in the segue.

First, you will need to add an #import directive to import the EditLocationViewController.h header:

```
#import "EditLocationViewController.h"
```

Then you can modify the prepareForSegue:sender: method to handle the case where you are using the showEditLocationViewController segue like this:

```
- (void)prepareForSegue:(UIStoryboardSegue *)segue sender:(id)sender
{
    if ([[segue identifier] isEqualToString:@"showEditTextViewController"]) {
        EditTextViewController* EditTextViewController =
            [segue destinationViewController];
        EditTextViewController.managedObjectContext = self.managedObjectContext;
        EditTextViewController.managedObject=self.managedTaskObject;
        EditTextViewController.keyString=@"text";
    }
    else if ([[segue identifier] isEqualToString:@"showEditPriorityViewController"]) {
        EditPriorityViewController* editPriorityViewController =
            [segue destinationViewController];
        editPriorityViewController.managedObjectContext = self.managedObjectContext;
        editPriorityViewController.managedTaskObject=self.managedTaskObject;
    }
    else if ([[segue identifier] isEqualToString:@"showEditLocationViewController"]) {
        EditLocationViewController* editLocationViewController =
            [segue destinationViewController];
        editLocationViewController.managedObjectContext = self.managedObjectContext;
        editLocationViewController.managedTaskObject=self.managedTaskObject;
    }

}
```

Build and run the program. You should now be able to view and modify the location for your tasks using the `EditLocationViewController` and create new locations as well.

Modifying Dates with the EditDateController

The last edit controller to implement is the `EditDateViewController`, which you can see in Figure 7-11. Like the `MasterViewController`, you need to create the interface for this controller using Interface Builder and the storyboard because the screen must hold a `UIDatePicker` control in addition to the table view that displays the selected date.

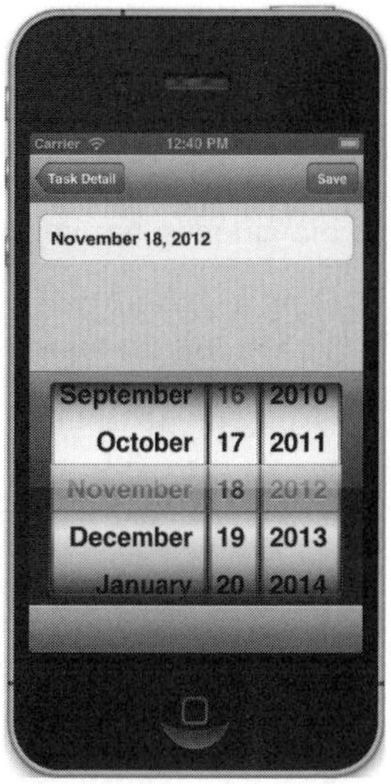

Create a new `UIViewController` subclass called `EditDateViewController`. Make sure you specify `UIViewController` as your subclass because the Subclass of drop-down list defaults to the last class you used, which was `UITableViewController`.

In the `EditDateViewController.h` header file, add an `#import` statement for your `Task` object:

```
#import "Task.h"
```

FIGURE 7-11: EditDateView Controller screen

Add references to the `UITableViewDelegate` and `UITableViewDataSource` protocols in the interface definition to indicate that you plan to implement these protocols:

```
@interface EditDateViewController :
    UIViewController <UITableViewDelegate, UITableViewDataSource>
```

Add properties for a `Task` object and the context. Then add `IBOutlet` properties for a `UITableView` and a `UIDatePicker`. Finally, add an action method, `dateChanged`, which runs when the user changes the date in the `UIDatePicker`. The finished header should look like this:

```
#import <UIKit/UIKit.h>
#import "Task.h"

@interface EditDateViewController : UIViewController
    <UITableViewDelegate, UITableViewDataSource>


@property (nonatomic, strong) Task* managedTaskObject;
@property (nonatomic, strong) NSManagedObjectContext *managedObjectContext;
@property (nonatomic, strong) IBOutlet UIDatePicker* datePicker;
@property (nonatomic, strong) IBOutlet UITableView* tv;

-(IBAction)dateChanged:(id)sender;

@end
```

Now it's time to move into Interface Builder and work on the UI in the storyboard. Open the `MainStoryboard.storyboard` file. Drag a new `UIViewController` from the Objects palette and drop it onto the storyboard. Make sure you grab a `UIViewController` and not a

`UITableViewController`. Using the Identity Inspector, change the class of the new view controller to `EditDateViewController`.

Drag a `UIDatePicker` control into the view widow and place it at the bottom of the view. In the Attributes Inspector for the date picker, set the Mode to Date. There are various date and time display modes, but you only need to allow the user to select a date.

Drag a `UITableView` into the view window and position it at the top of the view. Stretch the table view to fill the whole screen. Then send it to the back using Editor ➪ Arrange ➪ Send to Back.

Using the Attributes Inspector, change the table style to Grouped. You also need to configure the prototype cell so the table view knows how to display cells. Select the prototype cell. Then, using the Attributes Inspector, set the cell style to Basic. Next, set the reuse identifier to Cell.

Following that, you need to connect the interface to the code class. Hook up the table view's `dataSource` to the `EditDateViewController` by dragging the circle next to the `dataSource` outlet in the Connections Inspector and dropping it onto the icon that represents the edit date view controller below the view controller in the storyboard window. Do the same thing to connect the `delegate` outlet from the table view to the edit date view controller. Hook up the `tv` variable in the `EditDateViewController` header to the table view by Ctrl-dragging from the table view in Interface Builder and dropping onto the `UITableView` outlet in the code. Do the same to connect the `datePicker` variable to the `UIDatePicker` control. Finally, hook up the `UIDatePicker`'s Value Changed action to the `dateChanged:` method.

Now you need to set up the navigation from the Due Date cell in the view task controller to the edit date view controller. When a user taps the Due Date field in the view task controller, you want to segue to the edit date view controller with a push segue. So Ctrl-drag from the Due Date cell in the view task controller to the edit date view controller. Select Push from the pop-up menu to configure the push segue. You need to set the identifier for this segue. Click the segue and use the Attributes Inspector to set the identifier to `showEditDateViewController`.

You can now move on to the `EditDateViewController.m` implementation file. First, you implement the `viewDidLoad` method:

```
- (void)viewDidLoad {
    [super viewDidLoad];

    // Add the Save button.
    UIBarButtonItem* saveButton =
    [[UIBarButtonItem alloc]
      initWithBarButtonSystemItem:UIBarButtonSystemItemSave
      target:self
      action:@selector (saveButtonPressed:)];
    self.navigationItem.rightBarButtonItem = saveButton;

    // Set the date to the one in the managed object, if it is set.
    // Else, set it to today.
    NSDate* objectDate = self.managedTaskObject.dueDate;
    if (objectDate!=nil)
    {
        self.datePicker.date = objectDate;
    }
```

```
        else {
            self.datePicker.date = [NSDate date];
        }
    }
```

This method creates the Save button and adds it to the navigation bar. It also sets the date in the date picker control to the date in the Task object, if it exists, or to the current date.

The user invokes the saveButtonPressed: method when he clicks the Save button that you created in viewDidLoad. You need to implement saveButtonPressed: to save the currently selected date to the Task object. Here is the code:

```
-(void) saveButtonPressed: (id) sender
{

    // Configure the managed object.
    self.managedTaskObject.dueDate=[self.datePicker date];

    // Save the context.
    NSError *error = nil;
    if (![self.managedObjectContext save:&error]) {
        // There was an error validating the date
        // Display error information
        UIAlertView* alert =
        [[UIAlertView alloc]
         initWithTitle:@"Invalid Due Date"
         message:[[error userInfo] valueForKey:@"ErrorString"]
         delegate:nil cancelButtonTitle:@"OK" otherButtonTitles:nil ];
        [alert show];

        // Roll back the context to
        // revert to the original date
        [self.managedObjectContext rollback];

    }
    else{
        // Pop the view.
        [self.navigationController popViewControllerAnimated:YES];
    }
}
```

Because you are going to add a validation rule that includes the date, there is a possibility that the new date can fail the validation. If the validation fails, the save method will fail, so you need to roll the context back to its old state before the failed save. If the save method fails, you revert the dueDate to the originally selected date by calling the rollback method of the context. Then you show an alert to the user. If the save is successful, you simply pop the controller from the navigation stack.

Next, implement the dateChanged: method to reload the table view and update the date text:

```
-(IBAction)dateChanged:(id)sender{
    // Refresh the date display.
    [self.tv reloadData];
}
```

Because there is only one cell in the table, implement the `numberOfSectionsInTableView:` and `tableView:numberOfRowsInSection:` methods to return 1:

```
- (NSInteger)numberOfSectionsInTableView:(UITableView *)tableView {
    return 1;
}

// Customize the number of rows in the table view.
- (NSInteger)tableView:(UITableView *)tableView
 numberOfRowsInSection:(NSInteger)section {

    return 1;
}
```

Implement `tableView:cellForRowAtIndexPath:` to show the date that the user selected in the date picker:

```
- (UITableViewCell *)tableView:(UITableView *)tableView
        cellForRowAtIndexPath:(NSIndexPath *)indexPath {

    static NSString *CellIdentifier = @"Cell";

    UITableViewCell *cell =
    [tableView dequeueReusableCellWithIdentifier:CellIdentifier];
    if (cell == nil) {
        cell =
        [[UITableViewCell alloc]
            initWithStyle:UITableViewCellStyleDefault
            reuseIdentifier:CellIdentifier];
    }

    // Set up the cell...
    if (indexPath.row == 0)
    {
        // Create a date formatter to format the date from the picker
        NSDateFormatter* df = [[NSDateFormatter alloc] init];
        [df setDateStyle:NSDateFormatterLongStyle];
        cell.textLabel.text = [df stringFromDate:self.datePicker.date ];
    }

    return cell;
}
```

You can see that you are once again using an `NSDateFormatter` to convert the `NSDate` object into a string for display in the table view cell.

The final task is to modify the `prepareForSegue:sender:` method in the `ViewTaskController`. You will use this method to pass the task data to the `EditDateViewController` in the segue.

First, you need to add an `#import` directive to import the `EditDateViewController.h` header:

```
#import "EditDateViewController.h"
```

Then you can modify the `prepareForSegue:sender:` method to handle the case where you are using the `showEditDateViewController` segue like this:

```objc
- (void)prepareForSegue:(UIStoryboardSegue *)segue sender:(id)sender
{
    if ([[segue identifier] isEqualToString:@"showEditTextViewController"]) {
        EditTextViewController* EditTextViewController =
            [segue destinationViewController];
        EditTextViewController.managedObjectContext = self.managedObjectContext;
        EditTextViewController.managedObject=self.managedTaskObject;
        EditTextViewController.keyString=@"text";
    }
    else if ([[segue identifier] isEqualToString:@"showEditPriorityViewController"]) {
        EditPriorityViewController* editPriorityViewController =
            [segue destinationViewController];
        editPriorityViewController.managedObjectContext = self.managedObjectContext;
        editPriorityViewController.managedTaskObject=self.managedTaskObject;
    }
    else if ([[segue identifier] isEqualToString:@"showEditLocationViewController"]) {
        EditLocationViewController* editLocationViewController =
            [segue destinationViewController];
        editLocationViewController.managedObjectContext = self.managedObjectContext;
        editLocationViewController.managedTaskObject=self.managedTaskObject;
    }
    else if ([[segue identifier] isEqualToString:@"showEditDateViewController"]) {
        EditDateViewController* editDateViewController =
            [segue destinationViewController];
        editDateViewController.managedObjectContext = self.managedObjectContext;
        editDateViewController.managedTaskObject=self.managedTaskObject;
    }


}
```

Build and run the program. You should now be able to view and modify the date for your tasks.

Finishing Up the Editing Controllers

You have now finished implementing all the edit controllers. However, you still have some work to do in the `ViewTaskController`. First, you need to add an `#import` statement for the App delegate because you need to get a reference to the `managedObjectModel` to use your stored fetch request:

```objc
#import "AppDelegate.h"
```

Now you will implement the `didSelectRowAtIndexPath` method so that the user can activate the Hi-Pri Tasks and Tasks due sooner features. The Hi-Pri Tasks button demonstrates how to use a fetched property to get a list of high-priority tasks. The Tasks due sooner button shows you how to use a stored fetch request.

The following is the code for `didSelectRowAtIndexPath`:

```objc
- (void)tableView:(UITableView *)tableView
didSelectRowAtIndexPath:(NSIndexPath *)indexPath {

    // Deselect the currently selected row according to the HIG.
    [tableView deselectRowAtIndexPath:indexPath animated:NO];

    // Based on the selected row take some action.
```

```objc
if (indexPath.row==4)
{

    UIAlertView* alert =
    [[UIAlertView alloc] initWithTitle:@"Hi-Pri Tasks"
                               message:nil
                              delegate:self
                     cancelButtonTitle:@"OK"
                     otherButtonTitles:nil  ];

    // Use the Fetched property to get a list of high-priority tasks.
    NSArray* highPriTasks = self.managedTaskObject.highPriTasks;
    NSMutableString* alertMessage =
    [[NSMutableString alloc] init];

    // Loop through each high-priority task to create the string for
    // the message.
    for (Task * theTask in highPriTasks)
    {
        [alertMessage appendString:theTask.text];
        [alertMessage appendString:@"\n"];
    }

    alert.message = alertMessage;
    [alert show];
}
else if (indexPath.row==5)
{

    UIAlertView* alert =
    [[UIAlertView alloc] initWithTitle:@"Tasks due sooner"
                               message:nil
                              delegate:self
                     cancelButtonTitle:@"OK"
                     otherButtonTitles:nil  ];
    NSMutableString* alertMessage =
    [[NSMutableString alloc] init];

    // Need to get a handle to the managedObjectModel to use the stored
    // fetch request.
    AppDelegate* appDelegate =
    [UIApplication sharedApplication].delegate;
    NSManagedObjectModel* model = appDelegate.managedObjectModel;

    // Get the stored fetch request.
    NSDictionary* dict =
    [[NSDictionary alloc]
     initWithObjectsAndKeys:self.managedTaskObject.dueDate,
     @"DUE_DATE",nil];

    NSFetchRequest* request =
    [model fetchRequestFromTemplateWithName:@"tasksDueSooner"
                      substitutionVariables:dict];

    NSError* error;
```

```
NSArray* results =
[self.managedObjectContext executeFetchRequest:request error:&error];

// Loop through each task to create the string for the message.
for (Task * theTask in results)
{
    [alertMessage appendString:theTask.text];
    [alertMessage appendString:@"\n"];
}

alert.message = alertMessage;
[alert show];

}

}
```

The code takes some action based on the row that the user touched. When the user touches row 4, he wants to use the Hi-Pri Tasks feature, which uses the highPriTasks fetched property of the Task object that you defined in the previous chapter. If you don't remember, this property simply returns a list of all tasks that are marked as High Priority.

The interesting thing to notice about using the fetched property is that it returns an array of objects instead of a set. You can also see that using a fetched property is as simple as using a regular property. The code loops through each Task object returned from the fetched property and appends the Task name to a string. The code then displays the string using a UIAlertView.

When the user touches row 5, the code uses a stored fetch request to get a list of tasks that are due sooner than the current task. There are a couple of points of interest when using a stored fetch request. First, you need a reference to the managed object model because stored fetch requests reside in the model and not in your managed object class.

Next, if you specified substitution variables in the fetch request, you need to provide them to the fetch request in an NSDictionary that contains the objects and the keys. You can see that you are creating an NSDictionary using the dueDate property of the current Task object and the key text DUE_DATE. The key text is the same as the variable name that you specified in the previous chapter when defining the stored fetch request.

The code then creates an NSFetchRequest. It uses the fetchRequestFromTemplateWithName: method by supplying the name of the stored fetch request, tasksDueSooner, and the NSDictionary containing your substitution variables and keys.

The code then executes the fetch request against the context. Finally, the code iterates over the results, creating a string with the text from each returned Task object, and displays the string using a UIAlertView.

You are now ready to build and run the application. You should get a clean build with no errors or warnings. You should be able to add new tasks and edit all the attributes of your tasks. You should also be able to create new locations and delete existing ones. By clicking the Hi-Pri Tasks button in the task viewer, you use the fetched property to display all your high-priority tasks. The Tasks due sooner feature won't quite work yet because you have to implement date defaulting in the `Task` object. If you try to select Tasks due sooner and any of your tasks do not have due dates, you get an error. However, if all your tasks contain a due date, the code should function correctly and present a list of all tasks that are due sooner than the current task.

DISPLAYING RESULTS IN THE MASTERVIEWCONTROLLER

In this section, you implement the filtering and sorting buttons on the `MasterViewController`. The easiest way to implement this functionality is to modify the sort descriptor or predicate of the fetched results controller and then execute the fetch.

Sorting Results with NSSortDescriptor

When the user taps the Asc or Dsc buttons, the `toolbarSortOrderChanged` method runs. In this method, you get a reference to the fetch request used by the fetched results controller and change the sort descriptor to match the sort order that the user selected. Then you need to tell the fetched results controller to perform the fetch with the revised sort descriptor. Finally, you tell the table view to reload its data. Replace the stub code in the `MasterViewController` with the following, which is the code for the `toolbarSortOrderChanged` method:

```
-(IBAction)toolbarSortOrderChanged:(id)sender;
{
    NSLog(@"toolbarSortOrderChanged");
    // Get the fetch request from the controller and change the sort descriptor.
    NSFetchRequest* fetchRequest =  self.fetchedResultsController.fetchRequest;

    // Edit the sort key based on which button was pressed.
    BOOL ascendingOrder = NO;
    UIBarButtonItem* button = (UIBarButtonItem*) sender;
    if ([button.title compare:@"Asc"]== NSOrderedSame)
        ascendingOrder=YES;
    else
        ascendingOrder=NO;


    NSSortDescriptor *sortDescriptor =
    [[NSSortDescriptor alloc] initWithKey:@"text" ascending:ascendingOrder];
    NSArray *sortDescriptors =
    [[NSArray alloc] initWithObjects:sortDescriptor, nil];

    [fetchRequest setSortDescriptors:sortDescriptors];

    NSError *error = nil;
    if (![[self fetchedResultsController] performFetch:&error]) {
        NSLog(@"Unresolved error %@, %@", error, [error userInfo]);
        abort();
    }

    [self.tableView reloadData];
}
```

You use the same method regardless of which sort button the user tapped. At runtime, the code checks the title of the button to determine if the user wants the data sorted in ascending or descending order. Then you use the compare method of the NSString class to perform the sort.

You can also add sort descriptors to sort your data using multiple fields. Core Data applies the sort descriptors to the results in the order that you specify them in the array that you pass into the setSortDescriptors function. You will learn more about implementing sort descriptors in Chapter 8.

Filtering Results with NSPredicate

When the user taps the Hi-Pri button, your code should filter the list of tasks to show only high-priority tasks. Conversely, when the user selects the All button, you need to clear the filter to show all the tasks again. You can build these features as you did with the sorting functionality in the previous section. However, instead of modifying the sort descriptor, you are modifying the fetch request's predicate. You can use predicates to filter data in all types of data structures. Their use is not limited to Core Data. You learn more about predicates in the next chapter.

The toolbarFilterHiPri method needs to set the predicate used by the fetch request to return tasks with a priority of 3. Then the method has to tell the table view to reload its data. The following is the code for the toolbarFilterHiPri method:

```
-(IBAction)toolbarFilterHiPri:(id)sender{
    NSLog(@"toolbarFilterHiPri");

    // Change the fetch request to display only high-priority tasks.
    // Get the fetch request from the controller and change the predicate.
    NSFetchRequest* fetchRequest = self.fetchedResultsController.fetchRequest;

    // Clear the fetched results controller cache.
    [NSFetchedResultsController deleteCacheWithName:nil];

    NSPredicate *predicate = [NSPredicate predicateWithFormat:@"priority == 3"];
    [fetchRequest setPredicate:predicate];


    NSError *error = nil;
    if (![[self fetchedResultsController] performFetch:&error]) {
        NSLog(@"Unresolved error %@, %@", error, [error userInfo]);
        abort();
    }

    [self.tableView reloadData];

}
```

The code gets a reference to the predicate used by the fetchedResultsController. Then it clears the fetched results controller cache. You must clear the cache before changing the predicate that you use with the fetch request. After that, you create a new predicate with the criteria of priority == 3. Next, you set the predicate of the fetch request to your new predicate, perform the fetch, and tell the table to reload its data.

The `toolbarFilterAll` method simply removes the predicate from the fetch request. You do that by setting the predicate to `nil`, as follows:

```
- (IBAction) toolbarFilterAll: (id) sender
{
    NSLog (@"toolbarFilterAll") ;

    // Change the fetch request to display all tasks.
    // Get the fetch request from the controller and change the predicate.
    NSFetchRequest* fetchRequest = self.fetchedResultsController.fetchRequest;

    // Clear the fetched results controller cache.
    [NSFetchedResultsController deleteCacheWithName:nil] ;

    // nil out the predicate to clear it and show all objects again.
    [fetchRequest setPredicate:nil] ;

    NSError *error = nil;
    if (![[self fetchedResultsController] performFetch:&error]) {
        NSLog (@"Unresolved error %@, %@", error, [error userInfo]) ;
        abort () ;
    }

    [self.tableView reloadData] ;
}
```

This looks similar to the `toolbarFilterHiPri` method except that here, you set the predicate to `nil` instead of creating a new predicate to apply to the fetch request. Removing the predicate effectively unfilters the data.

GENERATING GROUPED TABLES USING THE NSFETCHEDRESULTSCONTROLLER

In Chapter 3, you learned how to use the `UILocalizedIndexedCollation` class to create a table view that organizes data within sections. When you work with Core Data, you can use the `NSFetchedResultsController` to achieve the same results. In this section, you build the `LocationTasksViewController`. The application displays the `LocationTasksViewController` when the user selects the Location button on the `MasterViewController`. The `LocationTasksViewController` displays all the tasks grouped by location.

The first step is to create a new `UITableViewController` without XIB that is a subclass of `UITableViewController`. Call the new class `LocationTasksViewController`. Modify the header file by adding properties for the context and a fetched results controller. Also, mark your class as implementing the `NSFetchedResultsControllerDelegate` protocol. The header should look like this:

```
#import <UIKit/UIKit.h>

@interface LocationTasksViewController :
    UITableViewController <NSFetchedResultsControllerDelegate>

@property (nonatomic, retain) NSManagedObjectContext *managedObjectContext;
```

```
@property (nonatomic, retain)
    NSFetchedResultsController *fetchedResultsController;

@end
```

Moving into the implementation file, add `#import` directives for the `Location.h`, `Task.h`, and `ViewTaskController.h` headers:

```
#import "Location.h"
#import "Task.h"
#import "ViewTaskController.h"
```

Now implement `viewDidLoad` to perform the fetch on the fetched results controller and set the title of the screen in the navigation bar:

```
- (void)viewDidLoad
{
    [super viewDidLoad];

    NSError* error;

    if (![[self fetchedResultsController] performFetch:&error]) {

        NSLog(@"Unresolved error %@, %@", error, [error userInfo]);
        abort();

    }

    // Set the title to display in the navigation bar.
    self.title = @"Tasks by Location";

}
```

Next, you write the `fetchedResultsController` accessor method. You have implemented this method several times before. The difference in this case is that you need to specify a `sectionNameKeyPath` when you initialize the `NSFetchedResultsController`.

The `sectionNameKeyPath` parameter allows you to specify a key path that the fetched results controller uses to generate the sections for your table. The fetched results controller contains the entire set of `Task` objects. You want the tasks grouped by location. Remember that the `Task` object has a `location` property that refers to a related `Location` object. The `Location` object has a `name` property that contains the name of the location. You really want the tasks grouped by the `name` property of the contents of the `location` property. Because you are holding a reference to a `Task` object, the key path to the `Location`'s `name` property is `location.name`. The following is the code for the `fetchedResultsController` accessor:

```
- (NSFetchedResultsController *)fetchedResultsController {

    if (_fetchedResultsController != nil) {
        return _fetchedResultsController;
    }

    /*
```

```
      Set up the fetched results controller.
      */
     // Create the fetch request for the entity.
     NSFetchRequest *fetchRequest = [[NSFetchRequest alloc] init];
     // Edit the entity name as appropriate.
     NSEntityDescription *entity =
     [NSEntityDescription entityForName:@"Task"
                 inManagedObjectContext:self.managedObjectContext];
     [fetchRequest setEntity:entity];

     // Edit the sort key as appropriate.
     NSSortDescriptor *sortDescriptor =
     [[NSSortDescriptor alloc] initWithKey:@"location.name"
                                 ascending:YES];
     NSArray *sortDescriptors =
     [[NSArray alloc] initWithObjects:sortDescriptor, nil];

     [fetchRequest setSortDescriptors:sortDescriptors];

     // Edit the section name key path and cache name if appropriate.
     // nil for section name key path means "no sections."
     NSFetchedResultsController *aFetchedResultsController =
     [[NSFetchedResultsController alloc]
      initWithFetchRequest:fetchRequest
      managedObjectContext:self.managedObjectContext
      sectionNameKeyPath:@"location.name" cacheName:@"Task"];

     aFetchedResultsController.delegate = self;
     self.fetchedResultsController = aFetchedResultsController;

     return _fetchedResultsController;
 }
```

If you look at the definition of the sort descriptor, you can see that you are also using the key path to the Location object's name property. For the fetched results controller to create the sections properly, you need to sort the result set using the same key that you use to generate the sections. As mentioned previously, the section key is set when initializing the NSFetchedResultsController in the sectionNameKeyPath parameter.

Next, you need to code the controllerDidChangeContent method to reload the data in the table view when the contents of the fetched results controller changes:

```
- (void)controllerDidChangeContent:(NSFetchedResultsController *)controller {
    // In the simplest, most efficient, case, reload the table view.
    [self.tableView reloadData];
}
```

The next step is to implement the table view methods. The numberOfSectionsInTableView method looks just like the corresponding method in the MasterViewController. However, because you are using sections on this screen, the fetched results controller does not just return 1 for the number of sections. Instead, the fetched results controller calculates the number of sections based on the number of different values in the location.name property.

The `tableView:numberOfRowsInSection:` method also uses the fetch results controller to populate the table view. In this case, you get an `NSFetchedResultsSectionInfo` object from the fetched results controller that corresponds to the current section. The section info object has a `numberOfObjects` property that returns the number of objects in the section. This value is returned as the number of rows in the section.

Here are the implementations for the `numberOfSectionsInTableView` and `tableView:numberOfRowsInSection:` methods:

```
- (NSInteger)numberOfSectionsInTableView:(UITableView *)tableView {
    return [[self.fetchedResultsController sections] count];
}

- (NSInteger)tableView:(UITableView *)tableView
 numberOfRowsInSection:(NSInteger)section {

    id <NSFetchedResultsSectionInfo> sectionInfo =
    [[self.fetchedResultsController sections] objectAtIndex:section];
    return [sectionInfo numberOfObjects];

}
```

The `tableView:cellForRowAtIndexPath:` and `tableView:didSelectRowAtIndexPath:` methods are the same as in the `MasterViewController`. You generate the cell text the same way, and the behavior is identical when a user selects a row. The following is the code for the `tableView:cellForRowAtIndexPath:` and `tableView:didSelectRowAtIndexPath:` methods:

```
// Customize the appearance of table view cells.
- (UITableViewCell *)tableView:(UITableView *)tableView
        cellForRowAtIndexPath:(NSIndexPath *)indexPath {

    static NSString *CellIdentifier = @"Cell";

    UITableViewCell *cell =
    [tableView dequeueReusableCellWithIdentifier:CellIdentifier];
    if (cell == nil) {
        cell = [[UITableViewCell alloc]
                initWithStyle:UITableViewCellStyleDefault
                reuseIdentifier:CellIdentifier];
    }

    // Configure the cell.
    Task *managedTaskObject =
    [self.fetchedResultsController objectAtIndexPath:indexPath];
    cell.textLabel.text = managedTaskObject.text;

    // Change the text color if the task is overdue.
    if (managedTaskObject.isOverdue==[NSNumber numberWithBool: YES])
    {
        cell.textLabel.textColor = [UIColor redColor];
    }
    else {
        cell.textLabel.textColor = [UIColor blackColor];

    }
```

```
        return cell;
    }

    - (void)tableView:(UITableView *)tableView
    didSelectRowAtIndexPath:(NSIndexPath *)indexPath {

        // Deselect the currently selected row according to the HIG.
        [tableView deselectRowAtIndexPath:indexPath animated:NO];

        // Navigation logic may go here -- for example, create and push
        // another view controller.
        Task *managedObject =
        [self.fetchedResultsController objectAtIndexPath:indexPath];

        ViewTaskController* taskController =
        [[ViewTaskController alloc]
         initWithStyle:UITableViewStyleGrouped];

        taskController.managedTaskObject=managedObject;
        taskController.managedObjectContext = self.managedObjectContext;

        [self.navigationController pushViewController:taskController animated:YES];


    }
```

You need to implement one additional method: `tableView:titleForHeaderInSection:`.
This method generates the titles for the sections of the table. Again, you use an
`NSFetchedResultsController` to get these titles. The fetched results controller maintains a sections array that contains the list of sections in the result set. You simply need to get the item out of
the array that corresponds to the section that the table view is asking for. Here is the code:

```
    - (NSString *)tableView:(UITableView *)tableView
    titleForHeaderInSection:(NSInteger)section
    {
        id <NSFetchedResultsSectionInfo> sectionInfo =
        [[self.fetchedResultsController sections] objectAtIndex:section];
        return [sectionInfo name];
    }
```

Now that you have built the `LocationTasksViewController`, you need to modify the
`MasterViewController` to call your new location controller when the user taps the Location button. In the `MasterViewController.m` implementation file, add an #import directive to import the
new controller:

```
    #import "LocationTasksViewController.h"
```

Modify the code in the `locationButtonPressed` method to create an instance of your new controller and push it onto the navigation stack:

```
    - (IBAction)locationButtonPressed:(id)sender
    {
        NSLog(@"locationButtonPressed");

        LocationTasksViewController* ltvc =
```

```
    [[LocationTasksViewController alloc]
     initWithStyle:UITableViewStylePlain];
    ltvc.managedObjectContext = self.managedObjectContext;
    [self.navigationController pushViewController:ltvc animated:YES];
}
```

You are now ready to build and run the application. You should be able to use all the buttons at the bottom of the `MasterViewController` to filter the data, sort the data, and bring up the tasks grouped by location screen.

IMPLEMENTING CUSTOM MANAGED OBJECTS

Up until this point, you haven't used any of the features of an `NSManagedObject` subclass. You could have written all the Core Data code that you have seen so far in this chapter using key-value coding and generic `NSManagedObjects`.

In this section, you learn about the additional features you can implement by using custom subclasses of `NSManagedObject`. These features include dynamically calculating property values at runtime, defaulting data at runtime, and single and multiple field validation.

Coding a Dynamic Property

You can use dynamic properties to implement properties that you need to calculate at runtime. In the data modeler, you should mark dynamic properties as Transient because you will compute their value at runtime and will not save this value in the data store.

In this example, you code an `isOverdue` property for the `Task` object. This property should return `YES` if a task is overdue and `NO` if it is not. You may notice that when you declare a `Boolean` property in the data modeler, Xcode translates the property into an `NSNumber` in the generated code. This is not a problem because a class method in the `NSNumber` class returns an `NSNumber` representation of a `BOOL`.

Open the `Task.m` implementation file. Add the following code to implement the `isOverdue` accessor method:

```
- (NSNumber*) isOverdue
{
    BOOL isTaskOverdue = NO;

    NSDate* today = [NSDate date];

    if (self.dueDate != nil) {
        if ([self.dueDate compare:today] == NSOrderedAscending)
            isTaskOverdue=YES;
    }

    return [NSNumber numberWithBool:isTaskOverdue];
}
```

This code simply compares the `dueDate` in the current `Task` object against the current system date. If the `dueDate` is earlier than today, the code sets the `isTaskOverdue` variable to `YES`. The code then uses the `numberWithBool` method to return an `NSNumber` that corresponds to the boolean result.

If you run the application now, any tasks that occurred in the past should turn red in the `MasterViewController`.

Defaulting Data at Runtime

Just as you can dynamically generate property values at runtime, you can generate default values at runtime. The Core Data framework calls a method named `awakeFromInsert` the first time you insert an object into the managed object context.

Subclasses of `NSManagedObject` can implement `awakeFromInsert` to set default values for properties. It is critical that you call the superclass implementation of `awakeFromInsert` before doing any of your own implementation to ensure that the managed object is configured correctly before you start working with it.

You should always use primitive accessor methods to modify property values while you are in the `awakeFromInsert` method. Primitive accessor methods are methods of the managed objects that are used to set property values but that do not notify other classes observing your class using key-value observing. This is important because if you modify a property and your class sends a notification that results in another class modifying the same property, your code could get into an endless loop.

You can set primitive values in your code using key value coding and the `setPrimitiveValue:forKey:` method. A better way is to define custom primitive accessors for any properties you need to access in this way. In this case, you are modifying the `dueDate` property in `awakeFromInsert`, so you need to define a primitive accessor for the `dueDate`. Fortunately, Core Data defines these properties for you automatically at runtime. All you need to do is declare the property in the `Task.h` header:

```
@property (nonatomic, retain) NSDate * primitiveDueDate;
```

Then add an `@dynamic` directive in the implementation file to indicate that Core Data will dynamically generate this property at runtime:

```
@dynamic primitiveDueDate;
```

Now you can set the `dueDate` property in the `awakeFromInsert` method without fear of any side effects that may occur because of other classes observing the `Task` for changes.

Implement the `awakeFromInsert` method in the `Task.m` implementation file to create an `NSDate` object three days from the current date, and use the primitive property to set the default date. The following is the code for the `awakeFromInsert` method:

```
- (void)awakeFromInsert
{
    // Core Data  calls this function the first time the receiver
    // is inserted into a context.
    [super awakeFromInsert];

    // Set the due date to 3 days from now (in seconds)
```

```
NSDate* defualtDate = [[NSDate alloc]
                      initWithTimeIntervalSinceNow:60*60*24*3];

// Use custom primitive accessor to set Due Date field.
self.primitiveDueDate = defualtDate ;

}
```

Before you build and run the application, delete the old app from the simulator because you may have tasks that do not have due dates. Now you can run the application. New tasks that you create have a default due date set three days into the future. You should now be able to use the "Tasks due sooner than this one" button on the task detail screen because all tasks will have defaulted due dates.

Validating a Single Field

Single-field validation in a custom class is straightforward. Core Data will automatically call a method named validateXxxx if you have implemented the method. The Xxxx is the name of your property with the first letter capitalized. The method signature for the validate method for the dueDate field looks like this:

```
-(BOOL)validateDueDate:(id *)ioValue error:(NSError **)outError{
```

A single field validation method should return YES if the validation is successful and NO if it failed. The method accepts an id*, which is the value that you are testing for validity, and an NSError** that you should use to return an NSError object if the validation fails.

Because this method receives an id*, you *could* modify the object that is passed into the validation function, but you should never do this. Users of a class would not expect validation to modify the object they submitted for validation. Modifying the object that a caller passed in would create an unexpected side effect. Creating side effects is usually a poor design choice that you should avoid. Treat the object passed in for validation as read-only.

In the validation of the dueDate of the Task object, you are going to enforce a rule that assigning past due dates is invalid. Here is the implementation of the dueDate validation function in the Task.m implementation file:

```
-(BOOL)validateDueDate:(id *)ioValue error:(NSError **)outError{

    // Due dates in the past are not valid.
    // Enforce that a due date has to be >= today's date.
    if ([*ioValue compare:[NSDate date]] == NSOrderedAscending) {

        if (outError != NULL) {
            NSString *errorStr = @"Due date must be today or later";
            NSDictionary *userInfoDictionary =
            [NSDictionary dictionaryWithObject:errorStr
                                        forKey:@"ErrorString"];
            NSError *error =
            [[NSError alloc] initWithDomain:TASKS_ERROR_DOMAIN
                            code:DUEDATE_VALIDATION_ERROR_CODE
                        userInfo:userInfoDictionary];
```

```
                *outError = error;
            }
            return NO;
        }
        else {
            return YES;
        }
    }
```

The first thing that you do is check the date that you receive as an input parameter and compare it to the current system date. If the comparison fails, you create an error string that you will return to the caller in the NSError object. Next, you add the error string to an NSDictionary object that you pass back to the class user as the userInfo in the NSError object. Then you allocate and initialize an NSError object with an error domain and error code. The domain and code are custom values that identify your error and can be any values you like. For this sample, I have defined them in the Task.h header file like this:

```
#define TASKS_ERROR_DOMAIN              @"com.Wrox.Tasks"
#define DUEDATE_VALIDATION_ERROR_CODE   1001
```

You pass the userInfo dictionary that you created to hold the error string to the initializer of the NSError object. Users of your Task class can interrogate the userInfo dictionary they receive in the NSError to get details about the problem and act accordingly. You return NO to indicate that validation has failed.

If the validation succeeds, the code simply returns YES.

Run the application now and try to set the due date for a task to a past date. You should get an error indicating that this is invalid.

Multi-field Validation

Multifield validation is slightly more complicated than single-field validation. Core Data calls two methods automatically if they exist: validateForInsert and validateForUpdate. Core Data calls validateForInsert when you insert an object into the context for the first time. When you update an existing object, Core Data calls validateForUpdate.

If you want to implement a validation rule that runs both when an object is inserted or when it is updated, I recommend writing a new validation function and calling that new function from the validateForInsert and validateForUpdate methods. The example follows this approach.

In this sample, you are enforcing a multi-field validation rule that says that high-priority tasks must have a due date within the next three days. Any due date farther in the future should cause an error. You cannot accomplish this within a single field validation rule because you need to validate both that the task is high priority and that the due date is within a certain range. In the Task.h header file, add a new method declaration for the function that you will call to validate the data:

```
- (BOOL)validateAllData:(NSError **)error;
```

Here is the function that enforces the rule in Task.m:

```
- (BOOL)validateAllData:(NSError **)outError
{
    NSDate* compareDate =
    [[NSDate alloc] initWithTimeIntervalSinceNow:60*60*24*3];
    // Due dates for high-priority tasks must be today, tomorrow, or the next day.
    if ([self.dueDate compare:compareDate] == NSOrderedDescending &&
        [self.priority intValue]==3) {

        if (outError != NULL) {
            NSString *errorStr =
                @"Hi-pri tasks must have a due date within two days of today";

            NSDictionary *userInfoDictionary =
            [NSDictionary dictionaryWithObject:errorStr
                                        forKey:@"ErrorString"];
            NSError *error =
            [[NSError alloc] initWithDomain:TASKS_ERROR_DOMAIN
                                        code:PRIORITY_DUEDATE_VALIDATION_ERROR_CODE
                                    userInfo:userInfoDictionary];
            *outError = error;
        }
        return NO;
    }
    else {
        return YES;
    }
}
```

The code first generates a date to which to compare the selected dueDate. Then the code checks to see if the dueDate chosen is greater than this compare date and that the priority of the task is high. If the data meets both of these criteria, it is invalid and you generate an NSError object just like in the previous section. A new error code is used and should be added to the Task.h header:

```
#define PRIORITY_DUEDATE_VALIDATION_ERROR_CODE  1002
```

The code then returns NO to indicate that the validation has failed. If the validation is successful, the method returns YES.

Now you have to add the two validation methods to Task.m that Core Data calls and code them to call your validateAllData method:

```
- (BOOL)validateForInsert:(NSError **)outError
{
    // Call the superclass validateForInsert first.
    if ([super validateForInsert:outError]==NO)
    {
        return NO;
    }

    // Call out validation function.
    if ([self validateAllData:outError] == NO)
    {
        return NO;
    }
```

```
        else {
            return YES;
        }
    }

    - (BOOL)validateForUpdate:(NSError **)outError
    {
        // Call the superclass validateForUpdate first.
        if ([super validateForUpdate:outError]==NO)
        {
            return NO;
        }

        // Call out validation function.
        if ([self validateAllData:outError] == NO)
        {
            return NO;
        }
        else {
            return YES;
        }
    }
```

Both of these methods call their superclass counterpart method. You have to call the superclass method because that method handles validation rules implemented in the model and calls the single-field validation methods. If the superclass validation routine is successful, the methods call your `validateAllData` method.

Build and run the application. If you try to set the due date for a high-priority task to more than two days in the future, or if you try to set high priority to a task that has a due date more than two days in the future, you get an error.

MOVING FORWARD

This chapter covered a lot of material. You learned how to implement the Core Data concepts that were discussed in Chapter 6.

At this point you have a fully functioning Core Data–based application that demonstrates many of the features of Core Data. You can use this application like a sandbox to play with these features or implement new functionality in the Tasks application on your own.

Now that you have built an entire application, I hope you have confidence in your ability to implement an application using the Core Data framework. You should be able to use Core Data effectively in your own applications.

In the next chapter, you learn more about some features of Cocoa Touch that you often use with Core Data. You explore key value coding and key value observing. You also learn more about predicates and how to implement sort descriptors using your own custom classes. Finally, you learn to migrate your existing data from one Core Data model version to another.

Core Data–Related Cocoa Features

WHAT'S IN THIS CHAPTER?

➤ Setting and getting data using key-value coding

➤ Implementing a loosely coupled application architecture with messaging and key-value observing

➤ Creating predicates in several ways and using them to filter data

➤ Building sort descriptors to order your data structures

WROX.COM CODE DOWNLOADS FOR THIS CHAPTER

The wrox.com code downloads for this chapter are found at `www.wrox.com/remtitle .cgi?isbn=1118391845` on the Download Code tab. The code is in the Chapter 8 download and individually named according to the names throughout the chapter.

In the previous three chapters, you learned about the fundamentals of the Core Data architecture — how to model your data and how to build a complete data-centric application using the Core Data framework. This chapter provides a more detailed look at some of the Cocoa functionality that you used with Core Data. In addition to their application in Core Data, you can use these features in other interesting ways.

In this chapter, you learn more about some important Cocoa technologies: key-value coding, key-value observing, predicates, and sort descriptors.

Although you have seen these features used with Core Data, they are an integral part of the Cocoa framework. You can use these concepts and their associated classes in ways that reach far beyond Core Data. For example, you can use predicates and the NSPredicate class to filter and query regular Cocoa data structures such as arrays and dictionaries. You can develop loosely coupled, message-based application architectures using the concepts of key-value coding and key-value observing. Adding a deeper knowledge of these Cocoa features broadens your knowledge of the development platform and provides you with more tools for your developer toolbox.

KEY-VALUE CODING

You have already seen key-value coding, also referred to as KVC, in previous chapters. When you used Core Data with an NSManagedObject directly, instead of using an NSManagedObject custom subclass, you used KVC to set and get the attribute values stored in the NSManagedObject. KVC allowed you to get and set the attributes of the managed object by name instead of using properties and accessor methods.

The term "key-value coding" refers to the NSKeyValueCoding protocol. This informal protocol specifies a way to access an object's properties using a name or key rather than by calling the accessor method directly. This capability is useful when you are trying to write generic code that needs to operate on different properties of different objects. For example, in Chapter 7, you designed the EditTextViewController as a generic controller that you can use to provide a text-editing capability. If you recall, you used this controller class to edit text attributes with different names in two different objects. The saveButtonPressed method in the EditTextViewController used KVC to specify the appropriate text field name for the object that you wanted to edit, as you can see in this code from Chapter 7:

```
-(void) saveButtonPressed: (id) sender
{

    // Configure the managed object
    // Notice how you use KVC here because you might get a Task or a Location
    // in this generic text editor
    [self.managedObject setValue:self.textField.text forKey:self.keyString];

    // Save the context.
    NSError *error = nil;
    if (![self.managedObjectContext save:&error]) {
        NSLog(@"Unresolved error %@, %@", error, [error userInfo]);
        abort();
    }

    // pop the view
    [self.navigationController popViewControllerAnimated:YES];

}
```

Keys and Keypaths

Keys are the strings you use to reference the properties of an object. The key is generally also the name of the accessor method that accesses the property.

Properties and accessor methods are closely related. When you type **@property NSString* name,** you are telling the Cocoa framework to create accessor methods for the name property for you. The framework automatically creates the `-(NSString*)name` getter method and the `-(void)` `setName:(NSString*)newName` setter method. You can choose to override one or both of these methods if the default implementation does not meet your needs. It is a general standard that property names start with a lowercase letter.

To get a specific value from an object using KVC, you call the `-(id)valueForKey:(NSString *)` `key` method. This method returns the value in the object for the specified key. The `valueForKey:` method returns the generic `id` type. This means it can return any Objective-C object type, which makes KVC ideal for writing generic code. The method is unaware of the type of object that it will return and can therefore return any type.

If an accessor method or instance variable with the key does not exist, the receiver calls the `valueForUndefinedKey:` method on itself. By default, this method throws an `NSUndefinedKeyException`, but you can change this behavior in subclasses.

Instead of passing a simple key, alternate methods allow you to use keypaths to traverse a set of nested objects using a dot-separated string. In the example in the previous chapter, you used keypaths to access a `Task`'s `Location`'s `name` property when you built the `fetchedResultsController` method for the `LocationTasksViewController`:

```
- (NSFetchedResultsController *)fetchedResultsController {

    if (_fetchedResultsController != nil) {
        return _fetchedResultsController;
    }

    /*
     Set up the fetched results controller.
     */
    // Create the fetch request for the entity.
    NSFetchRequest *fetchRequest = [[NSFetchRequest alloc] init];
    // Edit the entity name as appropriate.
    NSEntityDescription *entity =
    [NSEntityDescription entityForName:@"Task"
                inManagedObjectContext:self.managedObjectContext];
    [fetchRequest setEntity:entity];

    // Edit the sort key as appropriate.
    NSSortDescriptor *sortDescriptor =
    [[NSSortDescriptor alloc] initWithKey:@"location.name"
                                ascending:YES];
    NSArray *sortDescriptors =
    [[NSArray alloc] initWithObjects:sortDescriptor, nil];

    [fetchRequest setSortDescriptors:sortDescriptors];

    // Edit the section name key path and cache name if appropriate.
    // nil for section name key path means "no sections".
    NSFetchedResultsController *aFetchedResultsController =
    [[NSFetchedResultsController alloc]
     initWithFetchRequest:fetchRequest
```

```
    managedObjectContext:self.managedObjectContext
    sectionNameKeyPath:@"location.name" cacheName:@"Task"];

    aFetchedResultsController.delegate = self;
    self.fetchedResultsController = aFetchedResultsController;

    return _fetchedResultsController;
}
```

When addressing a `Task` object, you used the keypath `location.name` to get to the `name` property from the `location` attribute of the `Task` object (see Figure 8-1).

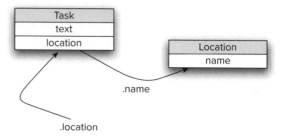

The first key in the keypath refers to a field in the receiver of the call. You use subsequent keys to drill down into the object returned by the first key. Therefore, when used with a `Task` object, the keypath `location.name` gets that `Task`'s `location` property and then

FIGURE 8-1: Accessing a value with a keypath

asks that object for its `name` property. As long as keys in the keypath return references to objects, you can drill down as deeply into an object hierarchy as you want.

You can use key-value coding to retrieve values from an object using a keypath instead of a simple string key by calling the `-(id)valueForKeyPath:(NSString *)keyPath` method. This works like `valueForKey` in that it returns the value at the given keypath. If anywhere along the keypath a specified key does not exist, the receiver calls the `valueForUndefinedKey:` method on itself. Again, this method throws an `NSUndefinedKeyException`, and you can change this behavior in subclasses.

Finally, you can use the `-(NSDictionary *)dictionaryWithValuesForKeys:(NSArray *)keys` method for bulk retrieval of values using KVC. This method accepts an `NSArray` of keys and returns an `NSDictionary` with the keys as the keys in the dictionary and the values returned from the object as the values.

Setting Values Using Keys

Just as you can retrieve values from an object using KVC, you can set values using KVC. You call the `-(void)setValue:(id)value forKey:(NSString *)key` method to set the value for a specified key. If an accessor method or instance variable with the key does not exist, the receiver calls the `setValue:forUndefinedKey:` method on itself. By default, this method throws an `NSUndefinedKeyException`, but you can change this behavior in subclasses.

You can also use a keypath to set a value in a target object using the `-(void)setValue:(id)value forKeyPath:(NSString *)keypath` method. If any value in the keypath returns a nil key, the receiver calls the `setValue:forUndefinedKey:` method on itself. Again, this method throws an `NSUndefinedKeyException`, but you can change this behavior in subclasses.

You can set a group of values in an object using KVC by calling the `-(void)setValuesForKeys WithDictionary:(NSDictionary *)keyedValues` method. This method sets all the values on all the key objects given in the dictionary. Behind the scenes, this method simply calls `setValue:forKey:` for each item in the dictionary.

Collection Operators

If your object contains an array or set property, it is possible to perform some functions on the list. You can include a function in the keypath in a call to `valueForKeyPath`. These functions are called collection operators. You call collection operators using the form `pathToArray.@function` `.pathToProperty`.

Following are the functions that you can use in a collection operator:

➤ **@avg:** Loops over each item in the collection, converts its value to a `double`, and returns an `NSNumber` representing the average

➤ **@count:** Returns the number of objects in the collection

➤ **@distinctUnionOfArrays:** Returns an array containing the unique items from the arrays referenced by the keypath

➤ **@distinctUnionOfObjects:** Returns the unique objects contained in the property

➤ **@max** and **@min:** Return the maximum and minimum values respectively of the specified property

➤ **@sum:** Loops over each item in the collection, converts its value to a `double`, and returns an `NSNumber` representing the sum

➤ **@unionOfArrays, @unionOfObjects, and @unionOfSets:** Function just like their distinct counterparts except they return all items in the collection, not just unique items

For further information on using these functions, see Apple's Key-Value Coding Programming Guide, which is included as part of the Xcode documentation set.

Additional Considerations When Using KVC

It makes no difference whether you access the properties of a class by using the dot syntax, calling the accessor method, or by using KVC. You can see this illustrated in Figure 8-2. You are calling the receiver's accessor method either way. You should be aware, however, that because there is an added level of indirection when using KVC, there is a slight performance hit. The performance penalty is small, so you should not let this deter you from using KVC when it helps to enhance the flexibility of your design.

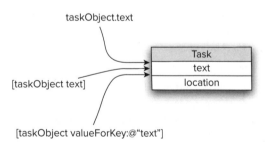

FIGURE 8-2: Accessing a value using different semantics

When building your own classes, you should pay attention to the naming conventions the Cocoa framework uses. Doing so helps to ensure that your classes will be key-value coding compliant. For example, the correct format for accessor methods i· -var for the getter and -setVar for the setter. Defining properties in your classes ensures that the accessor methods generated by the framework will be KVC-compliant.

There are additional rules for ensuring KVC compliance when your classes contain To-One or To-Many relationships. You should consult the Key Value Coding Programming Guide in the Apple documentation set for more detail on ensuring KVC compliance.

The `valueForKey:` and `setValue:forKey:` methods automatically wrap scalar and struct data types in `NSNumber` or `NSValue` classes. Therefore, it is not necessary to manually convert scalar types (such as `int` or `long`) into Objective-C class types (such as `NSNumber`); the framework does it for you automatically.

KEY-VALUE OBSERVING

In addition to obtaining property values using strings, you can take advantage of the `NSKeyValueCoding` protocol to implement another powerful feature in Cocoa: key-value observing (or KVO). Key-value observing provides a way for objects to register to receive notifications when properties in other objects change. A key architectural feature of this functionality is that there is no central repository or server that sends change notifications. When implementing KVO, you link observers directly to the objects they are observing without going through an intermediary server. If you need to implement a centrally stored publish/subscribe capability, the `NSNotification` class provides this capability.

The base class for most Objective-C objects, `NSObject`, provides the basic functionality of KVO. You should generally not have to override the base class implementation in your own implementations. Using KVO, you can observe changes to properties, To-One relationships, and To-Many relationships. By inheriting from `NSObject`, the base class implements KVO automatically on your objects. However, it is possible to disable automatic notifications or build your own manual notifications.

Observing Changes to an Object

To receive notifications for changes to an object, you must register as an observer of the object. You register your class as an observer by calling the `addObserver:forKeyPath:options:context:` method on the object that you want to observe.

The `Observer` parameter specifies the object that the framework should notify when the observed property changes. The `KeyPath` parameter specifies the property that you want to observe. Changes o this property cause the framework to generate a notification. The `options` parameter specifies hether you want to receive the original property value (`NSKeyValueObservingOptionOld`) or the v property value (`NSKeyValueObservingOptionNew`). You can receive both if you pass in both eyValueObservingOptionOld and `NSKeyValueObservingOptionNew` using the bitwise OR tor. The `context` parameter is a pointer that the observed object passes back to the observer a change occurs.

he property that you are observing changes, the observer receives a notification. ions come back to the observer through calls to the observer's `observeValueForKeyPath:` `change:context:` method. The observed object calls this method on the observer when l property changes. Therefore, all observers must implement `observeValueForKeyPath:` hange:context: to receive KVO callbacks. You can see the relationship between the ong with the methods used to set up the relationship in Figure 8-3.

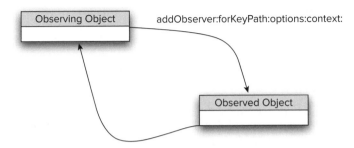

observeValueForKeyPath:ofObject:change:context:

FIGURE 8-3: The KVO relationship

When the observed object calls observeValueForKeyPath:ofObject:change:context:, the observer receives a reference to the object that changed. Also sent to the receiver are the keypath to the property that changed, a dictionary that contains the changes, and the context pointer you passed in the call that set up the relationship.

The NSDictionary that you receive in the callback contains information about the changes to the observed object. Depending on the options you specified in the call to set up the observer, the dictionary will contain different keys. If you specified NSKeyValueObservingOptionNew, the dictionary has an entry corresponding with the NSKeyValueChangeNewKey key that contains the new value for the observed property. If you specified NSKeyValueObservingOptionOld, the dictionary has an entry for the NSKeyValueChangeOldKey key that contains the original value of the observed property. If you specified both options using a bitwise OR, both keys are available in the dictionary. The dictionary also contains an entry for the NSKeyValueChangeKindKey that gives you more information describing what kind of change has occurred.

When you are no longer interested in observing changes on an object, you need to unregister your observer. You accomplish this by calling the removeObserver:forKeyPath: method on the observed object. You pass the observer and the keypath to the property that the observer was observing. After you make this call, the observer no longer receives change notifications from the observed object.

Automatic and Manual Implementations of KVO

The NSObject base class provides an automatic key-value observing implementation for all classes that are key-value coding compliant. You can disable automatic support for KVO for specific keys by calling the class method automaticallyNotifiesObserversForKey:. To disable keys, you need to implement this method to return NO for the specific keys you do not want the framework to automatically support.

You can implement manual KVO notifications for finer control of when notifications go out. This is useful when you have properties that could change often or when you want to batch many notifications into one. First, you have to override the automaticallyNotifiesObserversForKey: method to return NO for keys that you want to implement manually. Then, in the accessor for the property that you want to manually control, you have to call willChangeValueForKey: before you modify the value, and didChangeValueForKey: afterward.

Key-Value Observing Example

Now that you are familiar with the concepts behind key-value coding and key-value observing, you can work through a simple example. The example demonstrates how to use this functionality in practice. In this example, you implement an iOS version of a baseball umpire's count indicator. Umpires use this device to keep track of balls, strikes, and outs.

The sample application uses KVC and KVO to decouple the data object (`Counter`) from the interface (`ViewController`). Even though this example is simplified, it demonstrates how to use KVC and KVO to decouple your data objects from your interface. Keep in mind that this example is somewhat contrived to demonstrate using the principals of KVO and KVC in an application. You could easily implement this solution in many other, simpler ways, without using KVO and KVC. The `ViewController` uses KVC to set the values for balls, strikes, and outs in the `Counter` object. The `ViewController` also observes changes for these fields and uses the observation method to update the user interface.

Building the User Interface

The first task is to create the user interface storyboard for your application. Open Xcode and start a new project using the Single View Application template. Call your new application Umpire and make sure that Use Storyboards and Use Automatic Reference Counting are checked.

You should lay out the interface as shown in Figure 8-4. Open the `MainStoryboard.storyboard` interface file. Then add three Round Rect Buttons (`UIButton`) objects to the interface and change their titles to "balls," "strikes," and "outs." Add three `UILabel` objects, one above each button. Change the text in each one to the number 0.

Next, you need to modify the `ViewController.h` header file to add outlets for the UI controls and an action method that handles the action when the user taps on one of the buttons. Using the Assistant editor, Ctrl-drag each label from the user interface in the storyboard and drop them into the `ViewController.h` header. Set the connection for each label to `Outlet`. Name the labels **ballLabel**, **strikeLabel**, and **outLabel**.

At this point, your `ViewController.h` header file should look like this:

FIGURE 8-4: Umpire application user interface

```
#import <UIKit/UIKit.h>

@interface ViewController : UIViewController
@property (weak, nonatomic) IBOutlet UILabel *ballLabel;
@property (weak, nonatomic) IBOutlet UILabel *strikeLabel;
@property (weak, nonatomic) IBOutlet UILabel *outLabel;

@end
```

Now you need to wire up the balls, strikes, and outs buttons to an action method. Using the Assistant editor again, Ctrl-drag the balls button from the user interface in the storyboard and drop it into the `ViewController.h` header. This time, change the Connection to `Action` and name the action **buttonTapped**. Connect the strikes and outs buttons to the `buttonTapped` method by

Ctrl-dragging each button and dropping it on the `buttonTapped` method signature. You should now have each button connected to the `buttonTapped` method.

The finished header should look like this:

```
#import <UIKit/UIKit.h>

@interface ViewController : UIViewController
@property (weak, nonatomic) IBOutlet UILabel *ballLabel;
@property (weak, nonatomic) IBOutlet UILabel *strikeLabel;
@property (weak, nonatomic) IBOutlet UILabel *outLabel;

- (IBAction)buttonTapped:(id)sender;

@end
```

Now you need to open the `ViewController.m` implementation file. In the `buttonTapped` method, add a line of code to log that the user tapped a button. Modify the `buttonTapped` like this:

```
- (IBAction)buttonTapped:(id)sender {
    NSLog(@"buttonTapped");
}
```

Build and run the application. It should build successfully with no errors or warnings. In the iOS simulator, tap each button and verify that when you tap each button, you see the `buttonTapped` message in the console log.

The Counter Data Object

Now that your user interface is set up and working correctly, you will build a data object to hold the umpire data. Create a new class that is a subclass of `NSObject` and call it **Counter**.

Open the `Counter.h` header file. Add three `NSNumber` properties, one each for balls, strikes, and outs:

```
#import <Foundation/Foundation.h>

@interface Counter : NSObject

@property (nonatomic, retain)  NSNumber* balls;
@property (nonatomic, retain)  NSNumber* strikes;
@property (nonatomic, retain)  NSNumber* outs;

@end
```

You will be using this object in the `ViewController`, so you need to add a reference to the `Counter.h` header file in the `ViewController.h` header. Open the `ViewController.h` header file and add an #import statement to import the `Counter.h` header:

```
#import "Counter.h"
```

Also, in the `ViewController.h` header file, add a `Counter` property called `umpireCounter`:

```
@property (nonatomic, retain) Counter* umpireCounter;
```

The `umpireCounter` property holds the instance of the `Counter` to use to keep track of the ball and strike count.

Implementing Key-Value Observing

With the data object in place, you can connect your view controller to the data object using key-value observing. Open the `ViewController.m` implementation file.

You need to initialize the `umpireCounter` variable and set up the KVO observation in the `viewDidLoad` method. Here is `viewDidLoad`:

```
- (void)viewDidLoad
{
    [super viewDidLoad];
    Counter *theCounter = [[Counter alloc] init];

    self.umpireCounter = theCounter;

    // Set up KVO for the umpire counter.
    [self.umpireCounter addObserver:self
                         forKeyPath:@"balls"
                            options:NSKeyValueObservingOptionNew
                            context:nil];
    [self.umpireCounter addObserver:self
                         forKeyPath:@"strikes"
                            options:NSKeyValueObservingOptionNew
                            context:nil];
    [self.umpireCounter addObserver:self
                         forKeyPath:@"outs"
                            options:NSKeyValueObservingOptionNew
                            context:nil];

}
```

First, as usual, you call the superclass implementation of `viewDidLoad` to ensure that the object is set up properly and ready for use. Next, you create an instance of a `Counter` object and assign it to the `umpireCounter` property.

The next section sets up the KVO observation for each of the `balls`, `strikes`, and `outs` properties of the `Counter` object. Now you will take a closer look at the call to set up the observer for the `balls` property:

```
[self.umpireCounter addObserver:self
                     forKeyPath:@"balls"
                        options:NSKeyValueObservingOptionNew
                        context:nil];
```

Remember that `Counter` inherits the `addObserver:forKeyPath:options:context:` method from `NSObject`. You are calling this method to configure the `ViewController` as an observer of the `umpireCounter` object. Therefore, you pass `self` as the object that will be the observer. This particular observer will be observing the `balls` property of the `umpireCounter`, so you pass the string `balls` for the keypath. You don't really care what the old value of `balls` is; you are only interested in the new value when the value changes, so you pass the `NSKeyValueObservingOptionNew` option in the method call. Finally, you set the context to `nil` because you do not need context data.

Now that you've set up your code to become an observer, you need to implement the `observeValueForKeyPath:ofObject:change:context:` method that the observed object calls when observed properties change. Here is the method:

```
- (void)observeValueForKeyPath:(NSString *)keyPath
                      ofObject:(id)object
                        change:(NSDictionary *)change
                       context:(void *)context {

    // Change gives back an NSDictionary of changes.
    NSNumber *newValue = [change valueForKey:NSKeyValueChangeNewKey];

    // Update the appropriate label.
    if (keyPath == @"balls") {
        self.ballLabel.text = [newValue stringValue];
    }
    else if (keyPath == @"strikes") {
        self.strikeLabel.text = [newValue stringValue];
    }
    else if (keyPath == @"outs") {
        self.outLabel.text = [newValue stringValue];
    }
}
```

Remember that every time an observed property in the `umpireCounter` changes, the `umpireCounter` calls this method. The first line retrieves the new value from the change dictionary for the property that changed. Next, you examine the keypath that the `umpireCounter` passes in to determine which property has changed. Then you use that knowledge to set the text of the appropriate label.

In the `dealloc` method, you need to remove the KVO observers. Here is the code for `dealloc`:

```
- (void)dealloc {
    // Tear down the KVO for the umpire counter.
    [self.umpireCounter removeObserver:self
                            forKeyPath:@"balls"];

    [self.umpireCounter removeObserver:self
                            forKeyPath:@"strikes" ];

    [self.umpireCounter removeObserver:self
                            forKeyPath:@"outs" ];

}
```

Once again, you make a call to the `umpireCounter` object. This time, you call the `removeObserver:forKeyPath:` method to remove your class as an observer of the `umpireCounter`. You call this method once for each property that you are observing, passing `self` as the observer each time.

Updating Values with Key-Value Coding

The last thing you need to do is implement the `buttonTapped` method that executes each time the user taps one of the buttons in the interface. Instead of specifically setting the property values of the `umpireCounter` using dot notation, you use key-value coding in conjunction with the title of the button that was pressed to set the appropriate value. You also need to implement some business logic to limit the ball counter to a maximum of three and the strike and out counters to a maximum of two. Here is the code for the `buttonTapped` method:

```
- (IBAction)buttonTapped:(id)sender {

    UIButton *theButton = sender;
    NSNumber *value = [self.umpireCounter valueForKey:theButton.currentTitle];

    NSNumber* newValue;

    // Depending on the button and the value, set the new value accordingly.
    if ([theButton.currentTitle compare:@"balls"] == NSOrderedSame &&
        [value intValue] == 3) {

        newValue = [NSNumber numberWithInt:0];
    }
    else if (([theButton.currentTitle compare:@"strikes"] == NSOrderedSame ||
            [theButton.currentTitle compare:@"outs"] == NSOrderedSame )&&
            [value intValue] == 2) {

        newValue = [NSNumber numberWithInt:0];
    }
    else
    {
        newValue = [NSNumber numberWithInt:[value intValue]+1];
    }

    [self.umpireCounter setValue:newValue forKey:theButton.currentTitle];
}
```

First, you get a reference to the button that the user pressed to trigger the call to `buttonTapped`. Next, you use the title of that button as the key in a call to `valueForKey` to get the current value of that attribute from the `umpireCounter`. For example, if the user tapped the "balls" button, you are passing the string `balls` into the `valueForKey` method. This method then retrieves the `balls` property of the `umpireCounter`. This method works as long as the titles in the buttons match the property names in the data object.

The next line declares a new `NSNumber` to hold the value that you want to send back to the `umpireCounter`.

Next, you apply some business logic depending on which button the user pressed. If he pressed the "balls" button, you check to see if the old value was three, and if it was, you set the new value back to zero. It does not make sense for the balls counter to go higher than three because in baseball, four balls constitute a walk and the next batter will come up, erasing the old count.

The next line does a similar comparison for the strikes and outs counters, but you compare these values to two. Again, values greater than two make no sense for each of these properties.

If you do not need to reset the particular counter back to zero, you simply increment the value and store the new value in the local `newValue` variable.

Finally, you use key-value coding to set the new value on the `umpireCounter` using the `currentTitle` of the button that the user pressed as the key.

The application is now complete. You should be able to successfully build and run. When you tap one of the buttons, the application should set the properties of the counter object using key-value coding. It should then fire the key-value observing callback method and update the count labels on the interface using key-value observing. Notice how you never explicitly retrieved values from the umpireCounter using properties or valueForKey.

USING NSPREDICATE

In the previous chapter, you learned how to use predicates with Core Data to specify the criteria for a fetch. In general, you can use predicates to filter data from any class, as long as the class is key-value coding compliant.

Creating Predicates

You can create a predicate from a string by calling the NSPredicate class method predicateWithFormat:. You can include variables for substitution at runtime just as you would with any other string formatter. One issue to be aware of when creating predicates using strings is that you will not see errors caused by an incorrect format string until runtime.

When creating a predicate by calling the predicateWithFormat: method, you must quote string constants in the expression. For example, you see that you have to quote the string literal URGENT in this method call:

```
[NSPredicate predicateWithFormat:"text BEGINSWITH 'URGENT'"]
```

However, if you use a format string with variable substitution (%@), you do not need to quote the variable string. Therefore, you could create the previous predicate using this format string:

```
[NSPredicate predicateWithFormat:"text BEGINSWITH %@", @"URGENT"]
```

You can also use variable substitution to pass in variable values at runtime like this:

```
[NSPredicate predicateWithFormat:"text BEGINSWITH %@", object.valueToFilter]
```

If you try to specify a dynamic property name using a format string and %@, it fails because the property name is quoted. You need to use the %K (Key) substitution character in the format string to omit the quotes.

Say, for example, that you wanted to create a predicate at runtime but wanted the field you are filtering on to be dynamic, along with the value you want to filter. If you tried this code, it would be incorrect because the property you are trying to filter on would be incorrectly quoted by using the %@ substitution character:

```
[NSPredicate predicateWithFormat:"%@ == %@", object.property, object.valueToFilter]
```

The correct syntax for this predicate is as follows:

```
[NSPredicate predicateWithFormat:"%K == %@", object.property, object.valueToFilter]
```

You are not limited to creating predicates with keys. You can also create a predicate using a keypath. With respect to a Task object, the predicate location.name == "Home" is perfectly legal.

In addition to using the predicateWithFormat: method, you can create predicates directly using instances of the NSExpression object and NSPredicate subclasses. This predicate creation method makes you write a lot of code, but it is less prone to syntax errors because you get compile-time checking of the objects you create. You may also get some runtime performance increase because there is no string parsing with this method as there is with the `predicateWithFormat:` method.

To create the predicate text `BEGINSWITH 'URGENT'` using `NSExpressions` and `NSPredicate` subclasses, you code it like this:

```
NSExpression *lhs = [NSExpression expressionForKeyPath:@"text"];
NSExpression *rhs = [NSExpression expressionForConstantValue:@"URGENT"];
NSPredicate *beginsWithPredicate =
    [NSComparisonPredicate predicateWithLeftExpression:lhs
                            rightExpression:rhs
                            modifier:NSDirectPredicateModifier
                            type:NSBeginsWithPredicateOperatorType
                            options:0];
```

As you can see, this is quite a bit more than the simple one line of code shown previously. However, when using this method you do get the benefit of compile-time type checking.

The final method for creating predicates is to use predicate templates with variable expressions. You saw this technique in Chapter 7 when you built the `tasksDueSooner` predefined fetch request in your data model. With this method, you create your predicate template using either of the previously mentioned methods but with `$VAR` as variables in the predicate. In the case of `tasksDueSooner`, you created a predicate that said:

```
dueDate < $DUE_DATE
```

When you are ready to use the predicate, you call the `predicateWithSubstitutionVariables:` method on the predicate passing in a dictionary that contains the key-value pairs of the substitution variables and their values. In the example in Chapter 7, you used the predicate in the stored fetch request in the `tableView:didSelectRowAtIndexPath:` method of the `ViewTaskController`:

```
- (void)tableView:(UITableView *)tableView
didSelectRowAtIndexPath:(NSIndexPath *)indexPath {

    // Deselect the currently selected row according to the HIG
    [tableView deselectRowAtIndexPath:indexPath animated:NO];

    // Based on the selected row take some action
    if (indexPath.row==4)
    {

        UIAlertView* alert =
        [[UIAlertView alloc] initWithTitle:@"Hi-Pri Tasks"
                            message:nil
                            delegate:self
                        cancelButtonTitle:@"OK"
                        otherButtonTitles:nil  ];

        // Use Fetched property to get a list of high-pri tasks
        NSArray* highPriTasks = self.managedTaskObject.highPriTasks;
        NSMutableString* alertMessage =
        [[NSMutableString alloc] init];

        // Loop through each hi-pri task to create the string for
```

```objc
    // the message
    for (Task * theTask in highPriTasks)
    {
        [alertMessage appendString:theTask.text];
        [alertMessage appendString:@"\n"];
    }

    alert.message = alertMessage;
    [alert show];
}
else if (indexPath.row==5)
{

    UIAlertView* alert =
    [[UIAlertView alloc] initWithTitle:@"Tasks due sooner"
                               message:nil
                              delegate:self
                     cancelButtonTitle:@"OK"
                     otherButtonTitles:nil ];
    NSMutableString* alertMessage =
    [[NSMutableString alloc] init];

    // need to get a handle to the managedObjectModel to use the stored
    // fetch request
    AppDelegate* appDelegate =
    [UIApplication sharedApplication].delegate;
    NSManagedObjectModel* model = appDelegate.managedObjectModel;

    // Get the stored fetch request
    NSDictionary* dict =
    [[NSDictionary alloc]
     initWithObjectsAndKeys:self.managedTaskObject.dueDate,
     @"DUE_DATE",nil];

    NSFetchRequest* request =
    [model fetchRequestFromTemplateWithName:@"tasksDueSooner"
                      substitutionVariables:dict];

    NSError* error;
    NSArray* results =
    [self.managedObjectContext executeFetchRequest:request error:&error];

    // Loop through eachtask to create the string for the message
    for (Task * theTask in results)
    {
        [alertMessage appendString:theTask.text];
        [alertMessage appendString:@"\n"];
    }

    alert.message = alertMessage;
    [alert show];

}

}
```

Using Predicates

You can evaluate any object that is KVC-compliant against a predicate using the evaluateWithObject method of the predicate. The evaluateWithObject method returns YES if the object passed meets the criteria specified in the predicate.

For example, suppose that you build a predicate called thePredicate with the criteria text BEGINSWITH 'URGENT' as described previously. If you had a reference to a Task object called theTask that had a text attribute, you could call the function [thePredicate evaluateWithObject: theTask]. If the Task's text attribute started with the string URGENT, the call to evaluateWithObject: would return YES. You can see that this functionality has nothing to do with Core Data. Again, you can use predicates with any object that is KVC-compliant.

The NSArray class has a method called filteredArrayUsingPredicate: that returns a new filtered array using the supplied predicate. NSMutableArray has a filterUsingPredicate: method that filters an existing mutable array and removes items that don't match the predicate. You can also use filteredArrayUsingPredicate: with the mutable array to return a new, filtered NSArray.

SORT DESCRIPTORS

Like predicates, the use of sort descriptors is not limited to Core Data. You can use sort descriptors to sort other data structures such as arrays as long as the values contained within the array are KVC-compliant. As you may recall from the previous chapter, you use sort descriptors to specify how to sort a list of objects.

Sort descriptors specify the property to use when sorting a set of objects. By default, sorting using a sort descriptor calls the compare: method of each object under consideration. However, you can specify a custom method to use instead of the default compare: method.

Keep in mind that the descriptor doesn't do the sorting. The sort descriptor just tells the data structure how to sort. This is similar to the way an NSPredicate doesn't actually do the filtering; it simply specifies how to filter.

The first step in using a sort descriptor is to initialize a sort descriptor with the key that you want to sort on. You also need to specify whether you want to sort the resulting data in ascending or descending order. You initialize a sort descriptor by using the initWithKey:ascending: method.

Next, you create an array of descriptors by calling the NSArray arrayWithObjects: method and passing in one or more descriptors. You need to create an array so that you can sort on more than one field at a time. The framework applies the sort descriptors in the order that you specify them in the array.

For example, if you had an array of Task objects called theTaskArray, you could sort the array first on dueDate and then on text by creating an array containing two sort descriptors and calling the sortedArrayUsingDescriptors method:

```
// Create the sort descriptors.
NSSortDescriptor *dueDateDescriptor =
    [[NSSortDescriptor alloc] initWithKey:@"dueDate" ascending:NO];
NSSortDescriptor *textDescriptor =
```

```
        [[NSSortDescriptor alloc] initWithKey:@"text" ascending:YES];

    // Build an array of sort descriptors.
    NSArray *descriptorArray =
        [NSArray alloc arrayWithObjects: dueDateDescriptor, textDescriptor, nil];

    // Sort the array using the sort descriptors.
    NSArray *sortedArray =
        [theTaskArray sortedArrayUsingDescriptors:descriptorArray];
```

The `sortedArrayUsingDescriptors` method works by calling the `compare:` method on the type you are sorting. If the `compare:` method is not appropriate for your application, you can specify a different method to use when sorting by creating your sort descriptors with the `initWithKey:ascending:selector:` method.

Specifically, when comparing strings, Apple's String Programming Guide for Cocoa recommends that you use a localized string comparison. So instead of `compare:`, you should generally specify that the sort descriptor use the `localizedCompare:` or `localizedCaseInsensitiveCompare:` method using the `@selector (localizedCaseInsensitiveCompare:)` syntax.

Therefore, when sorting your `Task` objects based on the `text` field, which is a string, you should use a sort descriptor defined like this:

```
    NSSortDescriptor *textDescriptor =
            [[NSSortDescriptor alloc]
                initWithKey:@"text"
                ascending:YES
                selector:@selector(localizedCaseInsensitiveCompare:)];
```

The `localizedCaseInsensitiveCompare:` method of the `NSString` class uses an appropriate localized sorting algorithm based on the localization settings of the device.

MOVING FORWARD

In this chapter, you discovered how you could use some of the features of the Cocoa framework that you learned about in the context of Core Data, outside of Core Data.

You used key-value coding and key-value observing to build an application that has its user interface loosely coupled to its data model. Architecturally, loose coupling of application data and the user interface is generally a good thing.

Then you learned how to create predicates and use them to filter data in arrays. You also studied how to use predicates to do an ad hoc comparison of an object to some specific criteria.

Finally, you discovered how to create and apply sort descriptors to sort arrays.

You should now feel comfortable with using these features inside your Core Data–based applications. You should also be able to apply the same concepts and technologies to work with other data structures.

In the next chapter, you finish the exploration of the Core Data framework with a look at optimizing Core Data performance. You also look at versioning your database and migrating existing applications from one database version to another.

Core Data Migration and Performance

WROX.COM CODE DOWNLOADS FOR THIS CHAPTER

The wrox.com code downloads for this chapter are found at `www.wrox.com/remtitle .cgi?isbn=1118391845` on the Download Code tab. The code is in the Chapter 9 download and individually named according to the names throughout the chapter.

In the preceding chapters, you learned about the Core Data framework and how to use it to provide the data storage capability in your applications. In this chapter, you take a closer look at some advanced topics related to Core Data, including migrating from one database schema to another and optimizing the performance of your Core Data–based application.

In this chapter, you learn how to handle change in your application data model using model versioning and migration. You also learn how to effectively manage memory when building a Core Data–based solution, safely implement a threaded Core Data application, and troubleshoot and analyze your Core Data application using the Instruments tool.

MODEL VERSIONING AND SCHEMA MIGRATION

It is rare that a finished application turns out the way you imagined when you started. In fact, many applications are never truly finished. If your customers like your application, you will almost certainly want to enhance it and build upon its existing feature set. Often, you will get feature requests from customers and clients, which can be a continuing source of revenue for you, the developer.

When you first sat down to design your application, you reviewed the requirements and designed the database that would store your data. As the application development process moves forward, things change, and you may need to modify your data store by adding entities and attributes, changing data types, or modifying relationships between your entities. This is a normal part of the development cycle. Although you may occasionally get a nasty error message from Core Data about using an incompatible data store, this is not a big deal. While you're developing, you can simply blow away your old application and its data, and your application will create a new data store that works with the current schema. This is not an option once you have shipped your application.

In general, users will not be very happy if they try to open an updated version of your application and it crashes because the data store schema does not match the schema of the data file. They will be even less happy if they contact you for support and you tell them that they have to delete the old application and all their data to be able to run with the update. They will most likely not use your application, or any other applications that you build, ever again.

You are probably wondering how you can continue to extend your product while not losing all your customer's existing work when he or she upgrades to the newest version of your application. Fortunately, Apple has provided a solution with Core Data Versioning.

Core Data implements a feature called *model versioning*, which allows you to specify and label different versions of your data model in your Xcode project. You can have many versions of the data model in your project. You only need to specify which schema is the current model that your application should use.

Another tool provided by the framework is the *mapping model*. The mapping model lets you map the translation of data from one model into another. Finally, *data migration* is used with versioning and mapping to migrate a back-end data store from one schema version to another. I've illustrated this process in Figure 9-1.

The Core Data framework thus solves your application update problem. You can create a new version of your schema to support your

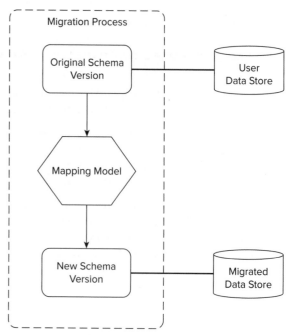

FIGURE 9-1: The data migration process

application enhancements and then use schema migration to migrate the existing data store on your customer's device to the new schema.

Model Versioning

To Core Data, two models are compatible if there are no changes to the model that will affect a change in the back-end data store. For instance, you can add a transient property while maintaining compatibility between the existing and the new data store. Remember, transient properties are not stored in the data store, so a change to a transient property does not break compatibility with the original data store.

If you make a change that alters the way your data is stored in the data store, however, you are breaking compatibility with the existing data store. Actions such as adding new attributes or entities, changing attribute types, and renaming entities or attributes will change the structure of the data store and will break compatibility.

There are some rules you can use to determine if two models will be compatible. For an entity, Core Data compares the `name`, `parent`, and `isAbstract` flags. Core Data does not care about `className`, `userInfo`, and validation predicates because these are not stored in the data store. These items are only available to the developer at runtime.

For every property, Core Data examines the `name`, `isOptional`, `isTransient`, and `isReadOnly` elements. For attributes, Core Data also looks at the `attributeType`, and for relationships, Core Data examines the `destinationEntity`, `minCount`, `maxCount`, `deleteRule`, and `inverseRelationship` elements. Core Data does not compare the `userInfo` and validation predicates.

If any of these attributes of a model differ for any entity or any property of any entity, the models are incompatible.

In Xcode, you can create and specify different versions of your application data model. You will look at this functionality now using the Tasks project. Although you will not be adding additional functionality, you will be modifying the database to purposely break compatibility with the existing data store to illustrate versioning and migration.

Find your existing Tasks application and copy it into a new folder. Open the new Tasks project in Xcode. Next, open the data model `Tasks.xcdatamodel`. To create a new version of the model, choose Editor ⇨ Add Model Version from the menu bar. In the dialog, accept the default version name of Tasks 2 and leave the Based on model drop-down set to Tasks.

If you look in the Resources folder in Xcode, you will notice that the `Tasks.xcdatamodeld` file now appears as a container holding `Tasks.xcdatamodel` and `Tasks 2.xcdatamodel`. `Tasks.xcdatamodeld` is actually a bundle and not a file. If you click on the disclosure indicator to open the bundle, you will see the two data model files, `Tasks.xcdatamodel` and `Tasks 2.xcdatamodel`, as shown in Figure 9-2. At this point, the two files are identical. You may also notice that the `Tasks.xcdatamodel` file has a little green checkmark on the file icon. The checkmark indicates that this file is the Current Version. This is the version of the model that Core Data will use at runtime.

FIGURE 9-2: Two versions of the Tasks model

You will be making some changes to the new version of the model, version 2. You will want to use the new version of the model in your application, so you have to set it as the current version. Select the `Tasks.xcdatamodeld` container in the Project Navigator. Then, using the File Inspector under the Versioned Core Data Model heading, set the Current model to Tasks 2. You should see the green checkmark move from the original model to the new version 2 model.

Now you will make a change to the model that will break compatibility with your existing Tasks data store. In the `Tasks 2.xcdatamodel` file, open the Location entity and add an `address` attribute of `string` type. Save the model. Make sure you have the `Tasks 2.xcdatamodel` file selected as the current versioned core data model. Clean your project by selecting Product ➪ Clean. Then build and run the application.

Because you have made a change to the model that breaks compatibility with the old data store, the application should raise an error and abort. In the console, you should see an error that looks like this:

```
2012-12-9 14:10:19.617 Tasks[9425:c07] Unresolved error Error Domain=NSCocoaErrorDomain
 Code=134100 "The operation couldn't be completed. (Cocoa error 134100.)"
UserInfo=0x8661f00 {metadata={
    NSPersistenceFrameworkVersion = 419;
    NSStoreModelVersionHashes =     {
        Location = <f8f7dab4 9e61e128 c44a7082 f6149d82 af48581c b9b2e6f8
21d073a1 0b5c204e>;
        Task = <40414517 78c0bd9f 84e09e2a 91478c44 d85394f8 e9bb7e5a
abb9be27 96761c30>;
    };
    NSStoreModelVersionHashesVersion = 3;
    NSStoreModelVersionIdentifiers =     (
        ""
    );
    NSStoreType = SQLite;
    NSStoreUUID = "292C13AC-B0FA-40C2-BD82-81AFE6E65050";
    "_NSAutoVacuumLevel" = 2;
}, reason=The model used to open the store is incompatible with the one used to
create the store}, {
    metadata =      {
        NSPersistenceFrameworkVersion = 419;
        NSStoreModelVersionHashes =          {
            Location = <f8f7dab4 9e61e128 c44a7082 f6149d82 af48581c b9b2e6f8
21d073a1 0b5c204e>;
            Task = <40414517 78c0bd9f 84e09e2a 91478c44 d85394f8 e9bb7e5a
abb9be27 96761c30>;
        };
        NSStoreModelVersionHashesVersion = 3;
        NSStoreModelVersionIdentifiers =          (
            ""
        );
        NSStoreType = SQLite;
        NSStoreUUID = "292C13AC-B0FA-40C2-BD82-81AFE6E65050";
        "_NSAutoVacuumLevel" = 2;
```

```
    };
    reason = "The model used to open the store is incompatible with the one
used to create the store";
}
```

The most important thing to notice in this error dump is the reason: `reason=The model used to open the store is incompatible with the one used to create the store`. The change that you made — adding a new attribute to an existing model object — broke the compatibility between versions of your core data model.

You'll fix this error in the next section.

Lightweight Migration

To make your existing data work with your new data model, you need to migrate the schema to a new data store. If the changes that you have made are not too drastic, you can easily accomplish this using a process called *lightweight migration*.

Lightweight migration is a feature of Core Data that helps you automatically migrate a data store from one model version to another. In the previous section, I briefly mentioned the mapping model. Core Data uses the mapping model to determine how to map data from one schema model into another. Lightweight migration allows Core Data to infer the mapping model based on the changes that you made to the model from one version to another.

Lightweight migration is particularly handy during development because you won't have to regenerate your test data every time you make a change to your model. It is also fast to implement because you don't have to go through the trouble of creating your own mapping model to map your data from one version to another.

For lightweight migration to work, the changes to your model have to be simple. Generally, if you add an attribute, make a required attribute optional, or make an optional attribute required and add a default value, lightweight migration will work for you. If you change the name of an entity or attribute, you need to set the renaming identifier for the renamed attribute in the user info pane to the old name of the attribute in the source model.

In the Tasks example, the model has changed, but you are still trying to use a data store that the user created with the old model. In this instance, you can use lightweight migration because you have only added a new attribute to the data store.

To use lightweight migration, you need to make a couple of changes to your application source code. If you recall from Chapter 5, the Persistent Store Coordinator is a Core Data object that associates a managed object model to a back-end data store. You can see this relationship in Figure 9-3. In your code, when you add a persistent store to the coordinator, you can specify an `NSDictionary` of options in the `addPersistentStoreWithType:configuration:URL:options:error:` method call. You will modify the code in the `AppDelegate.m` file to specify the options to initiate a lightweight migration.

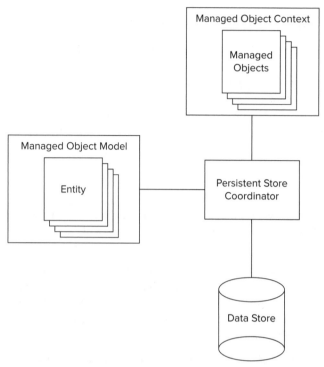

FIGURE 9-3: Core Data objects

Open the Tasks project and navigate to the `AppDelegate.m` file. You will be adding code to the `persistentStoreCoordinator` accessor method. The first thing you need to do is create an `NSDictionary` that contains the keys you want to pass into the coordinator. The two keys you will set are `NSMigratePersistentStoresAutomaticallyOption` and `NSInferMappingModelAutomaticallyOption`.

`NSMigratePersistentStoresAutomaticallyOption` tells the coordinator to automatically migrate the persistent store to a new model if the store is not compatible with the current model. Core Data searches the application bundle for a model that is capable of opening the existing data store, and then it searches for a model mapping from the model that can open the data store to the current model. Because you haven't created a mapping model, you have to add another option to your options dictionary.

You use the `NSInferMappingModelAutomaticallyOption` option key to tell Core Data to infer the mapping model from the differences between the model that can open the data store and the current model.

In the `persistentStoreCoordinator` method, after the line that allocates and initializes the `NSPersistentStoreCoordinator`, add the following code to initialize your options dictionary:

```
NSDictionary *options = [NSDictionary dictionaryWithObjectsAndKeys:
                            [NSNumber numberWithBool:YES],
                            NSMigratePersistentStoresAutomaticallyOption,
                            [NSNumber numberWithBool:YES],
                            NSInferMappingModelAutomaticallyOption, nil];
```

This code creates a new NSDictionary and populates it with the keys as discussed previously.

Next, you have to change the call to addPersistentStoreWithType:configuration:URL:options :error: to use the new options dictionary that you have created. Change the line to look like this:

```
if (![_persistentStoreCoordinator
        addPersistentStoreWithType:NSSQLiteStoreType
        configuration:nil URL:storeURL options:options error:&error]) {
```

The complete method should look like this:

```
- (NSPersistentStoreCoordinator *)persistentStoreCoordinator
{
    if (_persistentStoreCoordinator != nil) {
        return _persistentStoreCoordinator;
    }

    NSURL *storeURL = [[self applicationDocumentsDirectory]
                        URLByAppendingPathComponent:@"Tasks.sqlite"];

    NSError *error = nil;
    _persistentStoreCoordinator = [[NSPersistentStoreCoordinator alloc]
                        initWithManagedObjectModel:[self managedObjectModel]];

    NSDictionary *options = [NSDictionary dictionaryWithObjectsAndKeys:
                            [NSNumber numberWithBool:YES],
                            NSMigratePersistentStoresAutomaticallyOption,
                            [NSNumber numberWithBool:YES],
                            NSInferMappingModelAutomaticallyOption, nil];

    if (![_persistentStoreCoordinator
            addPersistentStoreWithType:NSSQLiteStoreType
            configuration:nil URL:storeURL options:options error:&error]) {

        NSLog(@"Unresolved error %@, %@", error, [error userInfo]);
        abort();
    }

    return _persistentStoreCoordinator;
}
```

Build and run your application. The migration should now succeed and the application should run just as it did before. Your error is gone, you've added a new field to the data store to support some new functionality, and your customer's data is intact.

> **WARNING** *Make sure you have a few tasks in your data store because you will be transforming the existing data in the next section. If you have no data, you will not see results when you apply the transformation.*

You can check in advance whether the lightweight migration will work by calling the `inferredMap pingModelForSourceModel:destinationModel:error:` method. If the mapping will work and the migration will succeed, you get a reference to the new model; if not, the method returns `nil`.

Generating a Mapping Model

If your model changes are too extensive or otherwise don't meet the criteria supported for performing a lightweight migration, you have to generate a mapping model. Remember that you use the mapping model to tell Core Data how to migrate your data from one store to another. You can also use the mapping model to perform data transformations as you move the data from one data store to another.

Because of the relationship between the mapping model and the data model, the classes used to build a mapping model correspond with the classes used to build a data model. `NSMappingModel` is like the data model, `NSEntityMapping` is like an entity, and `NSPropertyMapping` is like a property or attribute.

The `NSEntityMapping` class tells the migration process how to handle mapping a source entity in the destination data store. The mapping type determines what to do with the specific entity in the destination data store. The mapping types are add, remove, copy, and transform. Add mapping means that this is a new entity in the destination and should be added to the destination data store. Remove means that the entity does not exist in the destination and exists only in the source. Copy indicates that the mapping should copy the source object identically to the destination. Transform means that the entity exists in the source and the destination and the mapping should transform the source in some way to get from the source to the destination. Later in this chapter is an example of how to transform data as it is being migrated from one model to another.

The `NSPropertyMapping` class tells the migration process how to map source properties to destination properties. You can provide a value expression to transform values while moving the data from the source data store to the destination data store. You can specify a value expression in the mapping model editor in Xcode.

In some cases, you may want to do a custom migration when you use these classes, so it is good to have at least a cursory understanding of which classes are involved in performing a migration. More often, you will not work with the mapping classes in code because Xcode includes a graphical tool you can use to create and edit your mapping model. You will create a mapping model to migrate your data store to the original version of the data model. You will also transform some of the data in the data store along the way to demonstrate the transformation capabilities of executing the migration process using a mapping model.

In Xcode, select the `Tasks.xcdatamodeld` file and use the File Inspector to make Tasks the current model. You do this by setting the Current model in the Versioned Core Data Model section of the File Inspector to Tasks. To create the mapping model, select the Tasks folder in the Project Navigator and add a new file by selecting File ⇨ New ⇨ File from the menu bar. In the New File dialog, on the left side under iOS, select Core Data. In the right pane of the New File dialog, you should see an option for Mapping Model. Select the Mapping Model and click Next.

You should now see the Mapping Model Source Data Model dialog. You will use this dialog to tell the mapping model which data model is the source. Select the Tasks 2 model and click Next. Now you need to select the Target Data Model, so select the Tasks model. Remember that you have a data store that is compatible with the Tasks 2 model and you want to migrate it to be compatible with the Tasks model. On the next screen, enter the name for your new mapping model as **Map,** and click Create to have Xcode create your mapping model.

You should now see the mapping model tool. If you do not, make sure you have selected the `Map.xcmappingmodel` file in the Project Navigator in Xcode. You can see the mapping model tool in Figure 9-4.

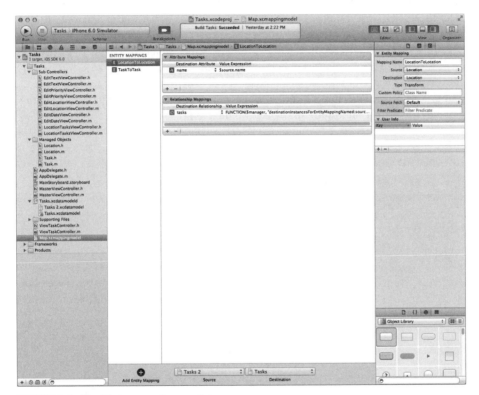

FIGURE 9-4: The Tasks mapping model

At the bottom of the screen, the tool lists the Source and Destination models. Above that is a three-column view. The left column displays the entity mappings, which the framework uses to migrate entities between data stores. The middle column displays the property mappings for the currently selected entity. The right column shows the details of the currently selected item.

The Mapping Model tool has created the default entity and property mappings for you. You can successfully run with the default mapping model. However, you will apply some transformations using value expressions to demonstrate how you can transform data while performing a migration.

In the mapping model are two entity mappings: one for Tasks and one for Locations. Select the TaskToTask entity mapping. This mapping maps Task entities in the source data store to Task entities in the destination. As you can probably guess, the LocationToLocation entity mapping maps Location entities in the source data store to Location entities in the destination.

Now you will create a few value expressions to learn how to transform your data during a migration. Value expressions are instances of the NSExpression class. If you recall from the previous chapter, this is the same class, with its subclasses, that you use as the right side of a predicate.

First, you will modify the priority value expression to set the priority of every task to Medium (priority 2). Select the TaskToTask mapping in the Entity Mappings pane. In the Attribute Mappings pane, select the priority attribute. The right pane is context sensitive: its contents change depending on the item you have selected in the left or middle pane. When you have an Entity Mapping selected, the right pane displays the mapping attributes that pertain to an Entity Mapping. When you select the priority attribute, the pane changes to display the fields that pertain to an Attribute Mapping. You can see in Figure 9-5 that when you have the priority attribute mapping selected, you can edit the priority mapping in the right pane.

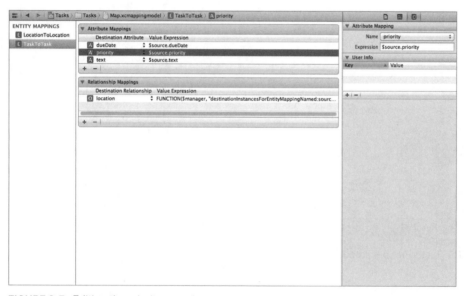

FIGURE 9-5: Editing the priority mapping

The default value expression for the priority attribute is $source.priority. This expression directly migrates the priority from the source to the destination. The special variable $source indicates that the value for this field in the destination should be taken from the corresponding source object. In the case of priority, the expression $source.priority gets the priority field from the source entity. However, instead of taking the value from the source, you want to change the priority for every task to 2. So, in the Expression field in the right pane, change the expression to the number 2.

Next, select the text attribute in the Property Mappings pane. The default value expression for the text property migrates the text from the source $source to the destination. You want to change the text of each task to **NEW TASK** so that you can see the effects of executing a transformation when the Tasks application opens. In the text property mapping, change the Expression field in the right pane to **NEW TASK**. Doing so changes the text of every task to NEW TASK.

Next, change the dueDate of all your tasks to today. Select the dueDate attribute in the Property Mappings pane. The default value expression for the dueDate property migrates the dueDate from the source to the destination. You want to set the new dueDate to today's date. You do not want to hard-code a date because you do not know when the user will run the migration on his data store. It would be better if you could specify the date using a function.

You can call arbitrary functions in a value expression using function expressions by using the FUNCTION keyword. The syntax is FUNCTION(receiver, selectorName, arguments, ...). In this case, you want the receiver to be NSDate, and the selector that you want to call is the date method, which returns the current system date.

This is not as straightforward to implement as you might imagine. Passing the string NSDate to the FUNCTION expression evaluates NSDate as a string literal and not the class NSDate. In effect, you would be executing a call that looks like this: [@"NSDate" date], which is not what you want to do. You need to convert the receiver into a class object, not a string.

There is another function expression you can use called CAST that accepts two strings and has the form CAST('string', 'type'). Therefore, you can call the function CAST("NSDate","Class") to get the class NSDate and not the string NSDate. Your final value expression for the dueDate mapping should be FUNCTION (CAST("NSDate","Class"), 'date'). This calls the method [NSDate date], which is what you want. Update the value expression and save the mapping file.

You are finished with the mapping model. You now need to go back into the AppDelegate.m file and make a code change. Because you have created a mapping model, you no longer need Core Data to infer the mapping model from the data model changes. In fact, if you have Core Data infer the changes, the framework does not execute your transformations.

In the persistentStoreCoordinator accessor method, change the options dictionary entry for NSInferMappingModelAutomaticallyOption to NO. This causes Core Data to search the application bundle for a mapping model instead of determining the mappings automatically. Again, you must do this to execute your data transformations and direct Core Data to use your mapping model. The options dictionary creation code should now look like this:

```
NSDictionary *options = [NSDictionary dictionaryWithObjectsAndKeys:
                         [NSNumber numberWithBool:YES],
                         NSMigratePersistentStoresAutomaticallyOption,
                         [NSNumber numberWithBool:NO],
                         NSInferMappingModelAutomaticallyOption, nil];
```

You are ready to build the application and run it. You should see the text of all the tasks change to NEW TASK, and if you click any task, it should have a priority of Medium and the due date should be set to today's date.

SAFELY THREADING WITH CORE DATA

As you work through designing and developing your iOS applications, you may begin to run into performance barriers that are difficult to overcome. For example, you may encounter situations where your user interface is unresponsive while waiting for a time-consuming operation to finish. Traditionally, moving these expensive operations to their own thread is a technique you could use to solve this and other performance issues. The iPhone and iPad are no exception.

Writing threaded code has typically been a difficult task. However, the iOS SDK includes a framework that simplifies the task of creating threads and using these threads to execute your code. You will look at the classes you can use in the iOS to implement concurrency in your application. Then you will build a sample application that executes a time-consuming process. First, you will run this process on the main thread; then you will move that process to its own thread, where you will see a significant improvement in the responsiveness of your application.

Designing for Threading

You should carefully consider the threading model for your application as early on in the design process as possible. It is somewhat difficult to retrofit threading into an application after you have completed the coding. If you can predict the operations that will be the most time consuming, or operations that are self-contained that you can run atomically in a concurrent fashion, you can design threading into your software from the beginning. Although you can implement threading in your application after you encounter a performance problem, your design will be better and your application code cleaner and more maintainable if you consider threading from the start.

As a designer, you should begin your consideration of threading once you have a thorough understanding of your application requirements. Based on these requirements, you should be able to determine the work that your application needs to perform. Once you understand this work, you should see if you can divide this work into atomic, self-contained operations. If you can easily break down a task to one or more atomic operations, it may be a good candidate for concurrency, particularly if the task is independent of other tasks.

A particularly useful case for implementing concurrency is to keep the main thread free to increase the responsiveness of your user interface. If you execute a long-running operation on the main application thread, the user experiences a frozen interface as the operation executes. This is potentially frustrating for users, because they cannot continue to work with your application while it is in this state.

In the example in this section, I graphically illustrate this point. First, you write an application that generates five random numbers and pauses for 1 second between each number. Because this operation runs on the main thread, you can see that your user interface freezes while you are generating these numbers. I have illustrated this scenario on the left in Figure 9-6. Then you take the random number generation and move it to its own thread. After you do this, the user interface is responsive as you generate the random numbers. You can see this expressed on the right in Figure 9-6.

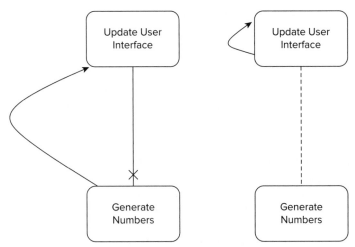

FIGURE 9-6: Threaded versus nonthreaded design

Threading and Core Data

As you could probably guess, you use Core Data to store the data in your sample. The problem is that Core Data is not inherently thread-safe, mostly because the managed object context is not thread-safe. If you modify a managed object in a thread that is different from the thread on which you created the context, the context does not know about the changes to the managed object. This can cause your application to contain stale data. It is also possible to introduce data inconsistencies if you attempt to modify the same managed object on different threads. For these reasons, you should avoid passing Managed Objects across thread boundaries.

One approach to threading with Core Data is to create a separate managed object context on each thread. You can easily achieve this by passing (or obtaining) a reference to the Persistent Store Coordinator and manually creating a context in the thread. Although the Persistent Store Coordinator is not thread-safe, the context knows how to lock the coordinator to enable concurrency using this method. You follow this approach in the sample application. If you need to perform many operations on the context, you should create a new Persistent Store Coordinator on the thread as well. You do not do this in your sample.

Although you never want to pass Managed Objects between threads, you can achieve a similar result by passing `objectID`s. The `objectID` uniquely identifies a managed object. You can obtain a managed object from the `objectID` by calling the `objectWithID:` method on the thread's context.

Threading with NSOperation

The concurrency model implemented in iOS does not require that you create individual threads directly. Rather, the developer creates operations designed to run concurrently and then hands them off to the system. The system then configures the optimal number of threads to use to run the specified concurrent tasks. You can create threads yourself, but if you do, you are responsible for determining the optimum number of threads to create based on the workload and the number of available processor cores. This is a difficult determination to make in real time. Additionally, by using this method, you can write your code to take advantage of future devices that have more than one core. By using the concurrency classes provided in the iOS, the system takes care of this complexity by creating and scheduling the threads for you.

When you decide that you need to move a particular block of code off the main thread and onto its own thread, look no further than the NSOperation class. NSOperation is an abstract base class that you subclass to define and implement atomic operations that you want to dispatch to a separate thread.

When deciding to implement an operation, you have a couple of architectural choices. If you have an existing method in a class that you want to execute asynchronously, you can use the NSInvocationOperation class. NSInvocationOperation is a concrete subclass of NSOperation that allows you to create an operation out of a class method and queue it for execution on a separate thread. If you are introducing threading into an existing application, NSInvocationOperation may be your best bet because you probably already have methods that perform the work you want to thread. It is also useful when you want to choose the method to execute dynamically at runtime because it accepts a selector as the method to run.

If you are building your threading model from scratch, you should implement threading by creating discrete subclasses of NSOperation. This gives you the freedom to implement your operations as you want and alter the way the operation reports status if your application calls for it.

To implement a subclass of NSOperation, at a minimum, you need to implement a custom initializer method to configure your object for use and a main method to perform the task. You can also implement other custom methods you need, such as accessor methods to get at the operation's data or dealloc to free memory allocated by the operation.

Once you have created your operation classes, you need to tell the system to execute them. You accomplish this by creating an instance of NSOperationQueue and adding your NSOperation subclasses to the queue. The system uses operation queues to schedule and execute your operations. It manages the queues, which handle the details of scheduling and executing your threads for you. It is possible to configure dependencies between operations when adding operations to an operation queue. You can also prioritize operations when you add them to a queue.

Core Data Threading Example

As I mentioned, this example application generates five random numbers and pauses for 1 second between each number to simulate a time-consuming synchronous operation. This code blocks the main thread, causing the user interface to become unresponsive while you are generating the random numbers. Then you take the random number generation and move it onto its own thread. Once you do this, the user interface remains responsive while you generate the random numbers.

> **WARNING** *This example involves inserting data into the Core Data context on an off thread. I would not generally recommend doing this; however, I am doing it in this example to demonstrate the mechanics of threading with Core Data. In production applications, you should generally use threads only to perform time-consuming reads and queries from Core Data, not to perform inserts or updates.*

To get started, open Xcode and start a new Master-Detail application. Make sure that "Use Core Data for storage" is checked. Call your new application **RandomNumbers**.

The first thing you will do is update the default data model to hold your random numbers. Open the data model file `RandomNumbers.xcdatamodeld`. In the Event entity, change the name of the `timeStamp` attribute to `randomNumber`. Change the type of the `randomNumber` attribute to `Integer16`. Your data model should look like Figure 9-7.

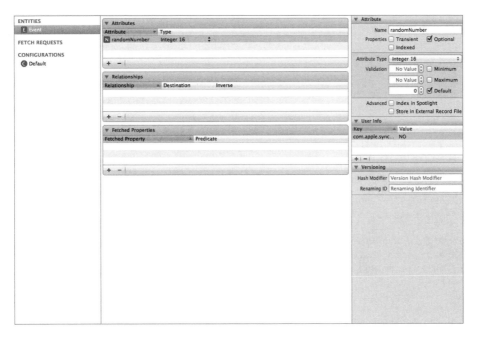

FIGURE 9-7: RandomNumbers data model

Next, you need to make some changes to the `MasterViewController.m` implementation file. In the `configureCell:atIndexPath:` method, change the reference to the old `timeStamp` attribute to `randomNumber`. The `configureCell` method should look like this:

```
- (void)configureCell:(UITableViewCell *)cell
        atIndexPath:(NSIndexPath *)indexPath
{
    NSManagedObject *object = [self.fetchedResultsController
                                objectAtIndexPath:indexPath];
    cell.textLabel.text = [[object valueForKey:@"randomNumber"] description];
}
```

You also need to make this change in the `fetchedResultsController` accessor method:

```
- (NSFetchedResultsController *)fetchedResultsController
{
    if (_fetchedResultsController != nil) {
        return _fetchedResultsController;
```

```objc
    }

    NSFetchRequest *fetchRequest = [[NSFetchRequest alloc] init];
    // Edit the entity name as appropriate.
    NSEntityDescription *entity = [NSEntityDescription entityForName:@"Event"
                            inManagedObjectContext:self.managedObjectContext];
    [fetchRequest setEntity:entity];

    // Set the batch size to a suitable number.
    [fetchRequest setFetchBatchSize:20];

    // Edit the sort key as appropriate.
    NSSortDescriptor *sortDescriptor = [[NSSortDescriptor alloc]
                                initWithKey:@"randomNumber" ascending:NO];
    NSArray *sortDescriptors = @[sortDescriptor];

    [fetchRequest setSortDescriptors:sortDescriptors];

    // Edit the section name key path and cache name if appropriate.
    // nil for section name key path means "no sections."
    NSFetchedResultsController *aFetchedResultsController =
        [[NSFetchedResultsController alloc] initWithFetchRequest:fetchRequest
                            managedObjectContext:self.managedObjectContext
                            sectionNameKeyPath:nil cacheName:@"Master"];
    aFetchedResultsController.delegate = self;
    self.fetchedResultsController = aFetchedResultsController;

    NSError *error = nil;
    if (![self.fetchedResultsController performFetch:&error]) {
        NSLog(@"Unresolved error %@, %@", error, [error userInfo]);
        abort();
    }

    return _fetchedResultsController;
}
```

Now you need to modify the fetched results controller delegate methods:
`controllerWillChangeContent:`, `controller:didChangeSection:atIndex:forChangeType:`,
`controller:didChangeObject:atIndexPath:forChangeType:newIndexPath:`, and
`controllerDidChangeContent:`. Fortunately, the change is simple; just comment those methods out.

The comment below the `controllerDidChangeContent:` method says, "Implementing the
above methods to update the table view in response to individual changes may have performance
implications if a large number of changes are made simultaneously. If this proves to be an issue,
you can instead just implement `controllerDidChangeContent:` which notifies the delegate that all
section and object changes have been processed." In this case, that is exactly what you are doing,
making a large number of changes simultaneously. So commenting out those methods prevents the
fetched results controller from calling them for each change you make to the table view.

Finally, uncomment the `controllerDidChangeContent:` method, which you can use to reload the
data in the table view after making bulk changes to the underlying data. If you do not comment out
the other delegate methods and leave `controllerDidChangeContent:` commented out, you will
notice that the app interface still freezes after moving the time-consuming code to another thread.

Blocking the Main Thread

You are ready to generate your random numbers and populate the Core Data database. You will implement the insertNewObject method, which runs when the user taps the plus button in the top-right corner of the application. Delete the existing implementation and add the following:

```
- (void)insertNewObject:(id)sender
{
    // Create a new instance of the entity managed by the fetched results
    // controller.
    NSManagedObjectContext *context =
    [self.fetchedResultsController managedObjectContext];
    NSEntityDescription *entity =
    [[self.fetchedResultsController fetchRequest] entity];


    // Generate 5 random numbers waiting 1 second between them.
    for (int i=0; i<5; i++){
        NSManagedObject *newManagedObject =
        [NSEntityDescription insertNewObjectForEntityForName:[entity name]
                                      inManagedObjectContext:context];

        [newManagedObject
         setValue:[NSNumber numberWithInt:1 + arc4random() % 10000]
         forKey:@"randomNumber"];

        //  Simulate long synchronous blocking call.
        sleep(1);

    }

    // Save the context.
    NSError *error = nil;
    if (![context save:&error]) {
        NSLog(@"Unresolved error %@, %@", error, [error userInfo]);
        abort();
    }


}
```

The method first obtains a reference to the context and then creates an entity description based on the entity that the fetched results controller manages. In the for loop, you create a new managed object to hold your random number. Then you generate a random number and assign it to the randomNumber attribute of your new managed object. After that, you call the sleep function to sleep the thread for 1 second. Sleep is a blocking call, so you use it here to simulate some code that takes a significant amount of time to execute. Finally, you save the context.

Build and run the application. When the application starts, tap the plus sign in the top-right corner of the interface to invoke the insertNewObject method and generate some random numbers. Try to scroll the Table View while you generate the random numbers. Notice how the user interface becomes unresponsive while you are generating the random numbers. The synchronous call to sleep is blocking the main thread, which controls the UI. After about 5 seconds, you see the random numbers appear in the interface as in Figure 9-8, and control returns to the user.

Moving the Blocking Call

Clearly, this is not a good situation for your application. Users become confused and disappointed when the application doesn't respond when they try to scroll the list while the application is generating random numbers. You can solve this problem by creating an `NSOperation` subclass and then moving the long-running code — in this case the code to generate the random numbers — onto a new thread.

Create a new Objective-C class that is a subclass of `NSOperation` and call it `RandomOperation`. In the header file `RandomOperation.h`, make sure the base class is `NSOperation`:

```
@interface RandomOperation : NSOperation
```

FIGURE 9-8: The running RandomNumbers application

Remember that Core Data is inherently not thread-safe. When you use Core Data with threads, the key is to create a separate context on each thread. You create a context against a Persistent Store Coordinator. You need to write an initializer for your operation that accepts a Persistent Store Coordinator. You then use that coordinator to create a new context into which you add your random numbers.

In the header file, add a property for the coordinator. You do not need to retain the coordinator because you will only hold a pointer to the shared coordinator. Finally, add an initialization method called `initWithPersistentStoreCoordinator` that accepts an `NSPersistentStoreCoordinator*` as an input parameter. Here is the `RandomOperation` header:

```objc
#import <Foundation/Foundation.h>

@interface RandomOperation : NSOperation

@property (nonatomic,weak) NSPersistentStoreCoordinator *coordinator;


-(id) initWithPersistentStoreCoordinator:(NSPersistentStoreCoordinator*)coord;

@end
```

Now you will move on to the `RandomOperation.m` implementation file. In the implementation, implement the `initWithPersistentStoreCoordinator:` method like this:

```objc
-(id) initWithPersistentStoreCoordinator:(NSPersistentStoreCoordinator*)coord
{
    if (self == [super init]) {
        self.coordinator = coord;
    }

    return self;

}
```

All you are doing in this method is calling the superclass `init` method and then storing the `NSPersistentStoreCoordinator*` input parameter in the class `coordinator` property.

You need to implement the `main` method to actually do the work:

```
-(void) main {

    // Create a context using the Persistent Store Coordinator.
    NSManagedObjectContext *managedObjectContext;

    if (self.coordinator != nil) {
        managedObjectContext = [[NSManagedObjectContext alloc] init];
        [managedObjectContext setPersistentStoreCoordinator: self.coordinator];
    }
    else {
        return;
    }

    // Generate 5 random numbers, waiting 1 second between them.
    for (int i=0; i<5; i++){
        NSManagedObject *newManagedObject =
        [NSEntityDescription insertNewObjectForEntityForName:@"Event"
                                        inManagedObjectContext:managedObjectContext];

        [newManagedObject
         setValue:[NSNumber numberWithInt:1 + arc4random() % 10000]

         forKey:@"randomNumber"];

        // Simulate long synchronous blocking call.
        sleep(1);
    }

    // Save the context.
    NSError *error = nil;
    if (![managedObjectContext save:&error]) {
        NSLog(@"Unresolved error %@, %@", error, [error userInfo]);
        abort();
    }

}
```

Most of this method is the same as the `insertNewObject` method from the `MasterViewController`. The major difference is that in the first part of the method, you use the class pointer to the Persistent Store Coordinator to create a new managed object context. There is some added safety code here to return from the method if you do not have a pointer to a valid coordinator. You then proceed to create Managed Objects containing the random numbers just as you did in `insertNewObject`. Finally, you call save on the context. You are now finished with the `RandomOperation` class.

Back in the `MasterViewController.m` implementation, you need to change the `insertNewObject` method to use your operation. At the top of the implementation file, add an `#include` for the `RandomOperation.h` header and another `#include` to include the app delegate:

```
#import "RandomOperation.h"
#import "AppDelegate.h"
```

You get a reference to the coordinator from the app delegate and pass it into your `RandomOperation` in the initializer.

Delete all the existing code from the `insertNewObject` method because you have moved this code into your `RandomOperation` class. You do, however, need to implement the `insertNewObject` method to use your `RandomOperation` class. The following is the implementation of `insertNewObject`:

```
- (void)insertNewObject: (id)sender
{
    // Create an instance of NSOperationQueue.
    NSOperationQueue* operationQueue = [[NSOperationQueue alloc] init];

    // Get a reference to the app delegate to get the coordinator.
    AppDelegate* appDelegate =
        [UIApplication sharedApplication].delegate;

    // Create an instance of the operation.
    RandomOperation* ourOperation =
    [[RandomOperation alloc] initWithPersistentStoreCoordinator:
        appDelegate.persistentStoreCoordinator];

    // Add the operation to the operation queue.
    [operationQueue addOperation:ourOperation];

}
```

First, you create an instance of the `NSOperationQueue` to hold and execute your operation. Next, you get a reference to the app delegate to obtain a reference to the Persistent Store Coordinator. Then you create an instance of your `RandomOperation` class and pass it a reference to the Persistent Store Coordinator. Finally, you call the `addOperation` method on the operation queue to add your operation to the queue and instruct the queue to execute your operation.

Delete your old version of the application from the simulator to delete the old Core Data database. Now run the program and click the plus button to add some new random numbers. If you try to drag the empty table into the application, you notice that the interface is responsive while you are generating the random numbers. However, there is one problem: the numbers never appear. If you wait a few seconds, quit the application, and then restart it, you see five new numbers in the table view. The problem is that the context in the `MasterViewController` is unaware that you have added records to the Core Data database on another thread, so the `FetchedResultsController` has not updated the table view.

Fortunately, there is a way to handle this. Whenever a context performs a save, the context sends an `NSManagedObjectContextDidSaveNotification` notification. The `NSManagedObjectContext` class has a method - `(void)mergeChangesFromContextDidSaveNotification:(NSNotification *)`

`notification` that accepts a notification and merges the changes contained in the notification into the context. Therefore, you need to write some code to listen for and handle the notification. When you receive the notification, you need to call `mergeChangesFromContextDidSaveNotification:` to merge the changes into the context on the main thread.

In the `viewDidLoad` method in the `MasterViewController`, you need to get a reference to the default notification center and add `self` as an observer for the `NSManagedObjectContextDidSaveNotification` message. You do this at the end of `viewDidLoad`. The following is the revised `viewDidLoad` method:

```
- (void)viewDidLoad
{
    [super viewDidLoad];
    // Do any additional setup after loading the view, typically from a nib.
    self.navigationItem.leftBarButtonItem = self.editButtonItem;

    UIBarButtonItem *addButton = [[UIBarButtonItem alloc]
            initWithBarButtonSystemItem:UIBarButtonSystemItemAdd
                            target:self
                            action:@selector(insertNewObject:)];
    self.navigationItem.rightBarButtonItem = addButton;

    // Add an observer for the NSManagedObjectContextDidSaveNotification message.
    NSNotificationCenter* notificationCenter =
    [NSNotificationCenter defaultCenter];

    [notificationCenter addObserver:self
                           selector:@selector(contextSaved:)
                               name:NSManagedObjectContextDidSaveNotification
                             object:nil ];


}
```

Any time that the `save` method is called on a context, Core Data generates an `NSManagedObjectContextDidSaveNotification` message. You are now listening for this message, and when you receive it, you execute the `contextSaved` method in the `MasterViewController`. Now all you have to do is implement the `contextSaved` method to take the notification and call `mergeChangesFromContextDidSaveNotification:` like this:

```
-(void) contextSaved:(NSNotification*)notification
{
    [self.managedObjectContext
        mergeChangesFromContextDidSaveNotification:notification];
}
```

The last thing that you need to do is implement `dealloc` to remove `self` as an observer on the notification center:

```
- (void)dealloc {
    [[NSNotificationCenter defaultCenter] removeObserver:self];
}
```

Delete your old version of the application from the simulator to delete the old Core Data database. Build and run the application. Click the plus button. Notice how the UI is still responsive. In a few moments, the save occurs, the notification is sent, contextSaved is called, the changes are merged into the context, and FetchedResultsController updates the table with the new random numbers. You have successfully moved a time-consuming blocking call off the main thread and onto another thread.

CORE DATA PERFORMANCE

When designing and building an application, one of your primary concerns should be performance. In the context of data-driven applications, you need to consider a few specific aspects of overall application performance.

The first aspect to consider is *perceived performance*. Perceived performance can be defined as how quickly your application appears to complete a task. The key word in this definition is *appears*.

The threading program that you built in the previous section is a perfect example of perceived performance. In the first phase of the example, when your user interface was frozen, you probably felt that the performance of the application was poor because it locked up for 5 seconds as it generated the random numbers. After you moved the random number generation to another thread, the application probably felt much snappier, even though the length of time from when you tapped the plus button to the time the random numbers appeared in the table view was the same. The difference was that the interface was responsive, so you perceived the application to be working more quickly.

You have already learned how to use threading as a tool for increasing the responsiveness and therefore the perceived performance of your application. In this section, I focus on another aspect of iOS programming that has a great impact on performance — memory management. On embedded devices such as the iPhone and iPad, you need to be particularly concerned about memory, because iOS does not currently support virtual memory or paging. If your application runs low on memory, the OS issues you a warning and tells certain parts of your application to unload. This causes a time-consuming reinitialization to occur when the user needs to use these parts of your application again. Additionally, it is possible that your application can run out of memory, causing the OS to terminate your application.

After you look at some memory management items, you will learn a few ways you can increase the actual speed of your applications.

Faulting

Core Data uses a technique called *faulting* to reduce the memory footprint of your application by keeping unused data out of memory. Faulted objects are instances of NSManagedObject or your NSManagedObject subclass that are retrieved in a fetch request, but not all the properties of the object are immediately loaded into memory. Core Data can conserve memory by loading only the parts of an object or a relationship that you need.

Core Data does not populate a faulted object's properties until you access them. This process, called *fault realization*, happens automatically. You do not have to execute a fetch to realize a fault, but behind the scenes, Core Data may need to execute additional fetches to realize faults.

Faulting most often occurs when objects are associated with relationships. If you recall the sample from Chapter 6, you had two entities, Task and Location, as illustrated in Figure 9-9. On the All Tasks screen, you queried Core Data for a list of all Tasks. Because the Task entity has a relationship entity, you would think that Core Data would load the related `Location` object into memory as well. However, it does not. The Location entity in this instance is faulted. Core Data has no reason to load a related `Location` object into memory unless the code asks for it.

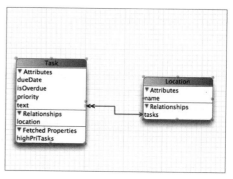

FIGURE 9-9: Tasks application data model

Core Data does not bring relationships to a faulted object into memory until you access them. This behavior allows Core Data to conserve memory by keeping unused objects out of memory until you need them.

In this example, Core Data is preventing only one object, the `Location`, from being loaded. You may be thinking that this doesn't save too much memory. That is true, but imagine if the location object were also related to a series of other objects, each with its own relations, and so on. In large object hierarchies, the memory conserved by faulting can be considerable.

Data Store Types

When using Core Data, you can specify the type of data store that Core Data uses to persist your data. Your options are SQLite, binary, and in-memory. Although you will usually use the SQLite store type, you will take a brief look at all of the types.

The in-memory store does not actually persist your data. As the name says, the data store is in memory. When your application quits, your data is gone. This could be useful when you want to use Core Data to manage your application data when that data does not need to be persisted from session to session. This is typically not very helpful in iOS applications because your application session could end at any time, particularly if the user of an iPhone gets a call.

The binary store type uses a proprietary binary format to store your data. The primary drawback of using the binary format is that all the data stored in the data store is loaded into memory when the data store is loaded. There is no provision to leave parts of the data on disk. In contrast, an SQLite database remains largely left on disk, and Core Data only brings the parts that you specifically query for into memory.

Although there is no "disk" on the iPhone or iPad, there is a difference between application memory and storage memory. When I say "on disk," I am referring to the space on the device that is used for data storage. The iPhone or iPad cannot use this storage space to execute applications, so there is a distinction between the application memory available for use by your application's execution and disk space, which is available for data storage.

Storing Binary Data

You may be tempted to store binary data such as images or sound clips in your Managed Objects using Core Data. In general, this is not a good idea. You are generally better off storing the binary data on disk and storing the path to the data in Core Data as you did in the catalog example earlier in the book. This is because you may store a large chunk of data in an object and not realize you are bringing all that data into memory when Core Data loads the object. For example, if you stored the images for each of your catalog items in the database but did not display them on the main catalog screen, these potentially large images would still be loaded into memory.

If you do store binary data in Core Data, do not store the data in frequently accessed rows. For example, you should not store an image in the same managed object that you use to display items in a table if you are not also displaying the image because the image will be loaded into memory regardless of whether you display the image.

Entity Inheritance

You may remember from Chapter 6 that you can implement an entity hierarchy in Core Data using inheritance and the parent field of an entity in the entity detail pane. I have illustrated a hypothetical entity hierarchy in Figure 9-10.

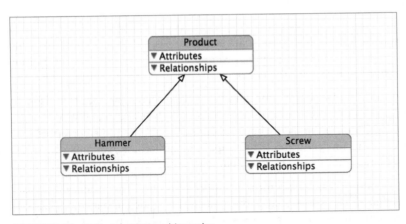

FIGURE 9-10: Entity inheritance hierarchy

Although this is a feature of Core Data, you need to be aware of how the implementation uses memory in the back-end SQLite data store. An entity hierarchy is not the same as the equivalent object hierarchy in an object-oriented design. In the entity hierarchy, all the attributes of all the entities in the hierarchy are stored in the same database table. This can lead to inefficiency in how the data is stored on disk, causing excessive memory usage.

To illustrate this, imagine that in the hierarchy illustrated in Figure 9-10, the Product entity has attributes P1 and P2, the Hammer has attributes H1 and H2, and the Screw has attributes S1 and S2. In the current implementation of Core Data, Core Data stores the data for all three of these entities in a single table, as illustrated in Figure 9-11. You can see that the Hammer entities have unused space in the table for the Screw-related fields and vice versa for Screw objects. Although this is a simple example, it illustrates the storage issue. The problem gets worse as your inheritance hierarchy gets larger and deeper. Therefore, you should carefully consider the storage and memory requirements of your Core Data store if you plan to implement a deep and complex entity hierarchy.

Record	Product		Hammer		Screw	
	P1	P2	H1	H2	S1	S2
Hammer 1	value	value	value	value		
Hammer 2	value	value	value	value		
Hammer 3	value	value	value	value		
Screw 1	value	value			value	value
Screw 2	value	value			value	value
Screw 3	value	value			value	value

FIGURE 9-11: Core Data storage for entity inheritance

Runtime Performance

Thus far, this chapter has covered improving perceived performance with threading and being conscious of how Core Data is using memory. This section lays out a few general tips that you can look to in an attempt to increase the runtime performance of your application.

First, when designing your model, avoid over-normalization of your data. Remember that you are not designing a relational database but an object persistence mechanism. Feel free to de-normalize your data if it makes building the displays for the application easier. You should try to find a balance between normalization and speeding up your queries for rapid display. Accessing data through a relationship is more expensive than retrieving an attribute. Consider this before normalizing your data. In addition, querying across relationships is expensive. Determine if you really need to do it, or de-normalize the data if it makes sense. For example, if you have an application that stores names and addresses, it may make sense from a UI perspective to keep the state name in the same table as the rest of the address as opposed to normalizing it out into its own table. You may not want to take the overhead penalty for following a relationship to a state table every time you need to look up an address if you will always be showing the address and state together.

I know it may seem obvious, but you should try to fetch only the data that you need when you need it. This tip ties in with the "Faulting" section from earlier in the chapter. Core Data will generally not bring in data that you are not going to use. Therefore, you should be careful to avoid building your queries in a way that forces Core Data to bring data into memory that you may not need.

Another thing you can do to increase your application performance is take advantage of Core Data caching. The Persistent Store Coordinator holds fetched results in its caches. This is particularly useful when you can set up a background thread to fetch data while the foreground remains responsive. Then the foreground thread can read the data from the persistent coordinator's cache when necessary, avoiding another trip to the data store.

The final tip has to do with the order of the items in your search predicate. Search order in predicates is important. Put likely-to-fail criteria first so the comparison can end quickly. The engine evaluates predicates in order, and if one part of the predicate fails, the engine will move on to the next record. You can potentially reduce query times by placing likely-to-fail criteria at the beginning of a predicate if it makes sense.

Managing Changes with the Fetched Results Controller

This section looks at how you can use an `NSFetchedResultsController` to update your table view based on changes to a result set.

When the data managed by an `NSFetchedResultsController` changes, the fetched results controller calls several delegate methods. You have the option to either use these delegate methods to update the associated table view based on each individual change or simply handle one delegate method and tell the table view to reload its data. You saw this earlier in the Core Data Threading Example.

Implementing the delegate methods to handle individual updates can yield better performance for changes to individual rows because you are not reloading all the table data each time there is an update. There is a trade-off, however, because if there are many simultaneous changes to the data, it may be cheaper to just reload all the data because presenting many individual changes can be time consuming.

To keep the Tasks application simple, I took the latter approach. In the `MasterViewController`, you implemented the `controllerDidChangeContent` delegate method to reload the data for the table view. Here is the implementation:

```
- (void)controllerDidChangeContent:(NSFetchedResultsController *)controller {
    [self.taskTableView reloadData];
}
```

Compare the way you just reloaded all the data for the table in the Tasks application to the way you handle individual cell updates in the default master-detail template. In the default template code, the fetched results controller processes each update individually. The delegate methods that the `NSFetchedResultsController` calls are `controllerWillChangeContent:`, `controller:did ChangeSection:atIndex:forChangeType`, `controller:didChangeObject:atIndexPath:forChange Type:newIndexPath:`, and `controllerDidChangeContent:`.

The fetched results controller calls the `controllerWillChangeContent:` and `controllerDidChangeContent:` methods to bracket the changes that are being made to the result set. You implement these methods to tell the table that changes will begin and end, respectively. You can think of these methods as beginning and committing a transaction to the table. Here is the implementation from the template:

```
- (void)controllerWillChangeContent:(NSFetchedResultsController *)controller {
    [self.tableView beginUpdates];
}

- (void)controllerDidChangeContent:(NSFetchedResultsController *)controller {
    [self.tableView endUpdates];
}
```

This code simply tells the table view that updates are coming and that updates are finished. The `endUpdates` call triggers the table view to display and optionally animate the changes to the data.

The fetched results controller calls the `controller:didChangeSection:atIndex:forChangeType` method when the sections of the table view should change. The two types of changes that you will receive in this method are `NSFetchedResultsChangeInsert` and `NSFetchedResultsChangeDelete`. Your code can determine if the changes to the data have added or removed a section from the table view. Typically, you implement a `switch` statement to handle these two cases, as shown in the template code:

```
- (void)controller:(NSFetchedResultsController *)controller
    didChangeSection:(id <NSFetchedResultsSectionInfo>)sectionInfo
            atIndex:(NSUInteger)sectionIndex
    forChangeType:(NSFetchedResultsChangeType)type {

    switch(type) {
        case NSFetchedResultsChangeInsert:
            [self.tableView insertSections:
             [NSIndexSet indexSetWithIndex:sectionIndex]
                     withRowAnimation:UITableViewRowAnimationFade];
            break;

        case NSFetchedResultsChangeDelete:
            [self.tableView deleteSections:
             [NSIndexSet indexSetWithIndex:sectionIndex]
                     withRowAnimation:UITableViewRowAnimationFade];
            break;
    }
}
```

This code simply inserts or deletes the section that it receives in the method call.

Finally, the fetched results controller calls the `controller:didChangeObject:atIndex Path:forChangeType:newIndexPath:` method when objects in the data store change. In this method, your code needs to handle these four operations: `NSFetchedResultsChangeInsert`, `NSFetchedResultsChangeDelete`, `NSFetchedResultsChangeMove`, and `NSFetchedResultsChangeUpdate`. Again, you usually handle calls to this method in a `switch` statement and make the appropriate changes to your table view. Here is the default template code:

```
- (void)controller:(NSFetchedResultsController *)controller didChangeObject:(id)anObject
        atIndexPath:(NSIndexPath *)indexPath
    forChangeType:(NSFetchedResultsChangeType)type
        newIndexPath:(NSIndexPath *)newIndexPath
{
    UITableView *tableView = self.tableView;

    switch(type) {
        case NSFetchedResultsChangeInsert:
            [tableView insertRowsAtIndexPaths:@[newIndexPath]
    withRowAnimation:UITableViewRowAnimationFade];
            break;

        case NSFetchedResultsChangeDelete:
            [tableView deleteRowsAtIndexPaths:@[indexPath]
    withRowAnimation:UITableViewRowAnimationFade];
            break;

        case NSFetchedResultsChangeUpdate:
```

```
            [self configureCell:[tableView cellForRowAtIndexPath:indexPath]
    atIndexPath:indexPath];
            break;

        case NSFetchedResultsChangeMove:
            [tableView deleteRowsAtIndexPaths:@[indexPath]
    withRowAnimation:UITableViewRowAnimationFade];
            [tableView insertRowsAtIndexPaths:@[newIndexPath]
    withRowAnimation:UITableViewRowAnimationFade];
            break;
    }
}
```

PERFORMANCE ANALYSIS USING INSTRUMENTS

When you are confronted with a performance issue in your application, the first place you should turn is Instruments. Instruments is a GUI-based tool that you can use to profile your application in myriad ways. Instruments features a plug-in architecture that allows you to pick and choose from a library of recording instruments to use in profiling your application, as shown in Figure 9-12. Additionally, you can create custom instruments that use DTrace to examine the execution of your application.

Once you have selected the recording instruments you would like to use, you can use Instruments to run your application, either in the iOS Simulator or on the actual device, and gather the data you need to optimize your application. After you start your application, Instruments profiles the application in the background as the application runs. As your application is running, you see the graphs in Instruments react to operations that you perform in the application.

The main feature of the tool's interface is the timeline. The premise is that you are recording the operation of your application in real time and can later go back and look at the state of your application at any time

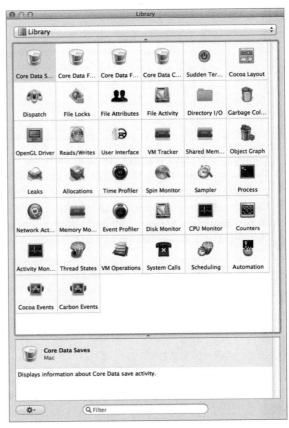

FIGURE 9-12: Instruments tool library

during your test run. This is an incredibly powerful tool to use when you are trying to find problems in your application.

Once you narrow down a particular problem to a specific time on the timeline, you can drill down into the application stack. The stack provides information on the code that was executing at the time that Instruments took the sample. You can select your code segments in the stack to view the source code.

Instruments is an incredibly powerful tool, and I cannot recommend it enough. If you have never used Instruments, you owe it to yourself to take a look at it. In this section, I walk you through the use of Instruments to profile your Core Data application using the Core Data–related tools.

Starting Instruments

In general, you can start the Instruments tool either by launching the application from the Xcode menu bar by selecting Xcode ⇨ Open Developer Tool ⇨ Instruments or by selecting Product ⇨ Profile from the menu bar.

Open the RandomNumbers project in Xcode. The easiest way to profile your project with Instruments is to use the Product ⇨ Profile menu item in Xcode. This finds your project binary and starts it in Instruments. Instruments then asks you to choose a trace template to use to profile your project as in Figure 9-13. *Trace templates* are predefined sets of tools you can use to profile certain areas of your application.

FIGURE 9-13: Instruments trace templates

Because you want to use the Core Data tools, select the Core Data trace template. This adds the Core Data tools to the instrumentation for your project. Click the Profile button to continue.

You are now ready to begin your test run. After you click the Profile button, Instruments launches the iOS simulator and starts your recording. You see the `RandomNumbers` application start up in the simulator. Once the application starts, you should see the timeline begin to move, indicating that Instruments is profiling your application. You should also notice a spike in the top instrument, Core Data Fetches. This indicates that a fetch has occurred in the application. Tap the plus button in the simulator to generate some random numbers. In 5 seconds, you should see a spike in the Core Data Saves instrument indicating that a save has occurred. Stop the recording by clicking the red button.

The Instruments Interface

Now that you have finished your test run, you should analyze your data. To do this, you need to understand how to use the Instruments interface. You can see the interface as it should look having completed your test run in Figure 9-14.

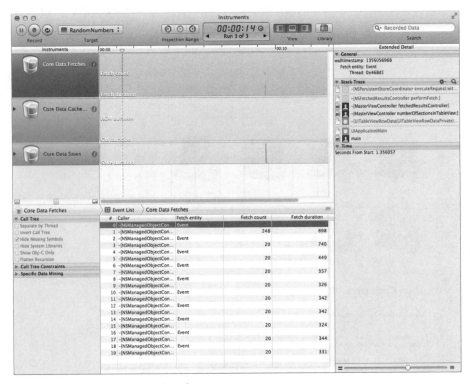

FIGURE 9-14: The Instruments interface

The Instruments pane on the left side shows all the instruments that are active for the current test run.

The Track pane in the middle shows a graph representing different things for different instruments. For the Core Data Fetches instrument, the Track pane shows the count of items fetched and the duration of the fetch. The Track pane displays the time that an event occurred during the test run. You can adjust the time scale using the slider below the Instruments pane. You can also scroll the Track pane using the scrollbar at the bottom of the pane.

Below the Track pane is the Detail pane. Like the Track pane, the Detail pane shows different details based on the tool you have selected in the Instruments pane. For the Core Data Fetches instrument, the Detail pane displays a sequence number, the caller of the fetch method, the fetched entity, the count of the number of items returned in the fetch, and the duration of the fetch in microseconds.

You can select an item in the Detail pane to view more detail about the item in the Extended Detail pane on the right side. The Extended Detail pane is particularly useful because it shows a stack trace for the method call you have selected in the Detail pane. Select a fetch in the Detail pane to view its stack trace.

I find it useful to display the file icons in the Extended Detail pane because doing this makes the calls in the stack that originated in your code obvious. You can enable the file icons by clicking the gear icon in the Extended Details pane. In Figure 9-14, you can see that the fetch selected in the Detail pane is initiated in the code in the `MasterViewController fetchedResultsController` method. If you double-click an item in the call stack that corresponds to one of your source code files, in this case the call to the `MasterViewController fetchedResultsController` method, Instruments displays the source code in the Detail pane, showing you the exact line of code that made the fetch request. Click the Event List View button at the top of the Detail pane to get back from the source code to the list of events.

The Core Data Instruments

Four instruments are available for use with Core Data: Core Data Saves, Fetches, Faults, and Cache Misses.

Core Data Saves reports the methods that invoke the Core Data `save` operation. It also reports the duration of the operation in microseconds. Opening the extended detail view shows the stack trace for the call and the time at which the call occurred.

You can use this tool to discover how often you are saving data and find a balance between saving too much and not saving enough. Each save operation causes a disk write, which can hurt performance, but not saving often enough results in using excess memory to hold the data in memory.

Core Data Fetches reports all fetches made against Core Data. The tool reports the name of the fetched entity, the caller, the number of records returned, and the duration of the fetch in microseconds. Opening the extended detail view shows the stack trace for the call and the time at which the call occurred.

Fetch operations are costly because they read from disk. You can use this tool to help optimize your search predicates to limit the number of rows returned by a fetch request.

Core Data Faults reports fault events that occur as the result of needing to realize object references in to-many relationships. The tool reports the method causing the fault, the object that was faulted, the execution duration in microseconds, the relationship fault source, the name of the relationship, and the relationship fault duration in microseconds. You can open the extended detail view to see the stack trace for the call and the time at which the call occurred.

As discussed earlier in this chapter, faulting is a memory-saving technique that comes at the expense of time when Core Data realizes the fault. If you find that Core Data is spending an excessive amount of time resolving faults, but your memory consumption is low, you could consider pre-fetching related objects instead of having them realized through a fault.

The Cache Misses tool reports fault events that result in cache misses. This is a subset of the information provided by the Faults instrument. The tool displays the method that caused the cache miss, the duration of execution for the fault handler in microseconds, the relationship cache miss source, the name of the relationship, and the relationship cache miss duration. Opening the extended detail view shows the stack trace for the call and the time at which the call occurred.

Similar to the remedy for extensive faulting, you can mitigate cache misses by pre-fetching data. If data is not in the cache, it leads to an expensive read from disk operation.

MOVING FORWARD

In this chapter, you learned how to version your data models and migrate between versions to add new features to your database and application. You also learned how to safely use Core Data in a threaded application with NSOperation to increase performance. You looked at some Core Data performance considerations and tips. Finally, you discovered how to use the Instruments tool to observe your application's performance when using Core Data.

This ends the section of the book on Core Data. You should now feel confident that you are able to implement a data-driven application using this exciting and useful technology. You should also have all the tools in your arsenal to be able to debug and troubleshoot problems that may arise while you are using Core Data.

In the next section of the book, you learn how to use XML and Web Services in your applications to communicate with other applications over the Internet.

PART III
Application Integration Using Web Services

10

Working with XML on the iPhone

WHAT'S IN THIS CHAPTER?

➤ Creating HTTP requests and receiving responses

➤ Understanding XML and how to use it in your applications

➤ Parsing XML to obtain the data that you need

➤ Using an external C library with your iOS SDK applications

➤ Generating XML using the libxml library

WROX.COM CODE DOWNLOADS FOR THIS CHAPTER

The wrox.com code downloads for this chapter are found at www.wrox.com/remtitle .cgi?isbn=1118391845 on the Download Code tab. The code is in the Chapter 10 download and individually named according to the names throughout the chapter.

In Part I of the book, you learned how to get data out of an enterprise database and store it on an iOS device with SQLite. You also learned how to display data on the device using the UITableView and customized UITableViewCell objects. In Part II, you learned how to create and manage data on iOS using Core Data. In this section, you learn how you can get your data off the device and into another system using XML and web services.

This chapter lays the groundwork for working with web services by showing you how to send data over the web using the HTTP protocol and how to deal with the returned data in XML format.

You learn how to communicate with external servers over the web and how to deal with the response from a web server. I cover the Cocoa classes to be used in the following chapter for working with web services.

IOS SDK AND THE WEB

This section provides a quick refresh of the architecture of a web-based application. Then you explore the classes in the iOS SDK and the Cocoa framework that support network communication over the web using the HTTP protocol. You finish this section by starting the chapter example, which gets data from the RSS feed for a website and parses the returned XML.

Web Application Architecture

The majority of content on the web, including web services, use HTTP (Hypertext Transfer Protocol) to communicate. HTTP is a standardized communication protocol that runs on top of the TCP/IP protocol that connects computers. HTTP implements a request-response design like that typically used in client-server applications. The web server that deals out web pages is the server, and the web browser or application is the typical client.

In a request-response design, the client makes a request to the web server. Then the web server processes the request and returns a response to the client, as illustrated in Figure 10-1.

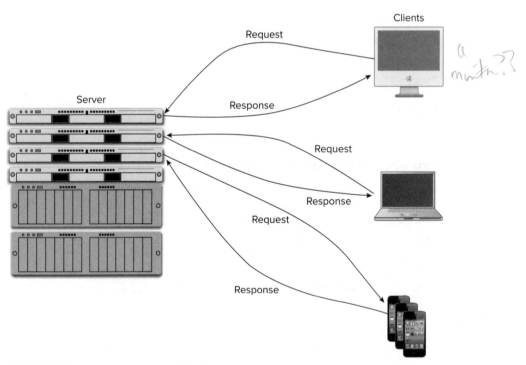

FIGURE 10-1: Request-response architecture

To initiate communication with a website, you need a couple of basic elements. First, you need to know the address or the URL of the server to which you would like to connect. A URL, or Uniform Resource Locator, is a text representation of the numeric address of a website. A name server then converts this text representation into a numbered IP address.

You can use a URL to create a request to ask a server for data. Then you need to make a connection to the server and submit your request. If everything goes according to plan, the server replies with a response that contains the data you requested.

Synchronous Data Retrieval

[handwritten: synchronous means one at a time, use A & b l'guide but "of"]

The Cocoa framework provides helper methods on common classes to assist you in quickly and easily retrieving data from a web page. For instance, the NSString class has a class method called stringWithContentsOfURL:encoding:error: that you can use to create a string with the contents of a URL. Similarly, NSData supports the dataWithContentsOfURL: method, which you can use to retrieve arbitrary data from the web.

As tempting as it may be to retrieve your web data with a single line of code, you need to be aware of some serious drawbacks when considering this approach. First and foremost is that these operations are synchronous. If you call one of these helper methods on the main thread, your application blocks until the call finishes. This may not seem like a huge limitation when running your iOS sample code on your computer with a fast Internet connection. However, on a slow Internet connection such as 3G, or if you attempt to retrieve a large amount of data, the main thread could be tied up for a significant amount of time. Remember that your UI runs on this thread and that any long-running operations on the main thread can cause your interface to become unresponsive.

Another issue is that these methods do not give you a lot of detail when a problem occurs with the call. Error handling is important when working with web-based services and networked calls in general. When writing networked code, you should code as defensively as possible. Network connections are notoriously unreliable. Your code should be able to handle dropped connections. You should also code with the expectation that the service you are calling may not be available or that it may return data you are not expecting.

The stringWithContentsOfURL:encoding:error: helper call on NSString returns a reference to an NSError object that you can interrogate for details about the error. However, the NSData method simply returns nil if it cannot retrieve the desired data. This is not good if you want to take different actions based on the type of error that occurs.

Although the aforementioned class methods may be appropriate for simply retrieving data from a website, you cannot use them to post data back to the site. Because the focus of this section of the book is on interacting with web services and exchanging data between the client and server, you won't be looking into these methods in any more detail. You should be aware that this functionality is available if you need or want to grab a little bit of data from the web in a quick and dirty manner. However, I would not recommend using these methods in a production application for the reasons just discussed.

The URL Loading System

Apple calls the set of Cocoa classes included in the iOS SDK for supporting communication using URLs and HTTP the *URL Loading System*. These classes support the request-response–based architecture described in the beginning of this section. You take a brief look at the classes that make up this system and then move on to an example where you use this framework to connect to a website and retrieve some data.

You use the `NSURL` and `NSURLRequest` classes to create the request to send to the server.

`NSURL` provides an object model that represents the address of a resource. You can use `NSURL` to reference local objects on the file system of a device as well as find resources on a local network or the Internet.

The `NSURLRequest` class represents all the data required to make a request to a web server, including its address as a URL. You typically initialize `NSURLRequest` objects by passing in an `NSURL` object. In addition, the request can contain other data specific to the protocol, such as the HTTP method to use when submitting the request and HTTP header fields. If you need to modify these properties before submitting your request, you must use the `NSMutableURLRequest` type. You will see this in the next chapter when you look at sending POST requests to a web server.

Next, you use the `NSURLConnection` class to make a connection to the server and submit your request. Once you submit your request via the connection, the framework calls the delegate methods of the `NSURLConnection` class based on the response received from the server.

Once enough data has come back from the server, the framework creates an `NSURLResponse` object and calls the delegate method `connection:didReceiveResponse:`. You can examine the response object to determine some information about the data the server sends you, including the expected content length and the encoding type of the incoming data.

Finally, you implement the `connection:didReceiveData:` delegate method to accept the data that the server returns. The connection object calls this method multiple times, as data flows to your application from the web server. When the server is finished sending the response, the connection object calls the `connectionDidFinishLoading:` delegate method, at which point you can release the connection to the server and go about processing the data you received. I have illustrated this process in Figure 10-2.

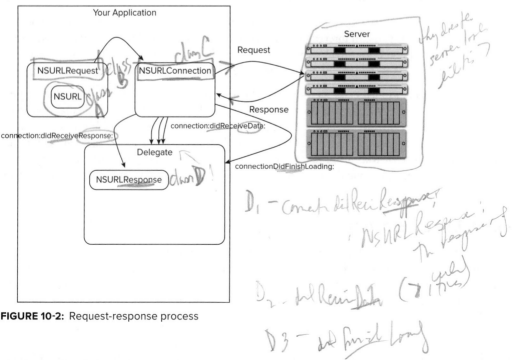

FIGURE 10-2: Request-response process

URL loading

classes for:
Caching
authentication & cookies

In addition to the basic set of classes you typically use to handle URL requests and responses, the URL Loading System provides some classes you can use to support caching, authentication to secure sites and services, and cookies.

Web Access Sample

You should now have an understanding of the architecture behind making calls to a server over the web and the classes that Apple provides to support this architecture. In this section, you build an application that goes out over the web and grabs the headlines from the RSS feed for CNN.com.

RSS stands for Really Simple Syndication. It is a well-defined schema for XML used to publish information to the web. Newsreaders are applications that can consume RSS feeds and present the feed data to users. Apple's Safari browser has basic newsreader functionality, as does Mail.app.

The only thing that you typically need to access an RSS feed is the URL for the feed. After creating and sending a request for the feed's URL, the server processes the request and returns the XML data corresponding to the feed that you requested.

The first part of the example uses the URL Loading System classes that I described in the previous section to make a request for the top stories from CNN.com. You simply dump the response to the console log in this example. After I cover parsing XML in the next section, you add code to the sample to parse the data returned from the feed and display the title of each story in your interface. This may not be the most groundbreaking newsreader application, but it introduces you to all the technologies you need to be able to use web services in the next chapter.

Starting the Application

Open Xcode and create a new Single View Application project. Call the new application **RSSSample**. Leave the Use Storyboards and Use Automatic Reference Counting checkboxes checked.

You need a data object to hold the data that the server returns after you call it with your request. You also need an action method to call when the user taps on a button in the application to start retrieving the feed data.

Open the `ViewController.h` header file. Add an `NSMutableData` property called **responseData**. This object will hold the data returned from the server in response to your web request.

You may not be familiar with the `NSData` class and its mutable subclass `NSMutableData`. `NSData` is a Cocoa wrapper for a byte buffer. Any time you expect to handle a series of bytes, you should probably use `NSData`. If you need to modify that buffer, as you do in this example, you must use `NSMutableData`. In this example, you receive the response data from the server in chunks. Each time you get a chunk, you append it to your `receivedData` object. This is why you need to use `NSMutableData`.

The following is the header for the `ViewController`:

```
#import <UIKit/UIKit.h>

@interface ViewController : UIViewController

@property (strong, nonatomic) NSMutableData *responseData;

@end
```

Building the Interface

The next step in building the sample application is to build the user interface. For the first part of the example, the user interface is very simple, consisting of only a single button, as you can see from Figure 10-3.

To build the interface, you need to open the `MainStoryboard.storyboard` file in Xcode. Add a Round Rect button to the view, resize the button as shown in Figure 10-3, and change the text of the button to read `Send Request`.

Next, use the Assistant Editor to open the `ViewController.h` header file next to the storyboard. Ctrl-drag the Send Request button from the storyboard and drop it into the `ViewController` header below the property definition. In the resulting popup, configure the connection as an Action and name the action **buttonTapped**. You can leave the Type as id, the Event as Touch Up Inside, and the Arguments as Sender. Click the Connect button to link the Send Request button to your code.

Your `ViewController.h` header should now look like this:

FIGURE 10-3: RSS sample application interface

```
#import <UIKit/UIKit.h>

@interface ViewController : UIViewController

@property (strong, nonatomic) NSMutableData *responseData;
- (IBAction)buttonTapped:(id)sender;

@end
```

It's time to move on to the `ViewController` implementation. Open the `ViewController.m` implementation file in Xcode.

If you recall from previous chapters, I like to add a stub method for any UI-based action methods. This way, you can run the application after you build the user interface and verify that you have all the actions and outlets properly connected. Implement the `buttonTapped:` IBAction method to log the name of the method:

```
- (IBAction)buttonTapped:(id)sender {
    NSLog(@"buttonTapped");
}
```

At this point in the example, that's all there is to the interface. To keep things simple, you send the response from the web server to the console log so that you can examine the output. When you get to the XML parsing section, you add a new interface element to display the headlines retrieved from the RSS feed.

You are now ready to build and run the application. Once the application comes up in the simulator, tap the button that you added in the storyboard. Make sure that you see the `NSLog` statement in the console log to ensure that you have correctly hooked up the button to the code.

Requesting Data from the Server

When someone taps the Send Request button in the application interface, you want to make a request to CNN.com and get the contents of the RSS feed. In this section, you will use the classes in the URL Loading System framework to make a request to the server and handle the response.

Creating the Request

To make a request to a web server, you have to create an NSURLRequest object. There is a convenience method on the NSURLRequest that you can use to create the request with an NSURL object. Remember that you use the NSURL class to represent URLs. You can create an NSURL object using an NSString.

You implement the buttonTapped method to create and submit the request to the CNN.com web server like this:

```
- (IBAction)buttonTapped:(id)sender {
    NSLog(@"buttonTapped");

    // Create the request.
    NSURLRequest *request = [NSURLRequest requestWithURL:
        [NSURL URLWithString:@"http://rss.cnn.com/rss/cnn_topstories.rss"]
        cachePolicy:NSURLRequestUseProtocolCachePolicy
        timeoutInterval: 30.0];

    // Create the connection and send the request.
    NSURLConnection *connection =
        [[NSURLConnection alloc] initWithRequest:request delegate:self];

    // Make sure the connection is good.
    if (connection) {
        // Instantiate the responseData data structure to store the response.
        self.responseData = [NSMutableData data];
    }
    else {
        NSLog (@"The connection failed");
    }
}
```

The first thing this code does is create an instance of an NSURLRequest object using the requestWithURL:cachePolicy:timeoutInterval: class method. You initialize the request by passing it an NSURL you create from a string that points to the URL you are interested in retrieving.

The cachePolicy parameter specifies how you want to handle obtaining the data for the request. You can either send the request directly to the server or attempt to retrieve the results from the cache. In this case, you specify the default caching policy specified by the protocol that you are using — in this case, HTTP.

You can pass another value in for this parameter to give you more fine-grained control of where the data for the request comes from:

➤ If you pass NSURLRequestReloadIgnoringLocalCacheData, the NSURLRequest object ignores locally cached data and sends the request to the server regardless of the data contained in the local cache.

➤ Passing NSURLRequestReloadIgnoringLocalAndRemoteCacheData has the same effect as passing NSURLRequestReloadIgnoringLocalCacheData, but it also instructs the object to ignore intermediary caches, such as those provided by proxy servers.

➤ NSURLRequestReturnCacheDataElseLoad instructs the request to always return data from the cache if it is available, and if it is not available to load the data from the server.

➤ Using NSURLRequestReturnCacheDataDontLoad instructs the request to use only cached data and not to attempt to get the data from the server if the data is not available in the cache. You could use this value to implement an Offline mode in your application.

➤ Passing NSURLRequestReloadRevalidatingCacheData allows the use of the cached data if the server validates that the cached data is current.

The final parameter in the requestWithURL:cachePolicy:timeoutInterval: method is the time-out interval. You use this to specify how long you want to wait for a response before failing with a time-out.

After creating the request, the code goes on to create a connection to the server by creating an instance of an NSURLConnection object. In the initializer, you pass in the request that you just created and declare the delegate for the connection to be self. Initializing the connection in this manner causes the NSURLConnection object to immediately send the request that you created to the server.

Finally, you test that the connection is valid and then instantiate your responseData property to handle the data that the server returns to your application.

NSURLConnection Delegate Methods

Once you send your request to the server, the connection object begins to call the delegate methods to inform you of the status of the request and response. You need to implement the delegate methods to handle the messages that the NSURLConnection is sending to you.

The first method you implement is connection:willSendRequest:redirectResponse:. The connection object calls this method when a redirect occurs based on the request made to the server. When making a request to a URL, the server sometimes redirects your call to another server. Implementing this method handles that case. To proceed normally, simply return the request that the NSURLConnection object passed into the method. This is the proposed URL to which you will be redirected. You can return nil to prevent redirects from occurring. You should be prepared to receive this message multiple times if the web server performs multiple redirects. Here is the implementation:

```
// Called when a redirect will cause the URL of the request to change.
- (NSURLRequest *)connection:(NSURLConnection *)connection
            willSendRequest:(NSURLRequest *)request
```

```
                     redirectResponse:(NSURLResponse *)redirectResponse

{
    NSLog (@"connection:willSendRequest:redirectResponse:");
    return request;
}
```

The next delegate method is `connection:didReceiveAuthenticationChallenge:`. You receive this message if the web server you are calling requires authentication to complete the request. Because I am trying to keep this example simple to show the basics of using the URL Loading System, the example will not use any authentication. However, in a production application, you are often required to authenticate to retrieve data from a URL.

When the `connection:didReceiveAuthenticationChallenge:` method is called, you can respond in one of three ways:

➤ Provide the necessary credentials by creating an `NSURLCredential` object and populating it with the data that the server expects. You can determine what the server expects by interrogating the `NSURLAuthenticationChallenge` object that you receive as a parameter to the `didReceiveAuthenticationChallenge:` method.

➤ Attempt to continue without passing credentials. You can do this by calling the `continue WithoutCredentialsForAuthenticationChallenge:` method on the sender of the challenge. Doing this typically causes the request to fail, but it may allow the user to retrieve a URL that does not require authentication.

➤ Cancel the request by calling the `cancelAuthenticationChallenge` method on the sender of the challenge. Doing this sends the `connection:didCancelAuthenticationChallenge:` message to your delegate.

You can find more information about authentication in the "URL Loading System Programming Guide" in the Xcode help and on the Apple developer website.

In this implementation, you just log that the `NSURLConnection` object invoked this method:

```
// Called when the server requires authentication.
- (void)connection:(NSURLConnection *)connection
    didReceiveAuthenticationChallenge:(NSURLAuthenticationChallenge *)challenge
{
    NSLog (@"connection:didReceiveAuthenticationChallenge:");
}
```

If you cancel the authentication challenge on the connection, the connection object calls the next delegate method, `connection:didCancelAuthenticationChallenge:`. Again, you implement this method by simply logging the call:

```
// Called when the authentication challenge is cancelled on the connection.
- (void)connection:(NSURLConnection *)connection
    didCancelAuthenticationChallenge:(NSURLAuthenticationChallenge *)challenge
{
    NSLog (@"connection:didCancelAuthenticationChallenge:");
}
```

The next delegate method, `connection:didReceiveResponse:`, provides some useful information about the response that you have received from the server. The connection object calls this method when the connection has enough data to create an `NSURLResponse` object. You can interrogate the response for some useful information such as encoding type and expected length:

```
// Called when the connection has enough data to create an NSURLResponse.
- (void)connection:(NSURLConnection *)connection
    didReceiveResponse:(NSURLResponse *)response {
    NSLog (@"connection:didReceiveResponse:");
    NSLog(@"expectedContentLength: %qi", [response expectedContentLength] );
    NSLog(@"textEncodingName: %@", [response textEncodingName] );

    [self.responseData setLength:0];

}
```

It is possible to receive this method more than once, so to be safe, you discard the data in your received buffer when you receive a call to this method by setting the length of the `responseData` buffer to 0.

The next delegate method to implement is `connection:didReceiveData:`. The connection object calls this method each time the connection receives a chunk of data. You receive calls to this method multiple times, as you receive data from the server. In the implementation, you append the data received in this method to the `responseData` `NSMutableData` instance. Remember that you need to use the mutable version of `NSData` because you append data to the object each time this method runs. Here is the implementation:

```
// Called each time the connection receives a chunk of data.
- (void)connection:(NSURLConnection *)connection didReceiveData:(NSData *)data
{
    NSLog (@"connection:didReceiveData:");

    // Append the received data to the responseData property.
    [self.responseData appendData:data];

}
```

You receive the `connection:willCacheResponse:` message before the connection caches the response. This method gives you a chance to change the cached response. There is a `userInfo` property that you can use to add information to the cached response before the connection object caches the response. You can implement this method to return `nil` if you do not want to cache the response. In the example, you simply pass along the cached response:

```
// Called before the response is cached.
- (NSCachedURLResponse *)connection:(NSURLConnection *)connection
                willCacheResponse:(NSCachedURLResponse *)cachedResponse
{
    NSLog (@"connection:willCacheResponse:");
    // Simply return the response to cache.
    return cachedResponse;
}
```

The last call that you receive is either connectionDidFinishLoading: or connection:didFailWithError:. In the case of connectionDidFinishLoading:, the connection object calls this method when the connection has successfully received the complete response. The implementation takes the response data and converts it to a string for display in the console:

```objc
// Called when the connection has successfully received the complete response.
- (void)connectionDidFinishLoading:(NSURLConnection *)connection
{
    NSLog (@"connectionDidFinishLoading:");

    // Convert the data to a string and log the response string.
    NSString *responseString = [[NSString alloc]
                                initWithData:self.responseData
                                encoding:NSUTF8StringEncoding];
    NSLog(@"Response String: \n%@", responseString);

}
```

The connection object calls the connection:didFailWithError: method when there is an error in receiving the response. This method simply dumps the error description to the log. In a production application, you probably want to handle the error a little more robustly by possibly allowing the user to retry the operation, or at least providing some feedback as to why the operation failed. Here is the implementation:

```objc
// Called when an error occurs in loading the response.
- (void)connection:(NSURLConnection *)connection
  didFailWithError:(NSError *)error
{
    NSLog (@"connection:didFailWithError:");

    NSLog (@"%@",[error localizedDescription]);
}
```

The completed code for the ViewController should look like this:

```objc
#import "ViewController.h"

@interface ViewController ()

@end

@implementation ViewController

- (void)viewDidLoad
{
    [super viewDidLoad];
    // Do any additional setup after loading the view, typically from a nib.
}

- (void)didReceiveMemoryWarning
{
    [super didReceiveMemoryWarning];
```

```
        // Dispose of any resources that can be re-created.
}

- (IBAction)buttonTapped:(id)sender {
    NSLog(@"buttonTapped");

    // Create the request.
    NSURLRequest *request = [NSURLRequest requestWithURL:
        [NSURL URLWithString:@"http://rss.cnn.com/rss/cnn_topstories.rss"]
        cachePolicy:NSURLRequestUseProtocolCachePolicy
        timeoutInterval: 30.0];

    // Create the connection and send the request.
    NSURLConnection *connection =
        [[NSURLConnection alloc] initWithRequest:request delegate:self];

    // Make sure that the connection is good.
    if (connection) {
        // Instantiate the responseData data structure to store the response.
        self.responseData = [NSMutableData data];
    }
    else {
        NSLog (@"The connection failed");
    }
}

#pragma mark - Connection Routines
// Called when a redirect will cause the URL of the request to change.
- (NSURLRequest *)connection:(NSURLConnection *)connection
            willSendRequest:(NSURLRequest *)request
            redirectResponse:(NSURLResponse *)redirectResponse

{
    NSLog (@"connection:willSendRequest:redirectResponse:");
    return request;
}

// Called when the server requires authentication.
- (void)connection:(NSURLConnection *)connection
didReceiveAuthenticationChallenge:(NSURLAuthenticationChallenge *)challenge
{
    NSLog (@"connection:didReceiveAuthenticationChallenge:");
}

// Called when the authentication challenge is cancelled on the connection.
- (void)connection:(NSURLConnection *)connection
didCancelAuthenticationChallenge:(NSURLAuthenticationChallenge *)challenge
{
    NSLog (@"connection:didCancelAuthenticationChallenge:");
}

// Called when the connection has enough data to create an NSURLResponse.
```

```objc
- (void)connection:(NSURLConnection *)connection
didReceiveResponse:(NSURLResponse *)response {
    NSLog (@"connection:didReceiveResponse:");
    NSLog (@"expectedContentLength: %qi", [response expectedContentLength] );
    NSLog (@"textEncodingName: %@", [response textEncodingName]);

    [self.responseData setLength:0];

}

// Called each time the connection receives a chunk of data.
- (void)connection:(NSURLConnection *)connection didReceiveData:(NSData *)data
{
    NSLog (@"connection:didReceiveData:");

    // Append the received data to the responseData property.
    [self.responseData appendData:data];

}

// Called before the response is cached.
- (NSCachedURLResponse *)connection:(NSURLConnection *)connection
                willCacheResponse:(NSCachedURLResponse *)cachedResponse
{
    NSLog (@"connection:willCacheResponse:");
    // Simply return the response to cache.
    return cachedResponse;
}

// Called when the connection has successfully received the complete response.
- (void)connectionDidFinishLoading:(NSURLConnection *)connection
{
    NSLog (@"connectionDidFinishLoading:");

    // Convert the data to a string and log the response string.
    NSString *responseString = [[NSString alloc]
                            initWithData:self.responseData
                            encoding:NSUTF8StringEncoding];
    NSLog(@"Response String: \n%@", responseString);

}

// Called when an error occurs in loading the response.
- (void)connection:(NSURLConnection *)connection
  didFailWithError:(NSError *)error
{
    NSLog (@"connection:didFailWithError:");

    NSLog (@"%@",[error localizedDescription]);
}

@end
```

Finishing Up

Build and run the application. When the application starts, tap the Send Request button. Make sure that you have the debug area displayed so that you can see the output console. If you have an active Internet connection, you should see a log entry in the console log for each delegate method as it runs. When the connection has finished downloading the data from the server, you should see the XML document that you retrieved from the CNN.com RSS feed.

> **WARNING** *You need to have an active Internet connection for this code to work correctly.*

XML AND THE IPHONE SDK

In this section, you learn about XML and how to integrate XML content into your application. You extend the sample project to parse the XML contained in the response from the CNN.com web server using the NSXMLParser class.

Brief Overview of XML

XML (the eXtensible Markup Language) defines rules for the electronic transmission and storage of data. The W3C web standards body defines the XML 1.0 specification. You can find the entire specification at www.w3.org/TR/REC-xml/.

The goal of XML is to provide software engineers with a tool that they can use and extend to define arbitrary data. XML is extensible in that, unlike HTML or other markup languages, the designer can introduce and include arbitrary tags that make sense for his application. In conjunction with an arbitrary schema, the developer can provide a formal definition of the schema via XSD (XML Schema Definition) or DTD (Document Type Definition) files. Users of the XML data can then use these schema definitions to validate the XML document and ensure that it conforms to the defined schema.

There are many standardized schemas currently in use, including RSS (which you used in the chapter example), SOAP, Atom, and XHTML. In addition, software vendors such as Apple and Microsoft use XML as the file storage format for many of their document-based software packages.

XML files are plaintext and human readable, which helps make them easy for developers to deal with. XML files typically define data in a tree structure, as shown in Figure 10-4. Because the tree is a common software paradigm, programmers typically have little problem parsing and using the data contained in an XML file with this structure. The fact that the designer can make up his own tags makes XML extremely flexible to use while you are designing the structure of your data and messages.

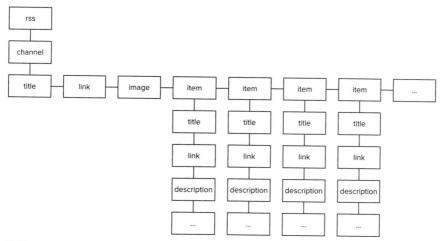

FIGURE 10-4: CNN.com RSS feed XML tree

You can use XML to store data locally. However, it is equally if not more common to use XML as a way to transfer data over the Internet. Many data transfer schemas, such as RSS and SOAP, rely on XML to exchange data. In the sample in the previous section, you received an XML response from the server in response to your request. In this section, you learn how to parse that response to obtain the headlines contained in the feed.

Parsing XML with NSXML Parser

After you make a call to a web service or, in this case, an RSS feed, you often must parse the XML response to get the data that you need for your application. There are a couple of different programming models when it comes to parsing XML: specifically, DOM and SAX.

DOM stands for Document Object Model. The DOM programming model represents the tree structure of XML as a tree of objects that you can access in your code. The objects in the DOM model represent nodes, attributes, comments, and other XML elements. In your code, you can recursively navigate the tree or perform queries to return all nodes with a particular name, attribute, and so on.

When you use a DOM parser, the entire XML document that you are parsing is loaded into memory at one time. For large XML documents, a DOM model can consume quite a bit of memory. Because memory is such a scarce resource on mobile devices such as the iPhone and iPad, Apple chose not to provide a DOM parser with the SDK. However, if you need the functionality provided by a DOM parser, you can use the C library libxml2. I cover the use of libxml2 later in this chapter in the section, "Generating XML with libxml." Before you settle on using DOM, make sure you consider the performance and memory implications of loading the entire XML document into memory.

The parser provided by Apple in the iOS SDK is SAX based. SAX stands for Serial Access Parser. SAX implements an event-driven parser that calls delegate methods as the parser moves through an XML document. The parser navigates the XML document sequentially and calls methods in a defined order when it finds things like tags, attributes, and text characters. Apple has provided an event-driven SAX parser with the `NSXMLParser` class. Although implementing the delegate methods to use a SAX parser can be cumbersome, it is far less resource intensive in terms of memory usage than using a DOM parser.

When you want to parse XML, you typically follow a few specific steps. First, you need to locate the XML that you want to parse. You can obtain the XML from the web through a URL, from a text file on a network or on the device, or from somewhere else and stored in an `NSData` object.

Once you have located your XML, you create an instance of the `NSXMLParser` class. When you initialize your instance, you pass in the XML data that you want to parse.

Once you have this code in place, you need to code the delegate methods that the `NSXMLParser` calls because it encounters certain elements in the XML file.

The parser calls the `parserDidStartDocument` and `parserDidEndDocument` methods when it begins and finishes parsing the document, respectively. You can add code to `parserDidStartDocument` to set up any variables that you intend to use during parsing. Likewise, you want to clean up any of these variables in the `parserDidEndDocument` method.

When the parser encounters a start element or tag, it calls the `parser:didStartElement:namespaceURI:qualifiedName:attributes:` method. In this method, you typically check to see which element was started and prepare to process the data within the element accordingly. The parser passes element attributes as a dictionary with the name of the attribute as the key in the dictionary and the value of the attribute as the value. The corresponding method that the parser calls when an element ends is `parser:didEndElement:namespaceURI:qualifiedName:`. In this method, you typically take some action when an element that you are interested in has ended.

When the parser finds characters contained within an element, it calls the `parser:foundCharacters:` method. The parser may call this method multiple times for a single element, so you should append any characters sent to this method to a mutable string until you receive a `didEndElement` call. This is similar to the way you handled the `connection:didReceiveData:` delegate method call from the `NSURLConnection` object earlier in this chapter.

If the parser encounters an error, it calls the `parser:parseErrorOccurred:` method. You should handle this method and provide some information to the user about the error that occurred.

Extending the Example, Parsing the XML

In this section, you extend the example code that you developed in the first part of this chapter to get the CNN.com RSS feed from the Internet. You take the XML document that you retrieve from the call to the website, parse it, and display the titles of the headline stories.

Starting Out

Before you begin, you need to know what you are looking for in the XML that you retrieve from the server. Figure 10-5 shows a representative sample of the XML that you retrieve when you call the CNN.com RSS feed website. You can download the complete XML file from this book's website.

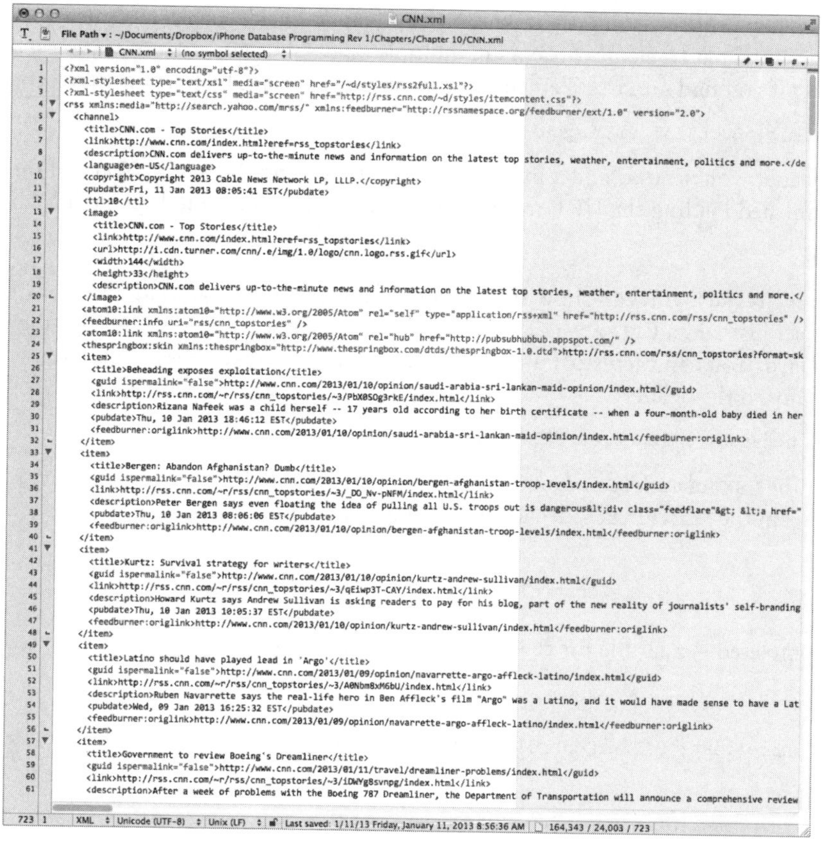

FIGURE 10-5: CNN.com RSS feed XML

You are interested in the `item` entities that encapsulate the information about a particular story item. Within the item, you only really want to grab the text inside the `title` element because your application only displays the title of each story. If you were building a more intricate application, you could create an item class with title, link, publication date, and description properties as well. However, for simplicity, you only capture and display the title of the article.

Setting Up to Parse

If you do not have the RSSSample project open, open it now. You need to add a property to the `ViewController` to hold the characters captured from the XML for the title. In the `ViewController.h` header, add a property:

```
@property (strong, nonatomic) NSMutableString *capturedCharacters;
```

Notice that you use an object of type `NSMutableString`. You must use a mutable string because you append to the current string each time you get a delegate method call to the `parser:foundCharacters:` method. Keep in mind that the `NSString` class is immutable, meaning that you cannot change it after its initial creation.

Next, you add a boolean flag property so that you know when you are inside an `item` element. You need to know this because the `title` element occurs in multiple places, but you are only interested in extracting the characters if you find a `title` element inside an `item` element. Here is the declaration:

```
@property (nonatomic) BOOL inItemElement;
```

While you are in the header, you need to add a method that starts parsing the XML. You call this method once you are finished loading the URL from the website. Call the new method **parseXML**:

```
- (void) parseXML;
```

Instead of just logging the results, you can show the output of your parsing in your application. To keep this example simple, just add a `UITextView` outlet to the interface so that you can access the property in the storyboard. You can then stuff all the headlines into that text view. Add a property variable for a `UITextView` to the header:

```
@property (weak, nonatomic) IBOutlet UITextView *textView;
```

Because you implement the `NSXMLParserDelegate` protocol to parse the XML in the `ViewController`, you need to indicate this in the `@interface` declaration. Modify the `ViewController`, `@interface` declaration like this:

```
@interface ViewController : UIViewController <NSXMLParserDelegate>
```

The following is the completed header file for the `ViewController` class:

```
#import <UIKit/UIKit.h>

@interface ViewController : UIViewController <NSXMLParserDelegate>


@property (strong, nonatomic) NSMutableData *responseData;
@property (strong, nonatomic) NSMutableString *capturedCharacters;
@property (nonatomic) BOOL inItemElement;

@property (weak, nonatomic) IBOutlet UITextView *textView;


- (IBAction)buttonTapped:(id)sender;

- (void) parseXML;


@end
```

Now you can move on to the implementation file. In `ViewController.m`, modify the `connectionDidFinishLoading` delegate method to call the new `parseXML` method. When you finish loading all the data from the URL, you want to parse and display it. Here is the `connectionDidFinishLoading` delegate method:

```
- (void)connectionDidFinishLoading:(NSURLConnection *)connection
{
    NSLog (@"connectionDidFinishLoading:");

    // Convert the data to a string and log the response string.
    NSString *responseString = [[NSString alloc]
```

```
                                initWithData:self.responseData
                                    encoding:NSUTF8StringEncoding];
    NSLog(@"Response String: \n%@", responseString);

    [self parseXML];

}
```

The next step is to implement the `parseXML` method to instantiate the parser, set the delegate, and begin parsing the XML:

```
#pragma mark - Parser Routines
- (void) parseXML {
    NSLog (@"parseXML");

    // Initialize the parser with the NSData from the RSS feed.
    NSXMLParser *xmlParser = [[NSXMLParser alloc]
                                initWithData:self.responseData];

    // Set the delegate to self.
    [xmlParser setDelegate:self];

    // Start the parser.
    if (![xmlParser parse])
    {
        NSLog (@"An error occurred in the parsing");
    }

}
```

Modifying the Interface

You need to add a text view to the user interface in the storyboard. You will use this text view to display the headlines that you retrieve from the RSS feed. Open the storyboard and add a `UITextView` to the interface, as shown in Figure 10-6. Clear the default text from the text view and move the Send Request button to the top of the screen. Finally, connect the outlet from the `UITextView` to the `textView` property in the `ViewController.h` header file. You can easily do this by using the Assistant editor to display the header next to the storyboard. Then, right-drag the text view and drop it on the `textView` property in the header.

Implementing the Parser Delegate Methods

As the `NSXMLParser` works its way through the XML document, it calls a series of delegate methods. You need to implement these methods to get the information that you need from the XML document.

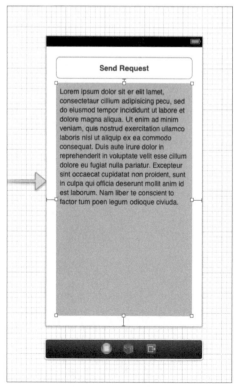

FIGURE 10-6: RSSSample user interface

First, you implement the start and end document methods:

```
// Called when the parser begins parsing the document.
- (void)parserDidStartDocument:(NSXMLParser *)parser {
    NSLog (@"parserDidStartDocument");
    self.inItemElement = NO;
    self.textView.text = nil ;
}
// Called when the parser finishes parsing the document.
- (void)parserDidEndDocument:(NSXMLParser *)parser {
    NSLog (@"parserDidEndDocument");
}
```

The code is relatively straightforward. First, for illustrative purposes, you log the name of the method that you are executing. This will prove instructive when you look at the console log. Examining the order in which the parser calls the delegate methods will help you to better understand how the parser works. Additionally, it is useful for debugging purposes should you encounter an error in your parsing logic.

In the `parserDidStartDocument:` method, you also initialize the `inItemElement` flag to `NO` because you are not currently in an `item` element. In the `parserDidEndDocument` method, you log that you have reached the end of the document.

Next, you implement the start and end element functions. Here is the `parser:didStartElement:namespaceURI:qualifiedName:attributes:` method implementation:

```
// Called when the parser encounters a start element.
- (void) parser:(NSXMLParser *)parser
didStartElement:(NSString *)elementName
   namespaceURI:(NSString *)namespaceURI
  qualifiedName:(NSString *)qualifiedName
     attributes:(NSDictionary *)attributeDict {
    NSLog (@"didStartElement");

    // Check to see which element you have found.
    if ([elementName isEqualToString:@"item"]) {
        // You are in an item element.
        self.inItemElement = YES;
    }

    // If you are inside an item element and found a title.
    if (self.inItemElement && [elementName isEqualToString:@"title"]) {
        // Initialize the capturedCharacters instance variable.
        self.capturedCharacters = [[NSMutableString alloc] initWithCapacity:100];
    }
}
```

This method receives the name of the element that has started as a parameter. You check the name of the element and set the `inItemElement` flag if you have started an `item` element. Next, check to see if you have started a `title` element. You may be wondering why you are checking to see if you have started a `title` element when you already know that you have started an `item` element. Remember that the parser calls this method each time an element begins. Because XML is typically organized as a tree data structure, you will almost certainly have elements nested within other elements. Therefore, each time that the parser calls this method, you could be starting a new element without having ended another element.

Notice that when you check for starting a `title` element, you also verify that you are in an `item` element. If you encounter a `title` element and you are not in an `item`, you don't need to do anything. If, however, you hit a `title` element and you are already in an `item` element, you initialize the `capturedCharacters` instance variable. You will use this `NSMutableString` to aggregate the characters from the `title` element in the call to `parser:foundCharacters:`.

You will do some similar processing in the `didEndElement` method:

```
// Called when the parser encounters an end element.
- (void)parser:(NSXMLParser *)parser didEndElement:(NSString *)elementName
   namespaceURI:(NSString *)namespaceURI qualifiedName:(NSString *)qName {

    NSLog (@"didEndElement");

    // Check to see which element you have ended.

    // If you are inside an item element and ended a title.
    if (self.inItemElement && [elementName isEqualToString:@"title"]) {
        NSLog (@"capturedCharacters: %@" , self.capturedCharacters);

        self.textView.text = [self.textView.text
                        stringByAppendingFormat:@"%@\n\n",self.capturedCharacters];

        // Clean up the capturedCharacters instance variable.
        self.capturedCharacters = nil;
    }


    if ([elementName isEqualToString:@"item"]) {
        // You are no longer inside an item element.
        self.inItemElement = NO;
    }

}
```

First, you check to see if you are in an `item` element and are ending a `title` element. If so, you log the characters that you captured, append them to the text view, and clean up the `capturedCharacters` property because you are finished with it for now. Next, check to see if the parser called this method because you are ending an `item` element. If that is the case, you set the `inItemElement` flag to `NO`. Remember that the parser calls this method each time an element ends. It is up to the developer to determine what element has ended and to act accordingly.

The last delegate method to implement is `parser:foundCharacters:`. In this method, you simply check to make sure that the `capturedCharacters` property is not `nil`, and then you append the characters passed into the method to the `capturedCharacters` mutable string. Keep in mind that the parser may call this method multiple times for the text inside a single element. That is why you are using a mutable string and appending the characters to it each time the parser calls this method. Here is the implementation:

```
// Called when the parser finds characters contained within an element.
- (void)parser:(NSXMLParser *)parser foundCharacters:(NSString *)string {
    if (self.capturedCharacters != nil) {
        [self.capturedCharacters appendString:string];
    }
}
```

You are now ready to build and run the application. As long as you have an active Internet connection, the application should download and parse the RSS feed and display the top headlines from CNN.com in the text view.

Generating XML with libxml

Sometimes when you are building a connected application, you need to generate XML from scratch. Thus far, you have only explored consuming XML. In this section, you learn how to build XML dynamically at runtime.

There are a several ways to build XML in your application. You should choose an appropriate method based on the needs of your application.

If you need to send a specific XML message with only limited dynamic data, your best bet is to build a format string using the XML and placeholders for your variables. For instance, if you were implementing an online address book, a message that you send to the server to add an entry may look something like this:

```
<address>
    <name>John Smith</name>
    <street>1 Ocean Blvd</street>
    <city>Isle Of Palms</city>
    <state>SC</state>
    <zip>29451</zip>
</address>
```

In this case, you do not need to build the XML document structure at runtime because you already know the structure of the message at compile time. Simply use a format string like this:

```
NSString *s = [[NSString alloc] initWithFormat:
                    "<address>"
                    "<name>%@</name>"
                    "<street>%@</street>"
                    "<city>%@</city>"
                    "<state>%@</state>"
                    "<zip>%@</zip>"
                    "</address>",name,street,city,state,zip];
```

On the other hand, if you are building an order entry system and the number of items in an order could change based on conditions in the application at runtime, you probably need to generate the entire XML tree dynamically. While generating XML with the NSXMLParser is possible as outlined in Apple's "Event-Driven XML Programming Guide for Cocoa," it is difficult and not intuitive.

It is far easier to build an XML document using the DOM model for XML parsing. Apple does not provide a DOM parser on iOS, but there is a C XML library called libxml installed on iOS that you can use for DOM processing. It is free and available under the MIT license, which you can find at www.opensource.org/licenses/mit-license.html.

While generating XML dynamically at runtime, using libxml is far easier than using NSXMLParser. Unfortunately, the library is in C, so it is a little more difficult to work with than an Objective-C library. If you think you will be building dynamic XML often, you may want to consider wrapping libxml in your own Objective-C wrappers. Additionally, there are several open source wrappers for libxml; however, you will not be looking at them. You will better understand how to use libxml by using the library directly in your code.

Using libxml in your project is as simple as adding the `libxml2.dylib` file to your project and editing your header search paths so that the compiler can find the headers. Then you only need to include the headers that you plan to use in your source code, and you are ready to go.

You may also want to use libxml if your application needs the capabilities of a DOM parser as opposed to the Apple-provided SAX parser. The libxml library also supports XPath. XPath is a query language that you can use to search your XML. In addition, libxml supports validating XML files against a DTD (Document Type Definition). You can think of a DTD as the specification for the XML used in a document.

XML Generation Sample

In this section, you will build a simple application that generates a simple XML document tree, as shown in Figure 10-7. The XML that you generate will look like this:

```
<?xml version="1.0"?>
<rootNode>
  <ChildNode1>Child Node Content</ChildNode1>
  <AttributedNode attribute1="First" attribute2="Second">
    <AttributedChild>Attributed Node Child Node</AttributedChild>
  </AttributedNode>
  <AttachedNode>Attached Node Text</AttachedNode>
  <!--This is an XML Comment-->
</rootNode>
```

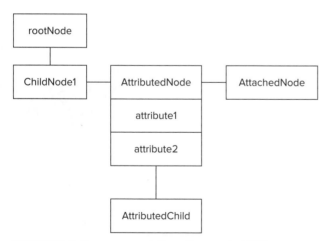

FIGURE 10-7: Tree representation of generated XML

Granted, this is not the most complex XML document, but the code will demonstrate everything you need to generate XML documents of limitless complexity.

Create a new Single View Application called **MakeXML**. The first thing that you have to do is tell Xcode that you will be using the libxml library. Right-click the project in the left pane of Xcode and select New Group. Call the new group **C Libs**. Next, add a reference to the `libxml2.dylib` dynamic library. Click the `MakeXML` project at the top of the Project Navigator. In the middle editor area, select the Build Phases tab. Find the Link Binary with Libraries section and click the plus sign at the bottom of the section to add a new library. In the Choose frameworks and libraries to add dialog, select `libxml2.dylib`. You should see `libxml2.dylib` appear in the Project Navigator. Drag the `libxml2.dylib` file and drop it into the C Libs group in the Project Navigator.

You now have to alter the search path in Xcode so that Xcode can find the headers for libxml2 when you are ready to compile. Click the `MakeXML` project at the top of the Project Navigator. In the middle editor area, select the Build Settings tab. In the Search Paths area, add the path `$SDK_DIR/usr/include/libxml2` to the Header Search Paths item. Enable Xcode to search this directory and below by changing the setting in the second column of the add file popup to recursive. Note that you will have to change the SDK in the path based on which SDK you are compiling with. This example assumes that you are using the iOS SDK version 6.0 and that you have installed the SDK in the default location.

Now you will build the UI for the application, as shown in Figure 10-8.

In the `ViewController.h` header, add a `UITextView` outlet property called **textView**. Add a method `generateXML` that you will call to generate the XML. Here is the complete `ViewController.h` header:

```objc
#import <UIKit/UIKit.h>

@interface ViewController : UIViewController
@property (weak, nonatomic) IBOutlet UITextView *textView;


-(void) generateXML;


@end
```

Next, open the `MainStoryboard` file and add a `UITextView` control. Resize and position the control to take up the whole screen. Connect the `UITextView` in the storyboard to the `textView` property in the `ViewController.h` header file.

FIGURE 10-8: MakeXML sample UI

In the `ViewController.m` implementation file, add the `import` statements for the libxml parser and libxml tree headers:

```objc
#import <libxml/parser.h>
#import <libxml/tree.h>
```

You construct the XML in the `generateXML` method. I want to demonstrate a few different things in this method, so it's long. I will walk through the method section by section, and then I will show the whole method in its entirety.

You first declare an `xmlDocPtr` object. `xmlDocPtr` is a `typedef` for a pointer to the libxml `xmlDoc` structure. This structure represents the entire XML document that you will be creating:

```
- (void) generateXML {
    xmlDocPtr doc;
```

Every XML document consists of a set of nodes. At the top of the tree of nodes is a special node called the *root* node. You need to declare the root node as an `xmlNodePtr` object. `xmlNodePtr` is a `typedef` to a pointer to an `xmlNode` struct. The library uses the `xmlNode` struct to represent all XML nodes. Here is the declaration of the root node:

```
xmlNodePtr rootNode;
```

Next, you call the `xmlNewDoc` library function to create a new document model. You assign the return to the doc object:

```
// Create a new XML document.
doc = xmlNewDoc(BAD_CAST "1.0");
```

You may have noticed the frightening-looking `BAD_CAST` parameter in the function call. `BAD_CAST` is simply a macro defined in the `xmlstring.h` header that you can use to cast a string to the `xmlChar*` type. You will likely use `BAD_CAST` anywhere that you use a string object with the library. Remember that libxml is a C library, so you should omit the @ symbol that you use when defining `NSString` objects in Objective-C. In this case, you are using a C-style `char*` string.

The next step is to create the root node. You call the `xmlNewNode` function to create a new node. The method takes an `xmlNsPtr` and an `xmlChar*` as its parameters. You can use the `xmlNsPtr` parameter to specify a namespace for your node instance. You use namespaces to ensure that the XML elements defined in your document do not conflict with elements with the same name in other XML documents. You do not use namespaces in this sample. The `xmlChar*` is the name of your new node. In this case, name the node **rootNode**:

```
// Create the root node.
rootNode = xmlNewNode(NULL, BAD_CAST "rootNode");
```

Because the root element is the starting point for the document, you must explicitly set the root element. Call the `xmlDocSetRootElement` function and pass in a pointer to the document and the root node:

```
xmlDocSetRootElement(doc, rootNode);
```

Now you are ready to start adding additional nodes to the tree. The easiest way to add new nodes to your XML document tree is to use the `xmlNewChild` function. This function accepts a pointer to the parent node for the new node, a namespace pointer if you are using namespaces, the name of the new node, and the textual content of the node. You create `ChildNode1` as follows:

```
// Create a new child off the root.
    xmlNewChild(rootNode, NULL, BAD_CAST "ChildNode1",
            BAD_CAST "Child Node Content");
```

This statement creates a node called `ChildNode1` that is a child of the `rootNode` and contains the string `Child Node Content`. Again, you can see that you use the `BAD_CAST` macro to pass string data into the library.

Next, you create a node that contains XML attributes. Attributes are another way to add data to an element node. Because you append a child to this node, you declare an `xmlNodePtr` so that you can hold a reference to the new node. Then you use the `xmlNewChild` function that you have already seen to create a new node. You call the `xmlNewProp` function to add two attributes to the `attributedNode`, as follows:

```
// Add a node with attributes.
    xmlNodePtr attributedNode;
    attributedNode = xmlNewChild (rootNode, NULL,
                              BAD_CAST "AttributedNode", NULL);
    xmlNewProp(attributedNode, BAD_CAST "attribute1", BAD_CAST "First");
    xmlNewProp(attributedNode, BAD_CAST "attribute2", BAD_CAST "Second");
```

So far, you have only added nodes as children of the root node. Part of the power of XML is the ability to express hierarchical data in a tree structure. To demonstrate this capability, add the next node as a child of the attributed node. You can accomplish this by passing the pointer to the attributed node into the call to `xmlNewChild`:

```
// Create a node as a child of the attributed node.
    xmlNewChild (attributedNode, NULL, BAD_CAST "AttributedChild",
            BAD_CAST "Attributed Node Child Node");
```

Instead of appending the new `AttributedChild` node to the `rootNode`, this code appends the `AttributedChild` node to the `attributedNode`.

Sometimes it may be more convenient to build the node and its associated text separately. You can do this and then add the node to the tree after you have populated it with text or other subnodes. A new node and its text content are created in this snippet. Then you add the text to the node and append the node to the root node, as follows:

```
// You can also build nodes and text separately and add them
    // to the tree later.
    xmlNodePtr attachNode = xmlNewNode(NULL, BAD_CAST "AttachedNode");
    xmlNodePtr nodeText = xmlNewText(BAD_CAST "Attached Node Text");
    // Add the text to the node.
    xmlAddChild(attachNode, nodeText);
    // Add the node to the root.
    xmlAddChild(rootNode, attachNode);
```

It is even possible to include XML comments using the `xmlNewComment` function:

```
// You can even include comments.
    xmlNodePtr comment;
    comment = xmlNewComment(BAD_CAST "This is an XML Comment");
    xmlAddChild(rootNode, comment);
```

Now that you have built the complete tree for the document, you have to tell the library to output the contents so that you can put the document into an `NSString`. Because libxml is a C library, there is a function that outputs the document to a memory buffer. You need to declare a memory buffer of type `xmlChar*` and an `int` variable to hold the length of the buffer. Once you have these variables set up, you can call the `xmlDocDumpFormatMemory` function. This function outputs the

XML document to the buffer that you pass in and returns the size of the buffer in a reference variable that you also pass in to the function. The last parameter to the xmlDocDumpFormatMemory function indicates that you would like space characters added to format the output. Here is the code:

```
// Write the doc.
    xmlChar *outputBuffer;
    int bufferSize;

    // You are responsible for freeing the buffer using xmlFree.
    // Dump the document to a buffer.
    xmlDocDumpFormatMemory(doc, &outputBuffer, &bufferSize, 1);
```

Fortunately, because Objective-C is a superset of C, Apple has created plenty of helper functions for getting data from C types into Objective-C types. For instance, the NSString class has a method called initWithBytes:length:encoding: that accepts a C char* buffer, a length, and an encoding type, and initializes an NSString with that data. You use that function to create an NSString from your XML document dump:

```
// Create an NSString from the buffer.
NSString *xmlString = [[NSString alloc] initWithBytes:outputBuffer
                                       length:bufferSize
                                       encoding:NSUTF8StringEncoding];
```

Next, you log the XML document string to the console and put the string in the text view in the user interface:

```
// Log the XML string that you created.
NSLog (@"output: \n%@", xmlString);

// Display the text in the text view.
[self.textView setText:xmlString];
```

Finally, you call some cleanup functions from libxml to free the memory that you allocated when creating your XML document. First, you free the output buffer that you just created with a call to xmlFree. Then, you free the memory used by the XML document with a call to xmlFreeDoc. You end with a call to xmlCleanupParser because you are completely finished with the XML parser:

```
// Clean up.
// Free the output buffer.
xmlFree(outputBuffer);

// Release all the structures in the document, including the tree.
xmlFreeDoc(doc);
xmlCleanupParser();
```

You should be careful to ensure that you are not using the XML parser anywhere else in your code before calling xmlCleanupParser. This method cleans up any remaining memory that the XML parser allocated, including global memory. You should only call this function when your application is completely finished using libxml and all documents that you have created with the library.

Listing 10-1 shows the entire generateXML method call.

```
- (void) generateXML {
    xmlDocPtr doc;
    xmlNodePtr rootNode;

    // Create a new XML document.
    doc = xmlNewDoc(BAD_CAST "1.0");

    // Create the root node.
    rootNode = xmlNewNode(NULL, BAD_CAST "rootNode");

    // Set the root of the document.
    xmlDocSetRootElement(doc, rootNode);

    // Create a new child off the root.
    xmlNewChild(rootNode, NULL, BAD_CAST "ChildNode1",
                BAD_CAST "Child Node Content");

    // Add a node with attributes.
    xmlNodePtr attributedNode;
    attributedNode = xmlNewChild (rootNode, NULL,
                                    BAD_CAST "AttributedNode", NULL);
    xmlNewProp(attributedNode, BAD_CAST "attribute1", BAD_CAST "First");
    xmlNewProp(attributedNode, BAD_CAST "attribute2", BAD_CAST "Second");

    // Create a node as a child of the attributed node.
    xmlNewChild (attributedNode, NULL, BAD_CAST "AttributedChild",
                BAD_CAST "Attributed Node Child Node");

    // You can also build nodes and text separately and add them
    // to the tree later.
    xmlNodePtr attachNode = xmlNewNode(NULL, BAD_CAST "AttachedNode");
    xmlNodePtr nodeText = xmlNewText(BAD_CAST "Attached Node Text");
    // Add the text to the node.
    xmlAddChild(attachNode, nodeText);
    // Add the node to the root.
    xmlAddChild(rootNode, attachNode);

    // You can even include comments.
    xmlNodePtr comment;
    comment = xmlNewComment(BAD_CAST "This is an XML Comment");
    xmlAddChild(rootNode, comment);



    // Write the doc.
    xmlChar *outputBuffer;
    int bufferSize;

    // You are responsible for freeing the buffer using xmlFree.
```

```
// Dump the document to a buffer.
xmlDocDumpFormatMemory(doc, &outputBuffer, &bufferSize, 1);

// Create an NSString from the buffer.
NSString *xmlString = [[NSString alloc] initWithBytes:outputBuffer
                                               length:bufferSize
                                             encoding:NSUTF8StringEncoding];

// Log the XML string that you created.
NSLog (@"output: \n%@", xmlString);

// Display the text in the text view.
[self.textView setText:xmlString];

// Clean up.
// Free the output buffer.
xmlFree(outputBuffer);

// Release all the structures in the document, including the tree.
xmlFreeDoc(doc);
xmlCleanupParser();

}
```

The last thing that you have to do before running the application is add a call to generateXML to viewDidLoad:

```
- (void)viewDidLoad {
    [super viewDidLoad];

    [self generateXML];
}
```

Now you are ready to build and run the application. You should see the XML generated in the console and displayed in the text view in the iPhone simulator.

Libxml supports many other features. I strongly encourage you to visit the libxml website at http://xmlsoft.org/.

MOVING FORWARD

In this chapter, you learned how to communicate with remote servers over the Internet using the Cocoa URL Loading System. You implemented the NSURLConnection delegate methods to handle asynchronous loading of data from the web. Then you discovered how to parse the XML that you receive as a response to a remote method call. Finally, you learned how to generate dynamic XML documents.

This chapter lays the foundation for integration with XML web services. The next chapter explores communication with XML web services; you build a sample project that queries a web service and then processes the response in an interesting way.

11

Integrating with Web Services

WHAT'S IN THIS CHAPTER?

➤ Learning about a web service and its usefulness

➤ Understanding how to send data to an XML web service using the POST and GET methods

➤ Parsing the response messages from a web service and using the resulting data from within an iOS application

➤ Building location-based applications using the GPS functionality in the Core Location framework and the mapping capability of the MapKit framework

WROX.COM CODE DOWNLOADS FOR THIS CHAPTER

The wrox.com code downloads for this chapter are found at `www.wrox.com/remtitle .cgi?isbn=1118391845` on the Download Code tab. The code is in the Chapter 11 download and individually named according to the names throughout the chapter.

In the previous chapter, you learned how to ask for data from a web server by sending HTTP requests. You also learned about XML and how to parse the XML that you receive from web servers in response to your HTTP requests. In this section, you take that knowledge a step further by integrating your application with Internet-based web services.

In this chapter, you learn about web services and how to use them in your iOS applications. You also explore a couple of other interesting features of the iOS SDK, including MapKit and Core Location.

This chapter builds on the knowledge that you gained from Chapter 10 to integrate iOS SDK applications with web services. I cover the use of the GET and POST HTTP methods to send data to a web service. You then create a couple of sample applications that use web services as an integral part of the program.

NETWORK APPLICATION ARCHITECTURE

When you set out to start work on a new project, one of your first decisions involves designing the architecture of your application and determining how the parts of your system should work together. Most data-oriented applications involve a database, and all iOS applications include a user interface. To get a better understanding of how to design applications where iOS and the database need to communicate, you take a brief look at a couple of typical network application architectures.

Two-Tier Architecture

The simplest network application architecture consists of a database and an interface. Architects refer to this design as *two-tier* or *client-server* architecture. You can see this design in Figure 11-1. In this design, the client application resides on the mobile device or computer and implements the application interface. Additionally, the client software includes the implementation of the business rules that govern the functionality of the application. The server tier is generally an enterprise database such as Oracle, SQLServer, or MySQL, which can share its data with many connected clients.

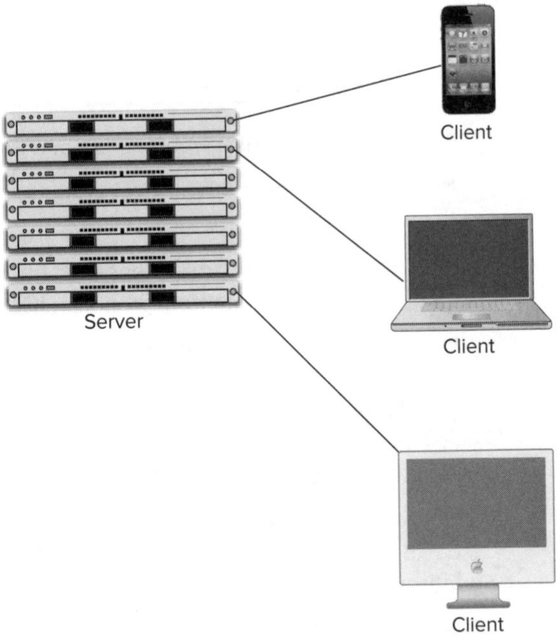

FIGURE 11-1: Two-tier architecture

You see this type of client-server architecture when you look at web servers — particularly web servers that serve simple HTML web pages. The client in this design is your web browser, and the server is the web server. Many clients connect to the same web server to get data. The client web browser hosts the user interface and the logic to display the HTML data.

This architecture is most appropriate for simple applications. However, as the business rules for your application become more complex, you are likely to outgrow this design. To maintain encapsulation of functionality, the client should be responsible for displaying data and the server for storing it. If minimal rules govern the logic and data of the application, you could implement them either in the database or on the client.

As the number and complexity of the rules that define the functionality of your application increase, you need to decide where you want to implement those rules. You can implement them on the client. If your client software is a "thick" desktop application, changing rules mean redeploying your application to your clients. If the client is a "thin" web-browser based client, you are constrained by the capabilities and performance of the browser and client-side languages such as JavaScript.

As the business rules of your application get more complex, you might need to add a third tier to your application architecture. It is in this tier where the business rules reside. In this design, you can decouple your business rules from both the display logic of the client software and the storage system of the database.

Three-Tier Architecture (*n*-tier)

As you learned in the previous section, you need to consider your application's ability to maintain a complex set of business rules in your design. As you design your system, think about the complexity of the rules that govern your application and the likelihood that these rules might change. For instance, if you are building an order entry system, keep in mind that customer discount percentages might change. You may not want to code these percentages into the user interface layer of your application because any changes to this data require a redeployment of your software. In instances like this, it is common for the designer to pull these business rules out of the interface and place them in their own logical software layer. The client-server design then evolves into a three-tier (or *n*-tier if more than one business layer is necessary) architecture (see Figure 11-2).

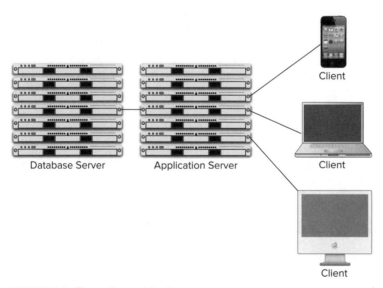

Database Server   Application Server   Client

FIGURE 11-2 Three-tier architecture

In a three-tier design, the application architect moves the business logic into its own logical and perhaps physical process. You can therefore decouple the business rules from the user interface and the database. This gives the designer more flexibility when it comes to designing the database, the interface, and the business logic. It also effectively encapsulates each of these important features of a system. It is easier to manage the business logic of your system if you do not tightly couple this code to the database or the user interface. This simplifies making changes to any one of the layers of the design without affecting any of the other layers. In this design, all the rules that govern what data can be added to the database and specific calculations that are performed on that data are moved out of the interface layer into their own tier. Many commercial application servers such as WebLogic, Apache Tomcat, and WebSphere perform this function.

Application Communication

Client applications need to be able to talk to the business tier or application server, and the application server needs to be able to talk to the database.

Typically, the application server and database reside on the same local network, although this is not necessary. These two layers generally communicate through an interface layer that knows how to call functions in the database. A common interface API for database communication is Open Database Connectivity (ODBC). Most programming languages provide support APIs for connecting to databases as well. The Microsoft .NET platform provides an API called ADO.NET, while the Java system provides JDBC.

For the client to business-tier communication, the designer can implement connectivity using a variety of methods depending on the languages and operating systems used in the implementation.

In the past, designers of Windows systems would have used DCOM, or Distributed Component Object Model. This technology allowed components on different computers to talk to each other. In a Java-based system, the designer could choose a similar technology called Java Remote Method Invocation (RMI). In this system, objects running in one Java virtual machine can call methods on objects in another virtual machine. CORBA, or Common Object Request Broker Architecture, is another technology that enables remote machines to execute methods and share data with one another. The advantage of CORBA is that it is language independent. There are CORBA implementations for most major computer languages and operating systems.

A more current technology enables the designer to implement the functionality of the business tier as a web service. With this technology, the designer can expose the business logic of the application using a web server. Client software can then use well-known methods of the HTTP protocol to access the services exposed by the application server.

INTRODUCING WEB SERVICES

When you use a web browser to visit your favorite website, you begin by sending a request to the site's server. If all goes well, the server accepts your request and returns a response. The response that you get is text in the form of HTML, which your browser renders into the page that you see on your screen.

Consumers of the HTML that a web server sends are generally people that view the HTML using a browser. Web services, on the other hand, respond to requests by sending back data that is intended for computers to consume.

Typically, most web services default to returning response data to you using XML. With some web services, however, you can request that your data be returned in other formats, such as JSON

(JavaScript Object Notation). JSON is a text-based format, like XML. Unlike XML, however, JSON can be used directly in browser-based web applications that are backed by JavaScript code. Coverage of JavaScript is beyond the scope of this book, as is using JSON in browser-based applications. What you should know, though, is that there are parsers available to consume JSON response data for many languages, including Objective-C.

In the previous chapter, you looked at a snippet of XML that could be used to add an address entity to an address book application:

```
<address>
    <name>John Smith</name>
    <street>1 Ocean Blvd</street>
    <city>Isle Of Palms</city>
    <state>SC</state>
    <zip>29451</zip>
</address>
```

Here is the JSON representation of the same address:

```
{
    "name": "John Smith",
    "street": "1 Ocean Blvd",
    "city": "Isle Of Palms",
    "state": "SC",
    "zip": "29451"
}
```

Unlike XML, whose structure is defined by its users, JSON relies on data structures defined in JavaScript. Specifically, JSON can use one of two data structures: the object or the array. Because these data structures are common in almost all modern languages, it is easy to convert JSON messages into data structures that can be used in almost any language. The object consists of a set of name-value pairs, and the array is a list of values.

Application architects can design web services to act as the application server for their particular application. Third parties also build web services to provide specific services to their clients. In this chapter, you develop two applications that use third-party web services from Yahoo! to implement some interesting functionality. The first service allows you to submit queries and returns the results based on proximity to the location of the search. The second service accepts a long string of text and returns a list of the most important words in the text.

In general, web services provide a way to expose some complex logic by using the simple and well-known interfaces of the web.

For example, a designer can easily expose an external interface to a database by building a web service that allows clients to create records or query the data store. Consider the product catalog from Part I of this book. You could build a web service that exposes an interface that accepts orders and enters them directly into the back-end database. You could then build an iOS order entry application that uses this web service to allow your sales force in the field to submit orders.

You can develop web services using many languages and frameworks such as Java, Microsoft .NET, and Ruby on Rails. Because of the variation in languages and platforms available, building a web service is beyond the scope of this book. This chapter teaches you how to integrate your application with existing web services.

SOAP Messaging

Two predominant protocols are used for exchanging data with web services: SOAP and REST. You look at SOAP in this section and examine REST in the next.

Microsoft originally developed SOAP (Simple Object Access Protocol) in the late 1990s, and the W3C standards body has standardized the protocol. The designers built SOAP to be platform and language-agnostic to replace technologies such as CORBA and DCOM. The designers chose XML as the format for the messages in an effort to avoid some of the problems associated with the binary-based messaging systems that SOAP would replace.

Unlike CORBA and DCOM, the designers of SOAP decided to send messages using the HTTP protocol, which makes network configuration easy. If users could see each other over the web using a browser, they could send messages to each other using SOAP.

SOAP messages share a common element with other messaging formats such as HTML in that the message contains a header and a body. The header contains details about the type of message, the format of the data, and so on. The body holds the "payload" or the data that the user intends to transmit.

One issue with using SOAP is the complexity of the messages. To transmit a little bit of data, users of SOAP often need to transmit long messages. For example, here is the SOAP request message that you would send to the eBay SOAP API to obtain the official eBay time (from eBay.com: "Using the eBay API to Get the Official eBay Time"):

```
<?xml version="1.0" encoding="utf-8"?>
<soapenv:Envelope xmlns:soapenv="http://schemas.xmlsoap.org/soap/envelope/"
    xmlns:xsd="http://www.w3.org/2001/XMLSchema"
  xmlns:xsi="http://www.w3.org/2001/XMLSchema-instance">
  <soapenv:Header>
    <RequesterCredentials soapenv:mustUnderstand="0"
        xmlns="urn:ebay:apis:eBLBaseComponents">
      <eBayAuthToken>ABC...123</eBayAuthToken>
      <ns:Credentials xmlns:ns="urn:ebay:apis:eBLBaseComponents">
       <ns:DevId>someDevId</ns:DevId>
       <ns:AppId>someAppId</ns:AppId>
       <ns:AuthCert>someAuthCert</ns:AuthCert>
      </ns:Credentials>
    </RequesterCredentials>
  </soapenv:Header>
  <soapenv:Body>
    <GeteBayOfficialTimeRequest xmlns="urn:ebay:apis:eBLBaseComponents">
      <ns1:Version xmlns:ns1="urn:ebay:apis:eBLBaseComponents">405</ns1:Version>
    </GeteBayOfficialTimeRequest>
  </soapenv:Body>
</soapenv:Envelope>
```

This is quite a verbose message, especially considering that you are not even passing any parameters. Although the API simply returns a timestamp that represents the current time, it is also quite verbose:

```
<?xml version="1.0" encoding="utf-8"?>
<soapenv:Envelope xmlns:soapenv="http://schemas.xmlsoap.org/soap/envelope/"
  xmlns:xsd="http://www.w3.org/2001/XMLSchema"
  xmlns:xsi="http://www.w3.org/2001/XMLSchema-instance">
  <soapenv:Body>
    <GeteBayOfficialTimeResponse xmlns="urn:ebay:apis:eBLBaseComponents">
      <Timestamp>2005-05-02T00:07:22.895Z</Timestamp>
      <Ack>Success</Ack>
      <CorrelationID>
        00000000-00000000-00000000-00000000-00000000-00000000-0000000000
      </CorrelationID>
      <Version>405</Version>
      <Build>20050422132524</Build>
    </GeteBayOfficialTimeResponse>
  </soapenv:Body>
</soapenv:Envelope>
```

While SOAP offers far more functionality than simple method calling, you can see why developers often mock the name "Simple" Object Access Protocol. Designers who simply needed to pass data between application layers or make basic method calls found that SOAP was overkill. This led to the development of a simpler messaging protocol called REST.

The REST Protocol

REST stands for REpresentational State Transfer. The designers of REST wanted to be able to call web service functions using the simple and well-known methods exposed by the HTTP protocol: GET and POST. The goal was to make it easy to invoke remote functions and provide response data in a more manageable format.

REST uses a simple URI scheme to communicate with web services. Developers who are comfortable using HTTP to make requests over the web already know how to call REST services. Typically, a client application can simply issue an HTTP GET request to a URL to make a method call. The developer can pass parameters to the call using query string parameters as if simply passing parameters to a regular website.

Because REST is not standardized, it is possible for the client to receive response data from a REST-based service in an arbitrary format. However, XML is commonly used. Typically, REST-based web services can also return data using the JSON format instead of XML. This is preferable if you are developing web-based applications.

To be able to easily determine the intent of a call, the HTTP GET method is used to query for data, and the HTTP POST method is used when you want to modify data such as in an INSERT or UPDATE to a database. This makes it easy to determine if the caller intends to simply query the service for data or make changes to the data that the service manages.

It is easy to build simple web services using REST. If you already know how to implement server-side web scripts, REST implementations are typically straightforward. Both of the examples in this chapter call web services based on the REST protocol. All the concepts in this chapter are equally applicable if your application needs to call a SOAP-based service. The only real difference is the format of the message that you are sending and the format of the response message.

EXAMPLE 1: LOCATION-BASED SEARCH

One of the great features of the iOS devices is the GPS. Even in Wi-Fi-only devices like the iPod touch, GPS data is often available based on the Wi-Fi access point to which the device is connected. Developers are able to use GPS to determine the current location of the device and build applications that use this data to provide a wealth of information to users. This leads to some creative applications.

In the first example in this chapter, you take advantage of the capability of the device. You use the Core Location framework to determine the current position of the device. Then you allow the user to input search terms into the application. After that, you call a Yahoo! web service using the REST protocol and the HTTP GET method to obtain businesses that meet the search criteria and are close to the current location. Finally, you use the MapKit framework to display the returned data on a map.

Don't worry if you don't have an iPhone. When you use Core Location with the iPhone simulator, the simulator conveniently returns the latitude and longitude of Apple headquarters in Cupertino, California, by default. You can also set the location for the GPS to return using Xcode.

The finished application looks like Figure 11-3.

Starting Out

Now that you have an idea of what the application can do and how it can look, you can get started. The first step, as always, is to open Xcode and create a new project. Because of a single view, you should create a new Single View Application project. Call the new application **LocationSearch**. Make sure that you have the Use Storyboards and Use Automatic Reference Counting checkboxes selected before you click Next. Choose a location to save your project, and click Create.

FIGURE 11-3: Completed LocationSearch application

You use the Core Location and MapKit frameworks in this example. These frameworks are not included in iOS projects by default, so you have to add references to the frameworks to the project. Click the `LocationSearch` project at the top of the tree in the Project Navigator. Then select the Build Phases tab in the editor pane. Next, click the plus sign at the bottom of the section with the heading Link Binary With Libraries. In the dialog that opens, select the `CoreLocation.framework` item, and click the Add button. Repeat this procedure to add `MapKit.framework` to your project as well.

You use these frameworks in your `ViewController` class. Therefore, you need to import the headers for these frameworks in the `ViewController.h` header. Add the following `import` statements to the `ViewController.h` header file:

```
#import <MapKit/MapKit.h>
#import <CoreLocation/CoreLocation.h>
```

The user interface for the application consists of a search bar to accept the search criteria from the user and a map view that you can use to display the search results. Because you need access to both of these interface items in your code, you must add instance variables and outlets for these elements.

In the `ViewController.h` header, add properties for an `MKMapView*` called `mapView` and a `UISearchBar*` called `searchBar` to the interface definition:

```
@property (weak, nonatomic) IBOutlet UISearchBar *searchBar;
@property (weak, nonatomic) IBOutlet MKMapView *mapView;
```

Building the Interface

This application has two elements in the interface: an `MKMapView` and a `UISearchBar`. Click the MainStoryboard in the Project Navigator to open the main storyboard for editing in the Interface Builder.

Make sure that you have the Object library palette open in the Utilities view. Locate the search bar item under the Objects ⇨ Cocoa Touch Storyboard ⇨ Windows & Bars heading. Drag the search bar to the top of the view. Make sure that you choose the search bar from the Library window and not the Search Bar and Search Display Controller.

Next, locate the map view under Objects ⇨ Cocoa Touch Storyboard ⇨ Data Views in the Library window. Drag a map view into the view and place it below the search bar. Stretch the map view to take up the rest of the view window. Figure 11-4 shows what your interface should look like in the interface builder.

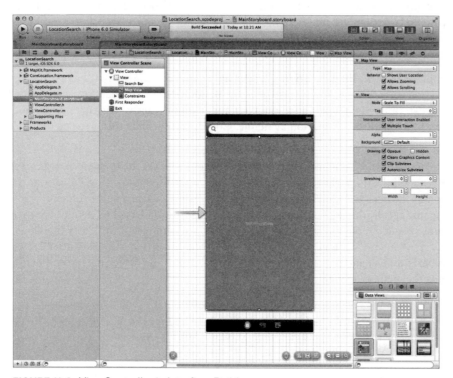

FIGURE 11-4: ViewController in Interface Builder

Now that you have visually defined your user interface, you need to connect the user interface elements to the code. Hook up the `UISearchBar` to the `searchBar` outlet in the `ViewController.h` header file by Ctrl-dragging the search bar and dropping it onto the property in the header file. Remember that you can use the Assistant editor to view the interface and the code side by side. Likewise, hook up the `MKMapView` to the `mapView` outlet in the `ViewController.h` header.

That's all that you need to do to build the interface and connect it to your code.

Core Location

The key ingredient in building a location-based application is getting the location of the user. Apple has built the Core Location framework to enable your applications to interface with the GPS hardware in the device. Using this framework, you can obtain the current location or heading of the device.

The Core Location Framework

Core Location is an asynchronous API that uses delegation to report location information for the device. To use this functionality, you first need to instantiate an instance of the `CLLocationManager` class. As the name implies, you use this class to manage the Core Location functionality. The class contains methods to start and stop location and heading updates as well as a property that returns the location of the device.

Once you have instantiated your `CLLocationManager` instance, you need to define a delegate. The delegate must conform to the `CLLocationManagerDelegate` protocol. This protocol defines methods that allow you to respond to location and heading change events as well as errors. You typically write code in the `locationManager:didUpdateLocations:` method to respond to changes in the device location.

In a production application, you should also implement the `locationManager:didFailWithError:` method. Core Location calls this method in case of error. In addition, Core Location automatically prompts the user to determine if he wants to allow your application to access his current location. If the user decides not to make this information available, Core Location calls this error method. Your application should be able to gracefully handle this situation.

After you have implemented the Core Location delegate methods and set the `CLLocationManager`'s delegate, you typically tell the manager to start updating the device's location. Core Location returns the location of the device as quickly as possible, often using a cached value if one is available. After the initial call, the device continues to hone the position based on a value that you can set using the `desiredAccuracy` property. You can control the number of callbacks that you receive to the `locationManager:didUpdateLocations:` method by setting the `distanceFilter` property. This property allows you to set the minimum distance that the device must move before the framework calls the method again.

Although the example does not use it, Core Location can also report heading information if the hardware of the device supports it. If you choose to enable heading data, your Core Location calls the `locationManager:didUpdateHeading:` method to report heading updates.

There are a few considerations to be aware of when developing software with Core Location. First, you should use the lowest level of accuracy that your application needs to implement its functionality. You can specify that the framework determine the device's location to the nearest three kilometers, one kilometer, one hundred meters, ten meters, or best possible accuracy. The default value is best possible accuracy. The GPS needs more power to determine the location of the device with higher precision. Power consumption on a mobile device is something you should consider when building mobile applications. Therefore, you should always specify the least accuracy that you can accept while still providing the desired functionality in your application.

Another consideration is when to turn off Core Location. As I mentioned, the GPS radio consumes a substantial amount of power. You should turn off location updates using the `stopUpdatingLocation` method as soon as is practical for your application. In the sample application, you only need to get the initial location of the device to perform your location search, so turn off location updates after you determine the device's location. Occasionally, you need to obtain frequent location updates while your application is running — for example, when the application is providing turn-by-turn directions. Just keep in mind that using the GPS consumes a lot of power and that you should keep it enabled for the shortest possible length of time.

Using Core Location

Now that you have an idea of how to use Core Location, you can add Core Location functionality to your application. In the `ViewController.h` header file, update the interface declaration to indicate your intention to implement the `CLLocationManagerDelegate` protocol:

```
@interface ViewController : UIViewController <CLLocationManagerDelegate>
```

You want to maintain a copy of the current location of the device. So, in the `ViewController.h` header, add a property for the current location:

```
@property (nonatomic, strong) CLLocation* currentLocation;
```

You also want to have a class-level instance of the location manager so that you can start and stop it at different points in your code. In the `ViewController.h` header, add a property for the location manager:

```
@property (nonatomic, strong) CLLocationManager *locationManager;
```

You are ready to start your implementation, so switch over to the `ViewController.m` implementation file. First, you add code to the `viewDidLoad` method to create the `CLLocationManager`:

```
- (void)viewDidLoad
{
    [super viewDidLoad];
    // Do any additional setup after loading the view, typically from a nib.

    // Create the Core Location CLLocationManager.
    self.locationManager = [[CLLocationManager alloc] init];
    // Set the delegate to self.
    [self.locationManager setDelegate:self];
    // Tell the location manager to start updating the location.
    [self.locationManager startUpdatingLocation];
}
```

In this code, you first allocate and initialize the `CLLocationManager` property. The `CLLocationManager` object controls all communication with the GPS in the device. Next, you set the delegate for the location manager to `self`. You can do this because you have declared that your class will implement the `CLLocationManagerDelegate` protocol. Finally, the code tells the location manager to start updating the device location using the GPS.

The final step is to implement the Core Location delegate methods. For now, you simply implement the `locationManager:didUpdateLocations:` method to store the location of the device in the `currentLocation` property. Additionally, you implement `locationManager:didFailWithError:` to log that you received an error. Here is the implementation:

```
// Called when the location manager determines that there is a new location.
- (void)locationManager:(CLLocationManager *)manager
     didUpdateLocations:(NSArray *)locations {
   self.currentLocation = [locations objectAtIndex:0];


}

// Called when an error occurs.
- (void)locationManager:(CLLocationManager *)manager
       didFailWithError:(NSError *)error {
   NSLog (@"locationManager:didFailWithError");
}
```

The Local Search API

You use the Yahoo! local search service API to get your search results. This is a REST-based API. The URL for the web service is: `http://local.yahooapis.com/LocalSearchService/V3/localSearch`.

This service enables you to search for businesses near a given location. The results include the name of the business, latitude and longitude, and Yahoo! user ratings.

The search API can accept many different parameters to help you narrow and filter your search. These include the radius from the base point to search for results, a route along which to search, or a specific category in which to search. To keep this sample simple, you only pass in the latitude and longitude of the device as the location to search and the query search terms that you are looking for.

The XML that you get in response to a query request looks something like this:

```
<?xml version="1.0"?>
<ResultSet xmlns:xsi="http://www.w3.org/2001/XMLSchema-instance" xmlns="urn:yahoo:lcl"
  xsi:schemaLocation="urn:yahoo:lcl
  http://local.yahooapis.com/LocalSearchService/V3/LocalSearchResponse.xsd"
  totalResultsAvailable="1101" totalResultsReturned="10" firstResultPosition="1">
  <ResultSetMapUrl>
    http://maps.yahoo.com/broadband/?q1=Cupertino%2C+CA&amp;tt=pizza&amp;tp=1
  </ResultSetMapUrl>
  <Result id="42965880">
    <Title>Pizza My Heart</Title>
    <Address>20530 Stevens Creek Blvd</Address>
    <City>Cupertino</City>
    <State>CA</State>
    <Phone>(408) 253-6000</Phone>
```

```
    <Latitude>37.322671</Latitude>
    <Longitude>-122.032921</Longitude>
    <Rating>
      <AverageRating>4</AverageRating>
      <TotalRatings>3</TotalRatings>
      <TotalReviews>3</TotalReviews>
      <LastReviewDate>1274534291</LastReviewDate>
      <LastReviewIntro>We go there all the time the pizza and salads are
      great. My only complaint is that the cashier serves the pizza with
      her hands after she/he takes all the money. I wish that they have
      special pieces of paper to handle the pizzas. Bills and coins are
      very dirty and there are so many virus around. Thanks in advance if
      you follow up on this review. Marcela</LastReviewIntro>
    </Rating>
    <Distance>0.67</Distance>
    <Url>http://local.yahoo.com/info-42965880-pizza-my-heart-cupertino</Url>
    <ClickUrl>http://local.yahoo.com/info-42965880-pizza-my-heart-cupertino</ClickUrl>
    <MapUrl>
      http://local.yahoo.com/info-42965880-pizza-my-heart-cupertino?viewtype=map
    </MapUrl>
    <BusinessUrl>http://pizzamyheart.com/</BusinessUrl>
    <BusinessClickUrl>http://pizzamyheart.com/</BusinessClickUrl>
    <Categories>
      <Category id="96926236">Restaurants</Category>
      <Category id="96926234">Carry Out &amp; Take Out</Category>
      <Category id="96926243">Pizza</Category>
    </Categories>
  </Result>
  <Result id="21557729">
    <Title>Jt Mc Hart's Pizza Restaurant</Title>
    <Address>19732 Stevens Creek Blvd</Address>
    <City>Cupertino</City>
    <State>CA</State>
    <Phone>(408) 255-0500</Phone>
    <Latitude>37.322736</Latitude>
    <Longitude>-122.018654</Longitude>
    <Rating>
      <AverageRating>4.5</AverageRating>
      <TotalRatings>19</TotalRatings>
      <TotalReviews>19</TotalReviews>
      <LastReviewDate>1317285711</LastReviewDate>
      <LastReviewIntro>We are so glad we went here because it has been
      the best sushi/sashimi dinner we have had yet. The food is very
      high quality and the fish is very fresh. Top notch in presentation
      couple with excellent selection of sake. Service is prompt and
      friendly. The ambience is relaxed and casual.</LastReviewIntro>
    </Rating>
    <Distance>0.96</Distance>
    <Url>
      http://local.yahoo.com/info-21557729-jt-mc-hart-s-pizza-restaurant-cupertino
    </Url>
    <ClickUrl>
      http://local.yahoo.com/info-21557729-jt-mc-hart-s-pizza-restaurant-cupertino
    </ClickUrl>
    <MapUrl>
```

```
         http://local.yahoo.com/info-21557729-jt-mc-hart-s-pizza-restaurant-
cupertino?viewtype=map
      </MapUrl>
      <BusinessUrl>http://mchartspizza.com/</BusinessUrl>
      <BusinessClickUrl>http://mchartspizza.com/</BusinessClickUrl>
      <Categories>
        <Category id="96926236">Restaurants</Category>
        <Category id="96926234">Carry Out &amp; Take Out</Category>
        <Category id="96926243">Pizza</Category>
      </Categories>
    </Result>
  </ResultSet>
```

In this instance, you sent a query for "pizza" with the latitude and longitude of Apple headquarters in Cupertino, California. This XML represents the first result returned from the web service. You can see that the response includes relevant information such as the name and address of the business, the phone number, the latitude and longitude, and the distance from the origin of the query. The response also contains review information submitted to Yahoo! by users of its web search services. Finally, you can see that there are several URLs if you want to use this information to allow a user to click a link in your application to bring up a map or to directly link to the site of the establishment.

If you look at the `ResultSet` element at the top of the XML, you notice that it has a few attributes of interest: `totalResultsAvailable`, `totalResultsReturned`, and `firstResultPosition`. Because there may be a large number of results for a query, the service returns the result set in batches. You can specify the batch size, up to 20 results at a time. You can also specify the start position of the results that you want to retrieve. In this particular case, there were 1,101 results, of which you received the first 10. Your application only handles the first batch of results. However, in a production application, you probably want to write some code to resend the query more than once so you can retrieve more results. It is up to you to keep track of the result position and to send back the next starting position to the service. Keep in mind that web services are stateless. They typically do not maintain any state on the server regarding your last request. It is up to you to implement whatever paging functionality meets the requirements of your application.

You can find complete documentation of the API at `http://developer.yahoo.com/search/local/V3/localSearch.html`.

Using the Search Bar

In this example, you added a `UISearchBar` control to your application. You use this widget to get the search criteria from the user. Unlike the other user interface elements that you have used thus far, the search bar works using the delegation pattern. Therefore, you need to declare your class as the delegate for the search bar and implement the `UISearchBarDelegate` protocol. Then, when the search bar text changes or the user presses buttons, the search bar calls your code through the delegate methods.

In your `ViewController.h` header file, you need to declare your intention to implement the `UISearchBarDelegate` protocol. Change the interface declaration to include this protocol:

```
@interface ViewController : UIViewController
    <CLLocationManagerDelegate,UISearchBarDelegate>
```

Now you need to tell the `searchBar` property that you want the `ViewController` to be its delegate. Add the following code to the `viewDidLoad` method in the `ViewController.m` implementation file:

```
// Set the delegate for the search bar.
[self.searchBar setDelegate:self];
```

The `viewDidLoad` method should now look like this:

```
- (void)viewDidLoad
{
    [super viewDidLoad];


    // Create the results array.
    self.results = [[NSMutableArray alloc] init];


    // Create the Core Location CLLocationManager.
    self.locationManager = [[CLLocationManager alloc] init];
    // Set the delegate to self.
    [self.locationManager setDelegate:self];
    // Tell the location manager to start updating the location.
    [self.locationManager startUpdatingLocation];

    // Set the delegate for the search bar.
    [self.searchBar setDelegate:self];

}
```

Next, write some code to handle the delegate events you are interested in handling. When a user taps the Search button, you take the text of the search bar and pass it to the location search web service. After submitting the request, you receive callbacks from the `NSURLConnection` using its delegate methods, as you learned about earlier in this book. To hold on to the response data that you receive from the connection, you set up a property called **responseData**. Add a property called **responseData** of type `NSMutableData*` to your `ViewController.h` header file:

```
@property (nonatomic, strong) NSMutableData *responseData;
```

You are now ready to implement your `searchBar` delegate methods in the `ViewController.m` implementation file. The search bar calls the first method `searchBarSearchButtonClicked:` when the user clicks the Search button. In this method, you create a request using the text in the search bar and send it off to the web service for processing. Here is the code:

```
- (void)searchBarSearchButtonClicked:(UISearchBar *)localSearchBar {
    NSLog (@"searchBarSearchButtonClicked");

    // Construct the URL to call.
    // Note that you have to add percent escapes to the string to pass it
    // via a URL.
    NSString *urlString = [NSString
        stringWithFormat:
            @"http://local.yahooapis.com/LocalSearchService/V3/localSearch?"
              "appid=YOUR_ID_GOES_HERE&query=%@&latitude=%f&longitude=%f",
        [localSearchBar.text
```

```
                    stringByAddingPercentEscapesUsingEncoding:NSASCIIStringEncoding],
            self.currentLocation.coordinate.latitude,
                            self.currentLocation.coordinate.longitude];

    // Log the string that you plan to send.
    NSLog (@"sending: %@",urlString);

    NSURL *serviceURL = [NSURL
                        URLWithString:urlString];

    // Create the request.
    NSURLRequest *request = [NSURLRequest
                            requestWithURL:serviceURL
                            cachePolicy:NSURLRequestUseProtocolCachePolicy
                            timeoutInterval: 30.0];

    // Create the connection and send the request.
    NSURLConnection *connection =
    [[NSURLConnection alloc] initWithRequest:request delegate:self];

    // Make sure that the connection is good.
    if (connection) {
        // Instantiate the responseData data structure to store the response.
        self.responseData = [NSMutableData data];

    }
    else {
        NSLog (@"The connection failed");
    }

    [localSearchBar resignFirstResponder];
}
```

You are using the same technique to send a request and receive a response from a web server, as I introduced in the previous chapter. I point out a few minor differences.

First, you create a string that represents the URL to be called. You are using the `stringWithFormat` method because you are plugging the search query text, latitude, and longitude in dynamically at runtime. Notice that you are using the standard HTTP method for passing parameters on the query string. That is, you give the name of the URL (`http://local.yahooapis.com/LocalSearchService/V3/localSearch`) and append a question mark (?) to indicate that parameters follow. Parameters are then passed as name-value pairs using the format `parameterName=value`. You separate your parameter pairs using the ampersand (&) character.

You can see from your URL string that you are passing four parameters: `appid`, `query`, `latitude`, and `longitude`. The `latitude` and `longitude` are the coordinates around which you want to center your search. The `query` is the item for which you want to search. The `appid` is a token that you receive from Yahoo! when you sign up to be able to use its web service. You can obtain a token to use the Local Search Service by going to: `https://developer.apps.yahoo.com/wsregapp/`. Make sure that you replace the text `YOUR_ID_GOES_HERE` in the definition of the `urlString` variable in the preceding code with the `appid` that you receive from Yahoo!. Otherwise, you cannot access the web service.

Another important thing to notice when examining your URL string is that you call the method stringByAddingPercentEscapesUsingEncoding on the text string that you obtain from the search bar. The HTTP protocol uses characters such as & and % in specific ways. If your text contains those (and several other) characters, they need to be "URL encoded." Calling this method on your string ensures that you are properly formatting the string to be able to pass it as a query string parameter.

The last part of constructing your string is to get the latitude and longitude from your currentLocation object and replace them in the URL.

The next line simply logs the string to the console so that you can verify that you are creating the request URL string properly.

Next, go on to create the objects you need to submit your query to the web service. You create an NSURL using the URL string that you built earlier. Then you create an NSURLRequest with the NSURL and specify the cache policy and time-out that you want. Finally, you create your NSURLConnection with the request, setting the delegate of the connection object to self.

Once you validate that the connection object is good, you instantiate the responseData property. Finally, you send the resignFirstResponder message to the search bar. This tells the search bar to dismiss the associated keyboard.

The next bit of code you write implements the searchBar:textDidChange: delegate method. The search bar calls this method any time the text in the search bar changes. Later on, you implement this function to remove the annotations from the map view if the search is changing. For now, you simply log a message indicating that someone called the method:

```
// Called when the search bar text changes.
- (void)searchBar:(UISearchBar *)searchBar textDidChange:(NSString *)searchText{
    NSLog (@"textDidChange");

}
```

Handling the Web Service Response

In this section, you look at the code you need to write to handle the response from the web service. First, you implement the NSURLConnection delegate methods to deal with the raw data that you receive from the web service. Then you define a new Result class that holds data about each result returned from the service. Next, you parse the XML and generate an array of Result objects. Finally, you use the MapKit API to plot the results on a map.

The NSURLConnection Delegate Methods

In the previous section, you wrote code to handle the user clicking the search bar. The code constructs the URL and uses the HTTP GET method to send the request to the web service. You need to implement the NSURLConnection delegate methods to handle the response data that the web service returns from your request. This code is similar to the code that you built in the previous chapter. To simplify this sample and focus on the web service–related aspects, I have removed some of the delegate methods that you do not need to handle.

First, you want to implement the connection:didReceiveResponse: method. The NSURLConnection calls this delegate method when there is enough data to create the response. The connection could call this method multiple times when there are server redirects from address to address. Therefore, you need to reset your response data each time the connection calls this method. Add this implementation to the `ViewController.m` implementation file:

```
- (void)connection:(NSURLConnection *)connection
didReceiveResponse:(NSURLResponse *)response {
    NSLog (@"connection:didReceiveResponse:");

    [self.responseData setLength:0];

}
```

Next, implement the `connection:didReceiveData:` method. The connection calls this method each time it receives a chunk of data, so you simply append the received chunk to your `responseData` buffer:

```
- (void)connection:(NSURLConnection *)connection didReceiveData:(NSData *)data
{
    NSLog (@"connection:didReceiveData:");

    // Append the received data to your responseData property.
    [self.responseData appendData:data];

}
```

Now you need to implement `connectionDidFinishLoading`. This method runs when the connection has finished loading all the requested data. Here you convert the response data to a string, clean up the connection, and call the method that you write to parse the XML:

```
- (void)connectionDidFinishLoading:(NSURLConnection *)connection
{
    NSLog (@"connectionDidFinishLoading:");

    // Convert the data to a string and log the response string.
    NSString *responseString = [[NSString alloc]
                                initWithData:self.responseData
                                encoding:NSUTF8StringEncoding];
    NSLog(@"Response String: \n%@", responseString);

    [self parseXML];
}
```

Finally, implement the `connection:didFailWithError:` method to log that an error occurred. Remember that you want to provide some more robust error handling and reporting in a production application. You also probably want to give the user some feedback as to why the error occurred. Here is the implementation:

```
- (void)connection:(NSURLConnection *)connection
  didFailWithError:(NSError *)error
{
    NSLog (@"connection:didFailWithError:");
    NSLog (@"%@",[error localizedDescription]);
}
```

Note that you don't have to call a web service or a URL asynchronously, but it is certainly my recommendation that you do so. Alternatively, you could retrieve the XML from a URL directly by calling the [[NSXMLParser alloc] initWithContentsOfURL] method. However, using this method causes a loss of responsiveness in your application, because the main thread blocks while waiting for the response from the server. Using the URL loading framework as you've done in this example is asynchronous and leaves your interface responsive as the application downloads the XML response. In addition, it gives you more control if you need to authenticate or handle errors more responsively, as I described in the previous chapter.

Defining the Result Class

The response XML that you receive from the web service contains a lot of information. Although you do not use all of that information in the sample, you parse it out and capture it. To hold this data, you create a new class that represents an individual result. Then, when you parse the XML, you create instances of this Result class, populate the data from the result of the web service call, and add the Result to an array.

Create a new class called **Result** that inherits from NSObject.

Here is the header for your Result class:

```
//
// Result.h
// LocationSearch
//
// Created by Patrick Alessi on 1/23/13.
// Copyright (c) 2013 Patrick Alessi. All rights reserved.
//

#import <Foundation/Foundation.h>
#import <MapKit/MapKit.h>

@interface Result : NSObject <MKAnnotation>

@property (nonatomic, copy) NSString *title;
@property (nonatomic, copy) NSString *address;
@property (nonatomic, copy) NSString *city;
@property (nonatomic, copy) NSString *state;
@property (nonatomic, copy) NSString *phone;
@property (nonatomic) double latitude;

@property (nonatomic) double longitude;
@property (nonatomic) float rating;

@end
```

One thing to notice is that you have included the MapKit.h header file. You need to do this because you use the Result class to provide annotation data for your map view. To accomplish this, you need to implement the MKAnnotation protocol. To implement this protocol, you must provide a coordinate property that returns a CLLocationCoordinate2D struct. This struct contains the coordinates of the point that you would like to annotate on the map. You also include a title property that displays a title for the map annotation, and a `subtitle` property that you can use to build the subtitle. Here is the implementation for the `Result` class:

```
#import "Result.h"

@implementation Result

-(CLLocationCoordinate2D) coordinate
{
    CLLocationCoordinate2D retVal;
    retVal.latitude = self.latitude;
    retVal.longitude = self.longitude;

    return retVal;
}

- (NSString *)subtitle {
    NSString *retVal = [[NSString alloc] initWithFormat:@"%@",self.phone];

    return retVal;

}

@end
```

The `coordinate` method implements the getter for the coordinate property that is required to implement the `MKAnnotation` protocol. You may have noticed that you did not declare a property called `coordinate`. In Objective-C, properties are simply a convenience. Behind the scenes, using properties and the dot syntax simply calls the appropriate getter or setter methods. Therefore, instead of defining a property, you simply implement the getter method that the `MKAnnotation` protocol requires.

The implementation of the `coordinate` method is straightforward. You take the latitude and longitude that you received from the web service call and package it up into a `CLLocationCoordinate2D` struct as defined by the protocol. Then you just return that struct.

You implement the `subtitle` property in the same way. Instead of defining it as a property, you simply implement the getter method. In this case, you want the subtitle to be the phone number of the business.

Parsing the Response XML

Now that you have defined your `Result` class, you can begin parsing the response XML and building your result set. Before you start, you need to make some additions to your `ViewController.h` header file. Add an `import` statement for your new `Result` class:

```
#import "Result.h"
```

Indicate your intention to implement the `NSXMLParserDelegate` protocol by updating the interface definition:

```
@interface ViewController : UIViewController
    <CLLocationManagerDelegate,UISearchBarDelegate, NSXMLParserDelegate>
```

Add a new `parseXML` method declaration to the class interface:

```
- (void) parseXML;
```

Add properties to hold an individual result, an `NSMutableArray` to hold the list of all the results, and an `NSMutableString` to hold the characters captured during the XML parsing:

```
@property (nonatomic, retain) Result *aResult;
@property (nonatomic, retain) NSMutableArray *results;
@property (nonatomic, retain) NSMutableString *capturedCharacters;
```

Move into the `ViewController.m` implementation file. Now you are ready to implement the `parseXML` method. You call this method from the `connectionDidFinishLoading` `NSURLConnection` delegate method when you finish receiving the XML response from the web service. Here is the implementation:

```
- (void) parseXML {
    NSLog (@"parseXML");

    // Initialize the parser with our NSData from the RSS feed.
    NSXMLParser *xmlParser = [[NSXMLParser alloc]
                              initWithData:self.responseData];

    // Set the delegate to self.
    [xmlParser setDelegate:self];

    // Start the parser.
    if (![xmlParser parse])
    {
        NSLog (@"An error occurred in the parsing");
    }


}
```

In this method, you first declare an instance of an `NSXMLParser` and initialize it with the response data that you received from the web service. Next, you set the parser's delegate to `self`. Then you tell the parser to start parsing the XML.

Remember that the `NSXMLParser` is a SAX parser, which is event driven. Therefore, you need to implement the `NSXMLParserDelegate` delegate methods that the parser calls as parsing events occur.

First, implement the `didStartElement` method. The parser calls this method each time a begin-element tag, such as `<Title>`, is found:

```
- (void) parser:(NSXMLParser *)parser
 didStartElement:(NSString *)elementName
    namespaceURI:(NSString *)namespaceURI
   qualifiedName:(NSString *)qualifiedName
      attributes:(NSDictionary *)attributeDict {
    NSLog (@"didStartElement");

    // Check to see which element has been found.
```

```
        if ([elementName isEqualToString:@"Result"]) {
            // Create a new Result object.
            self.aResult = [[Result alloc] init];


        }
        else if ([elementName isEqualToString:@"Title"]||
                 [elementName isEqualToString:@"Address"]||
                 [elementName isEqualToString:@"City"]||
                 [elementName isEqualToString:@"State"]||
                 [elementName isEqualToString:@"Phone"]||
                 [elementName isEqualToString:@"Latitude"]||
                 [elementName isEqualToString:@"Longitude"]||
                 [elementName isEqualToString:@"AverageRating"])

        {
            // Initialize the capturedCharacters instance variable.
            self.capturedCharacters = [[NSMutableString alloc] initWithCapacity:100];
        }
    }
```

In this code, you check the name of the element that you are currently processing. If the element is a Result, you create a new instance of your Result class to hold the result. If the name is another field that you are interested in, you allocate and initialize the capturedCharacters property in preparation for the characters to come.

Next, implement the foundCharacters method. The parser calls this method any time that it encounters characters inside an element. You implement the foundCharacters method to append the characters to the capturedCharacters property, if the variable is not nil. If capturedCharacters is nil, you are not interested in the characters, so you do nothing. Here is the code:

```
    - (void)parser:(NSXMLParser *)parser foundCharacters:(NSString *)string {
        if (self.capturedCharacters != nil) {
            [self.capturedCharacters appendString:string];
        }
    }
```

Now you need to implement the didEndElement method. The parser calls this method when an element ends. This method is a bit verbose, but its functionality is straightforward. When you use a SAX parser, you often find yourself writing a function like this that has a giant if/else if block. This is the nature of working with a SAX parser because you need to code one method to handle ending any element. Without further ado, here is the code:

```
    - (void)parser:(NSXMLParser *)parser didEndElement:(NSString *)elementName
      namespaceURI:(NSString *)namespaceURI qualifiedName:(NSString *)qName {

        NSLog (@"didEndElement");

        // Check to see which element has ended.
```

```objc
if ([elementName isEqualToString:@"Result"]) {

    // Add the result to the array.
    [self.results addObject:self.aResult];

}
else if ([elementName isEqualToString:@"Title"] && self.aResult!=nil) {
    // Set the appropriate property.
    self.aResult.title = self.capturedCharacters;

}
else if ([elementName isEqualToString:@"Address"] && self.aResult!=nil) {
    // Set the appropriate property.
    self.aResult.address = self.capturedCharacters;

}
else if ([elementName isEqualToString:@"City"] && self.aResult!=nil) {
    // Set the appropriate property.
    self.aResult.city = self.capturedCharacters;

}
else if ([elementName isEqualToString:@"State"] && self.aResult!=nil) {
    // Set the appropriate property.
    self.aResult.state = self.capturedCharacters;

}
else if ([elementName isEqualToString:@"Phone"] && self.aResult!=nil) {
    // Set the appropriate property.
    self.aResult.phone = self.capturedCharacters;

}
else if ([elementName isEqualToString:@"Latitude"] && self.aResult!=nil) {
    // Set the appropriate property.
    self.aResult.latitude = [self.capturedCharacters doubleValue];

}
else if ([elementName isEqualToString:@"Longitude"] && self.aResult!=nil) {
    // Set the appropriate property.
    self.aResult.longitude = [self.capturedCharacters doubleValue];

}
else if ([elementName isEqualToString:@"AverageRating"] && self.aResult!=nil) {
    // Set the appropriate property.
    self.aResult.rating = [self.capturedCharacters floatValue];
}


// So we don't have to release capturedCharacters in every else if block.
if ([elementName isEqualToString:@"Title"]||
    [elementName isEqualToString:@"Address"]||
    [elementName isEqualToString:@"City"]||
    [elementName isEqualToString:@"State"]||
    [elementName isEqualToString:@"Phone"]||
    [elementName isEqualToString:@"Latitude"]||
    [elementName isEqualToString:@"Longitude"]||
```

```
                    [elementName isEqualToString:@"AverageRating"])
        {
            // Clear the capturedCharacters property.
            self.capturedCharacters = nil;
        }
    }
```

As I said, it is verbose. However, it is actually simple. The first part of the `if` statement checks to see if you are ending a `Result` element. If so, you add the `Result` object to the results array. Every other `else if` clause of that `if`/`else if` block simply sets the appropriate property of your `Result` object. The last piece of the code sets the `capturedCharacters` property to `nil`.

The last delegate method that you implement is `parserDidEndDocument`. The parser calls this method when it has finished parsing the document. In this method, you call a method of your class, `plotResults`, which plots your results on the map:

```
- (void)parserDidEndDocument:(NSXMLParser *)parser {
    NSLog (@"parserDidEndDocument");


    // Plot the results on the map.
    [self plotResults];
}
```

You are now finished with the XML parser delegate methods. Next, you take a brief look at MapKit and then implement the `plotResults` method.

Using MapKit

The MapKit framework enables you to display maps within your application. You can programmatically add annotations to the map as you are doing in this example. The major feature of the framework is the `MKMapView` user interface control that you add to your views to make maps available in your application.

You are not limited to the basic annotation styles provided by the framework. You can build your own annotation view classes and use them as annotations on the map. For the sake of simplicity, this example does not do that.

Finally, the framework provides functionality to determine the user's current location and display it on the map. You implement this feature in the `viewDidLoad` method. You also implement the `MKMapViewDelegate` protocol to use colored pins for your annotations.

To get started, you have to modify the `ViewController.h` header file. You need to declare that you are implementing the `MKMapViewDelegate` protocol:

```
@interface ViewController : UIViewController
    <CLLocationManagerDelegate,UISearchBarDelegate,
    NSXMLParserDelegate, MKMapViewDelegate>
```

Next, you add the `plotResults` method to the interface:

```
- (void) plotResults;
```

You are now completely finished with the `ViewController.h` header file. Here is the complete header so you can verify that your code is coordinated with the example:

```objc
#import <UIKit/UIKit.h>
#import <MapKit/MapKit.h>
#import <CoreLocation/CoreLocation.h>
#import "Result.h"

@interface ViewController : UIViewController
    <CLLocationManagerDelegate,UISearchBarDelegate,
    NSXMLParserDelegate, MKMapViewDelegate>
@property (weak, nonatomic) IBOutlet UISearchBar *searchBar;
@property (weak, nonatomic) IBOutlet MKMapView *mapView;
@property (nonatomic, retain) CLLocation* currentLocation;
@property (nonatomic, retain) CLLocationManager *locationManager;
@property (nonatomic, retain) NSMutableData *responseData;
@property (nonatomic, retain) Result *aResult;
@property (nonatomic, retain) NSMutableArray *results;
@property (nonatomic, retain) NSMutableString *capturedCharacters;
- (void) parseXML;
- (void) plotResults;

@end
```

Now you need to move into the implementation file. The first thing that you want to do is center the map on the current location of the device. To do this, implement the Core Location delegate method `locationManager:didUpdateLocations:`. If you recall from the section titled "Core Location," the location manager calls this method when it determines that the device has moved. Here is the complete implementation:

```objc
- (void)locationManager:(CLLocationManager *)manager
    didUpdateLocations:(NSArray *)locations
{

    self.currentLocation = [locations objectAtIndex:0];

    // Create a mapkit region based on the location.
    // Span defines the area covered by the map in degrees.
    MKCoordinateSpan span;
    span.latitudeDelta = 0.05;
    span.longitudeDelta = 0.05;

    // Region struct defines the map to show based on center coordinate and span.
    MKCoordinateRegion region;
    region.center = self.currentLocation.coordinate;
    region.span = span;

    // Update the map to display the current location.
    [self.mapView setRegion:region animated:YES];

    // Stop core location services to conserve battery.
    [manager stopUpdatingLocation];

}
```

First, you set the `currentLocation` property to the location of the device. This is the location at position 0 in the input array `locations`. The array of locations that you receive in calls to `locationManager:didUpdateLocations:` always contains at least one object that has data on the current location.

Then you create an `MKCoordinateSpan` struct. This struct defines the area that you want to display on the map. You are declaring that you would like the map to display 0.05 degrees of latitude and longitude. The span determines how far in you want to zoom the map. A larger span results in a larger area displayed on the map, and thus a lower zoom factor. A small span zooms in on a small area, thereby producing a high zoom factor.

Next, you define an `MKCoordinateRegion` struct. You pass this struct to the `mapView` to define the region that you want to display. An `MKCoordinateRegion` consists of a span and a center point. You center the map on the coordinate that you receive from Core Location.

Next, you tell the `mapView` to set the region displayed on the map and to animate the transition to your new region. Finally, you tell the Core Location manager to stop getting location updates from the GPS. Because your application does not need extremely accurate resolution and you do not need constant updates from the GPS, you can conserve power by turning off the GPS.

For the next step, you need to make a couple of additions to the `viewDidLoad` method. You need to set the `mapView` delegate to `self` so that you can customize the pin colors for your annotations. In addition, for illustrative purposes, you can display the user's location on the map by setting the map view's `showsUserLocation` property to `YES`. Using the `showsUserLocation` property causes the map view to use Core Location to retrieve and maintain the user's location on the map. This forces the GPS receiver to remain on, consuming valuable battery power. You should carefully consider whether your application needs this functionality before using it. This example uses this feature to demonstrate a capability of the map view to display the user's current location. Here is the complete implementation of `viewDidLoad`:

```
- (void)viewDidLoad {
    [super viewDidLoad];


    // Create the results array.
    self.results = [[NSMutableArray alloc] init];


    // Create the Core Location CLLocationManager.
    self.locationManager = [[CLLocationManager alloc] init];
    // Set the delegate to self.
    [self.locationManager setDelegate:self];
    // Tell the location manager to start updating the location
    [self.locationManager startUpdatingLocation];

    // Set the delegate for the search bar.
    [self.searchBar setDelegate:self];

    // Set the delegate for the mapView.
    [self.mapView setDelegate:self];

    // Use Core Location to find the user's location and display it on the map.
```

```
    // Be careful when using this because it causes the mapView to continue to
    // use Core Location to keep the user's position on the map up to date.
    self.mapView.showsUserLocation = YES;

}
```

When the user clears the text from the search bar, you want to clear the old annotations from the map. You can do this by implementing the `searchBar:textDidChange:` delegate method like this:

```
// Called when the search bar text changes.
- (void)searchBar:(UISearchBar *)searchBar textDidChange:(NSString *)searchText{
    NSLog (@"textDidChange");

    // If the text was cleared, clear the map annotations.
    if ([searchText isEqualToString:@""])
    {
        // Clear the annotations.
        [self.mapView removeAnnotations:self.mapView.annotations];

        // Clear the results array.
        [self.results removeAllObjects];
    }

}
```

You implement this code to check to see whether the user has cleared the search string. If he has, remove the annotations from the map and clear your results array.

In the last bit of code, you implement the `mapView:viewForAnnotation:` delegate method. The map view calls this method when the map needs the view for an annotation. If you wanted to implement a custom view for your annotations, you would do it in this method. Instead of implementing a custom view, you use the `MKPinAnnotationView`; however, you can easily replace this with your own view. You change the color of the pin based on the user rating of the business that you are plotting on the map. Here is the code:

```
- (MKAnnotationView *)mapView:(MKMapView *)mapView
            viewForAnnotation:(id <MKAnnotation>)annotation
{

    // If you are displaying the user's location, return nil
    //   to use the default view.
    if ([annotation isKindOfClass:[MKUserLocation class]]) {
        return nil;
    }

    // Try to dequeue an existing pin.
    MKPinAnnotationView *pinAnnotationView =
    (MKPinAnnotationView *)
    [self.mapView dequeueReusableAnnotationViewWithIdentifier:@"location"];

    if (!pinAnnotationView) {
        // You could not get a pin from the queue.
        pinAnnotationView=[[MKPinAnnotationView alloc]
                            initWithAnnotation:annotation
```

```
                          reuseIdentifier:@"location"] ;

        pinAnnotationView.animatesDrop=TRUE;
        pinAnnotationView.canShowCallout = YES;

    }

    // You need to get the rating from the annotation object
    // to color the pin based on rating.
    Result *resultAnnotation = (Result*) annotation;

    if (resultAnnotation.rating > 4.5) {
        pinAnnotationView.pinColor = MKPinAnnotationColorGreen;
    }
    else if (resultAnnotation.rating > 3.5) {
        pinAnnotationView.pinColor = MKPinAnnotationColorPurple;
    }
    else {
        pinAnnotationView.pinColor = MKPinAnnotationColorRed;
    }


    return pinAnnotationView;

}
```

The first line of the method checks to see if the annotation is for the user location view. If it is, you simply return `nil` to tell the map to use the default annotation.

Next, you see the attempt to dequeue an existing annotation view. The map view works very much like the table view in this respect. It doesn't make sense to keep invisible map annotations in memory. Therefore, the map view creates and releases annotations as they become visible or disappear from the map, respectively. Instead of creating new annotation instances every time, the map view maintains an internal queue of annotation objects that it can reuse. Therefore, you first try to dequeue an annotation. If you cannot, you create a new pin annotation view with the correct reuse identifier. Then you set the attributes of this view.

Next, you cast the annotation that the map view is asking for to a `Result` object. Then you use the rating property of the `Result` to set the color of the pin. Finally, you return the `pinAnnotationView`.

The last thing you need to do is implement the `plotResults` method. This method calls the `addAnnotations` method of the map view to add the annotations to the map. Here is the implementation:

```
- (void) plotResults {

    // Annotate the result.
    [mapView addAnnotations:self.results];


}
```

Finishing Up

The code is now complete. You should be able to successfully build and run the application. If you attempt to run the application in the simulator, by default, you see that the device thinks that it is at Apple headquarters, regardless of where you are actually located. This is by design. Enter a search term in the search bar and watch the pins drop to show you the results. You can view the XML returned by the web service in the console.

You can modify the location used by the iOS simulator using the Debug ⇨ Location menu. This menu allows you to choose some predefined locations such as Apple, or Apple stores. You can also enter the latitude and longitude of your own choosing by selecting the Custom Location option. The City Bicycle Ride, City Run, and Freeway Drive options simulate the movement of the device along a bike ride, run, or drive, respectively.

EXAMPLE 2: CONTENT ANALYSIS

When making calls to a web service, you often use the HTTP GET method to send parameters to the service. When dealing with REST-based web services, you use GET to indicate that you are performing a query for some data from the server. Sometimes you need to POST data to the server. Many SOAP-based web services use POST to send data. REST uses the POST method to indicate that you are sending data to the server and intend to modify the database.

Sending a POST request is similar to sending a GET request with some minor exceptions, as you see in the example code.

In this example, you make a call to the Yahoo! Content Analysis service. According to Yahoo! the service "detects entities/concepts, categories, and relationships within unstructured content. It ranks those detected entities/concepts by their overall relevance, resolves those if possible into Wikipedia pages, and annotates tags with relevant meta-data." Because of the length of the string that you can submit to the service, it is not practical to use the HTTP GET method; therefore, the service requires that you use POST to send your string into the web service. You can apply the same principles that you use here to any web service that requires you to submit data using the POST method. The completed example looks like Figure 11-5.

FIGURE 11-5 Complete content analysis application

The content analysis service uses its own syntax called Yahoo! Query Language. Yahoo! describes YQL this way:

The Yahoo! Query Language is an expressive SQL-like language that lets you query, filter, and join data across web services. With YQL, apps run faster with fewer lines of code and a smaller network footprint.

Yahoo! and other websites across the Internet make much of their structured data available to developers, primarily through web services. To access and query these services, developers traditionally endure the pain of locating the right URLs and documentation to access and query each web service.

With YQL, developers can access and shape data across the Internet through one simple language, eliminating the need to learn how to call different APIs.

Getting Started

To get started, open Xcode and create a new Single View Application called **ContentAnalysis**. Make sure that you have the Use Storyboards and Use Automatic Reference Counting checkboxes selected before you press Next. Choose a location to save your project, and click Create.

In the `ViewController.h` header file, modify the `@interface` declaration to indicate your intention to implement the `NSXMLParserDelegate` protocol:

```
@interface ViewController : UIViewController <NSXMLParserDelegate>
```

Next, create properties for two `UITextView` variables:

```
@property (weak, nonatomic) IBOutlet UITextView *textToAnalyzeTextView;
@property (weak, nonatomic) IBOutlet UITextView *extractedTermsTextView;
```

Also, add properties for the response data that you receive from the server in response to your request and the characters that you capture during XML parsing:

```
@property (nonatomic, retain) NSMutableData *responseData;
@property (nonatomic, retain) NSMutableString *capturedCharacters;
```

Next, add an `IBAction` method called **analyzeContent** that you connect to a button that the user taps after he enters the text to send to the service. Finally, add an instance method called **parseXML** that you invoke to start the XML processing:

```
- (IBAction)analyzeContent:(id)sender;
- (void) parseXML;
```

The complete header should look like this:

```
#import <UIKit/UIKit.h>

@interface ViewController : UIViewController <NSXMLParserDelegate>

@property (weak, nonatomic) IBOutlet UITextView *textToAnalyzeTextView;
@property (weak, nonatomic) IBOutlet UITextView *extractedTermsTextView;
@property (nonatomic, retain) NSMutableData *responseData;
@property (nonatomic, retain) NSMutableString *capturedCharacters;
- (IBAction)analyzeContent:(id)sender;
- (void) parseXML;
@end
```

Building the User Interface

Now it is time to build the user interface for the application using the storyboard. Click the `MainStoryboard.storyboard` file in the Project Navigator to open the storyboard. Once the interface is open, add two `UITextViews`, two `UILabels`, and a `UIButton`, as shown in Figure 11-6.

Change the `title` attribute of the `UIButton` to read **Analyze Content**. Change the text of the top `UILabel` to read **Text to analyze:** and the bottom `UILabel` to **Extracted Terms:**

As default text in the Text to extract: text view, I set the text to the first part of the Declaration of Independence. I have included a text file containing the declaration, or you can use your own text or provide text at runtime. Delete the default text from the Extracted Terms text view.

Next, you need to hook up the text views from the interface to the proper outlets in the code. Hook up the Analyze Content button to the `analyzeContent IBAction` method in the `ViewController.h` header file by Ctrl-dragging the button and dropping it onto the method in the header file. Remember that you can use the Assistant editor to view the interface and the code side by side.

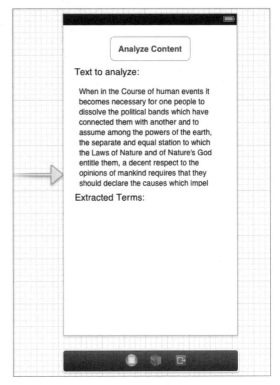

FIGURE 11-6: Term extract user interface

Likewise, hook up the text to analyze text view from the interface to the `textToAnalyzeTextView` outlet and the extracted terms text view from the interface to the `extractedTermsTextView` in the `ViewController.h` header.

In the `ViewController.m` implementation file, implement a stub `analyzeContent` method to log when someone calls the method. You use this to verify that you have correctly wired the button in the Interface Builder. Here is the stub code:

```
- (IBAction)analyzeContent:(id)sender {
    NSLog(@"analyzeContent");
}
```

Build and run the application. Click the `analyzeContent` button and verify that you see the log message in the console. This shows that you have correctly wired the button to the method. If you do not see the message in the console, make sure that you have properly wired the button to the message in the storyboard. You are now finished with the user interface.

Implementing the POST Call

You implement the `analyzeContent` method to POST the request to the web service.

The first thing that you do in this method is dismiss the keyboard by calling the `resignFirstResponder` method on the text view. Next, you clear the list of extracted terms to eliminate old results:

```
- (IBAction) analyzeContent:(id)sender
{
    NSLog (@"analyzeContent");

    // Hide the keyboard.
    [self.textToAnalyzeTextView resignFirstResponder];

    // Clear the old extracted terms.
    self.extractedTermsTextView.text = @"";
```

Now you create a string to hold the URL that you plan to call. This is the address of the Yahoo! Query Language web service. Next, you create an NSURL object with this string:

```
    // Create a string for the URL.
    NSString *urlString =
        @"http://query.yahooapis.com/v1/public/yql";

    // Create the NSURL.
    NSURL *url = [NSURL URLWithString:urlString];
```

The next line is where using the POST method differs from using GET. If you recall, when using the GET method, you simply set the URL string, set the parameter values inline, and send the request through the NSURLConnection. When using the POST method, you need to do things a little differently. After you create the NSURLRequest, you need to modify some of its properties. Therefore, you must use an NSMutableURLRequest instead:

```
    // Create a mutable request because you will append data to it.
    NSMutableURLRequest *request = [NSMutableURLRequest requestWithURL:url
                        cachePolicy:NSURLRequestUseProtocolCachePolicy
                        timeoutInterval: 30.0];
```

The first change that you make to the request is to set the HTTP method that you plan to use. Remember that you are using the POST method. The default method is GET, so you have to change this in the request to POST using the setHTTPMethod method:

```
    // Set the HTTP method of the request to POST.
    [request setHTTPMethod:@"POST"];
```

Next, you build a string to hold your parameters. In this example, there is only one parameter, but many parameters can optionally be passed using the POST method. You should note that parameters must be passed using the HTML parameter passing syntax name=value just like when using the GET method. Here is your parameter string:

```
    // Build a string for the parameters
    NSString *parameters = [[NSString alloc] initWithFormat:
                @"q=select * from contentanalysis.analyze where text='%@'",
                self.textToAnalyzeTextView.text];
```

Notice how you are using YQL to submit your query to Yahoo!. The syntax is similar to SQL in that you are selecting everything (*) from the `contentanalysis.analyze` table, where the text is the content that you want to analyze.

When you use the GET method to call a web service, you pass the parameters in the query string of the HTTP request. However, when you use POST, you pass those parameters in the body of the HTTP message. Therefore, you have to set the HTTP body using the `setHTTPBody` method:

```
// Set the body of the request.
    [request setHTTPBody:[parameters dataUsingEncoding:NSUTF8StringEncoding]];
```

The rest of the code for the method is the same as you have seen before. First, you create the `NSURLConnection`:

```
NSURLConnection *connection =
    [[NSURLConnection alloc] initWithRequest:request delegate:self];
```

Then you instantiate your `responseData` property:

```
// Make sure that the connection is good.
    if (connection) {
        // Instantiate the responseData data structure to store the response.
        self.responseData = [NSMutableData data];

    }
    else {
        NSLog (@"The connection failed");
    }
```

Here is the complete method implementation:

```
- (IBAction)analyzeContent:(id)sender {
    NSLog (@"analyzeContent");

    // Hide the keyboard.
    [self.textToAnalyzeTextView resignFirstResponder];

    // Clear the old extracted terms.
    self.extractedTermsTextView.text = @"";

    // Create a string for the URL.
    NSString *urlString =
    @"http://query.yahooapis.com/v1/public/yql";

    // Create the NSURL.
    NSURL *url = [NSURL URLWithString:urlString];

    // Create a mutable request to append data to it.
    NSMutableURLRequest *request = [NSMutableURLRequest requestWithURL:url
                                cachePolicy:NSURLRequestUseProtocolCachePolicy
                                timeoutInterval: 30.0];

    // Set the HTTP method of the request to POST.
```

```
[request setHTTPMethod:@"POST"];

// Build a string for the parameters.
NSString *parameters = [[NSString alloc] initWithFormat:
        @"q=select * from contentanalysis.analyze where text='%@'",
        self.textToAnalyzeTextView.text];

// Set the body of the request.
[request setHTTPBody:[parameters dataUsingEncoding:NSUTF8StringEncoding]];

NSURLConnection *connection =
[[NSURLConnection alloc] initWithRequest:request delegate:self];

// Make sure that the connection is good.
if (connection) {
    // Instantiate the responseData data structure to store the response.
    self.responseData = [NSMutableData data];

}
else {
    NSLog (@"The connection failed");
}


}
```

Receiving the XML Response

To receive the response from the web service, you need to implement the NSURLConnection delegate methods as you did in the previous example.

First, you implement the connection:didReceiveResponse: method. This delegate method is called when the NSURLConnection creates the response. The connection could call this method multiple times, so you need to reset your response data by setting its length to zero each time this method runs. Here is the implementation:

```
// Called when the connection has enough data to create an NSURLResponse.
- (void)connection:(NSURLConnection *)connection
didReceiveResponse:(NSURLResponse *)response {
    NSLog (@"connection:didReceiveResponse:");
    NSLog(@"expectedContentLength: %qi", [response expectedContentLength] );
    NSLog(@"textEncodingName: %@", [response textEncodingName]);

    [self.responseData setLength:0];

}
```

Next, you need to implement the connection:didReceiveData: delegate method. The connection calls this method each time it receives data, so you need to append the received data to your responseData buffer:

```
// Called each time the connection receives a chunk of data.
- (void)connection:(NSURLConnection *)connection didReceiveData:(NSData *)data
{

    NSLog (@"connection:didReceiveData:");

    // Append the received data to your responseData property.
    [self.responseData appendData:data];

}
```

Now you need to implement connectionDidFinishLoading. The delegate calls this method when the connection has completed loading the requested data. In this method, you convert the response data to a string and call the method to parse the XML:

```
// Called when the connection has successfully received the complete response
- (void)connectionDidFinishLoading:(NSURLConnection *)connection
{

    NSLog (@"connectionDidFinishLoading:");

    // Convert the data to a string and log the response string
    NSString *responseString = [[NSString alloc]
                                 initWithData:self.responseData
                                 encoding:NSUTF8StringEncoding];
    NSLog(@"Response String: \n%@", responseString);


    [self parseXML];
}
```

Parsing the Response XML

After you submit your request, you receive an XML response from the web service. The response contains the most relevant words and phrases from the text that you sent into the service, in order of relevance. The response that I received when I sent the declaration to the web service looked like this:

```
<?xml version="1.0" encoding="UTF-8"?>
<query xmlns:yahoo="http://www.yahooapis.com/v1/base.rng" yahoo:count="2"
yahoo:created="2013-01-24T15:21:47Z" yahoo:lang="en-US"><results><yctCategories
xmlns="urn:yahoo:cap">
    <yctCategory score="0.658057">Politics &amp; Government</yctCategory>
    <yctCategory score="0.5">Human Rights</yctCategory>
  </yctCategories><entities xmlns="urn:yahoo:cap">
    <entity score="0.878877">
      <text end="33" endchar="33" start="0" startchar="0">When in the Course of
human events</text>
    </entity>
    <entity score="0.79888">
      <text end="184" endchar="184" start="166" startchar="166">powers of the
earth</text>
    </entity>
    <entity score="0.62262">
      <text end="101" endchar="101" start="87" startchar="87">political bands</text>
```

```
      </entity>
      <entity score="0.532188">
       <text end="546" endchar="546" start="529" startchar="529">unalienable Rights</text>
       <wiki_url>http://en.wikipedia.com/wiki/Natural_and_legal_rights</wiki_url>
       <related_entities>
         <wikipedia>
           <wiki_url>http://en.wikipedia.com/wiki/All_men_are_created_equal</wiki_url>
           <wiki_url>http://en.wikipedia.com/wiki/United_States_Bill_of_Rights</wiki_url>
           <wiki_url>http://en.wikipedia.com/wiki/Hard_Promises</wiki_url>
           <wiki_url>http://en.wikipedia.com/wiki/Consent_of_the_governed</wiki_url>
           <wiki_url>http://en.wikipedia.com/wiki/Foundation_of_Freedom</wiki_url>
         </wikipedia>
       </related_entities>
      </entity>
    </entities></results></query><!-- total: 247 -->
  <!-- engine1.yql.bf1.yahoo.com -->
```

You need to implement the `parseXML` function, just as you did in the previous example, to parse this response XML:

```objc
- (void) parseXML {
    NSLog (@"parseXML");

    // Initialize the parser with your NSData from the RSS feed.
    NSXMLParser *xmlParser = [[NSXMLParser alloc]
                                 initWithData:self.responseData];

    // Set the delegate to self.
    [xmlParser setDelegate:self];

    // Start the parser.
    if (![xmlParser parse])
    {
        NSLog (@"An error occurred in the parsing");
    }


}
```

In this method, you first declare an instance of an `NSXMLParser` and initialize it with the response data that you received from the web service. Next, you set the parser's delegate to self. Then you tell the parser to start parsing the XML.

Finally, you implement your `NSXMLParser` delegate methods:

```objc
// Called when the parser encounters a start element.
- (void) parser:(NSXMLParser *)parser
didStartElement:(NSString *)elementName
   namespaceURI:(NSString *)namespaceURI
  qualifiedName:(NSString *)qualifiedName
     attributes:(NSDictionary *)attributeDict {

    // Check to see which element has been found.
    if ([elementName isEqualToString:@"text"]) {
```

```
              // Initialize the capturedCharacters instance variable.
              self.capturedCharacters = [[NSMutableString alloc] initWithCapacity:100];
       }
}

// Called when the parser encounters an end element.
- (void)parser:(NSXMLParser *)parser didEndElement:(NSString *)elementName
  namespaceURI:(NSString *)namespaceURI qualifiedName:(NSString *)qName {

      NSLog (@"didEndElement");

      // Check to see which element you have ended.

      // You ended a Result element.
      if ([elementName isEqualToString:@"text"]) {
          NSLog (@"capturedCharacters: %@" , self.capturedCharacters);

          self.extractedTermsTextView.text = [self.extractedTermsTextView.text
                                        stringByAppendingFormat:@"%@\n",
                                        self.capturedCharacters];

          // Clean up the capturedCharacters instance variable.
          self.capturedCharacters = nil;
      }


}

// Called when the parser finds characters contained within an element.
- (void)parser:(NSXMLParser *)parser foundCharacters:(NSString *)string {
      if (self.capturedCharacters != nil) {
          [self.capturedCharacters appendString:string];
      }
}
```

Because you are interested only in text elements, this code is straightforward. If you encounter the start of a text element, you initialize your capturedCharacters instance variable in the didStartElement method. In didEndElement, you check to see that you ended a text element. Then you append the capturedCharacters string to the extractedTermsTextView.

Finishing Up

The application is now complete. You should be able to successfully build and run the program. When you tap the Analyze Content button, you send the query to the web service. If you have an active Internet connection, you should receive an XML result set that contains the content analysis. You can verify this in the console log. The code takes the text contained in each text element, parses it, and appends it to the extractedTermsTextView in the user interface. Feel free to paste in any block of text that you find interesting to see what the Yahoo! service feels are the most significant words or phrases in the document.

MOVING FORWARD

In this chapter, you learned about the basics of XML web services. Then you saw how to call XML web services using both the HTTP GET and POST methods. This enables you to call any web service available on the Internet.

You also learned how to use the Core Location framework to access the GPS functionality and determine a device's location. Then you discovered how to use the MapKit framework to display and annotate maps.

Over the course of this entire book, you have explored the full spectrum of dealing with data in iOS. You have learned how to display data on the device, extract data from enterprise systems and store it on the device, use Core Data to generate and manage data on the device, and use web services to communicate from your application to other services.

You now have all the tools necessary to build robust, data-driven applications. I hope that you find the exploration of the frameworks and functionality available in the iOS SDK helpful in your daily work. I hope that you take this knowledge, go out, and build amazing applications, because the iPhone and iPad are amazing platforms for your software. These devices are only at their beginnings. As these technologies evolve, the capabilities of the devices will only get better, allowing you to build applications that are even more amazing!

Tools for Troubleshooting
Your Applications

In this book, I have covered various topics related to building data-centric iOS applications. Because most readers are already familiar with iOS software development, this book does not include in-depth coverage of the tools that experienced developers may already know about, such as Instruments and the Static Analyzer.

This appendix covers the other tools that can be invaluable when troubleshooting your applications. The techniques that you learn in this appendix are general. You should be able to use these techniques as-is with the current version of Instruments and apply the same principles to future versions of the tool. If you already know about these tools, perhaps you will learn a new tip or trick. If you have never used these tools, you will learn how to use them to effectively track down problems in your code.

INSTRUMENTS

Instruments is a graphical tool that helps you gather information about your application at runtime. You can then use this information to help track down difficult bugs such as memory leaks and network communication issues. Instruments is also valuable in profiling the performance of your application and helping you track down and fix bottlenecks. If your application is graphically intensive, you can use Instruments to measure graphics performance with the Core Animation or OpenGL tools. Many different tools are available in the Instruments application to help you troubleshoot a variety of application problems.

The Instruments application consists of a set of instruments to collect data about your application as it runs. You can see all the instruments that are available for use in Figure A-1. The instruments generally display their results graphically. You can have many instruments running concurrently, with their resulting graphs displayed together in the application interface. This can help you analyze the relationships between the data collected by different instruments.

You can also create custom instruments that use DTrace to examine the execution of your application. DTrace is a dynamic scripting tool that Sun created and Apple ported to OS X.

You cannot use DTrace custom instruments on the iOS directly, but you can use them in conjunction with the simulator when running your application on your development machine. While this reduces the usefulness of custom instruments because you cannot use them for performance profiling on the device, you can still build instruments to help you debug your applications in the simulator.

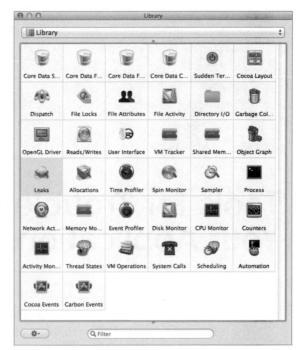

FIGURE A-1: Available instruments

Because DTrace instruments are of limited usefulness to iOS developers, I do not cover them in detail. You can refer to the Instruments user guide located at `http://developer.apple.com/library/ios/#documentation/DeveloperTools/Conceptual/InstrumentsUserGuide` for more details on creating custom instruments using DTrace.

Starting Instruments

You can start the Instruments tool directly from Xcode by selecting Xcode ⇨ Open Developer Tool ⇨ Instruments from the menu bar. You can also launch Instruments to profile the current application by selecting Product ⇨ Profile from the menu bar.

When you start the application, you see a list of templates for the trace document that you are about to start. The trace document holds the set of all your individual trace runs and the tools that you used during the trace run. You can save your trace documents so that you can review the data collected from your traces at any time.

The templates consist of default sets of instruments designed to assist you with specific tasks. For instance, you would select the Leaks template if you were interested in troubleshooting memory leaks in your application. After you select the Leaks template, the Instruments application appears with both the Leaks and Allocations instruments loaded into the trace document. The Allocations tool analyzes memory allocation and deallocation and records reference-counting events. The Allocations instrument is good to use in conjunction with the Leaks instrument because Allocations can give you insight into the history of an object that the Leaks tool reports as a leak.

The Trace Document

The trace document is the group of tools that you are using, along with any test runs. You can see an example of a trace document in Figure A-2.

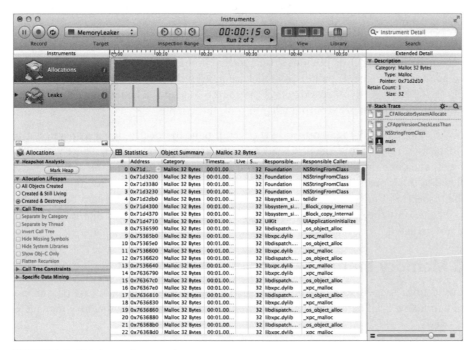

FIGURE A-2: The trace document

The Instruments pane shows the list of instruments that you are using for the current trace. Clicking the info button for an instrument displays that instrument's configuration options. You can add instruments to the Instruments pane by dragging them from the instruments library (displayed with Command+L) and dropping them into the Instruments pane.

The Track pane displays the graphical output of the instrument in a timeline. Each instrument records its data into its own track. The Track pane shows the time that an event occurred during the test run. You can adjust the time scale using the slider at the bottom of the Instruments pane. You can scroll the Track pane using the scrollbar at the bottom of the pane.

The small triangle that appears at the top of the Track pane is the playhead. The playhead indicates the current time of the test run. You can move the playhead to review the state of your application at any given time during its execution. You can add a flag at the current location of the playhead by clicking the Flag icon with the plus sign next to it in the toolbar. You can navigate forward to the next flag or back to the previous flag by clicking the Flag icons to the right or the left of the Add Flag icon, respectively.

The Detail pane shows the details of the currently selected tool. The Detail pane shows different details based on the tool that you have selected in the Instruments pane. You can select an item in the Detail pane to view more detail about the item in the Extended Detail pane. The Extended Detail pane is particularly useful because it shows a stack trace for the method call that you have selected in the Detail pane.

I find it useful to display the file icons in the Extended Detail pane because it makes the calls in the stack that originated in your code obvious. You can enable the file icons by clicking the gear icon in the Extended Details pane. If you double-click an item in the call stack that corresponds to one of your source code files, Instruments displays the source code in the Detail pane. Instruments highlights the line of code that was executing when it took the sample.

You can narrow the amount of data contained in the Detail pane by specifying an inspection range. To specify an inspection range, move the playhead to the location in the timeline where you want the range to begin, and click the left icon in the Inspection Range icon group in the toolbar. Next, move the playhead to the location in the timeline where you want the range to end, and click the right icon in the Inspection Range icon group in the toolbar. You should see the data in the Detail pane reduce to include only the data collected during the time window specified by the inspection range that you have created.

Objective-C Memory Management

In the upcoming section, you will explore the use of Instruments to discover the cause of a memory leak. First, you will take a brief detour to make sure that you understand how memory management works in Objective-C.

Automatic Reference Counting

For each example project that you have built during the course of reading this book, you have checked the Use Automatic Reference Counting checkbox when you created the project. Automatic Reference Counting, or ARC, is a feature of iOS that Apple introduced in iOS 4. ARC is a feature of the Objective-C compiler that frees you from most of the complexities of memory management that you would encounter when developing Objective-C applications prior to iOS 4. Memory management prior to iOS 4 is covered in the next section.

ARC is a compiler feature. The compiler adds memory management code at compile time. Contrast this with garbage collection in languages like Java, where memory management is done at runtime. The addition of the memory management code at compile time eliminates the burden of writing complex and bug-prone memory management code from the developer while maintaining excellent runtime performance. Garbage collection, in contrast, is a runtime technology that degrades application performance by using processor time for memory management instead of using those processor cycles to execute your code.

ARC works by evaluating the lifetime of all objects that you create. Then the compiler automatically adds code to release the memory that you have allocated when you can no longer use the object. You don't need to worry about when to retain or release objects because the compiler determines this for you.

Memory Management Prior to iOS 4

Prior to iOS 4, the developer was responsible for managing the memory consumed by the objects that you created in your applications. If you failed to properly free the memory that you allocate, the total amount of memory consumed by your application would grow as the application ran. This failure to clean up unused memory resulted in a memory leak. Eventually, if your program consumed too much memory, the OS would terminate your application.

There are still many applications written prior to iOS 4 and ARC. In addition, quite a few third-party libraries are not compatible with ARC. Therefore, it is important to understand how memory management worked before the introduction of ARC. The rest of this section assumes that you are not using ARC and that you have not checked the Use Automatic Reference Counting checkbox when you created the Xcode project.

All Objective-C classes that inherit from NSObject have a retain count. When an object is allocated using alloc or new, its retain count is set to 1. The retain count is a counter that indicates the number of bits of code that are interested in the object. When you need to hold on to a reference to an object, you increment the retain count by calling the retain method on the object. When you are finished with an object, you call release to decrement the retain count. The retain count determines when the object should be deallocated and its dealloc method called.

You need to be careful to balance calls to new, alloc, or retain with calls to release. If you have too few calls to release, the retain count for the object will never drop to zero, and the object will never be released, resulting in a memory leak. If you call release too many times, you will overrelease the object, causing a segmentation fault and an application crash.

In general, adding an object to a collection such as NSMutableArray increments the retain count. Likewise, removing an object from a collection decrements the retain count. Simply obtaining an object from a collection typically returns an autoreleased object. If you need to hold on to the reference to an autoreleased object, you need to call retain on it.

You can also send the message autorelease to an object. This indicates that the runtime should release the object at a point in the future, but not right away. You use autorelease pools to keep track of all autoreleased objects. The project template creates an application-wide autorelease pool automatically when you begin your application. You can create local pools yourself as well.

Autorelease is particularly useful for returning objects from methods. You can allocate the object that you plan to return from the method, configure it, and then autorelease it. It is then the caller's responsibility to retain the object to ensure that it has the proper retain count. The Objective-C runtime sends an autoreleased object to the release message one time for every time you call autorelease on it when the autorelease pool is drained or deallocated.

When you create an object with a helper method that has `alloc`, `new`, or `copy` in its name, it is your responsibility to release it. Objects created in this way, by convention, have a retain count of 1. If you use a method that returns an object such as `stringWithString` to get an instance of an object, you should assume that the object is autoreleased.

If you need to hold on to a reference to an autoreleased object, it is your responsibility to call `retain`. The default autorelease pool will deallocate autoreleased objects each time through the application's run loop. So, if you get an autoreleased object in a function, use it right away, and don't need it after the method call is complete, you do not need to worry about retaining it. However, if you plan to put an autoreleased object into an instance variable for access at a later time, you have to call `retain` on it or it will be deallocated at the end of the run loop and your application will crash with a segmentation fault when you try to send a message to the deallocated object.

You should use `release` instead of `autorelease` whenever possible because there is less overhead in calling `release`. If you are going to be creating and autoreleasing many objects, in a loop perhaps, you should wrap the loop in its own autorelease pool.

You can send the `retainCount` message to any `NSObject` to obtain the current retain count of that object. You generally won't use this method in a production application, but it can be helpful to log the retain count of an object as you are trying to debug memory problems.

The rules of memory management are simple. To summarize:

➤   If you create an object with `alloc`, `new`, or `copy`, the object has a retain count of 1, and you are responsible for calling `release`.

➤   If you get a reference to an object in any other way, you can assume that it has a retain count of 1 and has been autoreleased. If you need to hold on to a reference to the object, retain it.

➤   If you call `retain` on an object, you have to balance the call to `retain` with a call to `release`.

A memory leak occurs when you lose the reference to a pointer for an object that you have not deleted from the heap, or if you do not match the number of calls to `retain`, `alloc`, `new`, or `copy` to the number of calls to `release`. This is called overretaining an object. Overretaining results in the object's retain count never reaching 0, at which time the runtime frees the memory consumed by the object. Because you have not released the object, you have leaked the memory consumed by the object for the remainder of the life of the program.

Sample Memory Leak Application

Now that you have an understanding of memory management and Objective-C, you will build an application with a memory leak and then use Instruments to find and fix that leak. The application will be simple, with only a single button for the user interface, as you can see in Figure A-3. When you tap the Go button, a routine with a memory leak will run and log to the console.

FIGURE A-3: MemoryLeaker application

Start a new Single View Application project for iPhone called **MemoryLeaker**. Make sure that you uncheck the Use Automatic Reference Counting checkbox when you create the project. This is important, because you cannot compile the example code if you use ARC in the project. Click Next and select a location to save your project. Then click Create to create your project.

Open the `ViewController.h` header file, and add an action for the Go button as follows:

```
#import <UIKit/UIKit.h>

@interface ViewController : UIViewController

-(IBAction) goPressed:(id) sender;

@end
```

Now you need to build the interface in Interface Builder. Open the `MainStroyboard.storyboard` file in Interface Builder by clicking the `MainStoryboard.storyboard` file in the Project Navigator. Add a `UIButton` to the view. Wire the Touch Up Inside event to the `goPressed` method in the `ViewController.h` header using the Assistant editor. Save the storyboard.

Next, you are going to implement the `goPressed` method in the `ViewController.m` implementation file. Remember that this code has a memory leak, so don't use it in any of your applications. Here is the implementation of the `goPressed` method:

```
-(IBAction) goPressed:(id) sender
{

    NSMutableString *theString = [[NSMutableString alloc] init];

    [theString appendString:@"This"] ;
    [theString appendString:@" is"] ;
    [theString appendString:@" a"] ;
    [theString appendString:@" string"] ;

    NSLog(@"theString is: %@", theString);

}
```

This method simply creates an `NSMutableString` object, appends four strings to it, and logs the string to the console. Take a second to see if you can discover the memory leak on your own. The leak occurs because you allocated the `NSMutableString` object `theString` using a call to `alloc`, but you never released this object. After this method ends, the pointer to the string object disappears. This memory is now unrecoverable, resulting in a memory leak.

Build and run the application. When the simulator comes up, click the Go button. You should see this text in the console: `theString is: This is a string`.

Analyzing a Memory Leak in Instruments

Now that you have the sample application coded and ready to go, it's time to find the memory leak in the application using Instruments. In Xcode, select Product ➪ Profile from the menu bar. This launches the Instruments tool and prompts you to pick a trace template as in Figure A-4. Choose the Leaks template and click Profile. This starts the profiler and launches an instance of the iOS simulator.

FIGURE A-4: Instruments Trace Templates

Once the application starts in the simulator, you see a dark gray triangle at the top of the Track pane start to move from left to right. This indicates that Instruments is recording data from the running application.

The Leaks instrument is configured to autodetect leaks in your application every ten seconds. You can force manual detection of leaks at any time by clicking the Snapshot Now button that appears in the left side of the Detail pane when you have the Leaks instrument selected in the Instruments pane. After the application starts and Instruments is running, click the Go button in the iPhone simulator. In a few moments, when the leak check occurs, you see a red bar in the Leaks tool in the Track pane, as demonstrated in Figure A-5. You have now collected the data you need, so stop Instruments from collecting data by clicking the Stop button in the top-left corner of the application.

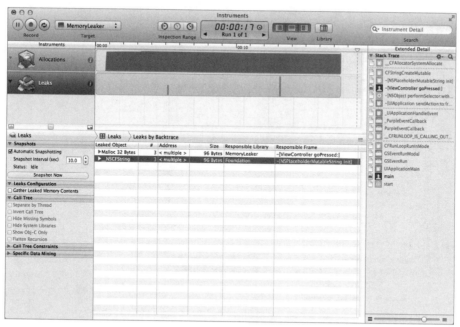

FIGURE A-5: Memory leak in Instruments

The red bar indicates that a leak was found, and in fact, it shows the number of leaks. For the sake of clarity, I have stopped Instruments on this run after triggering the memory leak two times. If you repeatedly tap on the Go button in the application, you see a stair-step pattern in the Leaks instrument, because memory is lost each time the button is pressed.

Make sure that you have the Leaks instrument selected by clicking Leaks in the Instruments pane. If you examine the Detail pane, you notice that there are two line items. Each line item in the Detail pane shows you a leaked block of memory. In this case, there were two leaked blocks. The first block is the NSCFString that holds your NSMutableString. The mutable string allocated the second block behind the scenes to hold the new contents of the string after you append data to your mutable string. If you had coded the application to release the NSMutableString, as you will in a moment, you would not see either of these blocks in the Detail pane.

Now you can test how Instruments can pin down where the leak has occurred. Make sure that you have the Extended Detail pane open. Then click the NSCFString line item in the Detail pane. The Extended Detail pane should show a stack trace that indicates the state of your application at the time the leak occurred. Notice that the fourth line down in the stack trace is in your code, specifically, in the View Controller goPressed method. When you double-click the line item in the Extended Detail pane, the source code for the View Controller goPressed method replaces the leaked blocks in the Detail pane, as you can see in Figure A-6.

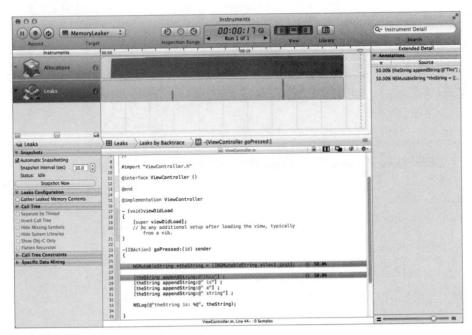

FIGURE A-6: Source code in the Detail pane

If you examine the Detail pane, you see the code fragment that Instruments is reporting as a leak. In this case, the Leaks instrument has flagged the line where you allocated `theString` as being responsible for 50.0% of the memory leak and the first call to the `appendString` as responsible for the other 50.0%. Instruments is telling you that you have allocated `theString` on the indicated line and then the object leaked. It is up to you to draw your own conclusion from there, but using the Leaks instrument has given you the origin of the leaked object. Now you just need to clean it up.

To fix the memory leak, you need to release the `NSMutableString` object when you are finished with it. So change the code in the `goPressed` method as follows:

```
-(IBAction) goPressed:(id) sender
{

    NSMutableString *theString = [[NSMutableString alloc] init];

    [theString appendString:@"This"] ;
    [theString appendString:@" is"] ;
    [theString appendString:@" a"] ;
    [theString appendString:@" string"] ;

    NSLog(@"theString is: %@", theString);

    [theString release];

}
```

Now rerun the application with Instruments. No matter how many times you press the Go button in the application, you should not see a memory leak. Congratulations! You just learned how to use the Instruments tool to track down and fix a memory leak, one of the most difficult types of bugs to locate!

THE STATIC ANALYZER

In the most recent versions of the Xcode toolset, Apple has included the Clang static analyzer. Clang is an open source tool that you can use to analyze your code for problems before you even attempt to execute it. You can do a one-time analysis of your code by selecting Product ⇨ Analyze from the Xcode menu bar. However, I recommend configuring your Xcode project to run the analyzer each time you build. You can do this by selecting your project file at the top of the tree in the Project Navigator. Then navigate to the Build Settings tab in the middle pane. Under Build Options, set the Run Static Analyzer option to Yes.

You see the static analyzer in action. Go back into the MemoryLeaker project and the `goPressed` method and remove the line that releases the `NSMutableString` variable `theString`. You have now reintroduced the memory leak into your application. Select Product ⇨ Analyze from the Xcode menu bar. You should see an icon in the left margin at the end of the `goPressed` method. This indicates that the static analyzer has found an issue. On the right margin of the same line, notice that the analyzer has noted a potential object leak. Click this notification, and you should see something like Figure A-7.

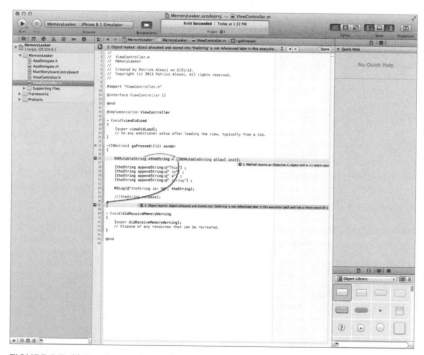

FIGURE A-7: Using the static analyzer

Sometimes a picture is worth a thousand words, and that is definitely the case with the static analyzer. The lines and arrows tell the story. The arrow on line 26 shows that you have created an NSMutableString. The line going from line 26 to the end of the method at line 37 shows that you have not released the string by the time you have reached the end of the method.

The comments that the static analyzer adds to the right margin explain the problem in detail. The comment associated with line 26 tells you that the alloc method returns an Objective-C object with a +1 retain count. This is also called the owning reference. On line 37, at the end of the method, the analyzer is reporting that the object allocated on line 26 is no longer referenced after this point, yet it still has a retain count of 1. Therefore, you have leaked the object.

Once again, add the line of code to release theString after the NSLog statement. Rerun the analyzer by selecting Product ⇨ Analyze from the Xcode menu bar. You should see the analyzer messages disappear because you have corrected the memory leak.

The static analyzer can find many other problems, too. For instance, it flags a dead store in which you write to a variable but never read the value back. To see this, change the goPressed method as follows:

```
-(IBAction) goPressed:(id) sender
{

    NSMutableString *theString = [[NSMutableString alloc] init];


    int i=0;
    i=5;

    [theString appendString:@"This"] ;
    [theString appendString:@" is"] ;
    [theString appendString:@" a"] ;
    [theString appendString:@" string"] ;

    NSLog(@"theString is: %@", theString);

    [theString release];

}
```

You can see that you are declaring the variable i, setting it to 5, and then never reading it again. If you run the static analyzer now, it raises an issue indicating that you never read the value stored in i. Dead stores are often a sign of a logic problem in your application.

Another logic error is using an uninitialized variable as the left-hand operand in an equality operation. Change the goPressed method as follows:

```
-(IBAction) goPressed:(id) sender
{

    NSMutableString *theString = [[NSMutableString alloc] init];

    '
    {
```

```
        [theString appendString:@"This"] ;
        [theString appendString:@" is"] ;
        [theString appendString:@" a"] ;
        [theString appendString:@" string"] ;
    }
    NSLog(@"theString is: %@", theString);

    [theString release];

}
```

In this case, you have declared the variable i, but you are using it in an equality test without assigning a value to it. Run the analyzer on this code, and you will get a flag on the line where you use the variable i saying that the left operand of the == operator is a garbage value.

There are many more problems that you can find even before you run your code using the static analyzer. Although it slows down your build slightly, you should definitely enable the analyzer to run during each build. It will save you many hours of debugging in the end.

INDEX

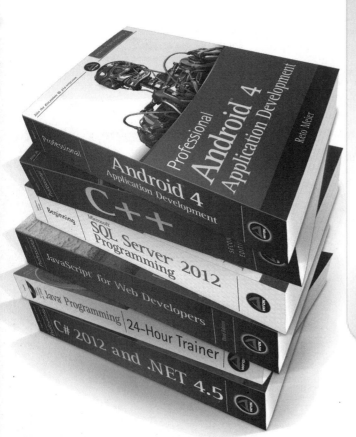